A Complete History of
The Negro Leagues
1884 to 1955

A Complete History of

——— The ———

NEGRO LEAGUES

——— 1884 to 1955 ———

Mark Ribowsky

A Citadel Press Book
Published by Carol Publishing Group

Carol Publishing Group Edition, 1997

A Citadel Press Book
Published by Carol Publishing Group
Citadel Press is a registered trademark of Carol Communications, Inc.

Editorial, sales and distribution, rights and permissions inquiries should be
addressed to Carol Publishing Group, 120 Enterprise Avenue, Secaucus, N.J.
07094

In Canada: Canadian Manda Group, One Atlantic Avenue, Suite 105, Toronto,
Ontario M6K 3E7

Carol Publishing Group books may be purchased in bulk at special discounts
for sales promotion, fund-raising, or educational purposes. Special editions
can be created to specifications. For details, contact: Special Sales Department,
Carol Publishing Group, 120 Enterprise Avenue, Secaucus, N.J. 07094.

Manufactured in the United States of America
10 9 8 7 6 5 4 3 2 1

Library of Congress Cataloging-in-Publication Data

Ribowsky, Mark.
    A complete history of the Negro Leagues, 1884 to 1955 / Mark
Ribowsky.
        p.   cm.
    Originally published: c1995.
    "A Citadel Press book."
    Includes index.
    ISBN 0-8065-1868-5 (pbk.)
    1. Negro leagues—History. I. Title.
[GV875.N35R53   1997]
796.357'0973—dc21   96-39793
                                                     CIP

For my beautiful son Jake,
who patiently waited to be born
while this book was written

Contents

Acknowledgments

This book represents a vindication of the belief that the Negro baseball leagues earned what they set out to gain—respect. This vindication extends beyond the men who played on the varying levels of obscurity in the Negro leagues and back to the prescient historians who made the case for blackball respect long before it was fashionable to do so. Facing a void in history carved by the neglect of several baseball generations, a small band of baseball archeologists concerned with saving the Negro leagues from permanent extinction began their arduous work two decades ago. Bit by bit, box score by box score, they have reconstructed a lost American society.

Because of them, flesh could be attached to bone in the writing of these pages, and I am particularly grateful to several of them for their invaluable assistance. Most of all, I am indebted to James Riley, the author of *The Biographical Encyclopedia of the Negro Baseball Leagues* for steering me through the turbulent crosscurrents of Negro league history. Even a few minutes of conversation with Jim Riley is like being on a riverboat through time. The same can be said of baseball historians like Jerry Malloy, James Overmyer, Neil Lanctot, and Bill Plott. All of these men have written extensively on various periods of the Negro league experience, and their works are must reading for any blackball aficionado.

No mere words can convey my deep appreciation for the surviving warriors of the Negro leagues, whose long and vivid memories form the tapestry of any honest work on the subject. To Buck O'Neil, Buck Leonard, Gene Benson, Max Manning, and the late Jimmy Crutchfield go my profound thanks for their reflections and their heroism.

Thanks as well to Bob Browning and Tom Heitz of the Baseball Hall of Fame and Museum in Cooperstown, New York, and to Steven Gietschier of *The Sporting News*, who combed through musty archival material documenting the earliest traces of African

Americans in baseball. To the Society for American Baseball Research in Cleveland. To Hillel Black, the editorial director of Birch Lane Press, who envisioned the need for this book and edited it with the same wisdom. And to my wife, Sandi, for all her faith, love, and support, just as always.

Introduction

For the better part of a century, Americans of equal ability played the game of baseball under the peculiarly American anomaly of unequal opportunity. On one side of the divide, descendants of European emigrants were given license to play this children's game for handsome wages and national acclaim. On the other side, descendants of African slaves were given license to do the same thing—as long as they did it without encroaching on the teams and the leagues of the Caucasian Americans. What was left over for African Americans in terms of renown and riches was meager. And yet for what seemed like an eternity, this system carried on without too many people believing there was anything terribly amiss about it, and if they did, that there was much they could do about changing it.

Given the ever-darkening complexion of baseball today, this rasher of sports and cultural history reads like a fable, which is likely why great numbers of current-day athletes and fans, black and white, are only remotely familiar with the particulars of what was known collectively as Negro league baseball. This book is a compelling reason why they should be more so—not only because the lessons of the Negro leagues are proud ones, but because they are also profane. Not to mention that knowing this story is absolutely essential in understanding the American experience and its schizoid pathology.

The first order of business is to specify terms. Black baseball—which can with sardonic irony be most appropriately dubbed "blackball," both for the hue and for the exclusion it engendered—came in many forms, including sandlot, semipro, industrial league, and unaligned pro teams that found it unnecessary to join a certified league. However, for the purposes of this book, the most beneficial lessons are those gleaned from the operations created in the name of mass organization—a favorite strategy, after all, within the civil rights movement.

For that reason, the term "Negro leagues" has become generic for the black game in toto. And while these pages cover important nonleague teams, especially in blackball's aboriginal years—when its players were uniformly known as "colored"—again, the emphasis obviates the need to get picky with the "Negro leagues" terminology.

Some readers may be surprised, even shocked, that some of this history will be dealt with harshly. This is because, quite possibly for the first time in the omnibus of Negro league literature, sentimentality has been excised for the sake of truth. That means the whole truth, an element hard to find in the normal Negro league tract, in which the retroactive shame of segregation overlooks the human frailties and deceits inherent in all history. Here, the almost physically painful saga of men deprived of their birthright has frequently turned the events of time into overripe drama and overromanticized folklore.

Nowhere in this book is the claim, for one thing, that any Negro league player should necessarily be considered as good as or better than one or another big league counterpart. Such claims are a waste of time even when applied to players within the same league; they are off the wall when so many Negro league statistics are unverifiable and embellished by the hyperbolic tales of blackball players.

Although much has been made about teams of Negro leaguers engaging, and routinely beating, aggregations of big leaguers in pre- and postseason exhibitions, it is wise to keep in mind that word *exhibition*. While the black players had everything to gain from whipping the big leaguers, the latter (often a motley collection of scrubs fronted by one or two name players) had nothing to gain but a little spare cash. Indeed, rather than settling anything about the level of ability on the field, all these matches really proved was that the vulgar rituals that pitted black against white in lucrative sideshows while big league segregation remained inviolate was a biracial disgrace. That some truly memorable baseball moments came out of these games—Satchel Paige's duels at sixty feet six inches with Dizzy Dean and Bob Feller, Josh Gibson's gargantuan home runs off Dean—only makes the privation of these gifted black men taste all the more acrid.

Of course, the possibility surely exists that by some means of measure Satchel Paige *was* better than Feller and Dean, and that

Gibson was better than, say, Bill Dickey. We'll never know. But my personal reaction, for example, to reading old clippings in which big league guys and white—and even black—sportswriters called Gibson "the black Babe Ruth" or John Henry Lloyd "the black Ty Cobb" is to be sickened by the condescension of it. It is also to understand part of why it was all but impossible for gifted players like these men to establish their own identities. Again by way of personal belief, that should have been a far more important crusade in the long run of the integration cause than any inflated batting averages or forced *tu quoques* with the majors.

As for the Negro leagues, they were schizoid in themselves. On the one hand, the players were magnificent creatures whose cultural contributions to race were a vital component of the entire civil rights picture, incarnating as they did the ambitious and perhaps unreachable dreams of black self-determination and full integration. In addition, black baseball was perhaps the first national black business, arising at a time when even local black business was a long shot at best to succeed.

The Negro leagues, with their plucky, bowlegged players and hopelessly utopian or cynical leaders, went about their business without ever cursing their fate. Even though teams, and leagues, could be here and gone from day to day, games were played as though by obsession; if a permit could be obtained for a game, the teams would find a vacant lot somewhere. If lodging couldn't be found, they'd prop their mitts under their heads and sleep on the field overnight, as though protecting their hard-won turf. And when they awoke, they'd go door to door in town drumming up ticket sales.

To latter-day students of the black game, standing amidst the curios of Negro league memorabilia and merchandising of team names and logos, this is the stuff of great picaresque charm; to the men who lived it, it was a matter of playing for their dinner. And yet, on a level that was in the haze way above them, some serious social history was being written here. Just as baseball was a common carrier of aspirations within the white working class in the late nineteenth century, the tides of blacks migrating from the rural South to the urban North identified strongly with the upward mobility embodied by teams playing for pay and representing the underclasses of Philadelphia, New York, Chicago, Detroit, Kansas City, and Pittsburgh. With blacks having little else to cheer for, these teams offered consolation and a rooting interest.

What's more, the business of baseball overlapped with, and gave impetus to, black participation in the fine arts; all "artists" by virtue of their manual talents and eye-winking nicknames, a Cool Papa Bell is an analogue of a Jelly Roll Morton, a Satchel Paige of a Satchmo Armstrong—though, unfortunately, in the eyes of white America, the notion of black artistry at the time was mainly the bow-and-scrape roles black actors played in Hollywood movies. Little wonder that, in dealing with how to cope in the white world, many blacks made the same equation as well.

Authentic black art, in its many forms, existed in a vibrant, sweaty underworld about which whites had a vague awareness. Louis "Satchmo" Armstrong's scatting, Cab Calloway's zoot suits, and Duke Ellington's big band—to say nothing of Langston Hughes's free verse—were wholly out of the mainstream; whites could, after all, perform a reasonably passable facsimile of jazz. And whites could, beyond a doubt, play baseball, without having to pretend that they could play it as well as or better than blacks.

Black expression was left to fend for itself, in honky-tonks, bar and grills, social clubs, and church choirs and on ball fields where grass never grew. In all these places, the black *glitterati* intermingled. A Sunday ball game brought out the cream of high-toned ebony society. The big leagues had Ladies' Day, but the Negro leagues had Easter every Sunday, a saint's day that might feature Bojangles Robinson hoofing before the game and Lena Horne throwing out the first ball. By owning a blackball team, as Bojangles Robinson and Louis Armstrong both did, esteem in the black community could be had at a very small price.

Whether simply out for a day of sun and baseball or tapping into the social phenomenon these games bred, black fans went batty over their heroes. A Sunday doubleheader in New York or Chicago boasting four elite Negro league teams often attracted up to forty thousand people and outdrew the big league games in town. Given this adulation, black players could take pride in their art, which seemed to them as legitimate as jazz and ragtime blues. Hall of Fame catcher Buck Leonard, who played in the Negro leagues for eighteen years, once said, with no sense of irony, "We hated the conditions, we hated not getting sixty cents on which to eat. But we loved to play. We wanted to play. Baseball was our game."

But it really wasn't their game, not even in the Negro leagues. While big league obstruction to integration was very much an economic issue—that of property values and fears of "there goes the neighborhood"—a number of white club owners with great influence within the big league inner sanctum coincidentally had side deals with Negro league club owners. The deal was that the white owners would provide blackball the use of major league stadiums in exchange for hefty rental fees and a cut of the gate and concessions. The New York Yankees, for one, were said to have earned around $100,000 a year on Negro league games at the mecca of Yankee Stadium.

Clearly, both white and black entrepreneurs had a stake in blackball's survival. But since forcing down the color wall was ostensibly the aim of the black leagues, one can only imagine how torn the black owners were when the white plutocrats, clinging to the last brick in the wall, professed their concern that the black game's own survival would be ruined by integration. Playing as it did on black owners' economic fears, this demagoguery found receptive ears. Caught on an ironic guy wire strung between the rights of black men and the rights of black capitalists feasting on the business of segregation, most of blackball vacillated as the day of reckoning came in 1947 in the guise of Jackie Robinson.

To many politically sentient blacks—great masses of whom immediately forgot about the black game the second Jackie Robinson set foot in the majors—it was sedition that, for a time, remnants of blackball pushed on, creating the incongruity of the Negro leagues sharing the same decade as the Freedom Riders in Mississippi and lunch-counter sit-ins in Alabama. Indeed, in the term "Negro" lay the seeds of blackball's doom. Where once an entire subculture doted on these teams, younger generations of Afrocentric leaders relegated the whole Negro league motif to the perdition of benign neglect.

Aside from the Negro leagues' legendary players, so were the leagues themselves ignored. While a dozen men denied their birthright have been inducted into the Hall of Fame, no man who ever owned a Negro league team or served a Negro league as commissioner or president has been so honored. This is reason enough to suspect that baseball's retrospective mea culpas have never been intended to ennoble the Negro leagues as an institution. Major league executives, who live by the atavistic codes of the baseball jungle, have carried on an embargo against the Negro league hierarchy that in another era was considered the enemy for exposing baseball's racial deceits. A magnificent innovator such as John Leslie Wilkinson—who as owner of the fabled Kansas City Monarchs rigged up light towers and fathered baseball's original night games—will likely never be bronzed at Cooperstown (even with the knowledge that Wilkinson happened to be white).

Unfair as this is, the tragedy of the Negro leagues was that there were too few J. L. Wilkinsons around to counterbalance the cast of plug-uglies, night riders, and hoodlums who held top positions in the Negro leagues in the thirties and forties. A case can be made that, in the name of purebred solidarity, soiled black seed money was preferable to no seed money at all—and that making accommodations with viperish white promoters, long a staple of blackball, was better than finding no accommodations available at which to play ballgames.

Conciliations like these were the price of keeping the Negro leagues up and running. Furthermore, the point is well taken that in the ethos of the 'hood, these men were revered as the beau ideal of the common man. This sentiment was expressed by the wife of Newark Eagles owner Abraham Manley, Effa Manley, who ran the affairs of the club. "He was in a one hundred percent illegitimate business," she once said in reference to Abe's numbers-running racket, "but the people loved him. He ended up losing a hundred thousand dollars in Negro baseball, but he enjoyed it and we had a wonderful team."

In the end, though, legitimacy in the baseball gentility could not be bought at any price by men whose social register was the police blotter. By extension, neither could the hastening of baseball integration. And though the Negro league mandarins would have taken great umbrage at the suggestion that they were in no great hurry themselves to reach the Elysium, history indicts them on the charge.

That the sins of the forefathers have been visited upon the child of their creation has been seen as well in black contempt for and apathy toward the Negro leagues today. Back when Negro league ball mattered as a black social requisite, its lifeline to the com-

munity was the black newspapers. These weekly journals, such as
the *Chicago Defender*, the *Pittsburgh Courier*, and the *Baltimore Afro-
American*, not only kept interest in the game high, but also kept
hope flickering that the black baseball sphere deserved inspection
by white fans who cared about good baseball, period. When these
papers became more race-militant, so did the course of baseball
integration.

And yet, mordantly, when the first retrospective literature was
published about the Negro leagues in the early seventies, the
works were those of white historians such as Robert Peterson,
whose book *Only the Ball Was White* broke the seal on the genre,
and John Holway, who has made a kind of cottage industry out of
piecing together quaint Negro league anecdotage. For a few years
after the virtual death of the Negro leagues, many black sportswriters who had abandoned covering the leagues' games felt a
terrible guilt about having helped to send blackball to the grave.
One, the *Pittsburgh Courier*'s Wendell Smith, who is in the baseball
writers' wing of the Hall of Fame, did a triple reverse on the
subject of the Negro leagues. During the black game's greatest
years, Smith practiced a see-no-evil style of coverage. After Jackie
Robinson's big league ascent, Smith—who was put on the
Dodgers' payroll to burnish Robinson's progress in white baseball—cursed the Negro leagues as a "slave trade." Then, in the
fifties, after the integration cause was won, Smith absolved men
like himself who had abandoned the black game; instead, he
disingenuously mourned the fact that "the big league doors
suddenly opened one day and when Negro league players walked
in, Negro baseball walked out."

But for Wendell Smith and other black scribes, guilt could not
erase their indifference. Amazingly, when Peterson's book appeared in 1970, blackball's corpse was still not cold. Still out there
on the musty old barnstorming trails was the final vestige of
baseball's Age of Unreason. Known simply as the Clowns, this
team in its salad years would send its players onto the field wearing
large red plastic noses and clown white smeared on their faces. For
years, the clowns had a sister team called the Zulus, who took the
field clad in grass skirts. Today, these quiddities of not-so-distant
racial realities seem like something out of a bad dream.

To some, blackball deserves to be left in that apparition, to rot
away in never-never land. But as the fans' persevering fascination

for the black game makes plain, there are too many lessons to be learned, too much history still to be gleaned from this allegory of deed and misdeed known as the Negro leagues. As weak, even venal as these motley leagues turned out to be, even their mock-heroics seem to be gallant in the long light of racial assimilation. If not for them, those wondrous, bowlegged men with the built-in legacy of their nicknames would have had no place to go.

Not that all of the breed could accept banishment to what amounted to a penal colony of American baseball. For some of the most talented players in the land, the ostracism of seemingly permanant second-class status burned too deep a scar into their self-worth. One such man, Luis Bustamente, was a Cuban whose dark skin condemned him to play at no higher level than the Negro leagues. Bustamente, playing for the Cuban Stars from 1905–1911, displayed the talent that earned him the sobriquet of "the Anguila" "the Eel" in the black press, and notices as "the world's greatest shortstop." But in 1912, a disillusioned Busta-mente drank glass after glass of straight whiskey until he collapsed and died. Next to the body was a handwritten suicide note that read:

"I'll drink until I become stupefied. Thus, I will eliminate myself [from baseball] as useless, keeping deep within me the conviction of what I am worth but what they won't let me prove simply because I have had the immense misfortune of being a Negro."

While few other black players felt so aggrieved over their lot in life, Negro league baseball stands as not just an ode to an undying spirit, as objectified by Satchel Paige, but is also the wail of embitterment and betrayal. The great Josh Gibson's death at age thirty-five in 1947—the year Jackie Robinson arrived in Brooklyn to play for the Dodgers—was not, as has been often theorized, the result of a heart broken by baseball's failure to promote him to the majors. But his death was a kind of suicide nonetheless, the slow torture of a strong but vulnerable man too weakened by the times to fight for his redemption.

But Jimmy Crutchfield was strong enough to fight for his, and in that he was in the majority of black players who refused to be lost souls. A sawed-off ingot of a man, Crutchfield spent nearly two decades living with the reality that he would never breathe big league air. But when he was old and stooped and young black jocks resided in the Forbes Five Hundred, there was no self-pity for Jimmy Crutchfield. In his time, he had found his own arcadia.

"When you're doin' something you love to do," he said, speaking in the present tense as though he had never hung up his spiked shoes, "there's nothin' lousy 'bout it. And, to me, I thought it was the first step toward the top of the world, man."

In truth, there was a whole lot lousy about it. But because it offered dreams and flight to men like Jimmie Crutchfield, black-ball established its nobility among its own. Forces they couldn't understand could take away their rights, but no one could take away their will. That was all they needed to play. And man, could they play.

A Complete History of
The Negro Leagues
1884 to 1955

1

Just Another Ballplayer

The challenge [for blacks is] to learn something about the game...in order that we will know what's going on out on the ball field, and won't humiliate Jackie by our lack of knowledge.
—*Pittsburgh Courier*, April 19, 1947

On April 15, 1947, when baseball heaven and earth parted for Jackie Robinson to take the field as a Brooklyn Dodger, the arrival of the first African-American player in modern major league history may have unleashed metaphoric fire and rain, but the mood at Ebbets Field on that afternoon was somewhat less ecstatic.

On this historic occasion—which had been otherwise intended as the Dodgers' Opening Day contest against the Boston Braves—no more than 26,673 fans were scattered over two-thirds of the cramped ballpark on Bedford and Flatbush Avenues. And while an estimated 14,000 black fans came out, more than had ever seen a Dodger game before, even they greeted Robinson's grand entrance with genteel, if loud, acclamation. No whoops, no war cries, no ovations.

As described in the normally overheated sports pages of the *New York Daily News* the next day, Jack Roosevelt Robinson had received "a pleasant reception from the fans and players."

This calm reaction, of course, belied the hideous pressures bearing on Robinson and the hell he would have to face as the 1947 season stretched out with so much uncertainty. When Robinson headed for his first-base position in his pigeon-toed gait, the anvil of centuries of black struggle and redemption was tied to

3

his neck. Clearly, Jackie felt the weight; according to another newspaper account, he "seemed frantic with eagerness, restless as a can of worms" in his first hours as a big leaguer. And yet what was really profound about these hours was that, in the end, they were just another in a thousand big league afternoons.

In all, Robinson went 0-for-4, and in his inauguration he was cursed by bad luck, if not by the Fates themselves. In the fifth inning, with a man on first, he drove a screamer up the middle of the diamond that the Braves' shortstop, Dick Culler, speared with a headlong dive. While sprawled on the ground, Culler dug the ball out of his glove and flipped it to second baseman Connie Ryan, who spun atop the bag and pegged to first to double up the bustling Robinson.

That Jackie Robinson was a sidebar even on this day was palpable. Trailing 3–1, the Dodgers roared back to win 5–3, the game-winning runs driven home by Pete Reiser. For the Dodger faithful, it was an old and comforting story. As the *New York Times* pointed out with not the slightest malice toward Jackie Robinson on the occasion of his coming-out, "Flatbush fans…had no problem about dividing their cheers. All of them went to an old hero, Pistol Pete Reiser."

In a strong sense, this quiet acceptance of the majors' first black player in fifty-five years was a victory for reason and inevitability. Baseball was going to carry on, same as ever, though with a conscience now alongside the ledger sheets. Still, there were some incidental factors at work in this muffled transition. For one thing, the integration of baseball was all but mandated by Branch Rickey, the flinty, canny Dodger chief executive, general manager, and quarter-owner who had lifted the lid on big league integration by signing Robinson to a minor league contract two years before.

Rickey's Machiavellian twists and turns had baffled both blacks and whites. He had held off making Robinson a Dodger until just seventy hours before Opening Day. With no bugles blaring, he had the announcement made in the press box during the sixth inning of an exhibition game. And the story ran only a close second to the *big* news in Brooklyn, which was Dodger manager Leo Durocher's suspension by the baseball commissioner for consorting with gamblers.

Rickey's orchestration of the event needed only a baton. As far-reaching as it was, Rickey kept his options open to the very last tick of the clock, and went to lengths to admonish the black community against getting too carried away. Two months before, at a black-tie dinner held by black civic leaders in New York, Rickey implored them not to make Robinson into a political cause celebre, not to stage "parades and welcoming committees" or to hold "Jackie Robinson Days."

If Rickey's main aim was to relieve some of the inordinate pressure from Robinson's shoulders, no less vital was his desire to relieve some of baseball's opprobrium from himself. This jounce would, he hoped, be but a small ripple in the baseball ocean, a shift of current, not a sea change.

To pound home the point, baseball's self-styled Great Emancipator was blunt, some might have said offensive. "You'll get drunk. You'll fight. You'll get arrested," Rickey lectured his audience of well-heeled blacks, part of the growing black bourgeousie. "You'll wine and dine the player until he's fat and futile. You'll symbolize his importance into a national comedy and an ultimate tragedy."

If things went down that way, Branch Rickey warned, "I will curse the day I signed him."

Both the black and white community obliged the terms of Rickey's fiat—though the mainstream press was clearly unaccustomed to the sight of a black man in a white man's game. The *Times*'s lead sports columnist, Arthur Daley, seemed to be pleasantly surprised by the rookie's poise. Daley wrote of Robinson:

> The muscular Negro minds his own business and shrewdly makes no effort to push himself. He speaks quietly and intelligently when spoken to and already has made a strong impression....
>
> A veteran Dodger said of him, "Having Jackie on the team is a little strange, just like anything else that's new. We just don't know how to act with him. But he'll be accepted in time. You can be sure of that. Other sports have Negroes. Why not baseball? I'm for him if he can win games." And that seems to be the general opinion.

If wary condescension and sobriety were the only price to pay for a smooth transition to the age of integration, the black newspapers were also willing to cater to Branch Rickey—though they were not willing to play down the story among black

Americans. The *Boston Chronicle*, for one, festooned its weekly edition of April 19 with the pulsating banner headline, "Triumph of Whole Race Seen in Jackie's Major-League Debut in Major-League Ball."

The watershed moment that occurred on April 15, 1947 could be gauged by the *Pittsburgh Courier*'s reportage a week before on rumors of Robinson's promotion:

> If Robinson fails to make the grade, it will be many years before a Negro makes the grade. This is IT! If Jackie Robinson is turned down this week, then you can look for another period of years before the question ever arises officially again.

When it became a fact, the *Courier* ran a large photograph of Robinson in his Dodger uniform, over a caption that read "Man of Destiny." And under an illustration of a clubhouse door with a Keep Out sign nailed to it, the paper emoted: "This is the door…that Rickey has finally opened. The Keep Out sign doesn't mean Jackie, or any other colored player who can make the grade. The great American pastime has really become American at last."

Still, most within the black press struck a cautious, reflective note, with caveats that Robinson didn't come with a guarantee of liberation, whether for himself or for other black ballplayers.

On its editorial page in the same issue, the *Courier*—echoing Branch Rickey's sentiments—issued to all blacks the challenge "to keep our mouths shut and give Jackie the chance to *prove* he's major league calibre! The challenge to conduct ourselves at these ball games in the recognized American way! The challenge to *not* recognize the appearance of Jackie Robinson as the signal for a Roman holiday, with the Bacchanalian orgy complex! The challenge to leave whiskey bottles at home or on the shelves of the liquor stores…and to leave our loud talking, obscene language and indecent dress on the outside of the ball parks."

An even more remarkable comment came via a snippety admonition in the April 25 *St. Louis Argus* that blacks should "act like human beings and not like a tribe of cannibals" at the ballpark.

Indeed, the national black monthly *The Crisis* cautioned black journalists against indulging in overtly parochial coverage that would make Robinson "the whole show," as "this kind of reporting and editing can do as much damage as a drunken, loud-mouthed fan."

The *Baltimore Afro-American* synopsized the prevailing attitude, beseeching readers in its April 19 edition to treat Jackie Robinson "as just another ballplayer, not as a phenomenon."

In line with the downsizing of the Jackie Robinson story, there was another common denominator in the reportage by both the black and white press. On that April 15, few baseball chroniclers of either color bothered to ruminate about what it would all mean to those still held hostage in the leper colony of baseball, the Negro baseball leagues.

For the black press, this was an irony beyond belief. Every spring and summer week for decades, the black tabloids had been black America's only pipeline to news about ballplayers and teams in these leagues that were merely a rumor in the white world. But for their coverage, the Negro leagues would probably have dried up long ago, preventing any chance for black men like Jackie Robinson to prove that their skills were big league. Yet now, in the rush to see Robinson through his perilous journey, when homage was called for, all that came up was silence, or worse, contempt.

Aside from brief citations of Robinson's one-year tour of duty with the Kansas City Monarchs of the Negro American League, the suffering caused to so many for so long by the major league's exclusionary traditions was no more than an afterthought. The *Courier*—which for years had annalized the glorious and sometimes tragic legends of such Pittsburgh-based Negro league legends as Josh Gibson, Satchel Paige, Cool Papa Bell, Gus Greenlee, and Cumberland Posey—found room only for a parenthetical reference:

> [D]iscrimination in [baseball] has always been felt keenly; more keenly because of the predominance of colored participants in more lines of sports, and the fact that in the colored baseball leagues were players who when they met white big-league players in off-season competitions, frequently came out on top.

Nonetheless, the *Courier*, by issuing another challenge to black fans—to "learn something about the game" so as not to "humiliate Jackie"—at once betrayed the years of black support and respectability it had helped to build for the colored leagues as big leagues in their own right.

In a black culture suddenly turned upside down, it seemed the entire scenario for the integration of baseball was being formulated with the understanding that no one was to ask what would become of the Negro baseball leagues that had spawned Robinson. Branch Rickey himself had made the case that there was no such thing as organized Negro leagues at all. And even as Rickey was trying to downplay Jackie Robinson as a candidate for sainthood, he was working to condemn the Negro leagues to perdition.

On the day Jackie Robinson took the field in Brooklyn, venerable Negro league teams like the Kansas City Monarchs, the Homestead Grays, the Birmingham Black Barons, and the Newark Eagles were beginning their own season—one given impetus by a shared sense within the leagues that they were all riding along with Robinson toward a better fate. But Jackie was the sole rider.

The first omen was the fourteen thousand black fans who streamed into Ebbets Field to see Robinson break in. Now, blacks began to queue up outside ticket booths, not just at Ebbets, but at National League parks across the country, snapping up ducats for the Dodgers' visits. In the Negro leagues, they could feel the draft created by the rush of fans fleeing their games.

This exodus would prove ironic, since the 1946 season had been the Negro leagues' apogee, and its best claim for continuance. That season had seen the two Negro circuits, the Negro National League and Negro American League, clear a combined $2 million in gate profits for the first time. Playing just across the Hudson River from New York City, the Newark Eagles successfully held their own turf in spite of the proximity of three thriving big league teams, drawing over a hundred and forty thousand fans.

But those same Newark fans who hadn't shown any interest in the Brooklyn Dodgers before were now among those lined up a mile long around Ebbets Field, or outside Shibe Park in Philadelphia, or at Forbes Field in Pittsburgh. By the end of the 1947 season, the Eagles' attendance had atrophied to fifty-seven thousand.

Similarly, longtime fans of the Kansas City Monarchs trekked to St. Louis to buy tickets to Dodger games against the Cardinals at Sportsman's Park. This same scene was being played out every day from Baltimore to Cleveland to Chicago, and was a major reason why Robinson's Dodgers would set National League attendance records both at home and on the road in 1947.

Correctly divining that the exodus was in full throttle, and that the Negro leagues had fallen from grace, the black press moved with the tide it had helped to swell by the tone of its Robinson coverage.

In early May, in anticipation of Robinson's first visit to Pittsburgh in a Dodger uniform, the *Courier* spread out four columns wide for Jackie. Under one of many Robinson-related pieces was a single three-paragraph item relating basic information about a Negro league clash between the New York Cubans and the Homestead Grays in Washington.

A week later, the *Afro-American* bannered page one of its sports section, "Record Crowd Watches Jackie in Philly Bow." At the bottom of the page was a two-paragraph inset in small type dispensing with a Negro league game between Baltimore and Homestead, under the headline, "Elites Break Even With Grays."

Once, these rousing Negro league games took second billing to no other league or sport in these pages, not even Joe Louis's championship fights. But by October, when Robinson's Dodgers were playing the New York Yankees in the World Series, the black papers could spare no more than a few paragraphs for the Negro World Series between the New York Cubans of Minnie Minoso and Luis Tiant Sr. and the Cleveland Buckeyes of Sam Jethroe and Quincy Trouppe. Not by coincidence, given the lack of press attention and the obsession with Jackie Robinson, few fans showed up for these games.

Now the Negro league leaders realized how illusory and self-defeating their dare-to-dream optimism had been, having learned the real lesson of 1947. By design and by necessity, and certainly by factors that were beyond black baseball's ability to control, when the earth parted for Jackie Robinson on April 15, 1947, it would begin to swallow up nearly a century of African-American baseball.

2

I Will Be Heard

I am not in favor of bringing about in any way the social and political equality of the white and black races. There is a physical difference between the races which I believe will forever forbid the two races living together on terms of social and political equality. I as much as any man am in favor of having the superior position assigned to the white race.

—Abraham Lincoln, 1858

Fowler, the crack colored second baseman, is still in Denver, Colo., disengaged. The poor fellow's skin is against him. With his splendid abilities he would long ago have been on some good club had his color been white instead of black.

—*Sporting Life,* December 30, 1885

As in every other area of social culture, blacks deprived of a shared march through history with whites turned to making their own history on the playing fields of an evolving America. Taking their cues from early nineteenth-century slaves who became "plantation champions" in bare-knuckled prizefights among themselves—a common leisure-time attraction for whites, who were loath to fight each other for sport but had no problem watching blacks do so—African Americans recognized that they had the talent to throw and catch round horsehide objects almost as soon as the English game of cricket mutated into baseball in the pre–Civil War years.

Indeed, according to baseball historian Harry Simmons, a black-versus-black game can be traced all the way back to 1860—only fourteen years removed from the first recorded baseball game, played between the Knickerbocker Base Ball Club of New York and the New York Base Ball Club at Elysian Fields in Hoboken, New Jersey, on June 19, 1846. Blackball's Elysian Fields was in the borough of Brooklyn in New York City. Here, on September 28, 1860, the Weeksville of New York engaged the Colored Union Club—the latter's name a self-consciously hubristic way of distinguishing it from a white Union club in New York. Weeksville won the game, a full nine-inning affair, 11–0, whereupon both teams receded into the void of ignored history.

At this stage of its genesis, baseball could hardly be called a sport, much less an organized one. Mostly, it was deemed a recreation around which social offerings were held at the fairgrounds that were used as diamonds. But then the game itself was very different from the one we know as baseball today. The dimensions of the field were the same, but other than there being nine players to a side and three outs to an inning, baseball was an alien form. Pitchers threw underhand from forty-five feet away and looked to tame the batter—or "striker," in the vernacular of the era—on four strikes.

The "new" wrinkle in baseball then was that the hitter was called out if a fielder caught a batted ball on the fly (a foul ball caught on one bounce was also an out). In many games, nine innings was just a number, the contest ending when one team got to twenty-one "aces," or runs. And no one thought it unusual that players performed bare-handed—even the catchers, whose gnarly hands resembled tree bark.

There was, however, one thing in common between then and now—baseball was generally played by wealthy men. The difference was that the players were *born* into wealth then, and played a game that was rigorously amateur in rule and in spirit. Even in the black sphere, in which there were few men of wealth and leisure and the participants were not bluebloods but typically blue-clad Union army soldiers, the games were a form of county fair entertainment.

One account of a black game of the day took note of the social amenities: "The women were interested and lent value by numbers and general attractiveness both at the games and in social features. There were picnics, dances and lunches [served] up to the players."

The end of the Civil War, and the apparent liberation, gave

blacks the notion that there could be mutual benefit in the existence of black teams, if not yet in open integration on the ball field. In 1865, a fully formed black baseball scene sprung up, especially in the East and middle Atlantic states. Stocked by ex-soldiers and promoted by some very prestigious black officers, teams were created with names like the Monitor Club of Jamaica (New York), the Bachelors of Albany (New York), the Excelsiors of Philadelphia, the Blue Sky Club of Camden (New Jersey), the Monrovia Club of Harrisburg (Pennsylvania), and the Unique Club of Chicago. There was even a black team playing out of Toronto.

By the late 1860s, the blackball capital was clearly Philadelphia. Following the lead of the Excelsiors, two ex-cricket players, James H. Francis and Francis Wood, formed the Pythians, whose promoter was a former army major, Octavius V. Catto, a teacher at the Institute for Colored Youth in Philadelphia. Because acquiring a permit for black games could be a problem in that city, the Pythians played many games in Camden, at the landing of the Federal Street Ferry.

In 1867, a full schedule of games was set between some of these seminal black clubs, and by agreement, the home team footed the expenses of the visiting clubs. This allowed the Bachelors to come from Albany to play both of the Philly teams. Later in the summer, the Mutuals and the Alerts came to Philadelphia from D.C., and this was a big deal since the Mutuals had some "name" players, including Maj. Charles R. Douglass—son of Frederick Douglass, the former runaway slave who rose to become the nation's leading black abolitionist voice—and Hugh M. Brown. Invariably, the Pythians prevailed in these marquee contests.

In an account of two 1867 games played at the Philadelphia County Prison yard at Eleventh and Wharton Streets, the Bachelors, "behind Captain James L. (Judge) Matthews, swamped the Excelsiors and the Pythians in a merciless way." If so, this was a major event, since the Pythians' record that year was said to have been 9 wins and 1 loss. So overpowering were the Pythians that the club's main man, outfielder John Cannon, was "considered by the white as a baseball wonder." Another Pythian player, George Brown, received a write-up hailing him as "a pitcher, the best amateur of his day, a strong and scientific batter and a fielder of much cleverness."

What's more, Octavius Catto was the George Steinbrenner of his day within black baseball. Catto also managed the team and was constantly firing team members in favor of promising or proven players from other clubs. Catto ruled by fear and arrogantly billed his team as "the Black Champion Pythians."

Octavius Catto didn't stop there. Baseball was booming in postwar America, and Catto wanted to participate. The structure that awaited Catto's entreaties, though, was so weak and so ham-handed that it was in no position to take a strong moral stand on such delicate matters as integration. Created in 1858 to further as well as protect the interests of amateur baseball in the New York City area, the National Association of Base Ball Players had grown into a national baseball umbrella; similar to a labor union, it governed the interests of ballplayers at the price of collected dues from member teams. Its duties included setting rules, settling disputes, and deciding which teams and players should have the privilege of being granted association eligibility. And while its actual powers were constantly breached, the baseball boom gave the association a magisterial bearing.

One thing the association certainly did *not* settle was the race question, probably because there was none—at least not until Octavius Catto decided to make it an issue in 1867. That December, the association held its annual convention in Philadelphia, prompting Catto to dispatch a representative named Raymond C. Burr to ask official recognition for the Pythians. Although Catto's petition was seconded by the white Philadelphia Athletics, Raymond Burr was ruled out of order by the court of white baseball; after holding several hurried and secret meetings, the association membership passed a resolution that excluded "any club which may be composed of one or more colored players." This move was taken, the association hastened to assure social activists and itself, not as the result of racial intolerance but in order to steer clear of "subjects having a political bearing."

Raymond Burr left the meeting hall euphoric. Dismissal was hardly appealing, but being treated deferentially—on the surface—by powerful whites struck Burr as a moral victory, or at least a moral gain. He later wrote that "all the delegates expressed sympathy and respect for our club." Burr was so flattered that when the convention leaders wondered if perhaps he could do a small favor for them—withdraw the Pythians' membership application, rather than "to have it on record that we were black-balled"—he was only too happy to comply.

But blackballed the Pythians—and all teams of color—surely were, which meant black baseball faced an obstacle course. One obstacle all along had been the failure of some very important black opinion leaders to get behind baseball as a means to achieve racial progress. One of the recalcitrants was William Still, the abolitionist leader who had created the Underground Railroad lifeline to free escaping slaves. Still could not understand why blacks were so agog over this silly game.

"Our kin in the South famish for knowledge, have claims [too] great and pressing...for frivolous amusements," Still wrote to the Pythians' secretary in 1869. "[I]t seems to accord more fully my idea of duty to give whence it will do the most good, and where the greatest needs are manifest."

But neither while intolerance nor black polemics could keep blacks off the ball field or away from the stands around the ball field, nor—witness Frederick Douglass, who could often be spotted watching his sons play—keep at least some black leaders away from the seductions of the game. When the Pythians hosted the Uniques of Chicago in 1869 for Octavius Catto's mythical "World's Colored Championship," over a thousand people from the Philadelphia area came out to the game, which was won by the Pythians to cap an undefeated, eleven-game season. Indeed, the association's dissing of the Pythians aside, there were still a few cockeyed optimists among baseball's early scribes. Covering the rousing activities on the other side of the baseball tracks in Philly, the white newspaper *New York Clipper* was clearly impressed by the black teams' ability to attract white opponents.

"White vs. Colored Clubs" blared the headline over a story that read: "The prejudices of race are rapidly disappearing. A week or two ago we chronicled a game between the Pythians (colored) and Olympics (white) clubs of Philadelphia. This affair was a great success, financially and otherwise. On the 16th the Pythians encountered the City Item Club, of the Quaker City, and defeated them by a score of 27 to 17. In Washington, on the 20th, the Olympics, of that city, were announced to play the Alerts, a colored club. The Unique Club, of Williamsburgh, composed of colored gentlemen, is anxious to get on a match with the Pythians. What say the Quakerdelphians?"

But this reverie, and momentum, went up in smoke when blackball lost its first messiah. After the Pythians had elevated Octavius Catto into a major political figure in black Philadelphia, he had become particularly active in the push for black voting rights in the city. That incendiary issue, the core of which was that blacks were shunted into separate polling places, had touched off riots in the streets in 1871, prompting the U.S. marshal for the eastern district of Philadelphia to call in the marines to keep the peace. On October 10, Catto was leaving the Institute for Colored Youth when he was accosted by a white man, who got into an argument with him and then shot and killed the thirty-one-year-old leader. The murderer was detained briefly, then let go.

When Catto went down it was only a matter of weeks before the Pythians did so as well; in fact, blackball's promising Philadelphia Story was in its final pages. Within a year, the Pythians and Excelsiors were in the grave. Amateur black teams all along the once-bustling eastern meridian evaporated. Thus, by the time baseball's first professional umbrella organization was born in 1870, the race question that was finessed into oblivion by the National Association of Base Ball Players in 1867 was fast becoming moot.

The new National Association of Professional Base Ball Players obviated the amateur federation once the pro boom trivialized the notion of sport as a county fair curio. Though the professional association too was wobbly (of the first twenty-five teams in its domain, only three—the Philadelphia Athletics, Boston Red Stockings, and New York Mutuals—were left standing six years later) some important innovations came about during this period of nascent professionalism. To speed up the game, umpires could now call strikes over the plate, and this seemed to juice up player impulses as well: Rather than just toss the ball up to the plate, pitchers were snapping off underhand curveballs, and hitters were practicing the new art of bunting to make the pitcher have to move off the mound. Since pitchers even then seemed to have the advantage, outs could no longer be registered on balls caught on one bounce, but only when caught on the fly.

The professional association, while not a true league—any team could play for the "championship" by filling out an application—could still make or break a team or a league by its recognition. However, by the mid-1870s, the progress of black baseball could be traced not by any team or league but by a handful of individual players scattered along the pro and semipro trails. The premier source in finding the spoor of these men is the archival material of *Sporting Life*, a weekly sports and leisure broadsheet that was published in Philadelphia. As this newspaper is regarded as the Rosetta stone of baseball's first generations, the black men who made its pages must be considered the sport's first professional African-American baseball players.

The earliest to be so pegged was a tall, reedy infielder named John Fowler, who was called Bud and who, with considerable irony, was born in Cooperstown, New York. This venue, of course, would later by mythologized as the cradle of baseball civilization by Albert Spalding—the game's first superstar and later a sporting goods czar and president of the Chicago White Stockings (forerunner of the Cubs)—who in 1889 spawned the dubious gospel of baseball: that it was the purebred American invention of a future Civil War general, Abner Doubleday, in that upstate New York village in 1839 (a claim Doubleday never made for himself). When the Hall of Fame was established a century later to commemorate the game's alleged centennial, Cooperstown went from myth to ivy-walled reality.

Albert Spalding and his fellow revisionists might have been astonished had they known they were unwittingly meting out poetic justice for pro baseball's first known black player—that is, if they had known who Bud Fowler was in the first place. Surely they didn't, as future historians would have to look hard to find Fowler playing second base in 1872 for a professional white team in New Castle, Pennsylvania, when he was apparently all of fourteen years old.

But *Sporting Life* came across Fowler often enough to make him a running item in small print. Its clippings of him form a paper trail through minor league rosters on teams from Lynn, Massachusetts, to Stillwater, Minnesota, to Keokuk, Iowa. Fowler was also known to have pitched with a Canadian team, the Maple Leafs of Guelph, Ontario, but when that team's white players objected to playing with him, he was released. This was not a popular move with the press and the fans, though. The Guelph newspaper groused that Fowler "has forgotten more baseball than the present team ever knew."

Indeed, coverage of Fowler in the white sporting press was

sympathetic wherever he went. *Sporting Life* made a practice in those back-page items of referring to Fowler as "the crack colored player" or, with simple color-blind matter-of-factness, as "one of the best players in the country." Honing in on the race barricade, the paper noted that "if [Fowler] had a white face he would be playing with the best of them."

While this was faint praise indeed compared with the endless toadying coverage of white heroes like Spalding and John Montgomery Ward, such accolades turned Fowler into a cult hero in the oddest of places. Finding his way to a team in Pueblo, Colorado, in 1885, Fowler reportedly made spare money giving walking and running exhibitions before ball games, and was said to have walked an eight-minute mile and run one in five minutes.

With all the teams and leagues Fowler joined, none could fairly be classified as "major league"—a term that arose in 1876, when the National Association of Base Ball Players was replaced by the National League of Professional Base Ball Clubs.

This transformation occurred when wealthier men became owners and began seeking ways to reduce the players' authority. It was the control-minded National League that was responsible for one of that most infamous of baseball phrases—the "reserve clause." Made a mandatory part of contracts in 1887, the clause bound all players to their teams for the life of their careers, unless the owners decided to trade them.

The fans felt a tightening of the old baseball structures as well. The National League forbade Sunday games and the sale of liquor in ballparks. For refusing to go along, the Philadelphia Athletics and New York Mutuals in 1876 and the Cincinnati Redlegs in 1880 were expelled from the league.

Yet, as draconian as the National League acted, its creation fully detonated the baseball boom in America. Now the game was professional without apology, and from its original seven teams the league would eventually include twenty-two clubs before the turn of the century, and would perform with an economic stability envied by the business community.

Even with the restrictions placed upon them, players earned up to $1,500 per month on most teams in the 1880s, and $2,500 in the 1890s—at a time when a factory worker was likely to earn under $500 a *year*. Indeed, there was regular talk about getting a salary cap on players, and in 1886, Al Spalding got the league to send private detectives to tail the players and file weekly dossiers so as to ensure that their social behavior justified their salaries.

African-American baseball players, of course, did not share in this windfall. If the game (as opposed to the business) of baseball was in a sense still in the dark ages—it was still played without fielders' gloves, a strikeout was still four strikes, a walk still credited as a hit—it was darkest for blacks, who had to scavenge through baseball's back alleys for work.

Even so, one black man did manage to attain big league status, by the sheerest of coincidences. His name was Moses Fleetwood Walker. Son of a doctor in Ohio, "Fleet" Walker and his brother, Welday, both attended Oberlin College, were scholars, and played on the school's baseball team. Then Fleet, followed for a brief time by Welday, played with the Toledo Blue Stockings in 1884, the year that club joined the American Association.

The year before, the thirteen-team association—the core of which was the three clubs booted by the National League—had forced an uneasy peace with the league after several years of raiding its players. The peace, codified in the Tripartite Pact and expanded later into the National Agreement, carved baseball's first major and minor league framework. Rules were made uniform and disagreements were resolved (save for the old sticking points—the National League still wouldn't play on Sunday or sell liquor in the park). And since adoption of the agreement's precepts was required by any league seeking official recognition, it was a way of regulating competition.

In 1884 the three "big" leagues consisted of the National League, the Union Association (which would last only that season), and the American Association. Thus, without anyone really taking much notice, this was the year that a Negro first gained status as a major leaguer.

All of which was quite irrelevant to the travels of Moses Fleetwood Walker, whose status began and ended with his color, though for a time even that had little impact on him—in the North, anyway. When Toledo played at home or on the nearby road, all went fine. But when the Blue Stockings went to the South, Walker took his life in his hands.

In Richmond, a typically baleful letter reached Walker promising that "75 determined men...have sworn to mob" him should he take the field. He did, scanning the crowd all the while for a lynch party that never came. Still, rather than back him up, the Blue Stockings looked for ways to end the tension by subtraction. When Walker cracked a rib in July of 1885—hardly a major injury—the club released him.

That left Fleet Walker, with two dozen or so other blacks, to vie for the very few spots open on teams in the minor leagues. Walker took up with the Waterbury team of the Eastern League in 1886. Another of the doughty clique, pitcher George Washington Stovey, attracted Bud Fowler–style notices playing with that league's team in Jersey City. Exhibiting a trait not often seen in pitchers of this primordial era of baseball, Stovey habitually vaulted from the pitcher's box to cover first base on slow rollers up the first-base line. This innovation led *Sporting Life* to proclaim that Stovey's "manner in covering first from the box is wonderful."

But a slight, 155-pound hob of a second baseman, Ulysses S. Grant—who wisely preferred to be called by the name of Frank— just may have been the best black player of his time. After Grant joined the Buffalo Bisons of the International League in 1886, hitting .340—third highest in the league—he became the first of a long line of black ballplayers to be made into not-quite-legal analogues of the game's greatest white players. Frank Grant, according to newspaper stories, was the "Black Dunlap"—after Fred Dunlap, the St. Louis Browns' second baseman whose talents had earned him baseball's first $10,000 salary.

Sporting Life, in one dispatch that never mentioned Grant's color, said he was "a great all-around player," a "very accurate thrower," "exceedingly hard to fool at the bat," and "the best all-around player Buffalo ever had."

Though their number was small, blacks seemed to be progressing rather well. Regularly in the mid-1880s, news of their activities ran in *Sporting Life* under the bold-faced heading "The Color Line"—the last word taken to be meant as "scene" and not "barrier." And these favorable reviews were not at all lost on some of the very scarce black businessmen, who began to see all-Negro leagues as a means of cashing in on the appeal of such men as Bud Fowler and Frank Grant.

An initial attempt to form such a league had actually been undertaken in the mid-1870s, in Pueblo, Colorado, in order to take advantage of Bud Fowler's popularity while he was playing and doing his walking exhibitions there. According to a *Sporting*

Life item, the brains behind this dream was one C. G. Kilpatrick, whom it described as "the well-known one-legged bicyclist and base ball umpire."

Intended to exist as a recognized minor league, with teams ranging over such black bastions as Cheyenne, Denver, Leadville, and Aspen as well as Pueblo, the circuit fell apart while still in the dream stage, before it could even find itself a name. Its epitaph may have been a *Sporting Life* note after the fall that C. G. Kilpatrick was now going back to "doing bicycle work at Wonderland," a local amusement park.

More serious moves were made in 1886 and 1887. The first was fueled by a black newspaper in Jacksonville, Florida, the *Leader*, which in March of 1886 placed blind ads in white newspapers across the South recruiting "colored baseball teams [with] a fair record and desire to enter the Southern League of Base Ballists." The only bond needed to post for membership was a five-dollar entry fee, which would go toward "printing, advertising, telegraphing, postal cards, stamps," and a subscription for each team to the *Leader*. As well, each team had to guarantee food, lodging, and carfare for visiting clubs.

The Southern League fielded ten teams: the Eclipse of Memphis, the Georgia Champions of Atlanta, the Broads of Savannah, the Eurekas of Memphis, the Lafayettes of Savannah, the Fultons of Charleston, the Athletics of Jacksonville, the Unions of New Orleans, the Florida Clippers of Jacksonville, and the Macedonias of Jacksonville. On April 8, the *Charleston* (South Carolina) *News & Courier*, reporting on the activities of the Fultons, carried an upbeat report that a basic plan for the league had been drawn up by a "board of twelve directors representing a capital of nearly $100,000"—which amounted to a lot of five-dollar bills and a good story.

The league, however, never applied for membership under the National Agreement, probably because the league fathers knew that it would not be able to begin play anywhere near its stated Opening Day of May 10. Instead, the first game, between the Eclipse and the Unions in New Orleans, was pushed back to June 7—whereupon it was rained out.

This ominous beginning notwithstanding, the Southern League endured, picking up some favorable coverage along the way. The story of the Eclipse-Unions game in the *New Orleans*

Times-Picayune, for example, read: "Judging from the first game, the colored clubs will furnish good sport, and the teams can play ball....The Eclipse boys all fielded well and threw the ball like the best professionals." The same couldn't be said for the Unions, who lost 3–1, allowing all the runs in the first inning "on missed third strikes [and] wild throws by the catchers and two passed balls."

As the season went on, most of the attention seemed to fall on the Fultons, or, as the *News & Courier* called them, "the much talked about Fultons [with] their showy uniforms, which consisted of dark blue shirts, white belts, light blue pants, red stockings and white caps with a double horizontal red bar." But if cool was the rule in this league, so was a high standard of play. A league directive ordered that no team was to play under "any regulations [other] than those published by Spaulding [sic] for professionalism. The ball is to be Peck & Snyder's dead red....No betting or pool selling will be allowed on the grounds and any persons found so doing will be ejected."

No directive was needed to locate a marquee attraction. Early on, newspaper coverage began to center on a young Charleston pitcher, B. B. H. Smith, who had played with the white semipro Manhattans of New York in 1884 and whose wunderkind aura earned him the nickname—possibly the first such christening in baseball—of Babe. According to an item in the *News & Courier,* Babe Smith "is said to be a host in himself."

Soon, three more teams entered the league: the Jerseys of Savannah, the Roman Cities of Jacksonville, and the Montgomery Blues. No team, however, was close to making a profit. Apparently, the Eclipse won the championship, or at least that was the claim in a late August dispatch in the *Memphis Appeal.* The team never got to defend its title. By the next year, the Southern League was itself eclipsed, having been unable to find enough small change in that alleged $100,000 stake to buy their Peck & Snyder dead reds.

Still, the concept of all-black pro teams—and by extension, all-black pro leagues—was close to reality. In fact, the first known black pro team was in clover in the middle and late 1880s, though with a certain bow to racial realities. They were the Cuban Giants, though the men of this team were about as Cuban as chitlins; actually, they were former waiters and porters at the Argyle Hotel in Babylon, Long Island, where the team was founded in 1885 as a summertime divertissement for white vacationers. Known as the Athletics in the beginning, the team went pro under a white promoter named John F. Lang, who even arranged for the club to play an exhibition against the New York Metropolitans of the big league American Association, who trounced the waiters 11–3.

But the real life of this club began when it caught the eye of a white businessman from Trenton, Walter Cook. Cook's design was clever: In order to attract white fans, he instructed his black players to act like Hispanics. Bounding onto the field, they would chirp pidgin *español* and cackle loudly, in a gross parody of everybody's idea of how Hispanics acted.

But while they played games against white amateur and semi-pro opponents, and won reams of attention in the press, it takes a leap of the imagination to believe that anyone who came to see them perform was really conned. Even frontier America would have had suspicions about Spaniards named George Williams, Abe Harrison, Bob Jackson, and Shep Trusty. Cook also regularly advertised the services of the great blackball pitcher George Stovey.

Not through a con but by playing superb baseball, by 1887 the Cubans had attained a level of notoriety that gave them the right to pick and choose which white teams they would play. In January 1887, Walter Cook wired an item to *Sporting Life* reading: "The Cuban Giants are now desirous of hearing from all the leading clubs in the country traveling this way, as we can pay good guarantees to first-class clubs. Our manager, S. K. Govern, care LaFayette Hotel, Philadelphia, has a few April dates not closed yet, and would like to hear from first-class clubs at once—college clubs in particular."

The Cubans could afford to preen. Barnstorming across the coal and steel towns of the Northeast from one sold-out game to the next, a number of their players were earning top dollar by bushball standards, up to $18 a week. While it would have sheer fantasy for a black team such as, say, the Eclipse of Memphis to believe it could ever play against a major league team, the Cubans slotted a game in the late fall of 1887 against no less than the National League champion Detroit Wolverines. According to one account, the Cubans led 2–1 in the eighth inning before their good fortune apparently grabbed them by the throat; making four errors in the eighth and ninth, they ended up blowing the game 5–2.

Even so, this sort of failure was rare. Winning by rote against their small-time competition, the Cubans' hauteur may have at least indirectly cost the second Negro league its life. Plans for this league—the National Colored Base Ball League—were formulated in March of 1887 at the Frederick Douglass Institute in Baltimore. By its very name—feeding off the National League while making perfectly clear to any threatened whiteball fathers that it was the colored version of the game—the National Colored League may have been solicitous, but it had high ambitions.

Eschewing black teams from the backwoods, league president Walter S. Brown, a black businessman in Baltimore, cultivated membership from the big cities, in emulation of the National League. Anteing up a $100 entry fee each, the starting lineup looked like this: the Keystones of Pittsburgh, the Capital Citys of D.C., the Gorhams of New York, the Lord Baltimores, the Resolutes of Boston, Falls City of Louisville, a reconstituted Pythians of Philadelphia, and the Browns of Cincinnati, who were represented at the meeting by the blackball legend Bud Fowler.

Ready to play, Walter Brown cut a deal with the Reach Sporting Goods Store in Baltimore to reward the league's best hitters and fielders at season's end with gold medals, in exchange for using Reach baseballs. Brown vowed that the players would earn up to $75 per month, and dashed off a series of releases to *Sporting Life* describing the Colored League in pointed terms that transcended baseball. The league, he waxed, was a sanctuary where "perfect harmony prevails."

Brown's intoxication with power was so great that he seemed to be slightly paranoid. Months before the league had even commenced play, he indignantly complained to *Sporting Life* that "some of the other [baseball] associations are tampering with our players. I look upon this as unfair and unjust; it looks to me as if some of the older associations are trying to cripple us in this manner. All we ask is to be treated fairly and given only half a chance and we will prove to the public that colored men are great ball players...and give satisfaction to the entire public."

Baseball people, at least those who cared about this netherworld of the sport, laughed at Walter Brown's Hamlet-like complaints.

Sporting Life defined the issue by deriding the notion that white teams would want or need to seduce black players, "owing to the high standards of play required and to the popular prejudice against any considerable mixture of the races." But, apparently every bit as sensitive as the old amateur association had been about concealing its racism, the National League took the extraordinary step of issuing the Colored League its official benefaction as a minor league under the National Agreement, so as to "protect" the black players from white teams who did not want them to begin with.

Accordingly, the Colored League, as a real live minor league, had been granted immunity from baseball's unwritten law of exclusion. Suddenly, maybe even too suddenly for Walter Brown, the future of blackball was now, riding on the success or failure of his league.

Whether or not anyone was truly aware of the import of this watershed moment, news of the Colored League was positive. And then, just as suddenly, the bottom fell out. Only a month into the season, *Sporting Life* noted that "it augurs ill for the success of the League that one club should already be in such financial trouble as to be unable to meet scheduled engagements."

That club, the Resolutes of Boston, had come to play in Louisville in early May, only to run out of money and have to fold on the spot. "At last accounts," read a seemingly smirky item in *Sporting Life,* the now-former Resolutes "were working their way home doing little turns in barber shops and waiting on tables in hotels."

A week later, only three teams were hanging on. By the end of May, the league was tapped out and funeral rites were being held in Walter Brown's Baltimore office, mourning the inglorious end of not just a league, but a chimera.

In his more dreamy moments, Brown may have imagined the Colored League as a prime trough of potential big league talent and a symbolic relationship with The Man. If Brown did hold such beliefs, he was merely the first black baseball entrepreneur to be bitterly disappointed.

Facing extinction as well was the hardy band of blacks clinging to their jobs in the white minor leagues. Small history was made in 1887 when these isolated pilgrims got to play in the biggest big league—in fleeting exhibition encounters against National League titans, with the minor league teams offering up good crowds and a cut of the house to the visiting big leaguers.

By the luck of the draw, the Newark Giants of the International League counted on their roster the dandy battery of George Stovey and Fleet Walker that year when the two New York National League teams, first the Brooklyn Bridegrooms (forebears of the Dodgers) and then the New York Giants, came across the Hudson River for games early in April. Hyping the impact of and the gate for these matches, it was announced in advance that George Stovey would start both games.

Stovey, though, didn't have it against Brooklyn, and was further doomed when Fleet Walker made throwing errors that allowed the Brooks to surge to a 12–4 win. But, facing the Giants days later, both men rebounded; Stovey's fast stuff whistled past the Giants' hitters most of the day, and Walker felt the rush of temporary fame when he gunned down John Montgomery Ward trying to steal second base. That, said the next day's *Newark Daily Journal*, was "something that but few catchers have been able to accomplish."

One would never know by this reportage that Newark lost this game as well, though by a competitive 3–2 score. As if sensing a dramatic irony—that of blacks competing against teams that ostracized them—the sporting press was only too delighted to aggrandize these players. One such account even presented the highly dubious scenario that John Montgomery Ward and his manager, Jim Mutrie, were so impressed by Stovey and Walker that they "made an offer to buy the release of the 'Spanish Battery,' but [the Newark manager] informed him they were not on sale."

The *Binghamton Leader*'s baseball man filed this metaphor-happy take on Stovey:

"Well, they put Stovey in the box again yesterday. You recollect Stovey, of course—the brunette fellow with the sinister fin and demonic delivery. Well, he pitched again yesterday, and...he teased the [Bridegrooms]. He has such a knack of tossing up balls that appear as large as an alderman's opinion of himself, but you cannot hit 'em with a cellar door....What's the use of bucking against a fellow that can throw at the flagstaff and make it curve into the water bucket?"

Fleet Walker was canonized in rhyme:

> *There is a catcher named Walker*
> *Who behind the bat is a corker,*
> *He throws to a base*
> *With ease and grace,*
> *And steals 'round the bag like a stalker.*

Frank Grant got similar treatment when his Buffalo team in the International League lost to the Philadelphia Athletics. "Grant, the colored second baseman," *Sporting Life* rhapsodized, "was the lion of the afternoon. His exhibition was unusually brilliant." Clearly, Grant had the ability to turn sportswriters' prose purple. Early in that 1887 season, after the Bisons beat the Toronto team, that city's baseball man may have set a record for adjectives in reporting that, on one play, Grant "made a double hook-action-compound-reversible-reflex slide."

But no contortions could save the blacks their jobs. It was during this season that noxious gases began bubbling to the surface of the race bog, not because the black players were black as much as because they were black and *good*—which of course they had to be, since unlike many whites they would never have been allowed in the league otherwise. George Stovey, for example, won 35 games for Newark in '87, setting an International League standard that stands to this day.

Such exploits evidently gave Stovey a shot of nerve. He went to Newark manager Pat Powers and demanded more money. Powers could hardly believe what he heard and, after turning Stovey down flat, issued some comments that were not designed to ensure Stovey a long life on any level of baseball. Stovey, Powers said, was "headstrong," "obstinate," and "hard to manage." While allowing that Stovey was "one of the greatest pitchers in the country," Powers added tersely and saliently, "I have more desirable men."

Letting blacks play in the International League was one thing; being shown up by them was quite another. Frank Grant laid waste to league pitching that season, leading the loop with a .366 average. This forced some whites to reach far afield in order to criticize him. When the Bisons played the National League's Pittsburgh Pirates in another of those high-visibility exhibitions, Grant roamed far across the infield to scoop up grounders most second basemen couldn't have touched. Rather than marvel at

Grant, the Pirates' manager, Horace Phillips, criticized him, saying that Grant "paid no attention to...running all over another man's territory." Ironically, Phillips's nickname happened to be Hustlin' Horace—though his own hustle, presumably, was more civil.

These verbal daggers must have stung, but not as much as the game-within-the-game that whites had been developing in response to dealing with black opponents. To many white players, these men were like tenpins, and it became sport to cut them down. Bud Fowler, who created more history than he probably ever knew, may have been responsible for the use of equipment as a baseball accessory when he was forced to start strapping wood splints over his shins while playing second base for Binghamton. It was either that or become a pincushion, since players slid into the bag with spikes flying and aimed at his lower legs. Soon, Frank Grant also donned the splints.

To be sure, nobody in the game said a thing about the civility of *this* style of play—including the blacks, who knew that to impugn white players might be a ticket right out of baseball. Still, for some whites, even those who had no love for integration, this sort of play was upsetting.

"While I myself am prejudiced against playing on a team with a colored player," an anonymous International Leaguer told *Sporting Life* in 1888, "still I could not help pitying some of the poor black fellows. I have seen [Bud Fowler] muff balls intentionally, so that he would not have to try to touch runners, fearing they might injure him. Grant was the same way. Why, the runners chased him off second base. They went down so often trying to break his legs that he gave up his infield position and played right field."

He went on: "About half the pitchers [in the league] try their best to hit these colored players when they are at the bat. One pitched for Grant's head all the time....Do what he could, he could not hit the Buffalo man, and [Grant] trotted down to first on called balls all the time."

The black players could dodge verbal and physical abuse from competitors, and lynch threats from some fans, but they could not sidestep social customs. That their fate was well beyond their control became obvious. Ignoring the incivilities of whites but concerned about the seepage of blacks into the minors, the normally supportive *Sporting Life* wondered in 1887, "How far will this mania for engaging colored players go? At the present rate of progress the International League ere many months may change its title to 'Colored League.'"

Then violence erupted in Syracuse that same season of 1887, when that team's manager, "Ice Water" Joe Simmons—who had once managed Fleet Walker—signed nineteen-year-old black pitcher Robert Higgins at the start of the season. In Higgins' first game, in Toronto, several of his teammates tripped all over themselves in the field, purposely throwing the game, so that Syracuse lost 22–8. The *Toronto World*'s baseball writer called the white players' actions a "disgrace" and a "most disgusting exhibition," pinpointing three Syracuse players in particular who "seemed to want the Toronto team to knock Higgins out of the box," so much so that they made errors "in the most glaring manner." The writer noted that "Higgins retained control of his temper and smiled at every move of the clique."

For the next ten games, the players—whom the *Sporting News* described as a "Ku Klux coterie"—did nothing more to sabotage Higgins, and he won two starts in that span, the second against Binghamton's William Renfroe, thus marking the first time that two black pitchers were said to have faced each other in the white minors.

Then, on June 5, Ice Water Simmons summoned his team to the P. S. Ryder gallery in downtown Syracuse to pose for a team picture. Everyone came except pitcher Dug Crothers and center fielder Harry Simon. Simmons eventually found Crothers, who told him he would not sit for a picture that included "that nigger." A furious Ice Water Simmons ordered Crothers to get his ass to the Ryder gallery or be suspended for the rest of the season. Crothers responded by smashing Ice Water Simmons's jaw.

Simmons did talk sense into Harry Simon, who allowed his picture to be taken (separate head shots were eventually used, rather than a group photo of the team). Within weeks, Crothers, who refused to relent, was fired, though more for mediocre play than the racial confrontation—which Crothers sought to explain in a newspaper interview.

"I don't know as people in the North can appreciate my feelings on the subject," he said. "I am a Southerner by birth, and I tell you I would have my heart cut out before I would consent to have my picture [taken with blacks]. I could tell you a very sad story of injuries done my family, but it is a personal history. My father would have kicked me out of the house had I allowed my picture to be taken."

Reports now appeared describing the behavior of some white players when a black teammate was on the mound. In Buffalo, a white pitcher refused to sign with the Bisons because of the presence of Frank Grant. The white press tended to place the onus on the black players. The *Toronto World* declared, "A number of colored players are in the International League, and to put it mildly their presence is distasteful to the other players."

Sporting Life even claimed that the black players of the International League had "not been productive of satisfactory result"— this in a year when its own pages revealed that Bob Higgins won 20 games and George Stovey 35, while Frank Grant hit .388 and Bud Fowler .350.

Given this depth of ill will, the National League's motives in sanctioning the existence of the Colored League are questionable in retrospect; since the Colored League was financially impoverished from the beginning, investing it with official recognition may have been a way of making its inevitable fall even steeper. Perhaps by white design, its demise would brand blacks as incompetent in the business of baseball. Now, with that failure as a backdrop, the campaign intensified to rid the nine New York teams and one New Jersey team of the International League of the spectre of black players. The most crippling blow would be delivered by a future major league Hall of Famer.

3

Jump, Jim Crow

Wheel about, turn about
Do jest so,
Every time I wheel about
I jump Jim Crow.
    —*Negro character in* The Rifle,
    by Thomas D. Rice, 1828

The feeling is pretty general among professional ballplayers that
colored men should not play with white men.
            —A member of the Buffalo Bisons,
            quoted in the *Buffalo Courier*,
            April 14, 1889

The racist backlash felt by the black players of the International
League in 1887 had little to do with that league per se; it had
everything to do with the national mood regarding racial relations.
In that year the routine subversion of civil rights laws was codified
when the U.S. Congress passed and President Grover Cleveland
signed the Compromise of 1887. This law officially ended Reconstruction, removing all legal obstacles to Jim Crow laws in the
South.

Now, even sophisticated journals in the North such as *The
Nation, Harper's,* and *The Atlantic Monthly*—which had expressed
liberal sensibilities in the matter of race—regularly published
articles depicting blacks as shiftless and unfit for white society.

The *New York Times* noted, without dissent, that "Northern men

30

no longer denounce the suppression of the Negro vote [in the South] as it used to be denounced in the Reconstruction days. The necessity of it under the supreme law of self-preservation is candidly recognized."

By 1896, the Supreme Court, in *Plessy v. Ferguson,* maintained that "legislation is powerless to eradicate racial instincts." By this decision, the Court articulated and made into law the doctrine supporting "separate but equal" accommodations.

Within this cultural maw, the social nature of baseball changed as well. No longer the bluebloods' game, baseball rapidly became a metaphor for the emergence of a new, competitive American middle class. Now, a new wave of first-generation Irish and Germans, who needed paychecks and had specific economic grievances against blacks, spilled onto ball fields clustered in the big teeming cities. On these fields, as in factory sweatshops, it wasn't so much racism at work as it was the pecking order for jobs.

Baseball itself would develop as a game and turn into a national pastime. The game we know today was born in the late 1880s. In 1888, a strikeout was set at three strikes; four balls was ruled a walk but no longer scored as a hit. Leather gloves became mandatory equipment, although they looked like pancakes with slits. In 1889, the two big leagues, the National League and the American Association—each with eight teams covering most of the big urban centers and a sprinkling of smaller markets (Indianapolis in the National League, Columbus and Louisville in the American Association)—drew over two million fans, who gorged on hot dogs and (in the Association only) guzzled beer. The Association, of course, also defied the blue laws and played on Sunday. Plainly, a cultural portent was taking shape on these manicured fields.

However, organized baseball refused to accommodate blacks. And one of the major leagues' biggest stars, Adrian "Cap" Anson, became the point man in the drive to hound blacks out of the game.

This came about in that same pivotal year of 1887, and it centered on the great black players George Stovey and Fleet Walker. On July 14, their Newark team was to play yet another exhibition with a National League team, the Chicago White Stockings (forerunner of the Cubs). Winner of five pennants in the eighties, the league's marquee franchise could boast that its player-manager, Cap Anson, at thirty-five had a record 187 hits and 147 RBIs in 1886 and would be the first man to collect 3,000 hits in a career.

Anson was the idol of little boys who saw him play, but he more properly belonged at the head of a lynch mob. Born to white parents but on a Potawatomi Indian reservation in Iowa, Anson openly loathed people of color. He saved some of his vitriol for the White Stockings' team mascot, a black song and dance man named Clarence Duval, whom Anson labeled a "no-account nigger" and a "chocolate-covered coon." He also leveled his enmity at players he had never met, such as Fleet Walker, whom Anson once tried to have removed from an exhibition game in 1884. Walker's Toledo team defied Anson, but now, Walker and Stovey's Newark team did not when Anson demanded that they be barred from the game.

That same day, July 14, the board of the International League met at the Genesee House Hotel in Buffalo. The purpose of the gathering was to have been the shift of one of the league's teams to another city. However, in response to the growing sense of unease over black players, the issue was introduced in concert by the six teams without blacks on their rosters. According to a newspaper report, "Several representatives declared that many of the best players in the league are anxious to leave on account of the colored element."A motion for the exclusion of all future contracts with blacks was put up for a vote. Owners voted, predictably, six to four for the motion, with only those teams that had black players voting against it. "Color Line Drawn in Baseball" was the headline in the *Newark Daily Journal* the next day.

Exclusion based on race had now become unwritten law in the International League, and a precedent for all levels of organized baseball. For the six active black players in the league (soon to be renamed the International Association), it was more like a purge. *Sporting Life,* which had seemingly endorsed limitations on black players, felt just a tad uncomfortable now that it was a fact. "[Blacks] are all good players and behave like gentlemen," the paper said, "and it is a pity that the line should have been drawn [around] them. Dod gast the measly rules that deprives a club of as good a man as Bob Higgins."

Other observers went beyond sympathy for the players and

wondered if the color line was an excuse for baseball executives to scour the game of anyone whose social background they disapproved of. "The fellows who want to prosecute the Negro," editorialized the *Rochester* (New York) *Post-Express,* "only want a little encouragement in order to establish class distinctions between people of the white race." What had happened at the Genesee House Hotel, said the paper, was a "manifestation of provincialism."

Indeed, baseball's provincialism was especially canting in light of white social lepers like Cap Anson being given the game's benediction, and the glaring inconsistency that welcomed black fans, in the North at least, to attend games. "Does the International League propose to exclude colored people from attendance at the games [as well]?" asked the *Binghamton Daily Leader.*

Since baseball was the perfect example of men in different positions seeking the same goal, the *Newark Call* wondered why the game's elders didn't approve this theme of commonality among all men: "If anywhere in this world the social barriers are broken down it is on the ball field. There many men of low birth and poor breeding are the idols of the rich and cultured: the best man is he who plays best. Even men of churlish dispositions and coarse hues are tolerated on the field. In view of these facts the objection to colored men is ridiculous.

"If social distinctions are to be made, half the players in the country will be shut out. Better make character and personal habits the test. Weed out the toughs and intemperate men first, and then it may be in order to draw the color line."

The *Newark Daily Journal* proved more adamant. Invoking the name of the first black big leaguer, the paper vouched, "It is safe to say that Moses F. Walker is mentally and morally the equal of any [International League] director who voted for the [exclusion] resolution."

Walker and the other black players returned to their "white" teams in 1888. But they walked into a revolving door. George Stovey, who won 35 games in 1887, was let go before the season began. "One of the greatest pitchers in baseball"—by white admission—would play with Trenton in the second-rate Middle States League. The other great pitcher, mild-mannered Bob Higgins, saw his salary boosted from $150 to $200 per month, yet at midseason, subjected to verbal abuse from teammates and fans, he quit and went home to Memphis, finding more peaceful work as a barber.

Bud Fowler, hearing the same abuse, voluntarily asked to be let out of his Birmingham contract before season's end, fleeing to the obscurity of state leagues in Illinois, New Mexico, Michigan, and Nebraska.

Fleet Walker and Frank Grant, meanwhile, remained in the International League, with opposite results. While Grant led Buffalo with a .326 average, Walker hit only .170. But now both men were considering other options. During the late fall of 1888, Grant played with the Cuban Giants, the independent black team. By the spring of 1889, Grant tested Buffalo's desire to have him back by demanding a raise to $250 a month. This made it easy for the Bisons to get rid of him and make it look like Grant's fault.

Finally, with exquisite irony, Fleet Walker—the first black big leaguer—was the last black man standing in the minor leagues. He played in 50 games with Syracuse in 1889, hit .216, then retired to work as a railroad mail clerk in Syracuse—all the while with a mounting indignation about white society, both because of what he had experienced in baseball and as the result of a terrifying incident in April of 1891 that left him facing murder charges.

Walker had been drinking in a Syracuse tavern when he and half a dozen white patrons got into a name-calling argument. When Walker went outside, the whites followed and surrounded him.

Refusing to retreat, Walker, according to newspaper reports, "applied insulting epithets to them." First the whites began punching Walker and throwing rocks at him. Walker reached into his waistband, pulled out a knife, and plunged it deep into the groin of one Patrick Murray just before the rest of the group chased him through the dark streets yelling "Kill him!" Walker escaped, but some hours later the police arrested him and charged him with second-degree murder.

By then, Walker was reportedly so drunk he couldn't recall what had happened. But after sobering up in the city jail, his head cleared.

"Who was that fellow I hit?" he asked the police. "He made a bad move when he came for me."

Considering the times, Walker might have spent the rest of his life in jail, with little legal recourse. However, at his trial in June, over thirty witnesses, some of them ex-teammates, cited Walker's dignified baseball career and gave examples of his courtly demeanor. On his part, the black player presented a convincing and eloquent case for acquittal on grounds of self-defense. When the jury returned with a verdict of not guilty, the gallery went wild. "[I]mmediately a shout of approval, accompanied by clapping of hands and stamping of feet, rose from the spectators," *Sporting Life* reported.

Vindicated, but now a deeply embittered man, Walker left Syracuse for good shortly thereafter. He and his brother Welday operated a hotel in their native Ohio, then published a black newspaper, *The Equator,* in the early 1900s.

Fleet Walker's chosen epitaph was not baseball, but the radical black nationalism baseball led him to advocate. In 1908, Walker wrote a forty-seven-page book, *Our Home Colony: A Treatise on the Past, Present and Future of the Negro Race in America,* which advocated a Back to Africa movement for African Americans, whom he said could expect "nothing but failure and disappointment" in America. Walker condemned whites for maintaining "a damnable and blighting caste spirit."

But the color line had found an ally in Fleet Walker, who ruminated that it was "the nature of man" to separate the races, and "almost criminal" to join them by the force of morality. The failure of pseudo-integration, he said, was "proof positive of an illegitimate association of the races."

The exclusion of blacks from the minor leagues vindicated Walter Cook's Cuban Giants. Having shied away from the enticing but risky National Colored League, the bogus Latinos now owned the patent for blackball success, such as it was. When Cook died in 1887, his successor, John M. Bright, kept the ruse intact—and now found that white teams who wanted no part of blacks on their rosters were eager to schedule games against the thinly veiled blacks posing as Cubans, allowing white teams to benefit from the Cubans' popularity. Even the big leagues could find it propitious to look the other way when it came to the Cubans. In 1887, the year of the great purge in the International League, the National League's Detroit Wolverines played an exhibition game against the Cubans, winning 6–4.

The Cubans did experience a Cap Anson-style obloquy in 1887, when another scheduled exhibition was canceled at the last minute by the big league St. Louis Browns of the American Association after eight Brown players wrote in a statement given to the team's owner, Chris Von der Ahe, on the eve of the game, "We, the...St. Louis Base Ball Club, do not agree to play against negroes tomorrow. We will cheerfully play against white people at any time, and think, by refusing to play, we are only doing what is right." Von der Ahe withdrew the St. Louis team from the field, leaving a full grandstand with no game to watch.

Still, the Cubans viewed this act as confirmation of their sovereignty—from where they sat, the big league players were *afraid* to play them. Now nothing could keep them from lording it over what was left of blackball. In 1888, the Cubans challenged three respected black clubs—the Keystones of Pittsburgh, the Red Stockings of Norfolk, and the Gorhams of New York—to enter a "black championship" tournament in New York. In short order, they vanquished them all.

Affronted by their defeat, and by the Cubans' arrogance, the Gorhams now sought revenge. But when both clubs entered the Middle States League, based in Pennsylvania, the Gorhams couldn't keep pace with the Cubans, who, despite owning the best record, were cheated when the Harrisburg Giants were ruled to be league champions because of some mysterious "forfeits" that no one around the league seemed to know about.

Still frustrated, the Gorhams tried to beat the Cubans in a similar fashion. The Gorhams—now managed by America's first celebrated black player, Bud Fowler—wired *Sporting Life* the news that the club had won the championship of the "New York State Colored League."

Incredulous, Giant owner John Bright wrote the paper, asking: "Who ever heard of a New York Colored League and where did the Gorhams win the championship title? There is but one colored organization now in existence that can lay claim to superiority over all other clubs of its race and that is the Cuban Giants club. They can knock the sox out of any colored club that could be pitted against them."

That season, Bright fitted his team with a new, properly regal nickname. Moving the Giants' base to York, Pennsylvania, they were to be called the Monarchs of York, though in several stories,

Sporting Life referred to them as the "Colored Monarchs of the Diamond," which could not have displeased John Bright. In character, the team—which stole the Gorhams' three top players—ravaged the Interstate League, the new name for the reformed Middle States League.

For a time, their only real competition was the defending champion Harrisburg club—which, in a tacit admission of the Monarchs' power, had fortified itself by signing Frank Grant. For Grant, though, this return to whiteball was no lark. Taunted from day one of his arrival, he was further degraded by having to live in segregated rooming houses instead of the team's regular hotels. In July, Grant abruptly dropped out of the league. Without his talents, Harrisburg quickly dropped from contention.

Strutting his stuff, at the end of the season John Bright wired *Sporting Life* that the Monarchs had finished the season with an 86–42 record, pointedly adding: "Every one of [our] players have conducted themselves as thorough gentlemen both on and off the field, and the earnest manner in which they played together, winning game after game, reflects great credit to the players."

In 1890, when the Cuban Giants went back to their original identity, and to playing independent ball, Frank Grant and George Stovey returned to the club as it barnstormed through the Northeast, reportedly winning 100 of 104 games in 1890, losing only to college teams in New Jersey and once to the hated Gorhams. But blackball was shriveling in the East, as black fans could count on fewer good-paying jobs and couldn't afford to attend ballgames. By 1892, only the Cubans were in operation on a full-time basis.

By the late 1880s, what had begun as a country club of weekend amateurs had metamorphosed into a monopoly. Chafing under the reserve clause, arbitrary fines, and blacklisting, a number of National League players had formed a splinter group, the Brotherhood of Professional Base Ball Players. By 1887, its membership had risen to over ninety disgruntled players, but still the National League refused to modify its policies. The players began a new league in 1890, the Players' National League of Baseball Clubs. Designed as a utopian model of profit-sharing between players and owners, the new league began raiding the National League of its best players.

Although the eight-team Players' League outdrew the National League in 1890, salaries and expenses left no profits to share; instead, it lost $340,000. While the National League lost $500,000 during that catastrophic year, its well-heeled owners had the means to survive, and ultimately the satisfaction of seeing the Players' League sue for peace. Only a year later, agreement was reached whereby several Players' League and National League teams merged, and the surfeit of Players' League performers were left to beg for jobs in the National.

The National League was now the proverbial thousand-pound gorilla; when the big league American Association failed in its small-town markets, it had to plead to the National for similar consolidation. In 1892, major league baseball began the season with a single twelve-team National League, the only concession the grand old league having had to make being its acceptance of Sunday games.

Surveying the baseball scene that year, the league's organ of public information, *Spalding's Glove,* approvingly reported that the sport of baseball was at last being operated on "true business principles."

Those principles, as reflected by the American ideology, were a death sentence to black teams and ballplayers. In 1892, the same year as the National League's predomination, the only facsimile of news concerning blackball involved a false start for integration in the Nebraska State League. Before the season, the league had invited a team from Hastings into the loop. But when word spread that the league was also considering allowing blacks to play, Hastings demurred. The club, reported *Sporting Life,* "stands ready to [enter] providing that [the league] is composed entirely of white players."

This did not, however, stop blackball from appearing in the American heartland and beyond. A team from Lincoln, Nebraska, was first to try, but after a summer of overwhelming victories in the weak Western and Nebraska State Leagues, the Lincoln Giants ran out of funds and stopped playing.

The peripatetic Bud Fowler, however, found fertile ground in the Midwest. In 1890, he signed with a black team in Findlay, Ohio. While the Findlays were playing in Adrian, Michigan, two white local businessmen, L. W. Hoch and Rolla Taylor, persuaded Fowler to move there. Financed by the Page Wire and Fence

Company, the new black ball club became a moving billboard—
the Page Fence Giants. Indeed, rather than representing a city,
they were a road act.

This was, in fact, the prototype of what would be perceived even
many years later as the overriding *modus operandi* of blackball. The
Page Fence Giants turned the almost uniformly white farm belt
into a black man's fantasy land. Rather than ask whites to pay to
see them play, they insisted on such attention. Riding through the
countryside in a custom-built Pullman railroad car, with a cook
and porters at their service, the players would arrive in a town
where they were scheduled to play and go door to door on bicycles
selling tickets to the game.

More than one player found himself facing two barrels filled
with buckshot. However, the game was played in a congenial way
whites understood. Always showing a lot of smiling teeth, performing on-the-field riffs such as double and triple windups and
juggling routines with the ball, the Page Fence boys played at least
as much for laughs as for wins.

When a newspaper in Adrian described pitcher Billy Holland as
"funnier than an end man on a minstrel show," it may not have
been imagery the players cared for, but to the fortunes of the team
it was like vespers. In fact, when one player, a center fielder named
Gus Brooks, collapsed while running after a fly ball during one
game, few in the stands or on the team could have known that
Brooks wasn't riffing. While everyone laughed, Brooks lay on the
ground, dying of a heart attack.

This was the new face of blackball, one that was finding a
context for its existence. Easing white anxieties by accepting the
identities of "Cubans" or "minstrels" could earn these men up to
$100 per month and their own Pullmans, and accommodations in
nice hotels. Even in the South, as the Ku Klux Klan sized hoods
and Jim Crow laws were being enacted, a black amateur team in
New Orleans, the Pinchbacks—proudly flaunting the name of a
black Reconstruction governor of Louisiana—drew large, multiracial crowds against white teams. The Pinchbacks, too, had an
effective gimmick: Their owner was a gambler who bet big money
on the games with other white promoters.

This was the price paid for mainstream legitimacy, so that
careers and paychecks could be extended. Bud Fowler, for example, used the Page Fence Giants to spring back into the minors for

a last shot, with the Adrian team in the Michigan State League in 1895.

But now another form of blackball would emerge. Up to now, even in the minor league sprinklings, this was a game suited to county fairs and bucolic picnics. As a new century beckoned, the geography of blackball was finding a more useful and appropriate context in the inner cities.

4

A Legitimate Profession

We repudiate the monstrous doctrine that the oppressor should be the sole authority as to the rights of the oppressed.
—W. E. B. Du Bois, 1905

Base ball is a legitimate profession.... It should be taken seriously by the colored player, as honest efforts with his great ability will open an avenue in the near future wherein he may walk hand-in-hand with the opposite race in the greatest of all American games—base ball.
—Sol White, in *Sol White's Official Base Ball Guide,* 1907

By the 1890s, African Americans had begun to flee the South. Blacks, representing a huge pool of cheap labor and recruited by northern industrialists, emigrated by the thousands to city ghettos like "Nigger Hill" in South Boston and "Little Africa" in Cincinnati.

Blacks, of course, had played baseball in the big cities, beginning with the Colored Unions-Weeksville match in Brooklyn in 1846. Walter Brown's National Colored League had foreseen the urban potential of blackball even when three-quarters of the black population was situated in the South. Brown's vision, though an immediate failure, carried long-term lessons. Indeed, as the Civil War century began to dim and the conventions of colonial America were turning upside down, one particular black man's passage northward could be seen as a touchstone of blackball's footpath.

By the late 1890s, Frank C. Leland had worked his way over the Mason-Dixon line, rummaging through the blackball wilderness

41

and serving an apprenticeship as the Napoleon of the black game. In 1887, the year he graduated from Fisk College in his hometown of Memphis, Leland played briefly with the Capital Citys of the National Colored League. Educated in prelaw, Leland then moved to Chicago to work as a clerk in the criminal court. But as a baseball man, he also shared Walter Brown's epiphany about blackball as business.

In 1888, Leland put together a combine of some of Chicago's black businessmen to sponsor the black amateur Union Base Ball Club. Unable to secure a permit to play in the city proper, the Unions played on some of the same prairie turf as the Page Fence Giants.

According to the world's first book of blackball history, *Sol White's Official Base Ball Guide,* published in 1907, the Unions became "the leading amateur colored team...against all kinds of odds, the umpires and crowds in general being against them. Nevertheless they won out and closed the season with a clear record of victories."

This experience fed Leland's obsession with baseball. Playing center field for the Unions that year, he was also the club's idea man. By his fiat, the next year the team was known as the Chicago Unions, and Leland had no intention of battling umpires as well as other teams. When the Unions played outside of Chicago, opponents had no choice but to accept the Unions' choice as home plate umpire: Frank Leland.

Leland's hand was behind every move of the team. Using his connections to the city government, he was given a permit to base the Unions at a ragtag field on Chicago's South Side, at Thirty-seventh Street and Langley Avenue, in 1889. Then, in 1894, the year after the Chicago Cubs (nee White Stockings) had vacated the five-thousand-seat South Side Park at Thirty-seventh and Butler, Leland obtained a lease on the grounds.

Earlier, Leland had also recruited Maj. R. R. Jackson, a local black businessman-politico, to help with the finances. Jackson, who knew almost nothing about baseball, said he would join Leland providing he could become the Unions' field manager. Leland promptly fired manager Abe Jones and put the major in charge of the players, who paid no attention to anything he said. The next season, Jackson, his fantasies met, was coaxed to leave the managing to first baseman William S. Peters, who would hold the job for the next ten years.

R. R. Jackson, meanwhile, was more then content to continue as the team's secretary, and Leland further aggrandized him some years later when he began publishing the Unions' yearbook—possibly the first team in all of baseball to highlight its players in print in an in-house organ. Year after year in this yearbook, Maj. R. R. Jackson would be shown in a full-page photograph, in a foppish mourning coat facing three-quarters with a baton in his hand and a carnation in his lapel. The caption, written by Leland, gushed:

> He was born and raised in Chicago, and is identified with every movement in which his race is interested and involved. The Major is known all over the United States as a soldier, good citizen, organizer, public speaker, promoter, financier, and successful business man. His genial disposition has won him a half million friends, and like Frederick Douglass, he believes that—
> "It is not the height to which you have attained,
> But the depths from whence you came."

Frank Leland luxuriated in his own growing notoriety as well. An immense man with cauliflower-sized ears, he slicked his pomaded hair to the sides of a razor-straight part right down the middle of his head and wore a mustache that spread on his lip like a tumbleweed. In keeping with his vision of black baseball, Leland took his Unions into the pro ranks in 1896, listing himself in the club directory as the traveling manager.

Leland's team played in Chicago only on Sundays, against semipro white teams in the Chicago city league, while continuing the club's barnstorming bonanza in the farm belt during the week. And while they were out there on trails crisscrossed by the Page Fence Giants, Leland was making mental notes on who were the best players on that powerful club.

Leland bided his time, building up his team and valuable chits. Leland's eye for talent was certainly rare, and the men with whom he stocked the Chicago Unions were catching the same attention as the best of the Page Fence boys. In fact, it was the latter team that made the first move in what became a battle of wits and wills between Leland and the Page Fence brass.

The blow came when L. W. Hoch and Rolla Taylor lured Leland's top pitcher, Billy Holland, away from the Unions in 1895. This move cemented Page Fence's killer roster, and in '96 the team was said to have amassed a record of 82 wins and 19 losses. The Page Fence Giants were riding so high now that Hoch and Taylor were ready to take on the other Giants of the times, John Bright's cocksure Cuban Giants.

Challenged to come out to Michigan for the still-mythical "Colored Championship" in September of 1896, Bright eagerly looked forward to defeating the Page Fence Giants as he had managed to do with his Cubans' old foes, the Gorhams. Adding to his effrontery, the last time the Cubans ventured west, they had whipped Frank Leland's Unions when the latter were still playing as amateurs in 1894.

But this trip proved to be the Cubans' Waterloo, as they fell victim to the long-ball hitting of shortstop Grant "Home Run" Johnson and the Page Fence pitching rotation of Holland, Harry Buckner, and George Wilson—the last a twenty-year-old phenomenon who had played with white teams in the Michigan State League, one of which was the Adrian squad that featured a young Honus Wagner. In the opener of the fifteen-game series the Cubans trounced Holland and won 20–14. Then, the Cubans suffered a 20–6 defeat in game two en route to losing ten of the fifteen games in a series played like a traveling carnival show across the upper Midwest.

But this series was the *commencement de la fin* of blackball's rustic, country fair incarnation. A national economic depression paralyzed much of the farm belt in the 1890s and hit especially hard at the region's spotty concentrations of black fans. The Page Fence Giants may have been the only team in history to win eighty-two straight games, as they claimed they did in 1897, and then have to quit playing.

Straggling back east, the Cubans had not only lost their swagger but the exclusive use of their name. In New York, a new black team called itself the Cuban X-Giants. Founded by white businessman E. B. Lamar, the X-Giants were only the first in a long litany of black teams to use the name with the hope of emulating John Bright's successful scam. Later, when *real* Cubans began to play in

America, their teams would have to borrow back the word "Cuban" from the non-Cubans.

Not amused by Lamar's larceny, Bright sued him for infringement. Answering the complaint, Lamar insisted, "We are informed legally that the name of the Cuban X-Giants is not incorporated, and that we have a perfect right to the use of same." The courts agreed.

Bright's only recourse was to defend his team's honor on the field. In September 1897, the two squads of ersatz Cubans engaged in a best-of-three match over three successive Sundays in Weehawken, New Jersey. Once again John Bright's ego took a battering, as the X-men won two of the three games and claimed yet another nonofficial "Colored Championship." But if Bright couldn't claim a championship, he could still insist on certain proprietary rights. When the team began the next season, they bore the name of the *Genuine* Cuban Giants.

Genuine or not, E. B. Lamar brushed off the fading Cuban Giants and took on a more formidable opponent, Frank Leland's Chicago Unions. For Leland, this was a risky challenge to accept. Though he had turned his players into a "professional" team, they were not yet ready for top-notch pro competition. With the demise of the Page Fence Giants, Leland was more interested in building up his team. To that end, he raided the corpse of the Page Fence Giants, reacquiring star pitcher Billy Holland. Then he landed another top pitcher, Bert Jones, who had won notices as a pitcher-outfielder with the Atchison team in the white Kansas State League in 1898. But Leland decided he couldn't pass up the opportunity of advancing his team, and agreed to meet the X-Giants in a fourteen-game series in and around Chicago.

According to *Sol White's Official Base Ball Guide,* "[T]he crowds on several occasions [were] enormous. The games were hotly contested all through the series but the superior hitting of the Cuban X Giants won for them the title of champions. They won nine of fourteen games played."

The overflow crowds, and the apparent vulnerability of the Unions, spurred other black businessmen in Chicago to invade Leland's lucrative territory. Fronted by Alvin H. Garrett, one team took the most efficacious route by reforming the Page Fence Giants under the new title of the Columbia Giants of Chicago. To Leland's dismay, the team that played in the Windy City in 1899 was virtually unchanged from the roster Leland had hoped to acquire for himself.

The Columbia Giants were able to find a home field close to Leland's, just a few blocks away at Thirty-seventh and Wentworth. And yet Leland and Alvin Garrett kept their distance, with Leland refusing to play the Giants. Instead, both fattened up on the same local and hinterland competition, while Garrett publicly challenged Leland to settle the question of which was the best team in Chicago. Goaded by Garrett, Leland finally acceded to a five-game match.

This contest became the first real intracity rivalry in pro blackball. Possibly, it was also the biggest baseball event to occur in Chicago up to that time, in part because it attracted hundreds of small and big-time gamblers. Indeed, to some fans, blackball's gambling infestation was a plus, since it paralleled the same trend in the white game. Blackball hucksters took pleasure in the fact that white men in expensive suits and bowler hats could wager small fortunes on the outcome of black competition—despite the fact that white gambling in black sports found its roots in the days of slavery, when plantation bosses would bet on their slave prizefighters.

Even so, it was with a certain pride that Sol White, recalling the Battle of Chicago, included the arcane information that the Columbia Giants "were favorites in the betting at ten to seven. The Unions were not without a following and were backed heavily at the prevailing odds. The rivalry was intense and spectators and players were worked to a high pitch of excitement."

Of the series, White went on: "The Columbia Giants were stronger in the box than the Unions and made less errors in their fielding. These qualifications won for the Columbia Giants the local Championship of Chicago and a big bunch of money. Of the five games played, the Unions did not win a game."

Frank Leland may have been beaten, but he was not about to go the way of the original Cuban Giants, who collapsed after losing to the X-Giants. Leland only accelerated his drive upward. When the X-Giants returned to the Midwest in the fall of 1899 and defeated the Columbia Giants in another challenge round, taking seven of eleven games in the series, Leland dauntlessly challenged the powerhouse X-Giants to another match in 1900, just a couple of years after his earlier humiliation by E. B. Lamar's club.

But in this time the Unions had acquired first baseman Bert Wakefield, who like Bert Jones had starred in the Kansas State League. Risky as it was, Leland's dare paid off. Taking nine out of fourteen games played over three weeks, the Chicago Unions could now claim to hold the colored championship of the whole world.

But even with this signal victory, Leland faced another crisis when Chicago rival Alvin Garrett's Columbia Giants signed star pitchers Harry Buckner and Billy Holland away from the Unions. Leland now needed a huge breakthrough to preserve his team and his ambitions. To achieve it, he enlisted people who were not in the habit of coming to the aid of black baseball—white big league owners.

In 1901, the Western League changed its name to the American League in order to broaden its purview and gain major league status. Under the league's thirty-seven-year-old president, Byron Bancroft "Ban" Johnson—who had played baseball on the Oberlin College team that had once been graced by black stars Fleet and Welday Walker—the American League expanded into a well-financed, lean, eight-team alliance, with the added inducement to the players of having no reserve clause.

As such, it was in a better position to challenge the sovereignty of the National League teams—whose owners had alienated large numbers of their players in the league's decade of monopoly rule—than had been the old American Association, Union Association, and Players' League. Though not yet officially a major league in 1901—that happened in 1902—the American League had signed no fewer than 111 disgruntled National Leaguers to its 182-man workforce. The National League had also lost many of its sycophants in the sporting press. *The Sporting News,* for one, upbraided the old league for its "gross individual and collective mismanagement," "cynical disregard of decency and honor," and "tyrannical treatment of the players."

By contrast, the American League club owners were more visionary. One of them was Charles Comiskey of the Chicago White Sox. Just two decades before, Comiskey had become one of the nation's baseball idols, as first baseman-manager of the American Association's St. Louis Browns. A Hall of Famer, he is often credited with having revolutionized the way first basemen played the position. Straying far from the first-base bag as the pitch was made in order to cover more ground, moving up or back according to the pitch and the game situation, Comiskey brought to the game an element of strategic placement in the field that by the late 1880s had become standard around baseball. (Black players, however, might have had a different memory of Comiskey—as the manager of the Brown team that surrendered to demands by five players to cancel that 1887 exhibition game against the Cuban Giants.) As founder of the White Sox—drawing on the name, in abbreviated form, of Cap Anson's old White Stockings—Charlie's authority was so pervasive that from 1901 until long after his death at age seventy-two in 1931, the Comiskey family would run the affairs of the team.

When the White Sox cast about for a ballpark that first year in Chicago, Comiskey chose to renovate South Side Park, which of course meant that Frank Leland's Unions would have to find a new place to play. But it also meant that Alvin Garrett's Columbia Giants had no field to play on, because their much inferior grounds at Thirty-seventh and Wentworth bordered on the White Sox construction site and they would not be allowed to play near Comiskey's team.

As the Unions' home was torn down, and as Alvin Garrett scrambled for a field, Frank Leland—who apparently had spies at city hall who'd told him about Charlie Comiskey's plans—had already found his new park.

The Unions' new field, Auburn Park, was a small, pleasant strip of green at Seventy-ninth and Wentworth, a couple of miles from South Street Park but close enough to make it plausible that Charlie Comiskey had been persuaded—or had his palm greased enough—to let Leland stay in the neighborhood. Garrett, however, wasn't so fortunate, or powerful. He never found a place suitable for the Columbia Giants. Without ever losing a game to Leland's team, Garrett knew Leland had beaten him.

Homeless now, with the barnstorming trails drying up and the inner-city baseball scene heating up, the Columbia Giants were simply boxed out of existence. On July 17, 1901, Leland filed papers for the creation of a new team, which he called the Chicago Union *Giants*. While this technically seemed to mean that Leland had merged the two teams, in fact his new club included not one former Columbia Giant player. Although Leland wanted to acquire several of these players, out of spite he did nothing, while they waited hopefully to hear from him as to whether they would be allowed to play on his team.

In 1902, Leland relented, making room for former Columbia third baseman William Binga and the team's ex-captain, left fielder John Patterson. For Billy Holland, though, the price of jumping twice from Leland's team was a longer time in perdition. Not until 1905 did Holland again wear a Union uniform.

It was none of these players, though, who drew historical attention to the Chicago Union Giants of 1902. Instead, it was the first recorded presence of a new pitcher from Texas named Andrew Foster. Though only twenty-one, Foster's reputation already preceded him. As it turned out, the reputation was a bit premature.

While Leland had described Foster as his prize protégé, and the youngster could throw a ball through a brick wall, he lost his first two starts. When the Union Giants barnstormed through what was left of bushball in rural Michigan, an unhappy Foster left Leland's Giants and joined a local semipro unit far removed from the pressures of Chicago's big-city baseball.

But Andrew Foster would be back, much to Frank Leland's regret.

5

King Rube

Frankly, I shall always feel that Rube's ability to thwart baseball's threatening skies was outstanding among the things which made him famous in the game's development. And yet, even Andrew Rube Foster was not without his faults.
—Black sportswriter Al Monroe, 1932

The last mile of the prehistoric age of blackball was walked by the Acme Colored Giants, a team based in the apple-farming community of Celoron, New York, who played in the Iron and Oil League. These Giants had been organized in 1898 by a white man, Harry Curtis, who promised the world, "We will have the strongest colored club in America."

According to one *Sporting Life* dispatch, the Acme Colored Giants "enlivened the air with singing and they can sing as well as they can play ball.... The negroes are a jolly, gentlemanly crowd, and an honor to the league."

But Harry Curtis was not happy on July 5, 1898. That day, the Giants lost to the Warren, New York, team 12–4, running their record to 8 victories and 41 defeats. Having seen enough, Curtis fired the entire team and presented a new Acme Giants, sans the word "Colored." He replaced the black players with a white team from Louisville that until recently had been part of the Southern League but that had been cast adrift when the league went bankrupt. Within two weeks, however, not only the new Acmes but the entire Iron and Oil League dissolved because of debt.

Another victim of the era was Bud Fowler. The great black

infielder's elliptical career made its final turns when he left the Page Fence Giants in the mid-1890s, first for the Adrian team of the Michigan State League, Fowler next joined an independent white club in Findlay, Ohio, in 1899. But, as with Frank Grant's last fling in whiteball in Pennsylvania, Fowler's stay in Findlay was dashed by the racism of the times.

In July of that year, *The Sporting News* reported that "the white members of the Findlay ball club have drawn the color line and have demanded of Dr. Drake, their backer, that Bud Fowler, colored, be ousted from the team. They will quit if their demand is not heeded."

When Bud Fowler disappeared into the haze of a semipro team in backwoods Pennsylvania known as the Smoky City Giants, it was the end of the line for blackball's first superstar.

Clearly, at the turn of the century, neither black players like Bud Fowler or Fleet Walker nor teams like the prototypical Cuban Giants mattered in the slow and serpentine progression of blackball. The focus now shifted to the convergence of migration and baseball in the inner city, first in Chicago and later in Philadelphia.

Like Cuban Giant owner John Bright and the Cuban X-Giants' E. B. Lamar, Walter "Slick" Schlichter was a white man who would set blackball on a course of its own. In 1902, Schlichter began to assemble a blackball team he called the Philadelphia Giants that would draw fans from the inner-city ghettos. A sports editor for the white *Philadelphia Item,* Slick had wealth as well as entree into the blackball underground. When Schlichter began to put a team together, he knowingly turned to Sol White.

Now thirty-four, the peripatetic White was a walking road map of blackball's first generation, having played in the National Colored League with the Gorhams, the Cuban Giants, and the Page Fence Giants. White had joined Alvin Garrett's Columbia Giants just in time to be left without a job when Frank Leland outmaneuvered that club, sinking it into oblivion. When Leland imposed his one-year moratorium on signing Columbia players, White didn't stand idly by. Heading east, he came to Philly, looking to hook up with the Cuban X-Giants, when he was intercepted by Slick Schlichter.

With White doubling as shortstop and manager, the team

rapidly came together. Looking back five years later in his *Official Base Ball Guide,* White revealed his initial reading of Slick Schlichter as a typical white scourge of black dignity. "At first glance," he wrote, "it might seem as if Schlichter's only idea was with the view of making money and that it was not to be taken seriously."

Slick would have admitted to mercenary impulses, but he would have pleaded not guilty to the era's exploitation of a race. Rather than standing in the way of black self-ownership, Schlichter positioned himself on solid ground as a race proxy, inasmuch as no segment of the black ownership class had gravitated to black-ball in the East. Like John Bright and E. B. Lamar before him, Schlichter was a white man living a baseball power trip through talented black men, and this inverted irony would be lost to future historians revivifying the ghosts of blackball. In revisionist history, the assumption is that all white owners of seminal blackball teams were no better than plantation bosses.

Walter Schlichter's Philadelphia Giants were built with no less attention to detail and care than Frank Leland's Chicago Union Giants had been. And a good deal of that effort came at the *expense* of the Unions. Exercising an option that had by now become standard operating procedure in blackball, Schlichter began a concerted effort to pry loose members of Leland's powerful team.

Unlike teams in the big leagues, blackball clubs were too busy trying to disembowel each other to put up a united front that would enforce the sanctity of the contract. Indeed, given how easily these teams could vaporize at a moment's notice, the concept of a reserve clause for their players was as logical as making Cap Anson their manager would have been.

As it happened, Walter Schlichter made his move just as Leland's heavy-handedness had led to an equally parlous threat from blackball's western front. In Iowa, a team called the Algona Brownies began raiding Leland's roster as well. The Algonas may have been the first team to have gone from a biracial to an entirely black lineup. The year 1903 was key to the transformation.

That year, the team's white directors lured that human pinball, Billy Holland, to jump from Leland one more time, along with black players like outfielder Bert Jones, catcher George Johnson, second baseman Harry Moore, and pitcher Walter Ball. At the same time, Walter Schlichter was coaxing the defections of second baseman John Patterson, pitcher Harry Buckner, third baseman William Binga, and catcher Robert Footes.

Now it was obvious that Leland had overplayed his hand in trying to teach the old Columbia Giants a thing or two about team loyalty. Many left in Leland's limbo joined the defectors from the Unions to give the Algona Brownies an unbeatable team. They proceeded to smash Leland's hapless club for what was billed as the "Western Championship" in 1903. But the true significance of this series was the fact that a regional delineation was made at all—a tacit recognition that the Midwest was no longer the center of the blackball universe.

In Philadelphia, Walter Schlichter and Sol White had done more than create a team; they had breathed life back into eastern blackball, so much so that E. B. Lamar's Cuban X-Giants were forced to upgrade to stay in the game. Lamar went on his own raiding parties in 1903, landing two major ex–Columbia Giants, second baseman Charlie Grant and shortstop Home Run Johnson.

Grant, in fact, may have been the player most in demand. He had just missed becoming the first black big leaguer since Fleet Walker. Two years before, Grant—a Cincinnati native who happened to have caramel-colored skin—had been working as a porter in Hot Springs, Arkansas, when the newborn Baltimore Orioles of the American League came to town for spring training. Spying Grant sucking up grounders for the black hotel team, Oriole manager John "Muggsy" McGraw—who was prone to underhandedness—hatched a plot to circumvent the barrier against men of color the way Walter Cook had with the Cuban Giants, by making Grant a man of less color.

Because Grant didn't look black, McGraw cast him as a Native American, complete with the identity of "Tokahoma" and the legacy of a full-blooded Cherokee. Tokahoma wore the Oriole uniform in practice games. But soon rumors of the ruse were spread by the now-retired and still openly racist Chicago White Stocking great Cap Anson, who was now an adviser to White Sox owner Charlie Comiskey. Comiskey, in turn, raised hell over the possibility that a black man or a Native American was being sneaked into baseball by McGraw.

"I'm not going to stand for McGraw bringing in an Indian on the Baltimore team," Comiskey railed. "If Muggsy really keeps this Indian, I will get a Chinaman of my acquaintance and put him on third. Somebody told me that the Cherokee of McGraw's is really Grant, the crack Negro second baseman from Cincinnati, fixed up with war paint and a bunch of feathers."

By this rather oblique remonstration, it was unclear whether Comiskey objected on grounds of race alone or because Baltimore would be getting its hands on a great black player by means of chicanery, thus snookering all the other clubs who would have loved to sign black players. But, seeing that his game was up, McGraw released Grant, who returned to Chicago, only to lose the opportunity to play when the Columbia Giants were run off the field by Frank Leland.

Walter Schlichter rescued him, but when in 1903 the Cuban X-Giants met the Philadelphia Giants for the eastern half of the World's Colored Championship—which Schlichter and E. B. Lamar insisted was indeed the *whole* world's Colored Championship—none of the veteran names would receive the accolades for having dominated the series. That claim to fame would go to black pitcher Andrew Foster.

Though it was barely a year since Foster had bailed out of Frank Leland's Unions, the interim had proven Leland's wisdom in bringing Foster up from the South. Leland knew at the time that Andrew Foster was a big man—six feet, two hundred pounds— with a fastball that melted bats and a "fadeaway"—the original term for the screwball. This pitch came out of his right hand and broke like a hard curveball in reverse, in to right-handed hitters, away from lefties, and paralyzing to all of them. But there was more to the Foster story, something that presaged titanic advances for black baseball.

First off, Foster had already earned himself a nickname and a legend. Although no one's ever been able to verify it, Foster came north on the wings of a story oddly similar to Charlie Grant's. Pitching for the very same Hot Springs hotel team in 1901, Foster, it was said—or at least Foster said—was invited to, as he put it, "fling 'em over" to Connie Mack's Philadelphia Athletics, who were training on the grounds that spring.

Supposedly beating Mack's ace, Rube Waddell, in an exhibition game, Foster left Hot Springs with the moniker of "Rube beater," which then became simply "Rube." Foster, however, was anything but a rube. Born in 1879, Foster was the son of a country minister from Calvert, Texas. The preacher man's son shied away from booze but packed an ivy-handled pistol under his belt. The gun and his cinder-block dimensions made Foster a truly frightening figure, an image which he seemed to enjoy, but Foster's wits and his burning ambition were aimed, however surreptitiously, at social climbing.

Foster was, by one account, "operating a baseball team in Calvert while he was still in grade school." At seventeen, Foster had made it to Waco, pitching for the black Waco Yellow Jackets and gaining a reputation thousands of miles away. Indeed, it wasn't Frank Leland but Leland's manager, W. S. Peters, who first attempted to bring Foster to Chicago. Playing hard to get, Foster demanded carfare. Peters wouldn't agree, but Leland was by now so intrigued and so convinced he had to have Foster that he wired the money.

That Rube Foster washed out with the Unions did not end the fascination about him. In 1902, looking to compete with the Philadelphia Giants, E. B. Lamar was the next to bring Foster north. Rube began with the X-Giants the same way he had with the Unions—he was blasted from the mound in a 13–0 loss to a team from Hoboken. But this was obviously a work in progress; learning to harness his stuff and to hold men on base, Foster's greatness arrived during the X-Giants' climactic championship series against the Philadelphia Giants.

This eight-game series was played at various fields in and around Philadelphia, bringing out the city's black population in force. Of the matchup, Sol White wrote: "These games were of the utmost importance and were fought with the bitterest feeling at every stage of the series." If so, the taste was especially bitter for White's club, which fell four times to Foster alone in the X-Giants' five-to-two-game series triumph. White confessed that his team was "outplayed in all departments of the game."

Walter Schlichter, though, would not lose gracefully. All during the 1904 season, Schlichter used his newspaper columns to dump on Lamar's team as inferior and lucky to have won. Sol White, on his part, passed off his club's loss as self-inflicted. "The Phillies," he wrote, "owing to dissension in the team were far from being satisfied with their defeat...and claimed that with proper harmony in their ranks, they could turn the trick on their much hated rivals."

The trashing and alibies—these trademarks of ballplayer behavior are plainly not modern inventions—set the backdrop of the rematch, a three-game series in Atlantic City in September 1904. (These so-called championship games were made all the more dramatic by the fact that these elite teams never met during the summer season, their priority being to rake in as much money as they could while barnstorming against both black and white semipros and amateurs.)

According to White, "Both players and spectators were worked to the highest pitch of excitement. Never in the annals of colored baseball did two nines fight for supremacy as these teams fought. Everything known to baseball was done by both nines to win."

However, what was done by Walter Schlichter before the season even began proved to be the difference. Knowing he would have to back up his bravado, and in the finest tradition of blackball, he stole Rube Foster.

Even so, few blackball experts believed the Philadelphia Giants would reverse the outcome of the previous year. The X-Giants still had such stars as second baseman John Patterson, pitcher Harry Buckner, and shortstop Home Run Johnson. But, unlike their timorous play of the last match, the "Phillies" displayed what Sol White called "the nerviest kind of ball playing."

Still, it would be Rube Foster—who came out of a sickbed to pitch, having caught a fever near the end of the season—who'd be responsible for the team's victory. The Cubans, playing head games to get an edge, had passed the word that Foster hadn't been sick at all, just scared. Which, of course, made this the crossroads of Foster's career. He *had* to pitch, lest he be called a coward. And so he came to Atlantic City, on his own, at the last minute, and when he took the mound for game one, the crowd went absolutely delirious.

As it turned out, this would become the first great mythical game of blackball's scarred life, as it lionized the achievement of one man above that of his team. Foster, keeping the X-Giants' heads spinning all day, struck out eighteen hitters—a number that, in the absence of any other reliable statistics, was immediately hailed as a blackball record, one that would stand up against decades of confirmable black games—despite the fact that the 8–4 win was far from his best game.

In fact, Rube had a better outing in game three—after the X-Giants won game two, propelled by four stolen bases by John Patterson—when he clinched the title by allowing just two hits in the 4–2 victory. Foster, who batted sixth in the order and often played right field on the days he didn't pitch, also led his team at bat, hitting .400 in the series.

Now blackball had a star who could inspire the national imagination and pump up a national agenda. His teammates, however, knew Foster was a hard man with a hard stare, an irritable fellow with a gun on his hip who kept to himself. Not that Foster was particularly disturbed that he was unloved. In his own vision of himself, Rube Foster was not equal among men, black or white. He was born to *lead* men.

For the next two decades, Foster and his obsessions would run roughshod over the black game. Like King Lear, he looked through those hard eyes and saw a world that would provide him with a hundred knights; wherever he went, whatever he did, blackball bowed to his wisdom, mostly in fear.

In his immediate wake, baseball became a stampede in inner-city Philadelphia. In the space of two years, at least nine new teams, all bearing the name "Giants," were born within a hundred miles of the city—as were two *genuine* Cuban teams based there, the Cuban Stars and the Havana Stars. Many of the players on these two teams had found jobs in blackball because of an adjunct boom, one touched off in Cuba when E. B. Lamar took his team on a playing tour throughout the island in the early 1900s, igniting a near-missionary zeal for the sport among the natives.

Entering the age of baseball, Cubans had their first American hero—Rube Foster, who dispatched Cuban league hitters by the dozens when the Philadelphia Giants toured the island in 1903.

Assuredly, Rube Foster wove black baseball into a permanent place in the American sports fabric. Yet nowhere in the Foster hype was the suggestion that he was possibly as much con as conqueror. Regarded far and wide as imperishable as a pitcher, it was obvious to those around him that by 1907, after just four seasons in the "bigs" of blackball, he was far more vulnerable than had been thought. By then, the cinder-block body had turned to cream cheese; capable only of sporadic starts, he looked like a flannel-covered beach ball in his uniform—which was why he rarely permitted anyone to photograph him until he could shimmy into one of his snazzy three-piece business suits and jaunty roadster cap.

Foster had the good sense to pack his storied pitching performances into those four formative years, though the fact remains that outside of those big postseason games, records on Foster during his career are lost in the great abyss that claimed so much of blackball's attempts at record-keeping; even Sol White could get no more specific than reporting that Rube had pitched "several no hit games and has struck out as high as 18 men in a single game [during those four seasons] against such teams as the Trenton YMCA...and the Cuban Stars."

What is left to fill the void is the first-person testament of Rube himself, who in 1907 gave an interview to writer Frederick North Shorey in the black *Indianapolis Freeman*. In this deposition, which was responsible for carving much of the Foster legend, Rube said he had won fifty-one out of fifty-five ball games in 1905, which he allowed "was doing pretty well."

And yet, as Rube was eating himself into a cream puff, other men of the Philadelphia Giants were burning up the barnstorming brambles. One was young pitcher Dan McClellan, who in his first year in the pros in 1903 had hurled the first recorded perfect game in blackball as, playing with the Cuban X-Giants, he mowed down the York team of the Tri-State League.

Jumping to the Philly Giants the next year, McClellan pitched key games, especially in 1906—a season that was a torture test for Sol White. Even before it began, White watched helplessly as, first, Home Run Johnson took over the managing reigns of the fledgling Brooklyn Royal Giants. Then, White saw his top players—Rube Foster, again, included—report sick or lame all summer long. As he recalled his travails, White's clipped and careful prose betrayed an edge of irritation that players were not playing because they weren't getting paid enough by Walter Schlichter—who had a habit of paying game expenses out of the players' cut of the gate.

White wrote, "With the many complaints of players and threats of quitting ringing in [my] ears every day," he had "passe[d] many a sleepless night."

Sol frequently donated his own money to soothe these players.

But it can be speculated that a man like Rube Foster, with megalomania on his mind, could not have been content, not at $400 a month and not while he was itching to broaden his horizon. In any case, it was McClellan and another former X-Giant, Home Run Johnson, who were said to have excelled when the Philadelphia Giants claimed their next "championship" in 1906.

This playoff round was actually high noon for the latest try at organizing a blackball league—though it was a Negro league with an asterisk. In what was essentially a vehicle by which E. B. Lamar could boost himself, the International League of Independent Professional Base Ball Clubs sought to exclude from blackball the superior Philadelphia Giants. Lamar admitted into the league new, feeble teams like the Quaker Giants and the two authentic Cuban clubs—and dressed the whole thing up as a serious portent of racial rapport by including two bland white teams, the Philadelphia Professionals and the Riverton-Palmyra (Pennsylvania) Athletics. He also anointed as a figurehead president and secretary two men with the conspicuously Caucasian names of Friehoffer and O'Rourke.

But Lamar's plans collapsed. By July, the Quaker team and the Havana Stars went bankrupt and Lamar had to swallow his pride and ask Walter Schlichter to aid his dying blackball league. Slick did, and in September of 1906 Sol White had the pleasure of watching his Phillies come together in the process.

Indeed, they took on all blackball challenges that year, trouncing the X-Giants in ten of fifteen games, and the Brooklyn Royal Giants in eleven of seventeen in the weeks prior to the International League title game. When they clubbed the X-Giants in that game, which was played on Labor Day, the growing imprimatur of Walter Schlichter's team was such that it was allowed to rent out the eighteen-thousand-seat Baker Bowl, the National League Phillies' home park—a mutual-gain arrangement with the big leagues that was a first for blackball—and drew over ten thousand fans.

For winning, Sol White wrote, the Giants were presented "a beautiful cup donated by President Friehoffer." But this was just a pit stop for the Philadelphia Giants. On September 30, 1906, they played three games in about eight hours. In the morning, they beat the Royal Giants—the newest home of the nomadic pitcher Billy Holland—6–1 in Elizabeth, New Jersey. At midday, they beat the X Giants again, 5–2, at Brighton Oval in Brooklyn. In midafternoon, they beat the Brooklyn Athletic Club on the same field, 6–2.

Exhilarated, Sol White went to press with his priceless guide to black baseball. Closing his narrative, he plumed his team, the black game, and the black race:

> September 30 marked the close of twenty years of professional Colored Base Ball. Taking lessons from the past, there seems to be nothing but the brightest prospects for great advancement in the future.

Sol White was only partly right. There would be room for advancement for blacks in baseball over the next several decades. But it would be only within the isolated forest of blackball, and even then only for a select few.

6

A Dangerous Predicament

The business end of the game has lagged along to such an extent that we now find ourselves in a dangerous predicament. We have a country full of colored ball players, well-developed as to playing; but the places for giving employment are being promoted with such an eel-like pace, and the majority are founded upon such an uncertain business principle, that it is having a tendency to throw a dense cloud over the Negro.

—Rube Foster, 1910

In his *Official Guide*, Sol White allowed Rube Foster to write a bylined article entitled "How to Pitch." Rube's dissertation was perhaps the first reference to pitching as the most critical component of baseball. "[I]t matters not how strong the infield or outfield may be, or how fast a team is on the bases," Foster declared. "The main strength of all base ball nines lies in their pitchers."

Going further, Foster offered an ingenious look inside a pitcher's head in describing the psychological game-within-the-game that few fans knew existed:

> The real test comes when you are pitching with men on bases. Do not worry. Try to appear jolly and unconcerned. I have smiled often with the bases full with two strikes and three balls on the batter. This seems to unnerve them. In other instances, where the batter

appears anxious to hit waste a little time on him, and when you think he realizes his position and everybody is yelling for him to hit it out, waste a few balls and try his nerve; the majority of times you will win out by drawing him into hitting at a wide one.

Foster's counsel for pitchers was radical for its day—and is no less so for many pitchers now:

Some pitchers when they have three balls and two strikes on a batter, often bring the ball straight over the plate and as the batter is always looking for it that way he will possibly "break up the game" for you. I use a curve ball mostly when in the hole. In the first place, the batter is not looking for it, and secondly, they will hit at a curve quicker as it may come over the plate, and if not, they are liable to be fooled. Most pitchers... use a fast ball close to the batter, which the batter can easily see will be on the in-corner of the plate and they get their eye on it very easy.

Finally, Foster said, "The three great principles of pitching are good control, when to pitch certain balls, and where to pitch them. The longer you are in the game, the more you should gain by experience. Where inexperience will lose many games, nerve and experience will bring you out the victor."

While no big league manager or pitching coach admitted to being influenced by Foster, his principles would evolve into the gospel of the pitching arts. Foster himself insisted that some teams sneaked him into their training camps to instruct pitchers on how to throw the fadeaway. One such sojourn, he said, came after Muggsy McGraw, hounded by Ban Johnson for his unending boorish behavior, quit Baltimore to take the reins of the National League's New York Giants. McGraw, the story went, brought in Foster, whose instructions turned Christy Mathewson into a Hall of Fame pitcher.

Another team that appeared in Rube's reveries was the Philadelphia Athletics. Foster liked to boast that Connie Mack had him on a kind of loose retainer, available at all times to analyze the Athletics' mound staff.

Foster's homilies would be repeated again and again by the

black press throughout the years. Unquestionably, he became a respected underground authority in the early years of the century; and it was just as certain that Rube used all his wily tricks in exhibition games against big league teams, games that he right-fully believed could create for himself enormous goodwill and good notices.

What's more, these testimonials could cross some serious color lines. After Foster hurled an exhibition game against the St. Louis Cardinals in 1910, the great Rogers Hornsby added fuel to the Foster legend by calling his fellow Texan "the smoothest pitcher I've ever seen"—which had an additional resonance, since "Rajah" Hornsby openly boasted of his Ku Klux Klan membership.

Still, as early as 1906, Foster's pitching was a means to an end, and that end was personal power. More and more now, his instincts veered from pitching and the tedious stream of ball games in the sticks. His impulse was to make blackball credible, to bring the black game to the same heights as the white one by the force of his will, his personality, and what he saw as his God-ordained rise in the black game.

In 1905, the white promoter Walter Schlichter, fully intending to ensure the racial purity of blackball, at least as he saw it, joined in a business affiliation with Nathaniel Colvin Strong, a thirty-one-year-old white promoter from New York.

Tall, bone-thin, and sharp-featured, "Nat" Strong was raised on the streets of Manhattan and began investing in local semipro teams after he graduated from City College in the mid-1880s and began selling sporting goods. His first team, the Murray Hills, featured a young Gene Tunney, the future heavyweight champ. Strong also bought the real estate on which sat ball fields such as Brighton Oval and Dexter Park in Brooklyn. In Dexter Park, part of the outfield was landscaped on a sloping incline, over the grave of a horse, so the story went, which is why right field there came to be known as Horse Heaven. Offering these fields to local competi-tion, Strong sold permits to semipro and black pro teams for escalating fees.

This became a lucrative side business for Strong, and then his principal endeavor. With John Bright's Cuban Giants and E. B. Lamar's Cuban X-Giants playing regularly at Brighton Oval and Dexter Park, Strong demanded a cut of the gate from any games played at these sites. By the early 1900s this operating system had grown into a monopoly in the East; now, any black and most semipro white teams had to work out an arrangement with Nat Strong if they hoped to play in New York. Nat would arrange the dates, place, and price, and routinely received 10 percent of the gate.

Until 1919, charging admission for a Sunday baseball game was prohibited in New York City. But realizing that Sunday ball could be a bonanza, Strong got around the law by letting people in free for Sunday games—and then charging for programs at the extravagant price of fifty cents each, more than the price of a ticket. Deposited in Strong's coffers, these spoils mounted. By 1900, Strong was renting office space in the prestigious World Building in downtown Manhattan.

One of his most frequent visitors was Walter Schlichter. Considering Strong to be a true friend of blackball, Schlichter had no qualms about paying Nat his meed when the Philadelphia Giants came to New York.

In 1905 Strong made Slick a partner in his booking operation. The sign on the door to room 46 now read Strong & Schlichter. Nat Strong further titillated newspapermen by appointing Walter Schlichter president of an organization with possibly the longest name in the history of sports: the National Association of Colored Baseball Clubs of the United States and Cuba. No one knew the actual function of the association, but Schlichter proudly displayed its name on his stationery and business cards.

Nat Strong had more important things on his mind than Walter Schlichter. Having secured the land rights to eastern blackball, he now made his goal owning teams that played on that land, though his first move may have been simply an exercise in raw power. When the Brooklyn Royal Giants came into existence in 1905, Strong would collect his usual rental and gate fees from the team's games. But as the team turned into a class act and a force in blackball, he craved more.

Thus began another of blackball's power struggles, to go along with the Cuban Giants versus the Cuban X-Giants and Frank Leland versus the Columbia Giants. This battle for the Royals involved the only eastern blackball power to actually be owned by a black man: John W. Connors, an ambitious black businessman who had formed the club with the profits from his supper club in Brooklyn, the Royal Cafe.

Over the next few years, Strong hiked the fees at Brighton Oval, leading Connors to correctly believe that Nat wanted to bankrupt him so that he could take over the club. Connors would try to resist Strong by fleeing Brooklyn and setting up the team's home base at Harlem Oval, at 125th Street and Lenox Avenue, while he looked desperately for support from the black men of blackball to help him keep control of his Royals. However, their timid response made it clear to him that his battle to remain a black owner of an Eastern blackball team faced long odds.

Rube Foster, sharp as his senses were, couldn't help but notice these events. Foster realized that blackball was now in danger of being defined by its white overseers, and he decided to play an active role in the game's future.

Providentially for Foster, the means to achieve his ambitions opened up before him in Chicago, where Frank Leland's kingdom was foundering. Leland had not been able to weather the raids of the early 1900s. However, he had been able to hire new players, including Billy Holland, who would head the pitching crew again. In 1905, taking to heart the theme of redemptive change, he gave the club a new name, the Leland Giants. That year, with Leland back at the helm and back in the dugout, the Lelands were said to have won 112 of 122 games, including 48 in a row.

While they were champions on the field, and whipping the competition in the Chicago City League and on their tours, the Leland Giants were losing money, due to the fact that Frank Leland's sense of decency undercut his business acumen. Booking games for his team, Leland had none of Nat Strong's viper instincts. Rather than driving up his team's cut to extortion levels, Leland allowed his opponents to collect almost as much of the profits as he did.

By 1906, a desperate Leland had to reorganize. This entailed incorporating the team and then creating a holding company with the title of the Leland Giants Base Ball and Amusement Company. Leland became the figurehead president of both concerns, selling $100,000 worth of stock to financial angels. Maj. R. R. Jackson invested, as did a number of black businessmen and a prominent black attorney and ward heeler with the aristocratic name of Beauregard Moseley.

These arcane machinations saved the team and even led Leland to talk about opening an amusement park on the Auburn Park grounds, but they did nothing to ameliorate the problem of Leland's magnanimity, nor the dearth of marquee names on his roster. But, now, having seen the goings-on back east, and remembering his onetime protege, Frank Leland sent money to Andrew Foster to come to Chicago.

Rube agreed to join the Lelands upon one large condition: that in addition to pitching, he would take charge of the booking chores. Leland may have been stunned by Foster's nerve, but he was in no position to reject his offer—especially when Rube told Leland that several other Philadelphia Giant players would bolt with him.

When Foster made his way to Chicago in the spring of 1907, his defection alone made the blackball earth move on a new axis. But Foster really stunned Walter Schlichter by delivering to the Leland Giants several other superb players, including outfielder Andrew "Jap" Payne, second baseman Nate Harris, and catcher James "Pete" Booker.

Eastern blackball responded by doing what all good black teams saw as their first option. Playing the same game, Schlichter's team raided the Brooklyn Royal Giants, stealing their best player, catcher Bruce Petway, and signing twenty-two-year-old shortstop John Henry Lloyd away from under E. B. Lamar's deteriorating Cuban X-Giants.

Lloyd was a prize catch. Born in Florida, with a reputation as a baseball wunderkind in Georgia that won him a ticket north, he was cast in the Rube Foster mold. When Lloyd, a lean and lanky man, began his career as a catcher, his face was smashed so often by foul tips that he fashioned a catcher's mask out of a waste-basket. Soon after E. B. Lamar brought Lloyd north, the catcher jilted Lamar's Cuban X-Giants and signed with the Philadelphia Giants, leading them to victory over the Cuban X-men for the eastern title in 1907.

But now that title carried less weight—literally, with Rube Foster in a Leland Giant uniform. At once, knowing that Foster's purview was magisterial and subject to no other authority, Frank Leland appointed him field manager, which gave more weight to his presence and drew hordes of people to games even when Rube wasn't on the mound.

The Leland Giants became masters of "raceball"—the kind

marked not by color but by men on the go all the time. The hit-and-run play had long been a part of the game, but Foster, a brilliant manager, made it nearly the whole game. Everybody ran, breaking from first on nearly every pitch. This whirl of men in motion drove pitchers nutty, and Foster tortured them further by playing bunt-and-run, which meant that, when the strategy was executed correctly, a man could go from first to third without the ball being hit beyond the pitcher's mound.

The Leland Giants were indoctrinated to take the extra base, and a dawdling fielder could prove fatal to his team's chances. Knowing that this fielder would overcompensate by hurrying his throw, Foster could reasonably expect to score extra runs on errors. Foster also instructed his men to wait out the pitcher, rattling the man's nerves. And his own pitchers were schooled in Rube's rules of geometry, physics, and psychology; often, the slightest alteration in a man's windup or stride to the plate could make him a winner, and Rube studied his pitchers from top to bottom, looking for structural flaws.

In short order, pitchers like Bill Gatewood, Billy Norman, and veteran Walter Ball became learned craftsmen, blending strong arms with sharp minds. While head-hunting and spitballs were an implicit part of the black game, they were not employed by Foster. Not only did Foster abhor such tactics, but he was putting his sense of honesty and probity on display for whiteball owners and managers, who he believed might find in him a shining exemplar of blackball too powerful to overlook for employment, if not now then someday soon.

Certainly Foster's profit-turning skills were making a statement of purpose, though it was more like the doings of Nat Strong than those of Connie Mack. Under Foster's sway, the Leland Giants received 40 percent of the gate and reaped around $500 per game, up from the $140 that had been collected during Leland's booking days. Subsequently, Foster's 40 percent extraction rose to 50 percent, at the same time that ticket prices rose to the major league level of fifty cents for a grandstand seat.

Indirectly, Foster's influence in Cuba made blacks important players there. In 1907, the island organized a winter league and Cuba became a back door to integration when American blacks vied for open spots there with American whites and the two races commingled—a frightening prospect to some white players back home. In 1909, when the Detroit Tigers toured the island after their pennant-winning season, Ty Cobb stayed home rather than face the black players who had been bogeymen to him by virtue of his youth in Georgia. Persuaded to accompany the Tigers on a return visit the next year, Cobb was outhit and overshadowed by John Henry Lloyd, Home Run Johnson, and Bruce Petway.

Such humiliations struck a raw nerve. After Mack's world champion Philadelphia Athletics made the tour in 1911, only to lose as many games as they won, Ban Johnson decided to take preventive measures, embargoing American League teams from, as he frankly admitted, "going to Cuba to be beaten by colored teams." Even so, big league players ventured to Cuba on their own, as did black players, who lived with them in a racially consonant atmosphere.

More directly, playing against Rube Foster's Leland Giants became a special event for major leaguers, even if they sometimes had to do so on the sly, by joining Chicago City League teams with names like the Logan Squares, the Donahues, the Red Socks, the Rogers Parks, the West Ends, and the Spaldings. The Chicago City League games were played on Saturday and Sunday mornings, before the major league games. White major leaguers in need of spare cash would play on the black professional teams using pseudonyms and pulling their hat bills down over their faces.

White Chicago Cub players, including Johnny Kling, Johnny Evers, and Joe Tinker, were regulars. It is questionable whether their manager, Frank Chance, knew what was going on. However, he was duly impressed by the Leland Giants, who dominated the Chicago City League, and by Rube Foster in particular. Chance said that, fat as he was, Foster was "the most finished product I have ever seen in the pitcher's box."

And so while big league teams were avoiding African Americans, Rube Foster had created a small opening. But even while confirming what big leaguers knew, and never denied—that there were some superb black country hardball players—the same hazy circumscriptions that had prevailed in the 1880s made coexistence possible only in the context of white *versus* black. Rather than being recognized as a vulgar exploitation of bigotry, then, these dubious concessions had to stand as social progress, since Ty Cobb's racist views reflected those of most major league teams.

In 1908, for example, the Chicago Leland Giants came off the road in August for a six-game series against a hastily assembled "All-Star" team of former major leaguers. Fronted by the New York Giants' hard-hitting outfielder Mike "Highlonesome" Donlin, the All-Stars included such big league rejects as Gus Munch, Percy Sullivan, and Jimmy Callahan, as well as local sandlot players. But the scent of a major league date with Rube Foster drew a huge advance sale at Chicago's Auburn Park. The pot grew so much that Leland, who regretted having made a prior arrangement with the white team to split the gate, made a $1,000 side bet on the outcome with Donlin.

Of the five thousand fans who jammed into Auburn Park for each game during the series, it seemed that all but a handful also had gambling on their minds. Bets were made on everything, down to who scored first and last and how many balls and strikes would accrue on each hitter—the betting game on Chicago's South Side being no less highly evolved than Rube Foster's game plans. Nearly lost in this insanity was the fact that Foster waddled to the mound and won the game 3–1, limiting the All-Stars to just three hits. In all, the Chicago Giants took four of the six games, with Rube providing the closure by starting and winning the last game.

Frederick North Shorey, the black reporter for the *Indianapolis Freeman* who had won Rube's trust, praised him repeatedly. Shorey saw a broader province spreading out under Foster's spikes. He wrote after the series:

> Rube Foster was the whole thing and, what is more, he knows it....[I]f it were in the power of the colored people to honor him politically and to raise him to the station to which they believe he is entitled, Booker T. Washington would have to settle for second place.

Not uncoincidentally, political power was exactly what Rube sought, but much more pronounced than Frank Leland's notion of political power, which consisted of the scraps that the local Chicago clubhouse threw his way. By 1908, Leland was a clerk in the circuit court, a clerk in the Board of Review, a deputy sheriff, and a member of the Cook County Board of Commissioners. Foster's appetite was much larger. Leland had wanted to make a black baseball team a valuable commodity; Foster wanted to dominate the business of blackball as a whole.

Foster considered himself the owner of blackball's future, and its eternal legacy. As it was, he figured he owned Cuba. In 1909, Rube informed Frank Leland that he wanted him to recuse himself from all facets of the business operation of the Leland Giants. Thus began a war of raw nerves that marred the season, which turned out to be less than profitable for the club after Foster reportedly injured his leg in July during a game against the Cuban Stars.

Could Rube have faked an injury and stayed out of the lineup as a pointed message to Leland? Consider that Rube Foster routinely froze the day's supply of baseballs prior to games to deaden them. He had his groundskeepers sodden the infield grass to slow down his team's bunts, and to embank the outer edges of the baselines to keep those bunts in fair ground. For Rube Foster, the point of all human endeavor was to come out ahead.

What's more, Foster chose the most dramatic time to pronounce himself fit to pitch again. After the Leland Giants had concluded two months of backwoods touring, the team arrived in the Windy City for a three-game exhibition series against the Chicago Cubs. The Cubs' owner, Charles W. Murphy, catered to Rube Foster's ability to attract fans by scheduling games against Leland's team. However, Frank Chance, the manager who had spoken so effusively of Foster, and Johnny Evers, who went undercover in the Chicago City League and played against Foster, both refused to play in an official capacity versus the black team.

Even so, it was of no small import that no other Cubs followed them out the door. The series commenced with the Lelands' veteran Walter Ball on the hill against the Cubs' outstanding Mordecai "Three Finger" Brown. The result, according to one report in the black press, was: "With the help of the umpires, who were more than favorable to the Cubs, the white boys won 4 to 2." But many fans would recall this game for a single moment of unbelievable courage by the Lelands' Joe Green. Trying to steal third, Green broke his leg, but when the ball trickled away from the third baseman Green got to his feet and half-hopped home- ward in a vain attempt to score. This was one blackball legend that was carved in pain, not myth.

The Leland Giants also dropped game two, 1–0, on a late error. Now, needing to save face, Rube Foster had an amazing recovery from what he had diagnosed as a broken leg. Taking the ball, he drank in a thunderous ovation from a full multiracial house of fans. If this was his message to Frank Leland, Rube reveled in its transmission.

Staked to a 5–0 lead against a pitcher with the catchiest name in baseball—Orval Overall—Rube cruised through most of the game. Though nicked for a run in the fourth on a Joe Tinker double, he was ahead 5–2 in the ninth. But the globular, sweating Foster was tiring, and loaded the bases with one out. He then forced in a run with a walk, but got the second out on a force at the plate.

Now, with the bases full of Cubs, Rube tried to bear down, only to give up a game-tying double to weak-hitting Del Howard.

What happened next has become a matter of conjecture. What is known is that Foster walked off the mound and to his dugout, in order, he said later, to remove himself and bring in a reliever, and only after calling time-out. But since no one on the field heard Rube call time, and with no sign from any umpire, the Cubs' Frank "Wildfire" Schulte bolted from third and crossed the plate with the winning run.

For years, Foster kept trying to explain his side of the bizarre ending, framing it in terms of white-umpire malice, while steering hard away from the impression of a gutless Foster lifting himself when a humongous game was on the line. In fact, the Foster scenario only added to his legend, as it starkly drew the racial lines he had hoped to exploit for his own use.

The whole gut-pounding experience certainly did nothing to interfere with his war of nerves against Frank Leland. Secure that he had made his case for absolute power, he gave Leland a final ultimatum in October: Either you go or I go and form my own "Lelands" team. Leland held firm; so did Rube.

But before Rube Foster quit, he laid careful plans. With quiet purpose, he had obtained loyalty pledges from two of Leland's most valued moneymen, the foppish Maj. R. R. Jackson and the wily attorney Beauregard Moseley. Knowing he was being out-maneuvered, Leland wasted no time in filing a lawsuit to enjoin Foster from forming any team under the Lelands name. Rube then countersued, claiming he had every right to appropriate the name.

It seems hard to imagine how Foster could have had this right. Nevertheless, Foster almost beat Leland. When the case was heard in the Chicago Circuit Court where Leland had once sat as a clerk, the verdict indeed gave Foster exclusive rights to the name "Leland Giants." But the judge saved Frank Leland's honor by giving *him* exclusive rights to the lease for Chicago's Auburn Park, and enjoined Foster from taking Leland's players.

In the shakeout that followed this bewildering decision, Foster and Major Jackson created their new version of the Leland Giants, while Leland renamed his suddenly no-name team the Chicago Giants. Leland was also able to prevent Foster's still-unassembled team from entering the Chicago City League.

But Rube Foster was too savvy to be co-opted after coming this far. He and Beauregard Moseley had made sure to have a ball field at their disposal, and now they leased Normal Park, about a half-mile from Auburn, at Sixty-ninth and Halstead. Within months, Foster had hired many top-notch players away from the Philadelphia Giants and—with no sympathy for John Connors's plight—the Brooklyn Royal Giants, claiming among others John Henry Lloyd, Home Run Johnson, catcher Bruce Petway, and pitcher Frank Wickware.

Indeed, Foster had been eager to raid blackball's eastern teams. In 1910 he told his favorite paper, the *Indianapolis Freeman*, about the "dangerous predicament" that was stunting blackball. In effect, Foster warned black club owners that they had better be prepared to cleanse blackball of its racial impurities. When Foster spoke of a "dense cloud hanging over the Negro," he may as well have been looking straight at the white promoter Nat Strong.

Strong was, of course, the second of the great obstacles in Foster's assured path to glory for himself and for blackball, after Frank Leland. And Rube would not be halted by the two thousand miles that separated them. In 1910, when by some accounts the Leland Giants won 109 of 118 games, Foster ensconced his club in a Pullman car and brought them east to battle a number of eastern teams, encroaching on Nat Strong's territory while Nat unsuccessfully tried to block the bookings.

Once his team won eighteen straight games in Strong's bailiwick, the war for blackball's soul was under way.

7

Five O'Clock Shuffle

Wherever the money was, that's where I was.
                                    —John Henry Lloyd

The irony of Rube Foster's Afrocentrism was that while he was prepared to fight Nat Strong's stranglehold on blackball's eastern wing, he readily accepted the implicit property privileges of class and race. Foster needed only to look around Chicago to know the score. There were no fewer than thirty stadiums used by pro and semipro teams, and not one was owned by black interests.

Looking a little closer, the plots of real estate most pertinent to Foster, Auburn Park and Normal Park, were owned by a white man, John Schorling. What was noteworthy about Schorling was that he was married to Charlie Comiskey's sister, which meant that Schorling had the long arm of the White Sox behind his baseball forays. A bartender by trade, John Schorling by 1910 found himself king of Chicago's bush league teams.

Out of deference to Frank Leland, and then Foster, Schorling removed himself from blackball promotions, beyond collecting rent on the two ballparks. But both he and his baronial brother-in-law had kept tabs on the skyrocketing growth of the Leland Giants and their lucrative matches with the Cubs and other white teams, and had cautiously considered tapping into the team's fortunes at a safe distance.

Now, events were playing out that made such a link inevitable. As it happened, both Foster and Comiskey were looking for greener fields in 1910. The Sox found theirs—Comiskey Park— moving to this brand-new, twenty-eight-thousand-seat facility on

73

the South Side at Thirty-fifth and Shields on July 1, 1910. This meant that South Side Park, which Comiskey had taken from Frank Leland a decade before, was sitting vacant—at precisely the same time that Rube Foster was fretting about the rural conditions at Normal Park.

This presented John Schorling with an intriguing opportunity. Schorling wanted very much to add South Side Park to his baseball freehold. The problem for Charlie Comiskey was that it seemed easier and cheaper to raze the facility than to pay for its upkeep.

For Schorling, the only way to make an accommodation with blackball work for Comiskey and himself was to install an attraction like, say, the Leland Giants. And the only way to do that was to enter into a business relationship with Rube Foster. This scheme meant Charlie Comiskey would become a partner in blackball—a ticklish situation, to say the least, for a major league bigwig in 1910.

Once Schorling had gotten Foster's and Beauregard Moseley's okays on concession and gate splits, Comiskey gave his approval, but under an elaborate scheme that allowed Schorling to secretly stand in for Comiskey. While Comiskey would still own the stadium, Schorling would front for him as the operator of record. To make the point, the name of the field was changed to Schorling Park. According to the plan, Rube owned the title to the eight-thousand-seat grandstand while Comiskey (with Schorling as façade) retained the deed to the overall grounds—which, with a little stretching of the truth, let Foster stake the claim that he "owned" his own ballpark.

This tremendous public relations bauble was designed to mask the nasty little hypocrisies not just of the deal but of Rube Foster's racial stratagems. And, to unprying eyes, it did. Foster was assumed far and wide to be the lord temporal at Thirty-ninth and Wentworth, his affiliation with Comiskey nonexistent and with Schorling only incidental. If the members of the white press knew otherwise, Comiskey prevailed on them not to report the information. And if the black press knew, it apparently was deemed far more important to fudge the issue (in the name of a black self-achievement that had not really been achieved).

Not everyone in the black press kept quiet, however. In 1912, a tiny black newspaper with the curious name of the *Chicago Broad Ax* blew the whistle on Foster, revealing the Schorling connection and upbraiding him (the paper did not trace the link back to Comiskey) for taking profits that "should be received by the Race to whom the patrons of the game belong."

Foster denied collaborating with the enemy while quietly redoing the contracts to excise Schorling's name, though his and Comiskey's roles remained intact. Foster would insist in future years that there were no contract at all, that he and Schorling conducted whatever business they did by handshake agreement.

Further consolidating positive coverage and his broad designs, with great fanfare Foster changed the team name he had fought like a bobcat to purloin from Frank Leland. Now, the club became the Chicago *American* Giants, a true national investment for the race. Not again did anyone dare to raise the issue of hypocrisy in Rube Foster's commandments.

For Foster, the new name was like a dip in the River Jordan. Foster had every intention of making the black game—through the vessel of his team—an *American* game, with black men standing toe to toe with each other, at least figuratively, on the footstool of the American Pastime.

To do this, Foster had his American Giants begin to emulate the rituals of and walk the same turf as major league teams, intending to force-feed black professionalism into white consciousness as a first step toward integration, while at the same time grounding a black counterstructure that could stand on its own—with Rube Foster in total command and someone with whom the major leaguers would eventually have to deal.

As early as 1910, Foster began to talk about reviving the concept of Walter Brown's National Colored League. "In my opinion," Foster wrote in the *Indianapolis Freeman* that year, "the time is now at hand when the formation of colored leagues should receive much consideration. In fact, I believe it is absolutely necessary."

This statement was a corollary to Foster's carefully worded pronouncements about the "dangerous predicament" posed by blackball's "uncertain business principles." Playing to the conscience of black capitalists, while challenging them to act, Foster threw down the gauntlet. He said:

> The players have, through all sorts of adverse conditions, been able to bring our race to the notice of thousands who are interested in the game. Now would

our businessmen and friends of the profession make an effort to help us reach our coveted goal of complete success, or will they stand by and see us fail? Which shall it be?

Unfortunately, Foster's first experience with a black league exposed him to the same problems that had destroyed Walter Brown's league. Charging Beauregard Moseley with the task of sounding out other midwestern and southern black clubs about joining in a league, by early 1910 the attorney had made tentative plans with seven teams—the Louisville (Kentucky) Cubs, the Orleans Eagles, the Mobile (Alabama) Tigers, the St. Louis Giants, the Kansas City (Kansas) Giants, and teams from Kansas City, Missouri, and Columbus, Ohio—to play with the Leland Giants in the Negro National Base Ball League.

As Foster's stalking horse, Moseley felt free to state the league's mission in slightly more militant terms than Foster could have. Because blacks were "already forced out of the game from a national standpoint," the league would see to it that "the Negro comes to his own rescue by organizing and patronizing the game successfully." Moseley also promised that this success "would of itself force recognition from minor white leagues to play us and share in the receipts."

Although this goal reflected Foster's one-step-at-a-time approach to possible integration, it nonetheless raised the stakes of the Negro National League. Consequently, Foster was no doubt relieved he had let Moseley do the talking when the league collapsed from a lack of proper funding—the very nugget of Foster's discontent about blackball—and expired before a single game was played.

Now, Foster had to retreat, even as he went about turning the American Giants into a one-term paradigm of blackball potential. While Schorling Park was being renovated, the Giants plowed through the barnstorming trails and—according to Foster—won 123 of 129 games in 1910, breaking some impressive ground by going where few black teams had dared to play.

Most notably, Foster went south. Pointedly imitating the major league teams, he took the Giants below the Mason-Dixon line for spring games in such daunting places as Alabama, Mississippi,

Arkansas, Florida, Tennessee, Kentucky, and Texas—where in his home state, Foster found he was treated like a visiting potentate.

Ignoring Jim Crow, Foster proved a lot about blackball—mainly that in finding amateur, semipro, and pro black competition all across the Deep South, blacks were refusing to downplay their devotion to the game. Not incidentally, he also cultivated a minor league of his own, scoping out the local talent and signing up the best of it for the Giants.

Having taken the South, Foster headed west, extending the new blackball trail to outposts like Seattle and Tacoma and Butte and Portland. And when the long summer was done, he led his men down the Pacific rim to play in the California Winter League. Then it was back across the continent to Cuba for another Rube Foster coronation on the island.

Even when Schorling Park was ready for them, Foster kept his Giants away from Chicago for all but a few games. He realized the local competition in Chicago had faded. He also did not want to face the Frank Leland–inspired interdiction by the Chicago City League. But, more critically, Foster understood that it was on those endless expeditions throughout the country that the Chicago American Giants had become the first team to merge the sport and the symbolism of blackball. That had been Foster's plan all along, and the long road through the Black America being left behind in the urban transition must have made him feel like an apostle.

For sure, there was an oracular scent to these dashing men in their seersucker suits riding the rails in their private Pullman car, led by the hard-staring man sucking on a meerschaum pipe. As they emerged onto the playing field in their crisp red and white uniforms emblazoned with the CAG logo, the locals would be lined up around the block to buy tickets.

One such young black man to bear witness to the majesty of the American Giants during those years was a student at New Orleans University named David Malarcher. Waiting for the team to come through Louisiana, he saved his money for weeks to wait in line to buy tickets, and when he handed them in and entered the ballpark he was transformed.

"I shall never forget the first time I saw Rube Foster," Malarcher told author John Holway. "I never saw such a well-equipped ball club in my whole life. I was astounded. Every day they came out in a different set of beautiful uniforms, all kinds of bats and balls, all the best of equipment."

Malarcher related a story he had heard about Foster and the team's arriving at the train station. The white stationmaster, it seems, knew that a great team called the American Giants was due, but didn't know they were black. Seeing them step off the Pullman, he did a double take and called to them, "Hey, what're you niggers doing getting out of Mr. Rube Foster's car?"

Foster, not even blinking, drew out every word slowly and contentedly as he approached. "I just happen to be Mr. Rube Foster," he said, brushing past the startled stationmaster.

Such incidents, apocryphal or otherwise, would remain etched in the minds of several generations of blackball players. For many Nirvana came when Foster asked them to play with his team. Some, like catcher George Dixon, shortstop John Beckwith, and pitchers Ben Taylor and Smokey Joe Williams, were personally hired by Foster. One trick in catching Rube's eye was to win a reputation on another team, because he liked to seduce and hire other owners' stars. According to Foster, raiding wasn't thievery; rather, he was rescuing men lost in the wilderness.

Accordingly, in the decade 1910–1920, Foster loaded up on the stars of blackball's first generation. One was the wide-eyed New Orleans boy who had lined up to buy American Giant tickets, Dave Malarcher, whose nickname—"Gentleman Dave"—earmarked him as a perfect fit for Foster's highly regimented, no-back-talk system. Having put in time with teams in Indianapolis and Detroit, he joined the American Giants in 1920; for the next fifteen years, Malarcher would live the principles taught by Rube Foster.

Although the American Giants rarely played in Chicago, Frank Leland's Chicago Giants were quickly eclipsed by Rube's enormous shadow. Managed by the plucky Joe Green, they pushed on with aging players and with Leland defiantly taking back the Leland Giants name that Foster had dumped. Blithely, Leland billed the club as the "Colored World's Champions," though his team's only "championship" contest came in 1911 when the Lelands went to Kansas and played a series with the black Kansas City Giants—and lost.

In 1914, losing money profusely, Frank Leland suffered a heart attack and died at age forty-five. Their chieftain gone, and with the Chicago City League breaking up, Joe Green sought relief from Leland's nemesis. Rube Foster agreed to take over the ailing team. But, in a last slap at Leland that reached into the grave, he used it as a "traveling club," a kind of minor league refuge for unproven or has-been American Giant players.

By the midtwenties, the club, like Frank Leland himself, was a faded blackball memory.

So too was Walter Schlichter. The second decade of the century saw the collapse of Schlichter's Philadelphia Giants, the death blow having been the defection of the indefatigable Sol White.

Fed up with Schlichter's penny-pinching, and seeing Rube Foster steal so many of his star players, this last honorable man accepted an offer by John Connors to manage the struggling Brooklyn Royal Giants in 1911. The following year, the Philadelphia Giants—the team that had ignited a blackball renaissance—went out of existence after a nine-year run.

With the incipient demise of John Bright's Cuban Giants and E. B. Lamar's Cuban X-Giants, not one pro team was left in Philadelphia from that joyous bedlam of the early 1900s.

For Sol White, the Brooklyn Giants were no sea of tranquility either. Having himself lost many of his players to Foster, John Connors could no longer fight the takeover advances of Nat Strong. With other local teams being pressured by Strong to boycott the Royals, Connors could not get games, and by 1911 he was forced to sell his franchise to Strong.

Now, as the owner of Brighton Oval, Dexter Park, the Brooklyn Royal Giants, and the Cuban Stars, Nat Strong completely dominated small-time ball in the East. And while Foster's notices were still confined to the black press, Strong had won praise for himself in the white papers.

In 1914, the *New York Age* ran an obsequious portrait headlined "King Nat of the Bushers." Describing Strong's newest booking sodality—the Inter-City Association—as "the big league of bush baseball," the *Age* parroted Strong's wild claims as to the number of players under his control:

Five-thousand semi-professional ball players hail Nat C. Strong as "King of the Bushers," and perhaps more than any other man he has extended the popularity of the sport outside the regular fire-spitting ball fan in this country....

The salaries of the semi-professionals in Strong's circuit range from $7 to $50 per week. Collegians also play...Chinese, negro and Cuban teams, says Strong, draw big gates in the East.

"King" Strong denied that he intended to extend the field of his operations, saying the eastern games from March to October keep him as busy as a sane man ought to be.

Foster despaired that under the white promoter blackball was merely a "semiprofessional" pastime and reduced to a sideshow of racial attractions and other geeky entertainment. In 1909, for instance, Strong promoted the American tour of Henri St. Yves, a French marathon runner, and in 1913 he sponsored a touring Chinese baseball team. Despite Strong's denial of expansion, he had in fact started booking his bushball games in Detroit and Chicago—close enough for Rube Foster to feel Strong's hot breath.

Most ominously, Strong was definitely extending his influence over eastern blackball, even though it could seem at times that Strong was *reducing* the prestige and local loyalties of the black game. Take, for example, his treatment of the poor Brooklyn Royal Giants. Shortly after buying the team, Strong turned it into a traveling club, keeping Sol White's squad almost entirely away from Brooklyn.

What's more, at a time when Foster was paying up to $150 a month to his players, Strong was quoted as saying that in his opinion no black ballplayer was worth more than $75 a month.

In 1911, a second blackball front opened in New York when white boxing promoter Roderick "Jess" McMahon—who with his younger brother Edward once had a minor interest in Walter Schlichter's Philadelphia Giants—formed the Lincoln Giants (not to be confused with the earlier black team of that name in Nebraska).

Rather than cater to Strong, McMahon found his own ballpark,

Olympic Field, at Fifth Avenue and 136th Street in Harlem. He then solicited the services of a man with a heavy grudge against Strong—Sol White.

White, who had watched Strong conquer and then nearly banish the Brooklyn Royal Giants, agreed to head up the Lincoln club. Having seen fratricide become the norm in blackball, White was prepared to play hardball. His first order of business was to nail the coffin shut on his old Philadelphia Giants, procuring the defections of that moribund club's last stars, pitchers Dan McClellan and Dick "Cannonball" Redding, catcher Louis Santop, and outfielder Spotswood Poles.

Then, repaying Rube Foster in kind, McMahon went and snared three of the main men Foster had stolen from the Philadelphia Giants: John Henry Lloyd, Home Run Johnson, and James Booker.

It surprised no one that the Lincoln Giants immediately became a major force. Because Strong had a clamp on New York bushball, the team became pretty much a traveling club, but its star names allowed it to bypass much of the semipro circuit and schedule lucrative exhibition games, *a la* Rube Foster's American Giants, with white big league barnstorming teams.

Out of those contests, in fact, came some of early blackball's storied—and mostly unverifiable—lore. John Henry Lloyd took center stage in these legends, which had him outhitting an aging Honus Wagner when the Pirates' future Hall of Famer toured with big league All-Star aggregations—a matchup pitting what some historians believe are the two greatest shortstops of all time.

Lloyd may indeed have shone in these games, which the blackball contingents certainly took more seriously than the often loafish white big league barnstormers. In games of which newspaper accounts existed and survived, Lloyd is shown to have made a single and double of the Philadelphia Athletics' Chief Bender in a 7–3 Lincoln win over a National League All-Star squad in 1913, and two more hits (with two stolen bases as well) against the Athletics' famous ace Grover Cleveland Alexander when the Lincoln Giants tore apart Connie Mack's team 9–2 in an exhibition game that same year.

However, of more importance to John Henry Lloyd, and to all of the other blackball men at the time, was that little if any of the proceeds of these games reached their pockets. Although Jess

McMahon paid his players relatively high wages, they knew McMahon, in the style of Nat Strong, was making a fortune.

Worse, McMahon was an alcoholic whose sour temper and lavish spending habits antagonized many players, including John Henry, who quit the Lincoln Giants to join Rube Foster's Leland Giants in 1914. Lloyd took with him the brilliant six-foot-five pitcher Smokey Joe Williams and several others.

Lloyd returned east when McMahon cut his losses by selling the Lincolns to two other white promoters, James Keenan and Charles Harvey, in 1915—but when John Henry arrived he found he was trapped, as the deal, reminiscent of the peculiar court resolution of the Foster-Leland power struggle, gave McMahon control of the Giant players under the name of the Lincoln Stars.

Lloyd stayed for the year, leading the Stars into a nasty battle against Foster's American Giants that was declared a draw at the end after the two teams had split ten feral games. This gritty performance impressed even Foster, who while not normally given to aggrandizing his opponents was also not unmindful that the Lincoln Stars had defied his enemy Nat Strong. "I am one who takes his hat off to [them]," he said. "Their great playing and wonderful defense was never surpassed, if equaled, on any diamond."

But when Lloyd once again joined Rube Foster's team, Jess McMahon's time in the sun was about over. In September of 1917, the American Giants—fortified not only with Lloyd but with Cannonball Redding and Louis Santop—took the reeling Stars in a best-two-of-three series. Now McMahon, exhausted as the result of Rube Foster's buccaneering, folded his team and took a job as the assistant to boxing promoter Tex Rickard, never again to return to baseball.

The biggest beneficiary of the Lincoln Stars' death was a relieved Nat Strong. He now lured the money-hungry Lloyd, as well as Cannonball Redding, to the de jure Brooklyn Royal Giants. While not taking back his assessment about the worth of most black players, Nat Strong did give the Royal Giants the use of two Pierce-Arrow Cadillacs to get them to and from games in the countryside.

But nothing could disguise the fact that the black game was becoming comatose in New York. Thus, if Nat Strong was to have a real say in blackball's future, he would have to set his sights beyond the Hudson River.

Considering the constant and absurd shuffle of team-jumping players between New York and Chicago, a better model of a workable blackball was flourishing not in either of those places but in the flatlands of the now-dying American frontier. In the 1910s, the prairie legacy of the Page Fence Giants and Algona Brownies was being resurrected in evolving inner-city basins that awaited the black migration.

Actually, before there were inner cities in those parts, the Page Fence–style public relations gimmickry was being imitated with success by the first semipro black team in Kansas, the Topeka Giants. This club was almost all show, as typified by the manager, one Topeka Jack Johnson, whose name wasn't Jack Johnson at all until he stole it from the mountainous black prizefighter who won the heavyweight title on the day after Christmas in 1908. He watched in awe as the real Jack Johnson flaunted his color and the white women he ran around with. All the commotion sparked a national clamor to find a "Great White Hope" to defeat Johnson in the ring, and this maelstrom gave birth to Topeka Jack Johnson's identity.

Topeka Jack tried his hand at prizefighting, but was more successful when he formed the Topeka Giants. With Topeka Jack at the helm, and acquiring a cult following, the team was able to lodge in fine hotels and play against white teams regularly, the potential racial tensions eased by nonthreatening advance work. One of the Giants' players, Arthur Hardy, once described to author Robert Peterson how the club eased the black-white passages:

> We always liked to get into town at least by the middle of the morning for advertising purposes. As a rule, when we went into a town, we would placard it and uniform up and go out and practice so the people could get it noised around that we were in town.
>
> Sometimes they set up a parade. Both teams paraded. That was in Smith Center and Blue Rapids and Frank-fort, Kansas. That was the regular program. They had very good bands. Most of those little towns had a

municipal band, you know—the band concert once a week was a big event then—and they would lead the parade and we'd march out to the baseball park....

[I]n those little towns, we would average $15, $20 a man for a game. The admission charge was 50¢ or 75¢, kids a quarter...and expenses were at a minimum. In those days you could get a good meal for 25¢, and you could get lodging for 50¢....

[W]e did some clowning on the field. But it was done like this: As you know, some people might resent what they might consider you making fun of them....Johnson always insisted that we didn't want to humiliate anybody....After all, we were pros and the other teams were fellows who were playing once a weekend...and so Topeka Jack would always talk to the local people. He'd say, "Now what about you folks here? Do you want us to put on some funny kinds of act? Or do you think they would resent it?"

Here was one of the stunts: The pitcher would throw the ball and maybe it would be a little low but the umpire would call it a strike; all right, you'd get down on your knees at the plate. Or some guy would hit a ball out of the park and run to third base and around the bases backward, that sort of thing....

We did have a little act on the Topeka Giants, though, that was in addition to baseball. We had four fellows who made up a topnotch [singing] quartet, and in the evenings, around the hotel, those guys would make $25 or $30 sometimes. They did especially well if they caught a bunch of traveling men in there, because, you know, there wasn't anything to do in those small towns; at that time, they didn't even have picture shows.

In time, Topeka Jack's cachet was supplanted by that of an erudite black man named Tobe Smith, who owned the Kansas City (Kansas) Giants. Smith, following the real estate blueprint of Nat Strong and Rube Foster, secured grounds for his team at 430 Washington Boulevard, and assumed instant status booking games against powers like the two Chicago teams.

Consolidating blackball in the heartland, Smith strung together a loose alliance of lesser black teams such as the Topeka Giants, the Minneapolis Keystones, the St. Paul Gophers, and the Dayton Marcos. In 1910, when Topeka Jack Johnson went to manage the Kansas City (Missouri) Royal Giants, Smith's Giants played and beat the Royals for the "Kansas City Colored Championship," and the series became big news in the local papers.

But now other Midwest cities were discovering baseball's seductions. Cross-state, a black tavern owner, Charles Mills, made the St. Louis Giants succeed by overtly appealing to white fans. And this applied not only to games against local white opposition, which normally drew nearly all-white crowds; a game against the Chicago American Giants in 1910 brought out around three thousand fans to the St. Louis Giants' bandbox field, Kuebler Park on North Broadway, and at least a third of the crowd was white.

Rather than being met with alarm, this development was greeted as a clarion call by some people who lived west of the Mississippi. In 1912, the *St. Louis Post-Dispatch* was moved to take a position so ahead of its time that most white fans around the country would have gagged reading it.

"[We wonder] if baseball is, after all, the great American game," read its editorial page. "We play it, to be sure, but the colored people play it so much better that the time is apparently coming when it shall be known as the great African game."

In similarly benign fashion, in all-white Indiana, a black team called the ABCs was the Hoosier State's top sports draw. Sponsored in the 1890s by the American Brewing Company, the club found its watermark in 1908 when a white barkeeper named Ran Butler (as demonstrated by John Connors and John Schorling, the cash spilled by hard-drinking city folk during hard times could stoke a fair-sized investment) purchased both the ABCs and a ball field for them, Northwestern Park in Indianapolis.

But it was another Midwest team that pushed the entertainment quotient of blackball to the limit. This was the All Nations, an ingenious design in ethnic exploitation begun in 1912 in Des Moines by John Leslie Wilkinson, a white man with high standards in baseball and camp.

When J.L., as he was known, was playing amateur and semipro ball around Iowa—under an assumed name, so as not to offend his father, a college president—he landed on one squad billed as an all-girls' team; in truth, the players were men in drag. This high concept, which made John Bright's Cuban capers seem dignified, set off a brainstorm inside Wilkinson's head; while ethnic tomfoolery had paid off for the Page Fence Giants and Topeka Giants, the team that Wilkinson christened the All Nations would rewrite the primer on ethnic chic. He created a rainbow coalition of whites, blacks, Cubans, Asians, Native Americans—and one woman, whom he called Carrie Nation.

Wilkinson, a stickler for honest detail, insisted that all of these people be exactly what he portrayed them to be. And as the decade stretched on and the club moved its base to Kansas City in 1915, the black and Cuban contingents were represented by some superb ballplayers—notably pitchers John Donaldson, Bill "Plunk" Drake, and Jose Mendez, and outfielder Cristobal Torriente.

This was rather astonishing, given that every player on his All Nations team had to perform in an additional capacity, either with the wrestlers or the dance band that traveled with the club. Jose Mendez, for example, brought down the house playing guitar and cornet with the band on the field after the last out was made.

Eventually J.L. Wilkinson decided to get rid of the frivolous aspects of the All Nations and play good solid ball. This change probably occurred along about 1915, when the team beat the mighty American Giants of Rube Foster and won national recognition in *Sporting Life*. The All Nations, said the paper, were "an outfit that baseball sharps claim is strong enough to give any major league club a nip-and-tuck battle." From here on, J. L. Wilkinson too saw blackball as a means to accumulate power.

While it was a standard, and necessary, procedure for black clubs to gain a large part of their income by playing white teams and pulling in white fans, this paradox was just one of the many unresolved conflicts within the black game, which while selling black self-reliance was still reliant on white business. Both Rube Foster and St. Louis Giant owner Charles Mills were deeply troubled by the dilemma. On June 12, 1909, Mills wrote to blackball's main tribune, the *Indianapolis Freeman*, apologizing for the startling fact that to date his Giants had played only two black teams during the season.

This conundrum would be partially resolved, at least somewhat, but the great bugaboo of blackball—white ownership—would rage on without solution. Indeed, even in the Midwest world of black self-rule, self-rule would prove transitory. In Indianapolis, for example, the ABCs changed hands in 1912 when Ran Butler was bought out by a white man named Tom Bowser. But Bowser had good sense, and in 1914 he imported as his manager Charles I. Taylor, a bird dog of a man who could spot talent and leadership abilities in other men as dependably as Rube Foster.

C. I. Taylor, in fact, had already begun to lay the groundwork that would keep blackball growing for decades. Born in South Carolina in 1872, the slight, priggish Taylor had risen from poverty to attend Clark College in Atlanta and serve in the army during the Spanish-American War. Drawn like J. L. Wilkinson to blackball, he and his three brothers formed the Birmingham (Alabama) Giants in 1908.

That team, only in its infancy, sported names that now reek of blackball majesty: Gentleman Dave Malarcher, Taylor's brother and pitcher Candy Jim Taylor, and center fielder Oscar Charleston. Years later, Malarcher described the stocky Charleston as "all muscle and bone...perfect broad shoulders, fine strong legs, strong muscular arms, and powerful hands."

Others simply called him mean. With his scowl and brawling tendencies, Charleston was a baleful man, and he enjoyed watching people gulp when he got mad and, so the tales went, tore the horsehide cover right off the baseball with his bare hands.

In 1910, the black migration swept the Birmingham Giants to the racially consonant fields of Indiana to be recast as the West Baden Sprudels. Tom Bowser realized he needed C. I. Taylor as an ally. Bowser gave him co-ownership and the managing job of the ABCs in 1914. Taylor also did the blackball boogie-woogie, lifting some other wondrous players from their teams: second baseman Bingo DeMoss from Topeka, infielder Frank Warfield from St. Louis, Cannonball Redding from Lincoln, and pitcher Dizzy Dismukes from the Mohawk Giants of upstate New York.

Rube Foster, warily eyeing the ever-shifting Midwest scene, found his eyes fixated on C. I. Taylor. While Taylor came across to most as courtly and likable, Rube could see a different Taylor, a man with blood lust in his eyes.

Where normally this might have impressed Foster because it would have reminded him so much of himself, instead it irked him that C. I. Taylor had no intention of standing in Rube's shadow and that C. I. flatly refused to give away 50 percent of the gate when the two discussed a possible visit by the American Giants to Indianapolis.

And so by the spring of 1916, Rube Foster couldn't worry too much about Nat Strong—not while he and C. I. Taylor were on a collision course.

8

Out of the Wilderness

Make way for Democracy! We saved it in France, and by the Great
Jehovah we will save it in the U.S.A. or know the reason why.
—W. E. B. Du Bois, *The Crisis,* May 1919

The white man now, and has in the past secured grounds and
induced some one in the role of the good old Nigger to gather a lot
of athletes and then used circus methods to drag a bunch of our
best citizens out, only to undergo humiliation, with all kinds of
indignities flaunted in their faces, while he sits back and grows rich
off a percentage of the proceeds.
—Dave Wyatt, *Indianapolis Freeman,* January 27, 1917

Of all the grudge battles fought within blackball, the unofficial
"Colored World Series" of 1916 was the closest that any of
these competitions ever came to a gang war. Not by coincidence,
this one marked the first clash between Rube Foster and C. I.
Taylor, and the year long buildup of their mutual enmity ensured
that there would be ugliness on the field.

Rube had verbally attacked Taylor when Taylor refused to
accede to his terms in order to facilitate an ABCs-American Giants
match during the 1916 season. Using his privileged forum in the
Indianapolis Freeman, Foster claimed that Taylor had come to him
for advice on players in the past and that they each had promised
not to raid the other's clubs. But once Taylor went to Indianapolis,
Foster claimed, he broke his word. To Rube, such effrontery not
only was disrespectful, but had "ruined" black baseball in West
Baden and was emblematic of Taylor's win-at-any-cost tactics on
the field.

89

Although Rube Foster too could be accused of such tactics, he was on safe ground in contrasting the ABCs' games with his own team's. Blackball people still clearly recalled a 1915 game between the ABCs and a white major league All-Star team in Indianapolis that turned into a riot when a white baserunner was called safe on a close play at second base. Bingo DeMoss, the ABCs' second baseman, was so enraged by the call that he ran at the umpire and tried to punch him. He missed, but the frightening Oscar Charleston charged in from center field and smashed the ump in the face, knocking him to the ground with a split lip. In the next instant, fans came streaming out of the stands to join the brawl, which was quelled only after an eighteen-man police squad was called to the stadium. For starting the fight, DeMoss and Charleston were thrown in jail and charged with assault and battery.

Taylor publicly tried to make amends by calling the two players "cowardly." He asked that "the people do not condemn the ABCs baseball club nor my people for the ugly and unsportsmanlike conduct of two thoughtless hotheads." But Foster believed the incident did irreparable harm to blackball, especially since the game had been against a white minor league team and caused racial fears to erupt in heretofore placid Indianapolis. Soon thereafter, the city banned interracial games.

Besides, Rube believed C. I. Taylor was a liar and a jackal underneath the gentleman's pose. By chance, Foster's Chicago American Giants came through Indianapolis in July 1915, just after the DeMoss-Charleston flare-up. Playing against a white local semipro team at Federal League Park before the ban was enacted, an American Giant player got into an argument with an umpire, whereupon a policeman ran onto the field waving his gun at the player and at Foster. Freaked out by this treatment, Rube—who wisely kept his own gun out of sight—held C. I. Taylor responsible for having created such paranoia among the local white citizens.

In Rube's harshest indictment, he charged that by turning them into hoodlums, C. I. Taylor had lost his ballplayers' respect. Whatever ethical infraction Rube Foster committed, such as stealing players from other teams, no one, he contended, could claim that his players did not respect him—*love* him, he wouldn't hesitate to say—or that they failed to play according to the rules the way all men should, and the way black men *had* to play.

For his part, Taylor believed Foster to be a great baseball man but also a blowhard who had bamboozled black sportswriters into deifying him. He knew however, that he had to be careful in his public criticisms of Foster. When he responded, it was with an eye to Foster's reputation and power. On August 14 and 15, C. I. Taylor took to the pages of the *Freeman* as well. But instead of replying to Foster's direct criticism, he sought to generate sympathy by implying that Foster had unfairly taken all the credit for blackball's success.

"No one will deny that [Foster] has done a great deal for baseball," Taylor wrote, "but he has not worked single handed."

Both men knew that the only way to settle the argument was on the field. And so in October, 1916, they contracted to play a series of games for a fifty-fifty split of the gate. The length of the series would later become an issue in itself. Before game one, the two bosses posed for photographs, but refused to stand next to each other; instead, the sports editors of Indianapolis's two black newspapers took turns standing between them.

All remained calm for the first two games, which were split by the teams. Then, in game three, the silliest of squabbles made Foster lose his cool. Rube had decided to manage from inside the first-base coaching box. He spotted the glove that his first baseman had left on the field at the end of the previous inning (as pro players, from the big leagues on down, were wont to do). The glove was too close to the bag. Picking it up, Foster slid the mitt on his hand and went on coaching.

But now Ben Taylor, the ex–American Giant who had defected to play first base for his brother C. I., raised a point of order with the umpires about the legality of a coach wearing a mitt. After a long discussion, the umpires asked Foster to return the glove to the field. Not accustomed to taking orders from umpires, Foster erupted. After arguing with all the umpires, he threatened to bar them from working future games. Then he threw his arms skyward in a great shrug and waved his team out of the dugout. En masse, they stalked off the field.

And while their departure resulted in a forfeit, Foster returned the next day to the coaching box—with a glove on his hand. When the ABCs offered the same objection, the umpires inexplicably reversed their previous ruling and declared that Mr. Foster could wear whatever he wanted on his hand. Rube Foster then announced to the press that he had been "vindicated" and that the forfeit had been rescinded.

This claim would be debated later. When the ABCs won the fifth of nine games, counting the disputed forfeit, C. I. Taylor insisted that his team had won the series outright. Foster, however, refused to concede, either on the forfeit or what he said had been his understanding that this series was to have been a best-of-twelve affair. Rube Foster would never give in on these points.

Even the *Indianapolis Freeman,* however, would not accept their hero's whining, which the paper described as a "pitiful sight." When Foster and the American Giants boarded their train, the newspaper declared, "The mighty Rube locked himself in his state room and said, 'Don't bother me until we get to Chicago.' With that, he went to bed and thought over the incidents of the past week. It's hard but it's fair, Rube.... The best team won."

Even so, Foster had lost none of his clout, as C. I. Taylor quickly learned. When the 1917 season got under way, Cannonball Redding—who had won three of those five games for the ABCs—was signed to the American Giants. In another year, so were Oscar Charleston, Bingo DeMoss, and none other than C. I. Taylor's most talented brother, Candy Jim.

In classic Foster style, Rube had also picked up other stars from other blackball teams, including outfielder Floyd "Jelly" Gardner from the Detroit Stars, pitcher Jose Mendez from J. L. Wilkinson's All Nations, and outfielder Jimmie Lyons, from the St. Louis Giants.

Foster was again ready to resurrect his vision of a national Negro league, the objectives of which were to force Nat Strong to leave the black game and to force the white major leagues to accept some manner of sanctioned integration. In 1917, Foster believed the time was propitious for a baseball reformation.

In April, the opening of the baseball season, the United States entered World War I. Even with the tribulations and deprivations they imposed, the war years actually served to advance black enterprise. Manpower needs in defense plants and industrial factories accelerated the migration from the South. Within three years, around half a million African Americans had moved northward, and blacks became essential to the war machine.

Though placed in separate units and subjected to overt racism by white officers, over 367,000 black men served in the military with distinction. The black 369th Division became the first unit of the Allies to reach the Rhine. When the 369th returned, they were given a parade through Harlem, cheered by a million people.

As a microcosm, colored baseball teams were hit hard by wartime losses. C. I. Taylor's ABCs lost sever players to the draft, and Rube Foster lost eight, including Cannonball Redding. Yet Rube saw these contributions as the unfolding of social progress, as did many other influential black leaders. Taking note of the mutual sacrifice of the races, W. E. B. Du Bois, editor of the monthly *Crisis,* averred: "Let us not hesitate. Let us...forget our special grievances and close our ranks shoulder to shoulder with our white citizens...fighting for democracy."

In theory, the view that democracy could not be unconditional abroad and conditional at home made perfect sense. But American racism, never tempered by reason, continued on its venomous course. In 1917 at least thirty-eight blacks were lynched; fifty-eight were lynched during the following year. A race riot broke out in St. Louis because whites objected to black employment in a defense plant. Only because the Germans exploited these gross inconsistencies in propaganda flyers did President Woodrow Wilson issue a public statement that decried lynching.

In fact, propinquity to blacks only made for greater hostility among many whites. By the early twenties, with the country eager to return to prewar conventions, not only did Klan membership skyrocket, but northern labor unions—which still refused to accept blacks—stood by as industries cast blacks out of jobs by the thousand. In 1919, the year the world was made safe for democracy, there were at least twenty-five race riots in America. Those black leaders who spoke of militant solutions were generally branded Bolsheviks.

Many blacks were so disillusioned by the false promises of the war that—as Moses Fleetwood Walker, the first black major leaguer, had suggested years before—they maintained that the only solution was to establish a home colony in the African motherland.

Rube Foster was not among that legion. In fact, at war's end he was determined to pursue assimilation by getting his Negro league into the starting blocks. Part of his impatience was due to the huge wartime infusion of blacks into the big cities, enlarging the pool of fans for blackball.

Back east, new blackball men were riding that human wave, and doing so well that this forsaken turf again came alive. The migration swept one whole team north, the Jacksonville (Florida) Duval Giants. That club's players were relocated in Atlantic City, New Jersey, in 1916 under the aegis of two white aldermen, Thomas Jackson and Henry Tucker, and renamed the Bacharach Giants after the city's white mayor, Harry Bacharach.

Within the eastern corridor, yet another revival of Philadelphia blackball within the power circle came to pass, especially when another team, the Hilldale Field Club, began the 1917 season with a whole new look. A popular amateur club since 1910, the Hilldales turned pro, having self-incorporated that winter.

This was a triumph for the newest of blackball lords, Ed Bolden. A clerk in Philadelphia's Central Post Office, Bolden took over the Hilldales in 1911. While there was little to distinguish this amateur club, which played in the borough of Darby, Pennsylvania, just across the Delaware county line, Bolden made it a hot team.

Working the pages of the black *Philadelphia Tribune* the way Rube Foster did the *Indianapolis Freeman* and the budding *Chicago Defender,* Bolden's vivid stories about the Hilldales brought in crowds of up to three thousand people at the nonenclosed field Bolden had requisitioned at Ninth Street and Cedar Avenue. Charging only a dime for admission, Bolden's minuscule profits were only $40 a game. But Bolden held raffles—a ton of coal as first prize, $5 in gold as second—that upped the team's take to as much as $217.89 a game in 1914.

By that year, Bolden's amateurs were able to schedule three games against Connie Mack's Philadelphia Athletics. And, playing Rube Foster in miniature, Bolden would routinely steal players away from other sandlot clubs around the area, a practice that, as with Foster, did nothing to crimp Bolden's opinion that he was a "clean" baseball man. Threatening to fine any player who participated in the common blackball spectacle of on-field brawling, Bolden also required his players to attend practice twice a week and a thirty-minute practice *before* games. Anyone caught AWOL was fined $5.

Bolden issued this all-inclusive warning as well: "No player shall indulge in any intoxicating liquor before the game nor at any time during his sojourn upon the field, nor on his way to or from the field. Neither shall he come upon the field under the influence, or smelling of alcoholic liquors."

As a matter of fact, Bolden reeled in disgust at what he considered to be a sewerlike atmosphere at Schorling Park, where fans at American Giant games openly bought and sold whiskey in the rest rooms, used vulgar language, and routinely hopped the railing to join player brawls. In July, 1916, the *Chicago Defender* chastised the Schorling Park scene as "a fright. Sunday someone threw a cushion into the box seats...and it knocked a woman's hat off. Too bad that some people never know how to act."

Ed Bolden could not rid his park of the scourge of gambling. For that matter, no one on any level of baseball seemed to be able to do so. However, he ringed the stands with security guards; and in 1916, when four fans caused a disturbance, he swore out arrest warrants on them.

All of this was done in preparation for Bolden's team to compete with the famous black clubs. The last step came in November 1916 when—in a move straight out of the Frank Leland playbook—he incorporated the team as the Hilldale Baseball and Exhibition Company, of which Ed Bolden was president.

Thus stoked, Bolden jumped into the maelstrom of blackball. For the 1917 season, he stocked the club with veteran pros lifted from some of those blackball powers, including pitcher Doc Sykes, outfielder Spot Poles, catcher Bill Pettus, sawed-off second baseman Bunny Downs, and right fielder Otto Briggs. As the leadoff hitter, Briggs, a C. I. Taylor find, would become so entrenched in Philadelphia that he was eventually hired as circulation manager at the *Tribune* (after he married the daughter of the publisher).

Bolden's biggest score was enticing Louis Santop to leave the Brooklyn Royal Giants in 1918—by paying "Top" the stratospheric salary of $450 per month. That year, too, a roguish spitball pitcher, Phil Cockrell, came over from the Lincoln Giants.

That season's Hilldale roster is most notable because it included an eighteen-year-old third baseman with the nondescript name of William Johnson, who would wash out after only a few games.

As a boy in Maryland and Delaware, Johnson had been smitten by the Hilldales' huge local communion. After playing ball in the sandlots, he got a break during the war when Bolden lost four starters to the draft—including catcher Specs Webster, who died of pneumonia in France—and needed bodies, not just for the Hilldales but for the Bacharach Giants, whose owners came to him to save their team. At times, in fact, the Hilldale players would participate in a game in the morning, then put on Bacharach uniforms and play another in the afternoon.

One of the new bodies was Johnson. He was paid $5 a game. But when he failed to make the team, Johnson honed his talents with a nearby semipro club known as the Madison Stars. When he returned in 1920, he carried more weight and a new identity. He was now "Judy" Johnson, having been dubbed with the strange nickname—which no one could ever quite figure out—by a Madison outfielder named Robert "Jude" Gans, who had made Johnson his protégé.

For $100, which was all that Bolden had to pay the Madison club for the boy named Judy, he got a ballplayer with a psychotic passion for getting on base. Judy would meticulously let out the seams of his left uniform sleeve, the one facing the pitcher, so he could be hit with the pitch. When third baseman Oliver Marcelle failed to show up at the park, Bolden installed Judy at third. It would be a decade before any other man would play there for the Hilldales.

One indicator of the Hilldales' stature was that in their first pro year, 1917, all of the big Eastern blackball clubs paid visits to Darby, hoping to sponge up some of the large houses that had led Bolden to enlarge his field to eight thousand seats and rename it Hilldale Park. One by one, the Lincoln Giants, the Brooklyn Royal Giants, and the Cuban Stars came through. The real indicator, though, was Nat Strong's eagerness to court Bolden as an ally (or conquest). Though he could plainly see that Ed Bolden was no toady like Walter Schlichter, this "courtship" was essential to Strong's worldview.

Impressed with Bolden's straight-arrow image and money-making operation, the white major league teams came calling as well, though not for long. Buffeted by wartime player losses of their own, the majors were suffering grave losses at the box office. But while games with popular black teams were desirable, it did nothing for big league egos that both the Phillies and the Athletics were regularly being outdrawn as biracial crowds continued to jam Hilldale Park on Saturdays and holdiays. (With Sunday ball illegal in Pennsylvania, Bolden brazenly defied the law and played his home games only on these two days.)

Thus, some white major league clubs now began to shy away from direct competition with black teams. Moreover, some major league club owners ordered players who joined up with ragtag barnstorming units to withdraw from games against the black-ballers. Brooklyn Dodger owner Charles Ebbets laid down this law to his star pitcher, Rube Marquard, when the hurler went out to tour with one such "All-Star" aggregation after the 1917 season. Marquard ignored the order and pitched against the Lincoln Giants, who drove him from the mound in a lopsided win. An apoplectic Charlie Ebbets then fined Marquard $100. Ebbets explained the reproof in the following:

> The Brooklyn team is averse to permitting its team, or any of its players, participating in games with Negroes. There are only semiprofessional Negro teams, and when there is an outcome like yesterday's game, when Rube was beaten, President Ebbets believes it tends to lower the calibre of ball played by the big leagues in the eyes of the public, and at the same time make the major league team the subject of ridicule at the hands of the more caustic fans.

Ebbet's canards are today painfully obvious—he had ascribed third-rate status to Negro teams even though they'd beaten the stuffing out of his star pitcher. Rather than holding blacks to the standards to which they held whites, losing to them in any competition was simply considered the ultimate insult, and close to sedition, among white club owners.

In a game against Hilldale, a touring team fronted by Boston Red Sox pitcher Joe Bush held a one-run lead when Bush loaded the bases in the ninth inning. Rather than face the heart of the Hilldale batting order, Bush used his spikes to tear the cover off the ball and then refused to accept a new ball from the umpire and walked off the field. Hilldale won, by forfeit.

A prime concern now for the major leagues was to avoid just such embarrassing moments, and the uptight behavior it caused among players and owners. The solution came in 1920, after the "Black Sox" World Series gambling scandal disgraced the game, and the owners appointed the majors' first commissioner, Kenesaw Mountain Landis.

A tough, at times uncouth federal judge from Illinois, the fifty-four-year-old Landis was a hollow-faced wafer of a man with a mane of unruly white hair and a mulishly stubborn streak. He had distinguished himself with the baseball owners by refusing to hear a lawsuit filed in the early 1900s by the Federal Baseball League to force entry into the major league circle, after its petition had been rejected by the major league powers. Landis refused to hear the case not on legal grounds but because, as he said, his "expert knowledge of baseball obtained by more than thirty years of observation of the game as a spectator convinced me that if an order had been entered it would have been, if not destructive, at least vitally injurious to the game of baseball."

Landis was known to order people into court without sub-poenas, and to hold others without warrants, leading one court-room observer to say that the judge "blandly ignored the law in the interests of what he conceived to be justice."

For the next two decades, Landis served the club owners well. Baseball experienced a boom unparalleled in its history, and not at any time was anyone permitted to question segregation. By the early 1920s, Landis knew how to hide baseball's real intent: to remove blackball from the world of baseball. He decreed that no team could compete in bush league games in the offseason. For most white fans, this embargo was painless. For blackball, it was a swift kick in the groin.

Rather than a war-fed communality, then, armistice ushered in a new level of racial antagonism. Until the war, small but significant gains in the white major leagues by men of color—though not African Americans—could have been construed as a step toward acceptance. Although John McGraw had failed to pass off Charlie Grant as "Chief Tokahama," McGraw had little trouble signing a real Native American in 1903 to the New York Giants: Charles Albert "Chief" Bender, a catcher from Crow Wing, Minnesota, who would play in the majors for sixteen years and be elected to the Hall of Fame in 1953. Another Native American (and all-American) of some note—Jim Thorpe—played for six years, from 1913 to 1919, in the major leagues.

More adventurous moves occurred in 1911, when the Cincinnati Reds signed two members of the Cuban Stars, outfielder Armando Marsans and third baseman Rafael Almeida. Not by coincidence, all of these men were relatively light-skinned.

The white *New York Age* stated: "Now that the shock is over it would not be surprising to see a Cuban a few shades darker than Almeida and Marsans breaking into the professional ranks...it would then be easy for colored players who are citizens of this country to get into fast company." The paper went on: "Until the public got accustomed to seeing native Negroes on big league [teams], the colored players could keep their mouths shut and pass for Cubans"—in other words, behave the way black players had for John Bright years before.

However, even these sprigs of hope were broken. While Marsans played eight big league seasons and Almeida three—and another caramel-colored Cuban, catcher Miguel Angel Gonzalez, played from 1912 to 1932 with five teams and later managed in the big leagues as well—not only did the black wave not materialize, but the Cuban wave ebbed as well.

The renewed color sanctions led Rube Foster to change course, but not his ultimate destination. His immediate concern now was reform within the black game. As Foster knew, all the petty squabbling and backbiting among blackball brothers was making it impossible to rebut the major league indictment that black baseball was synonymous with "low calibre" baseball. Professionalism concerned Foster as much as legitimacy. Consequently, he was determined to keep Ed Bolden out of the orbit of Nat Strong and his claque of semiprofessionals and bush leaguers.

At the same time, Foster continued to attract white fans and white opponents. Postwar America was awash with industrial and company league teams, many of which existed in the environs of Chicago and became fodder for the American Giants. A dismayed *Chicago Defender* scribe taking note of the trend, wrote that it would not be surprising if black American Giants "depended on the other race altogether."

Strutting across a guy wire run between white emoluments and black self-interest, Foster called for a league that challenged white provincialism and at the same time provided the opportunity for his black teams to have the option to play their white counterparts.

In campaigning for a Negro league in the April 26, 1919 *Defender*, Foster's main target was expressly *not* the white major leagues, whom he did not want to alienate, but rather white promoters like Nat Strong. In print, Foster urged black club owners to join "in not allowing white men to own, manage and do as they feel like doing in the semipro ranks with underhand methods."

And Foster knew there were able men around blackball to answer the call. In contrast to circa 1910, blackball was being graced by other savvy men like Ed Bolden and J. L. Wilkinson; where Frank Leland's incorporation stratagem was once a mystery to his compatriots, by 1920, the St. Louis Giants, Winston-Salem Giants, Pittsburgh Giants, Baltimore Black Sox, and Madison Stars had joined Bolden in the corporate game, all selling shares ranging from $1 to $100.

Foster was the driving force behind the formation of the Negro National League and its governing body, the National Association of Colored Professional Base Ball Clubs. The owners' meeting to ratify the creation of the league was held on February 13 and 14, 1920, at Kansas City's Street Hotel. From the start, Foster's plans also called for the coronation of Rube Foster.

When he arrived in Kansas City, Foster had invited as privileged witnesses selected members of the Negro press: Dave Wyatt and Elwood C. Knox of the *Indianapolis Freeman*, Cary B. Lewis of the *Chicago Defender*, and A. D. Williams of the *Indianapolis Ledger*. Owners in the new Negro National League included men who were either vanquished Foster adversaries—C. I. Taylor of the Indianapolis ABCs and Joe Green of the Chicago Giants—or old trucklers eager to please him anew—John Matthews of the Dayton Marcos, and Charles Mills of the St. Louis Giants. There was also one man who could fairly be called a stooge—John "Tenny" Blount, for whom Foster had helped exploit the promising, untapped turf of Detroit.

To help Tenny Blount get started in Detroit, Foster had sent a number of his American Giants to play on the Detroit Stars team in 1919. To everyone's astonishment, Blount turned a $30,000 profit that year. Although a good portion of it was given back to Foster by prior agreement, Tenny Blount was the kind of black "entrepreneur" Rube Foster detested as antithetical to the cause.

Complying with Rube's wishes, the black press depicted Blount as a "typical" black businessman. The real story was that Blount's businesses included gambling and prostitution in the Motor City. Blount was a career vice man and numbers runner, and his wealth came from draining hard-earned money from the ghetto. But Tenny, like most other black numbers men, was popular on the street, by dint of the fact that he had made it big in a white man's world. Men like Tenny Blount were often idolized as *the* symbol of the black leisure class; as a consequence, Rube Foster, and the other "clean" blackball men, would have to learn to live with them.

Just as important, though, Rube Foster had also allied himself with one of the two Cuban teams on the edges of blackball, the Havana Cuban Stars. This team was materially owned by the Cuban promoter Abel Linares, but Foster's standing as an icon on the island had turned Abel Linares into Rube's agent.

Linares knew well that the Cuban teams in the States—the other, the New York Cuban Stars, was being overseen by a Harlem version of Tenny Blount, a numbers man and Nat Strong toady named Alex Pompez—were poor relations in the black game. These teams were denied home grounds, forced to travel all the time, and paid substandard wages, and to them a nod from Rube Foster meant far more than the odd signing of a Cuban by the Cincinnati Reds. And so Abel Linares was thrilled to be offered a place within the grandest of blackball dreams, and gladly allowed Foster to act as his proxy in Kansas City. But barely consulting Linares, Foster looked to plant the team in a city where he thought it would be accepted; given its acceptance of Cubans, that city was Cincinnati.

One Foster protagonist purposely did not appear in Kansas City. While Ed Bolden was invited, the Hilldale owner refused to come, no doubt still irked by a recent meeting between the Hilldales and American Giants.

In fact, Foster had ignored Hilldale for years. When Foster had taken his American Giants east, he pointedly played another Darby club, the Peerless American Giants, at their field just across the street from Hilldale Park. Finally, in 1919, Rube foresaw a huge payday and scheduled three games at Hilldale Park, gaining rare concessions from Bolden. Rube's team drilled the Hilldales in the first two games but were rousted in the third, which did not sit well with Rube or his retainers in the black press. In his stories on the games, Dave Wyatt of the *Indianapolis Freeman* dubbed the Hilldales the "Hill-billies" and attributed their lone victory to "umpirical robbery, hostility of the police force and wrathfulness of the crowd, who seemed unusually inhumane."

Rube, though, could not begrudge Bolden's rise in blackball, and sent him a number of complimentary letters throughout the 1919 season. With the Negro National League fast becoming a reality, Foster was deathly afraid of Bolden taking his business to Nat Strong.

Not by coincidence, Strong began to court Bolden, offering the owner a variety of concessions to align with him in a mighty league Strong wanted to form in the East. Strong saw this alliance as essential, and yet he had to take valuable time out from his effort to create it to cope with yet one more challenge in his own home grounds.

In 1918, Strong's major irritation had once again become John Connors, who had been lying in wait ever since Strong had taken the Brooklyn Royal Giants away from him in 1912. Now, in the Bacharach Giants of Atlantic City, Connors found a means to plot his revenge. The Giants, Strong's major rival in the East, had gone under in 1918, and now Connors purchased the club and moved it to Harlem, using the aid and economic leverage of a man who could not only pierce Strong's monopoly but terrify him. This was the elegantly named Baron Wilkins, a notorious gangster and owner of a nightclub in Harlem called the Exclusive Club. In reorganizing the Bacharachs, Connors took Baron Wilkins in as his co-owner.

A decade before, Wilkins had helped bankroll Jack Johnson (the prizefighter, not the Topeka Giant manager), and had reportedly won $250,000 betting on Johnson when he beat James Jeffries in 1910. Wilkins's money enabled Connors to pry Cannonball Redding and Jess Barber from Rube Foster, and Bill Pettus and Oliver Marcelle from Ed Bolden, as well as a number of players from Strong's Royal Giants.

When the Bacharachs began playing in New York, Connors's own connections in Brooklyn scored a real coup—several games between the Bacharachs and the Hilldales were held at Ebbets Field, and several more at Shibe Park in Philadelphia, marking the first time that black teams were able to rent white major league stadiums for all-black games since the early 1910s, when black teams had played games at Comiskey Park in Chicago, Columbia Park in Philadelphia, and the Polo Grounds and Hilltop Stadium in New York.

In his usual diplomatic fashion, Nat Strong attacked Connors and Wilkins for offering "coons" more money than *he* could. Unhappy as he was that his other local rivals, the Lincoln Giants, were still playing to good crowds around New York, Strong saw the Hilldales as his trump card. Strong made overtures to Ed Bolden to "amalgamate" with the Royal Giants in 1919. But Bolden, who could not have been displeased being wooed by the two most powerful blackball men in the country, declined the entreaties. Livid, Strong tried to retaliate by re-forming the old Philadelphia Giants and setting them up to play at the Delaware County Athletic Park in Darby. The Giants, however, did not live out the season, leaving Bolden indomitable.

Now it was Foster's turn to woo Bolden. In the months prior to the Kansas City meeting, Bolden was repeatedly invited to attend. Foster turned spiteful when Bolden refused and further twitted Rube by signing three American Giant players after the 1919 season. He declared that Hilldale—along with the Bacharachs, Lincoln Giants, and Brooklyn Royal Giants, all of whom had also rebuffed his new league—was "outlawed." Accusing Bolden of fomenting dissension within the black game by encouraging contract-jumping, Foster enjoined Negro National League teams from scheduling games with the four leper teams.

While Bolden warned that the league's teams would regret passing up lucrative games in Darby, Foster believed that he had neutralized a bigger threat than Bolden, by getting white promoter J. L. Wilkinson to join the league with a new club Wilkinson was developing from the remnants of the All Nations.

Wilkinson's inclusion, however, presented another conundrum for Foster, since Rube had previously called for all black teams to be owned by black entrepreneurs. Still, allowing a place for this particular Caucasian promoter made sense. For one thing, it was imperative that the new league mine the fertile pool of Kansas City blackball players, thereby pushing the new league's influence westward. And of all the blackball pioneers in those parts, none had the financial wherewithal—or the genius—possessed by Wilkinson. Not incidentally, only Wilkinson could pony up the $500 league entry fee.

For another thing, the call was made easier by the fact that many blackball people considered Wilkinson to be a true friend of the black game and its aspirations. He had built his All Nations teams with respect not only for black talent but for black *men*. Then, too, Wilkinson would never indulge in the condescension toward and outright put-downs of the black race that were so typical of Nat Strong. Instead of billing himself as "the king," J. L. Wilkinson remained in the background with the All Nations, sending his traveling secretary, Quincy J. Gilmore, or a Kansas City businessman named Howard Smith—both black men—to public functions, not merely to front for him but to strengthen the team's ties to the black community.

When Wilkinson created the Kansas City Monarchs for the new league, he again stayed in the shadows during Opening Day ceremonies in Kansas City. It was Quincy Gilmore who rode in the owner's car during the pregame parade. A year later, when Rube Foster needed an accomplished front man to head a white-funded team in Columbus, Ohio, he chose Howard Smith.

As this last move plainly shows, Foster was the last one to become overly technical about the question of racial purity within blackball, especially given his long partnership with Charlie Comiskey's brother-in-law John Schorling. In fact, the black game had been heavily infiltrated by white entrepreneurs. For example, while black businessman Charles Mills was the titular owner of the St. Louis Giants, the incorporation of that club in 1920 effectively placed it under the control of white financiers.

And so while Foster called for all-black enterprises, the real issue for him was not really black versus white, it was "good" white versus "bad" white. And later, it would also be "good" black versus "bad" black.

At the Kansas City convocation, the dirty little secrets and hypocrisies were kept hidden from the public as Rube played the role carved out for him by Dave Wyatt in the *Freeman*, that of "Moses to lead the baseball children out of the wilderness."

While the white major leagues had appointed a commissioner, it was a given that no such office could possibly retain any manner of authority over Foster. The constitution of the Negro National League bound all member clubs to play when and where Foster directed, and against whichever teams he selected, and mandated that all equipment must be purchased from Foster, including bats, balls, and uniforms. As Rube explained, this collective purchase would translate into savings for all. What he didn't say was that he received a discount from the dealers, allowing him to make a profit on the owners. What's more, Rube shipped the same number of balls to each team, and if for some the consignment proved too large, they still had to pay for them.

Even so, Foster was sensitive to potential charges of his skewing the league to the benefit of his own team. And so, wielding his inordinate power, he began moving players from team to team like so many tin soldiers, trying to create some manner of parity between league clubs. By this time, Rube also intended to hammer home league bylaw number one—the unconditional prohibition of team-jumping and team-raiding. In effect, this was blackball's first application of a reserve rule, and under Foster's aegis all league teams were to be protected financially, from a pool of league dues, in case the eastern teams stole any players.

Thus, Foster took the great outfielder Oscar Charleston off his own roster and returned him to C. I. Taylor's Indianapolis ABCs. He sent pitcher Jose Mendez from Detroit back to J. L. Wilkinson. He sent pitcher Sam Crawford from Detroit back to Wilkinson. As part of the evening-up process, he sent the quicksilver outfielder Jimmie Lyons from the American Giants to Detroit, shifted pitcher John Donaldson from Kansas City to Detroit, and so on.

With Foster's fingerprints all over every piece of league business, the ratification of the Negro National League bore witness to the nova of Rube Foster at its highest point. In the past, some blackball owners had squirmed about his highway-robbery cut of American Giant games played in their towns; now they codified it in the league charter by agreeing to pay 5 percent of the gate to the league office in Chicago—meaning that 10 percent of each and every league game was to be tithed to Foster. Though Foster took no salary as league president, he demanded these spoils as the league's booking agent, under the category of operating expenses.

Rube Foster in his resplendence looked very much like Nat Strong in his. Accordingly, it could now be seen that Foster's argument with Nat Strong had nothing to do with methodology but everything to do with who had the implicit right to hold blackball in a hammerlock. Indeed, a strong case can be made that the ulterior motive behind Foster's league was not racial hegemony but the economic hegemony of Foster's booking office. Not coincidentally, when Foster embroidered the stationery of the Negro National League preparatory to its first season, it carried in big bold letters the name of the Western Booking Agency—owned by Andrew Foster.

That masthead in general was a Rube Foster gasconade. It proclaimed "A. R. Foster" as "Chairman" of something called the "Base Ball Commission" (Tenny Blount, C. I. Taylor, and J. L. Wilkinson were the other members) and as "Chairman of the Board of Directors" (Wilkinson, Taylor, and a St. Louis Giant official named Sam Shepard were the others). The cable address was—naturally—RUBEFOS. And sprawled across the width of the paper was the swashbuckling motto We Are the Ship...All Else the Sea.

Which was pretty much what Rube Foster had been saying, using the first person singular, throughout his adult life.

9

A Decided Disadvantage

Close analysis will prove that only where the color line fades and cooperation instituted are our business advances gratified. Segregation in any form, including self-imposed, is not the solution.

—Ed Bolden, 1925

The logistical nightmare that awaited the inaugural Negro National League season was no more daunting a hurdle than the racial conditions of the day. Though Rube Foster tried to ignore the realities, he could not fail to perceive the omens when he and the American Giants returned from a long road trip in July 1919 and found Chicago an armed camp following the eruption of a race riot over the denial of factory jobs to blacks. With the city under martial law, Foster had to feel particularly uneasy that Schorling Park—the center of his very world—was occupied by National Guard troops.

These social realities of postwar America forced Foster to cancel all home games for almost a month, including a lucrative rematch with the Hilldales. And yet, guided by the sheer force of his own will, Foster would not allow the American Giants and his new league to be deterred.

Although the Negro National League was scheduled to begin operating as late as 1921, the first game was played on May 2, 1920, when the Indianapolis ABCs beat the American Giants 4–2. However, most league clubs were not ready to open their seasons; some would not begin playing until July, in some cases because ballparks hadn't been found to accommodate them.

The ballpark situation, in fact, threatened to become a huge embarrassment for Foster. Only by controlling property could Rube's messianic march against Nat Strong gain a foothold. Foster recognized this fact with an early directive that each league franchise have a park, "either leased or owned."

However, only Foster in Chicago, Tenny Blount in Detroit, and Charles Mills in St. Louis could claim they possessed a permanent place to play. In all the other league cities, games at white-owned parks were dependent on there being gaps between other amateur and semipro games, and those contests might be scheduled at the last minute. Foster expected that the Cuban Stars would find home grounds in Cincinnati, but they failed to do so. Foster had to revise his ballpark dictum so that the Stars could play exclusively on the road in 1920, as they had before.

As a result, the Negro National League schedule, originally a hundred games for each of the eight league teams, became catch-as-catch-can. At one point the American Giants had played twenty games and the Dayton Marcos only six. While all of the clubs continued to fill out the preponderance of their schedules with games against white teams—which provided the biggest pay-days—some teams began skipping Saturday and Sunday dates set aside for league contests, especially if they were supposed to make a long trip to play an unprofitable game against an unattractive team.

Foster spent long hours in his office, seeking to solve every problem in the operation. When teams ran out of money and were stranded on the road, Rube would wire them enough to get home. When teams were on the verge of going bankrupt, Rube would send a payroll advance to keep them afloat. Still trying to pump up weak clubs, he continued to rearrange player rosters.

All of these problems disrupted Foster's carefully calculated disbursement plan, which had the home team guaranteeing 35 percent of the gate to the visiting team. The problem was, 35 percent would amount to nothing when the crowd was small, and this forced the home team—or Foster—to kick in money to keep the visitors' happy. In time, strong home clubs began to skimp on the weaker teams' expense money in order to guarantee the 35 percent, leading some teams to refuse to come back.

Growing more obsessed with making the Negro National League work in spite of these difficulties, Foster had to cut back on his American Giant duties. By 1922, he would step aside as manager, handing that gem of a job to his protégé, third baseman Gentleman Dave Malarcher. Soon Rube Foster's obsessions would cost him more than a seat in the dugout.

By August of that first Negro National League season of 1920, any hope of keeping statistical records, even won-lost records, over the course of an unbalanced schedule and without corroborative press coverage was abandoned, leaving history with a dearth of information regarding that blackball year. Rube Foster, however, went unchallenged when he unilaterally crowned the American Giants the winner of the league's first pennant.

Curiously, though—or maybe not, given the mercenary under-currents of Foster's strategies—detailed financial records were meticulously kept. During that season, the eight league teams drew over 616,000 paid admissions; every team actually made money, and Foster's 10 percent exaction of all league games yielded an $11,000 bonanza for the Western Booking Agency.

And, for a change, the players shared in the good fortune. With clubs able to save money without offering large sums to select stars to jump to their teams, the salary pool would rise from $30,000 in 1920 to $275,000 within five years. In 1920 alone, the average salary of each league team soared by over $2,000, to around $200 per month.

Foster had come into the season on a high. He'd predicted that the warp and woof of blackball affiliated with the Negro National League would more than resemble "the same identical plan as both big leagues and all minor leagues." Structurally, he was correct. On the periphery of the Negro National League, but protected from raiding parties as a dues-paying member of Foster's National Association of Colored Professional Base Ball Clubs, a regional black semipro league had begun operating in the pivotal year of 1921.

The Negro Southern League fielded teams in Knoxville, Montgomery, Atlanta, Birmingham, New Orleans, Nashville, and Jacksonville. And while none of these clubs was under any agreement to serve as a minor league funnel for any Negro National League team, they formed an important adjunct to Foster's empire. Linking North and South, the league meant Rube had annexed even more territory (the Southern League teams did not have to kick back any gate proceeds to Western Booking, however) and resulted in more black-versus-black competition under one roof. But it also meant that, mired in the Jim Crow South, these teams could only play other black teams and the continued inability of the Southern League teams to draw white fans, and to take in enough capital from indigent black attendees, was another bitter lesson for Rube Foster.

Meanwhile, in Darby, Pennsylvania, Ed Bolden's black team, Hilldale, played almost no black teams. Bolden also became the only black member to be elected to the board of directors of the Philadelphia Baseball Association, which oversaw the affairs of sixty-five white amateur and semipro teams in the area.

Clearly, Ed Bolden was seeking a heavy symbolic kick in his middle-of-the-road stands against Foster and Nat Strong. In October 1920, using his new connections, Bolden was able to book a six-game series against two white major league All-Star barnstorming teams. One of these teams had a puckish Phillie outfielder, at least for that one season, named Casey Stengel. The other had none other than Babe Ruth, coming off an unheard-of 54 home runs in his first season with the Yankees.

The Ruth games especially turned on the locals, black and white, who couldn't wait to see the white star go head-to-head with black slugger Louis Santop. Bolden specifically timed these games to compete with an American Giants-New York Bacharachs game during the same week at Shibe Park, and he prevailed when his contests put more people into the stands at Phillies Park. What's more, while the Hilldales won only one of the six games, Santop impressed the white major leaguers. In the opener of the set against Ruth, he hit two singles and a double, though the Babe would ultimately win the personal battle when in the next game he jerked one clear out of the park onto Broad Street.

Bolden's appetite was surely whetted by what white booking partners could bring to Darby. Thus, as wary as he was about it, Bolden came to an accommodation with the biggest of all white bookers, though in truth, it might have been Rube Foster who finally drove Bolden to make peace with Nat Strong.

All through the 1920 season, Bolden and Foster had battled long-distance, with the first volley fired by Bolden. In April, the American Giants came through Darby again, to play not the "outlawed" Hilldales but the semipro Madison Stars. Meaning to repay Bolden for his dismissal of the Negro National League, Rube showily offered the Stars membership in and the protections of, the National Association of Colored Professional Base Ball Clubs as well.

That, however, was only the beginning of Rube Foster's vindictiveness. Next he offered his belated help to John Connors in his seemingly endless struggle with Nat Strong. Foster struck an agreement with Connors and his gangster partner Baron Wilkins by which the Bacharach Giants would enter the Negro National League as an "associate member."

This backdoor access to the league would prove providential for Connors. True, Foster had doubled the original league entry fee to $1,000, but the Bacharachs were now indemnified by Foster's league against player raids by the western clubs. And while the Bacharachs were not formally a member of the Negro National League, the team could schedule league teams to boost attendance, though 5 percent of the gate for these games went back to Foster.

This arrangement allowed Rube to infiltrate Nat Strong's turf. Starting in 1921, the American Giants of Chicago and other league clubs played the New York Bacharachs at Dyckman Oval in upper Manhattan, right under Strong's nose. Though the Bacharachs were really a pawn in Foster's power games, Connors was so grateful for Rube's forbearance that he apparently believed it was incumbent upon him to cripple another Foster foe: Ed Bolden. Though Connors had now pledged to respect player contracts in the Negro National League, he soon raided the Hilldales of some of their top players. He brought to the New York Bacharachs catcher Yank Deas, shortstop Dick Lundy, and outfielder Jess Barber, who had just settled in with Hilldale after Bolden had stolen him from Foster.

Fuming, Bolden filed suit against Deas and Lundy—but not Barber—for breach of contract; incredibly, he cited a 1902 Supreme Court ruling that upheld baseball's reserve clause, which of course was the last thing Bolden wanted to include in blackball contracts. Bolden won a temporary injunction against Deas in the Philadelphia Court of Common Pleas. But the court also required that Bolden post a $2,000 bond to protect Deas from any loss of income until a final hearing. Hoisted on the blackball petard of avarice, Ed Bolden let the matter drop.

Now Bolden's court became the forum of pubic opinion. On August 21, 1920, he wrote an open letter to Foster in the *Philadelphia Tribune,* berating him for taking a "belligerent attitude toward our club." Bolden declared that the Bacharachs' incursion on his team was part of a plan whereby Foster "sought to place us in disfavor" in the east by trying to persuade its teams to boycott Hilldale.

Seeing the walls closing in on him, Bolden felt he had no other option but to seek an accommodation with Nat Strong. Actually, when he met with Strong in November, it was evident that Bolden had grown quite bigger than Strong and had the upper hand now. Instead of an amalgamation of teams, all Strong got was a neutrality agreement allowing games to be played between Hilldale and Strong's Brooklyn Royal Giants.

Chagrined that Bolden had thrown the fading Strong a life preserver, Foster was at the same time impressed once again by his canny moves, especially since they were so similar to his own. Indeed, Bolden was furthering blackball's growth within the parameters Foster had set up. It may even have been Bolden's agenda all along to make connections in New York, through Strong, to leverage himself in any future dealings with Foster.

To be sure, that prospect loomed larger even as he and Foster battled each other throughout 1920. Clearly, Bolden knew he could not ignore the Negro National League once it passed muster that first season. Aware of the vulnerability of his team to raiding forays in the name of league sanctity, Bolden too craved the protection Foster had given the New York Bacharachs.

Bolden signaled his amenability in his open letter to Foster in the *Philadelphia Tribune,* by appealing for cooperation between east and west. And just days after his truce with Nat Strong, Bolden—acting more like Machiavelli than Rube Foster did—shocked his new ally in New York by turning his back on Strong and coming to terms with *Foster.* Anteing up his $1,000, Bolden obtained associate membership status in the Negro National League—at once *preventing* Hilldale from playing Strong's out-lawed Royal Giants.

The *Chicago Defender* depicted Bolden's tense meeting with the Negro National League barons in Indianapolis that fall as a lovefest. "The magnates acted more than fair and treated Bolden as if he had been a member all the time," the paper warmly reported. But in reality, Foster remained wary of Ed Bolden's loyalty.

For now, the 1921 Negro National League season began with a broader purview, though the widening borders were created by the shifting of franchises that could not survive even the prosperous season of 1920. Unable to carry on, the Dayton Marcos were moved to Columbus, with a black front man—J. L. Wilkinson's crony Dr. Howard Smith—and a new star player-manager in thirty-seven-year-old John Henry Lloyd. Given permission to leave the Bacharachs to take the job, "Pop" Lloyd hit a reported .337, but the club disappeared after the 1921 season—as did Charles Mills' St. Louis Giants.

Moreover, the Negro National League was still mired in logistical mud. While the American Giants won the pennant again with a record of 41–21, the busier Kansas City Monarchs came in second at 50–31. Foster's showcase team never made it to St. Louis for even a single game, but went to Darby, Pennsylvania, in October to meet Hilldale in a six-game series. Those games between the two East and West superpowers were so important that they, in effect, constituted blackball's first World Series.

The opener, played before a full house of five thousand people at Baker Field in Philadelphia on October 4, was another in-your-face exercise in Rube-ball. Running wild on Hilldale catcher Jim York, Foster's American Giants stole *ten* bases en route to a 5–2 win.

But now the Hilldales rose up for Ed Bolden. Phil Cockrell won game two to get his team even, and after the Giants took game three, Hilldale didn't lose again once the series shifted to Hilldale Park. Keeping the Giants off the base paths, the former "Hillbillies" stormed back with timely hitting to conquer Foster's men with three wins, two losses, and a tie.

Pumped up by the victory, Ed Bolden contemplated his next bold move. As it became clear over the coming months, that move would be to turn against Rube Foster the way he had turned against Nat Strong.

Bolden had come to regret the Hilldales' associate membership in the Negro National League. The odd American Giant date proved profitable, but Bolden couldn't play natural-rival eastern clubs Foster held as outlaws, and a trip to the Midwest for a handful of games would have cost him a fortune in 1922. Bolden complained to the press in January 1923, "[W]e have received more money for a twilight engagement in Philadelphia, where the players could walk to the park, than a Sunday game in the West, with over a thousand miles of railroad fare to cover!"

These same factors had by then already broken the back of John Connors. Even with infusions of Baron Wilkins's money, Connors couldn't keep the Bacharach Giants solvent. After the team broke up, it was reclaimed by its creators, Thomas Jackson and Henry Tucker, who planned to start it up again, though no sooner than 1923. Now deprived of another eastern ball club to play, Bolden spent the winter before the 1922 season dropping hints that he would withdraw from the Negro National League—but backed down in the face of threats that appeared in the *Chicago Defender* and which obviously reflected Foster's thinking.

"[U]nless Manager Bolden comes into the fold he may find his club wrecked," the paper editorialized in the March 4 edition.

Bolden read this statement as a warning that his team would be raided, and quickly renewed his associate membership for 1922. But all the while, he was looking to get past Rube Foster's league.

The American Giants may have won the league crown in 1921, but the year really belonged to Oscar Charleston, the big and nasty outfielder who played with the St. Louis Giants that season. Because Foster had pushed hard for more comprehensive coverage in the black press, Negro league historians Dick Clark and John B. Holway were, decades later, able to reconstruct a near-complete statistical rendering of the season for the 1985 *Journal of the Society for American Baseball Research*. Today, this argosy, subject to the usual caution about information found in Negro league game box scores, offers a periscope view of some legendary men.

Oscar Charleston began that season with the soon-to-be-defunct St. Louis Giants, having been sold by C. I. Taylor's Indianapolis ABCs to St. Louis in the offseason. Not only did Charleston thrive in St. Louis, but as a team the Giants hit .286, by far the best in the league, with Charleston (.446) and outfielder Charles Blackwell (.418) finishing one-two in the batting race. The ABCs' first baseman, Ben Taylor, also reached the .400 plateau, hitting .415 with a league-high 86 hits. This triumvirate ravaged the league in different ways as well. While Taylor's specialty was pushing hits through the infield, the muscular Charleston hit 14 home runs, and Blackwell followed him with 9, in addition top a league-best 13 doubles. Amazingly, Oscar had a slugging average of .774— and 28 stolen bases, more than anyone else.

By contrast, Rube Foster's American Giants were dead last in hitting, at .237, with only two men—the Cuban Cristobal Torriente and the repatriated Jimmy Lyons—over .300. And yet this was actually one of Foster's best teams, its speed and pitching without peer. In one rather astounding game, the American Giants fell behind the ABCs 18–0 but rather than swing away they dropped eleven bunts and executed six squeeze plays. In the end, they had scrambled back to tie it 18–18 when darkness halted the game.

Rube Foster's ace that year was southpaw Dave Brown, who went 10–2, had five shutouts, and one-hit the Kansas City Monarchs. But for Dave Brown, the glory would fade three years later, when he murdered a man in a bar brawl and lived out his life as a fugitive, never to be found.

This season was one of crucial transition for blackball. That the black game had a genuine tradition could be seen by the inclusion of near-turn-of-the-century players like Pop Lloyd, Detroit's Pete Hill and Bruce Petway, and St. Louis Giant pitcher Bill Gatewood, one of the Philadelphia Giants Rube Foster had taken with him to Chicago in 1909. Gatewood, a super pitcher, had long ago developed a habit of downing a bottle of corn whiskey before games in full view of the crowd and the other team's hitters; he later admitted that the bottles contained only water and that he carried out the charade to amuse the crowd and psyche out the hitters.

The 1921 season also saw the end of the career of the ubiquitous manager of that Philadelphia team jilted by Foster and Gatewood—Sol White, who took his final turn at bat at age sixty in twelve games as a player-coach with the Columbus Buckeyes, hitting .167.

But now a new core of young players appeared, led by ABC catcher Raleigh "Biz" Mackey. A large man with nimble feet and a howitzer for an arm, Mackey came out of Texas as a revelation: a switch hitter who could discourse on the science of hitting the way Foster did pitching.

In his rookie year, Mackey hit eleven home runs, and his arm

was a stop sign for base stealers. Mackey's only weakness seemed to
be his great fondness for liquor. Often he played while drunk, and
if opponents smelled whiskey on his breath when they came up to
hit, then they knew they could challenge him on the bases. But
even pie-eyed, Mackey could gun them down.

Even the Negro Southern League paid a dividend for Foster's
league. In Montgomery, Alabama, a cobralike outfielder, Norman
"Turkey" Stearnes, was ripping up league pitching. All arms and
legs, Stearnes was a pastiche of oddities; in his batting stance he
leaned way forward and his back foot pointed straight up. When
he ran, his elbows flapped in and out—thus his nickname. He
choked up on a light, thin bat, yet he hit moon-shot home runs.
On Bruce Petway's recommendation, in 1922 Tenny Blount became the first National League owner to give Turkey Stearnes a
contract. Stearnes would go on to have a twenty-year blackball
career.

At the conclusion of that 1921 season, the Negro National League
had made it through two years, almost purely on Rube Foster's
will. But serious cracks had begun to show in Foster's fortress.
Despite his constant manipulations to bail out sinking teams,
Columbus went under, driving Pop Lloyd back east, to the
Hilldales. The St. Louis Giants also died, to be replaced by
another team, the St. Louis Stars, which came in along with the
Pittsburgh Keystones and Cleveland Tate Stars. But within a year,
the latter two were also gone.

While the core teams in Chicago, Kansas City, and Indianapolis
continued to make money, the ABCs were rocked when C. I.
Taylor died suddenly on March 2, 1922, at age fifty. And Foster
had to admit that attendance was down by 25 percent in 1922 and
that half the league's teams had gone into the red.

Foster himself was becoming less stable as well. Over the past
year, his young daughter had died of pneumonia, and an increasingly volatile Foster seemed less interested in league harmony
than in what the league could mean to his legacy. Instead of
bailing out anemic teams, he took to blaming those teams for
keeping "slack business records." By making a new appeal to black
businessmen to enter the league, he implicitly denigrated the
league's white seed money.

Among observers who had harbored Foster's little deceits, this was a clear betrayal. Writer Ollie Womack of the black *Kansas City Call* was the first to question Foster in print. Noting that the American Giants played at home almost every Sunday, Womack wrote: "[They] make one trip around the league circuit, while several other clubs, especially the Monarchs, make from two to five."

But, incredibly, it was Rube Foster's lackey in Detroit, Tenny Blount, who inadvertently came closest to blowing Foster's racial pretense. Blount told the black *Pittsburgh Courier* that, because of Rube's Sunday advantage, "Foster and Schorling got theirs and looked wise"—thereby dropping the name of Foster's silent white partner, whose involvement with the American Giants was not widely known.

Carefully sidestepping the John Schorling issue, Foster pointed out that he was paying rent ranging from $945 to $1,346 a month to his "landlord" at Schorling Park. Besides, he said, these Sunday affairs in Chicago made more money for the visiting league clubs than they made at home.

This quiet grumbling followed by a year Ed Bolden's anxieties about Foster's methods and the overall value of league membership. And nothing in the past year had eased Bolden's mind.

Just as Bolden feared, the loss of dates with the Brooklyn Royal Giants and New York Lincoln Giants were not made up, despite the expensive road trip the Pennsylvania Hilldales took in August to play Chicago's American Giants and the Detroit Stars. Only four western teams had played the Hilldales in Darby, Pennsylvania, during the 1921 and 1922 seasons. Bolden was further pained that his team lost six of the nine games on that western swing, though Phil Cockrell pitched a no-hitter against the American Giants. In all, Bolden's Hilldales lost seventeen of twenty-eight games against Negro National League clubs over 1921 and 1922.

In December 1922, a disgruntled Ed Bolden submitted a letter of withdrawal to the Negro National League office. He said he was at a "decided disadvantage of ownership" in the league. Bolden also asked that his $1,000 entry fee be returned.

Unlike the year before, Foster could not flatter or cajole Bolden into relenting. But he could make Bolden pay for walking out—by refusing to return the money. Claiming that this exaction had not been an entry fee but rather a "deposit" to cover expenses, Foster

pointed out that a recent amendment to the league constitution—
which Bolden never knew existed—made all "deposits" unrefund-
able, to be used as insurance against potential raids from the
eastern teams.

To Ed Bolden, the explanation was not only crude but an
unimaginable affront. Believing Foster's interpretation to be a
"legal shakedown," he threatened at first to sue the league. Then,
well aware of the uncertainties of the court system, Bolden
decided to hit Foster where it would hurt most. Again he turned to
Nat Strong.

The irony in this reconciliation was that it would make Strong
seem like the villain who undid blackball just as it seemed to be
uniting—when in fact a black man had exacerbated the tensions
and racial conflicts Rube Foster had managed to keep submerged.

While Bolden's revanche bought him great power for a time, in
the end it would retard the black game, and nearly kill it off. And
yet history would be kind to Ed Bolden; Negro league revisionists
would routinely overlook Bolden's perfidies in order to make Nat
Strong seem responsible for blackball's failure to unite. Indeed,
the main source for this view were the words of Rube Foster
himself, a man who played the race card with cunning and
duplicity in defense of his territory.

In the real world of 1923, Nat Strong could not have done
anything without the graces of Ed Bolden. Having already laid the
groundwork two years earlier, Bolden dwarfed Strong in influence
when they spawned another alliance.

Strong's power within blackball had been eroding for years, to
the point where he could fairly be called a minor hand booking
the Brooklyn Royal Giants and Alex Pompez's Cuban Stars at
Dexter Park in Brooklyn. As other bookers had broken his
monopoly, Strong had begun spending almost all his time booking
the white semipro Brooklyn Bushwicks.

Thus, Strong was overjoyed when Bolden came back to revive
him. And Bolden surely needed Strong to form what was essentially a self-defense society for the eastern teams that had been left
out in the cold by the Negro National League. As Bolden formally
stated this premise—notably absent of any reference to race—in
the December 1, 1923 *Philadelphia Tribune:* "The fans have loyally
supported the club and there is little doubt they will continue

doing so, but I think they are entitled to better competition among our clubs; and the best way to secure it is through an organized circuit."

But Bolden had more in mind than a free-trade zone among outlaws. He wanted to challenge Foster's Negro National League—in numbers, as a bloc. Bolden could thus offer his own league as a working exemplar of "big league" blackball, without its crude Rube Foster aspects—and offer himself as the Anti-Foster.

With Strong in his pocket, Bolden did not need to be distracted by the usual blackball clefts. The New York market was now undivided, opening up free travel in the Northeast corridor for the first time in years. From the start, the Hilldales, Royal Giants, and Cuban Stars were on line; and Bolden easily signed on two more clubs that in the past had experienced bad blood with Strong, James Keenan's New York Lincoln Giants and Tom Jackson's Atlantic City Bacharach Giants. Bolden took in a sixth and final eastern member, the Baltimore Black Sox, a newly turned pro team owned by two white barkeepers, Charles Spedden and George Rossiter.

Bolden sewed these teams together without regard to the complexion of the owners. As it happened, Bolden was the only African American among them, and Alex Pompez the only other non-Caucasian. First and foremost, what Bolden needed was a war fund, and that he got mainly from white moneymen—à la the Negro National League—which meant that the nagging conflict between black baseball and its white angels would not be resolved soon, if ever.

But now it was Bolden's turn to hold a historic meeting of blackball owners and their agents. On December 16, 1922, representatives of the six teams of the brand-new Mutual Association of Eastern Baseball Clubs met at the YMCA Building in Philadelphia to ratify the league's hierarchy: chairman of the board Ed Bolden and secretary-treasurer James Keenan.

With the Eastern Association's constitution signed, its aims certified, and its coffers full, blackball's night of long knives would now begin.

10

Farewell, Rube Foster

As generally befalls a giant, Rube Foster proved his own undoing.
—Al Monroe

Although the reserve clause and the constitution of the Mutual Association were identical to those of the Negro National League, none of the new league's owners felt compelled to broaden the spirit of harmony and cooperation beyond the league's borders. Where Negro National League men had refrained from raiding the rosters of outlawed eastern clubs to prove their commitment to a new class act in blackball, the men of the new circuit came out of the Philadelphia meetings with no such scruples.

James Keenan of the New York Lincoln Giants began by attacking Rube Foster's roster. In February 1923, he signed the ill-fated pitcher Dave Brown. Ed Bolden struck next, reeling in the Detroit Stars' outfielder Clint Thomas and second baseman Frank Warfield, as well as the Kansas City Monarchs' pitcher Rube Currie and outfielder George Carr. Then Bolden bought his biggest plum by culling the budding superstar catcher Biz Mackey from the Indianapolis ABCs.

During the next two years, Foster helplessly watched eighteen Negro National League players defect to Eastern Association teams. With each defection, Rube's only recourse seemed to be to shame the new league by trying to cover it with the devil's cloak of Nat Strong.

While Strong didn't actually sign anyone from the West to his Brooklyn Royal Giants, Ed Bolden had arranged with Strong to consolidate the booking mechanics of league competition. Bolden alone profited from Hilldale games, but the five other clubs ceded varying portions of their gate receipts from league games to Strong and Bolden.

To make this diminished income acceptable to the others, the two men stopped collecting excessive fees from teams visiting Dexter Park and Hilldale Park; instead, all league teams, including visitors, were paid a flat fee per game—normally $500 to $600. But this also meant that teams would no longer receive a cut of the gate for well-attended games that might yield far more money.

These practices became a target for the power bloc in the west. The *Chicago Defender*, again doing Foster's bidding, wrote of the new league's opening series of games that "colored baseball in the East has gone back a decade when Nat Strong offered ball clubs $100 flat and two 15–cent meals for a Sunday game."

Even before the Philadelphia meetings, Foster was taking dead aim at Ed Bolden's league as purveyors of racial impurity. In the October 13, 1922 edition of the *Kansas City Call*, Foster charged, "There can be no such thing as black baseball with four or five of the directors white any more than you can call a street car a steamship. There would be a league all right, but the name would have to be changed," he told the black paper.

Several months later, Foster declared unconditional war, growling to the *Defender* on January 13, "There can be no peace in [black] baseball as long as the quislings back East are bucking the ship of the [Negro] National League."

Shortly after Foster's "no peace" declaration, Bolden used his own middlemen in the black press to respond, mainly to the growing criticism involving Nat Strong. He insisted to the black *New York Amsterdam News* that, on his part, he "never paid Mr. Strong one cent for booking the Hilldale Club." What Bolden failed to say was that this arrangement only applied to the Hilldale Club; all other league teams did pay a ransom—to Strong and Bolden.

Still, Bolden now made a non-too-subtle alteration in the nomenclature of the league: Right before the circuit began play, the operative name for the Mutual Association was changed—just as Rube Foster had said it would be—to the Eastern Colored League.

While the Eastern Colored League was plagued by the same logistical tangles as the Negro National League, its creation marked another milestone for blackball. For the first time, a means now existed by which to quantify the relative strength of teams that had at one time or another been regarded as the best in the East.

That first season of 1923, Ed Bolden's Hilldales cleared the field against Eastern Colored League teams, winning 32 games and losing 17 while compiling a reported overall record against all levels of competition of 137–43–6. What's more, Bolden's connections with whiteball paid off. That same year, the Philadelphia Athletics somehow slipped through Judge Landis's unofficial ban on team barnstorming in order to play Hilldale in a six-game exhibition series—though the Hilldales, in winning five of the six, may have further hardened Landis's attitudes against such affairs.

To Strong's dismay, his Brooklyn Royal Giants could do no better than win half of their thirty-six league games and finish third behind the 23–17 Cuban Stars but ahead of the Bacharach Giants, Lincoln Giants, and Baltimore Black Sox. Still, while Strong's team did not fare that well in the 1923 season, he probably enjoyed serving as the lightning rod for Rube Foster's foamy tirades in the black papers.

Both Strong and Bolden knew that such enmity only elevated them and the Eastern bloc, and the only question that remained as both leagues chugged unsteadily on was which side would have the most influence when and if an accommodation would be made to save blackball yet again.

That crossroads, and who would get there in sounder shape, was the hidden reality within the two blackball worlds in 1923. Even Foster eventually seemed to be resigned to a new order. By 1924, Rube tried to weed out some of the more unsavory members of the Eastern Colored League faction in time for the coming rapprochement. His new target was the Baltimore Black Sox.

That team certainly had become an embarrassment to Bolden's regime. Even with the league's race-neutral mindset, the two Black Sox owners, Charles Spedden and George Rossiter, were pushing the limits of toleration. The two white men housed the team in a sewer known as Maryland Park, which featured broken seats, holes in the roof, nonworking toilets, and a weed-covered field.

Even more unsightly, Spedden and Rossiter actually had a "special reservation" section of box seats *for whites only*. They also refused to hire blacks to work in the box office—an important secondary virtue of blackball as a business—because the owners had "not found them satisfactory in the rapid handling of change" and were "most always short when the count up is made," according to a story in the *Baltimore Afro-American* on May 16, 1923.

Yet even with these slanders, blacks in Baltimore supported the club, and the owners rewarded the fans by at least spending money on players and putting quality teams on the field. To Bolden, this was an effective rejoinder to Foster, whose "blacks only" league was rife with owners presiding over withering franchises.

And so Bolden stood with Spedden and Rossiter, as he did with the vilified Nat Strong. Hanging together, the Eastern Colored League turned a profit just as Foster's league was hitting the skids.

Still racked by instability, the Negro National League had lost four teams in 1923, Toledo and Milwaukee going down with the Pittsburgh and Cleveland clubs by the end of the season. Then, a month into the 1924 season, the significant but sad tale of the Indianapolis ABCs came to an end. Destroyed by the death of C. I. Taylor and the sneak-attack raids of the Eastern League—which took ten of its players away—the club disbanded.

An exasperated Foster now dispersed the expatriated players around the league and, reaching again into the Southern League, pulled up the Memphis Red Sox to replace the ABCs. He also put a short-lived team in Cleveland, the Browns. To ease the way for both of these teams, he waived the league's $1,000 entry fee- "deposit."

Foster was horrified by the beating the Negro National League was taking. Figures for 1923 placed gate receipts at $193,669, down from $251,774 in the break-in year of 1921. All the teams made money that first year; they would all lose money in 1924.

Even the imperial American Giants were in trouble. Though the Chicago team collected roughly $25,000 at the gate every season, Foster had to dip into the team's coffers to bail other teams

out of bankruptcy. Foster kept league expenses low enough—
about $162,000 in 1923—to turn a $31,000 profit on paper. But
his out-of-pocket expenses were enormous, and by borrowing
from Peter to pay Paul, he drained all the profits.

Foster, who had ignored the on-field schedule of the American
Giants, now had to watch the team recede as the cynosure of black
baseball. Accordingly, other club owners felt a decreasing compulsion to blindly accede to Rube Foster's demands. In the past two
years, Foster had not only drawn up these teams' schedules but
often filled out their lineup cards as well. One of his main orders
was that they had to save their best pitcher for those lucrative
Sunday games, no matter the competition—and this often led to
inferior pitchers losing important league games that weren't
played on Sundays. Now, in 1924, with Foster losing clout, the
grumbling grew audible.

As he had done before, Tenny Blount rebelled openly. In 1924,
Detroit's Blount told Foster he would no longer comply with his
orders. Infuriated, Foster pulled back from pursuing Nat Strong
while he obsessed about destroying his onetime lackey. Foster
withheld league monies from the Detroit Stars and canceled
attractive dates he had scheduled for them; meanwhile, he found
new owners ready to take over the Stars when Blount could no
longer afford to go on. A year later, Tenny Blount was gone from
blackball.

This internecine coup blunted further criticism among the
owners, even though Blount convinced black sportswriter Al
Monroe of the *Chicago Defender* that he should expose Foster's
manipulations of the schedules.

As Monroe later recalled of his work, "The articles were a
source of worry for Rube, and were published in several outstanding papers. Many club owners wrote Blount, commending him for
his stand. 'We'll demand a showdown at the next meeting,' they
said. They did not, however, and instead sat through Foster's
meetings saying nothing. They were all afraid of baseball's
Mussolini."

Monroe went on: "Foster planned and did crush Blount as a
method of reaction. When Blount left baseball...he had been
crushed by Rube, financially and spiritually."

Still, Foster was not blind to his league's declining fortunes, and
by mid-1924 he had become tired of fighting blackball's eastern

front. During the summer he and the Kansas City Monarchs' J. L. Wilkinson met several times with Ed Bolden about agreeing to a covenant—and when it happened, it proved how much Foster's power had ebbed. Rube went into the meeting prepared to fight for the repatriation of players taken from the Negro National League, the return of games with the attractive Eastern League teams, and a no-raid pledge from that League.

Foster also believed he could collect some of the profits from the Eastern League teams, thereby taking Western Booking to its apogee. As Al Monroe related: "Having captured the West, South, and Middle West, [Foster] decided to extend his power to the East. 'I'll have a hand in all the games Baltimore, Philadelphia, Atlantic City and New York play before long,' he used to boast." Presumably, this grand design would have left Rube in charge, as czar-cum-commissioner of the black big leagues.

But when a concord was reached, Foster came away with little that was on his wish list. The only contact between East and West was to be an annual World Series, to commence October 1924. No players were sent back to the West, and Bolden kept the autonomy of his league intact. This actually advanced Foster's original design of a blackball structure that mirrored that of the white majors, but it did nothing to align the two black leagues. One league had an openly condoned raiding policy; the other didn't. One had a central authority to mediate disputes; the other didn't. One had Rube Foster; the other didn't.

Foster did draw the line on the return of Bolden's $1,000 deposit, but that was a small, pyrrhic victory. If Foster believed he could root out Nat Strong's role in black game, he was badly mistaken. Wallowing in Rube Foster's weakness, Strong, who profited from the Negro World Series (through Ed Bolden), had come farther onto the black stage than even Strong might have hoped.

Symbolic of Foster's decline, when the World Series was played, Ed Bolden's team participated, but not Rube Foster's Chicago American Giants. J. L. Wilkinson's Kansas City Monarchs, who went 55–22 that season, beat out the American Giants with their 49–24 record to win a berth against Bolden's Hilldales of Darby, Pennsylvania.

Foster seemed to treat the pennant-winning Monarchs as an

afterthought. As cocommissioner with Bolden of the World Series Commission, Rube scheduled a best-of-nine series with maximum profitability and exposure. Rather than hold all the games in the contestants' cities, the games were to be a traveling show. According to Foster's schedule, two games would be played in Philadelphia, two in Baltimore, two in Chicago, and *then*—provided they were necessary—the last three in Kansas City; in addition, not one Sunday date was set in Kansas City.

Although J. L. Wilkinson was an understated man, he too had learned to use the black press as a sounding board. Thus, on September 9, the *Kansas City Call* upbraided Foster, asking, "Whose World Series is this anyway?" and mocking him for having saved "the World Series apple" for Chicago, while Kansas City got "the core—if there is one." Should Foster deprive the city of at least one Sunday game, the paper warned, "he will be the most unpopular man who ever walked out of the Union Station Plaza."

Rube Foster didn't need any further dissension, especially from the savvy Wilkinson. He dropped his pretext—that Kansas City's Muehlebach Stadium might not be available because white teams had first call on the field—and booked the three Kansas City dates for games five, six (a Sunday), and seven; any spillover games would then go to Schorling Park in Chicago.

The first black World Series in 1924 dramatically etched the exhilarations and pitfalls of the black game. This was the year that J. L. Wilkinson surpassed Rube Foster. His Kansas City Monarchs were a paragon of homegrown talent. Aside from pitcher Plunk Drake and the brilliant catcher Frank Duncan—who began his career with Foster's American Giants—nearly all of the Monarchs were Wilkinson finds, most notably second baseman Newt Allen, pitchers Cliff Bell and "Bullet" Joe Rogan, left fielder Heavy Johnson, shortstop Dobie Moore, utilityman Carroll "Dink" Mothell, and third baseman Newt Joseph.

Befitting the Series motif of blackball worlds in collision, Ed Bolden's Hilldales were composed mostly of mercenaries—the checkbook having bought the loyalties of men like pitchers Phil Cockrell and Rube Currie, catcher Biz Mackey, and outfielders Louis Santop and Clint Thomas, though the great Judy Johnson could logically be called a homeboy.

The up-and-down attendance for the Series attested to blackball's still-tenuous hold on the black community. For the opener, played on October 3, 1924 at Shibe Park, over 5,300 fans saw Bullet Rogan beat Cockrell 6–2; in game two, a Sunday affair at the same site, the crowd jumped to over 8,600 as Hilldale creamed Plunk Drake 11–0 to even the series. When the series shifted to Baltimore, the game drew all of 584 people and was halted by darkness after thirteen innings with the score tied 6–6. Replayed on the following Sunday, Hilldale won 4–3 when Newt Allen threw the ball away with the bases loaded in the ninth.

Now, at Kansas City's Muehlenbach Stadium, Bolden seemed to have Wilkinson's number when Judy Johnson slammed a three-run homer in the ninth to give Hilldale a 5–3 victory. The Monarchs then won game five 6–5 when Bullet Rogan—who pitched the entire game—singled in the winning run in the twelfth inning.

Game six would endure as one of blackball's most mythical contests. Played before about 8,800 on the Sunday date in Kansas City Wilkinson had fought for, the hero was the great Cuban pitcher, Jose Mendez, who was now also the Monarchs' manager, When Mendez the manager ran out of pitchers, he put Mendez the pitcher—thirty-six years old and his old speed gone—on the mound. Mendez won the game 4–3, scattering seven hits.

The series, now deadlocked at three games apiece, reached its conclusion in Chicago. First the Monarchs won another close game, 3–2, behind the tireless Rogan, this time when Frank Duncan lined a two-out, bases-loaded single in the ninth. Then Hilldale came back, winning 5–3 with two in the ninth before 6,200 fans on Rube Foster's Sunday date.

Now down to a one-game series, Jose Mendez pushed his luck and his body. With his pitching staff burned out, Mendez made himself the starter against Hilldale's Scrip Lee. Using junk and smarts, Mendez stood up to Lee and thirty-degree cold that held the crowd at Schorling Park to around 1,500. After seven scoreless innings, the Monarchs blew the game open with five runs, and old man Mendez won with a three-hit shutout.

Rube Foster had reason to be smug about the first black World Series. In all, the games—with a top ticket of $1.65 for a box seat, $1.10 for a grandstand seat—took in about $52,000, clearing $30,000 after expenses. The Monarchs earned almost $10,000 of that amount—half of which was pocketed by J.L. Wilkinson. Half went to the players, whose share came to $308 apiece. Ed Bolden distributed his team's $6,500 cut the same way, leaving the players with $193 each. (By comparison, major league World Series shares ran about four times as much.) Foster and Bolden took 5 percent more each as cocommissioners, and 6 percent went to each league's runner-up teams, Baltimore and Chicago. The last 4 percent went to the third-place clubs, the Detroit Stars and Lincoln Giants.

Feted at a victory party and entertained by black singers Billie Young, Blanche Calloway, and Amon Davis, the Monarch players and their courtiers in the Kansas City press partied hard and dug into Rube Foster even harder.

"Let no hint of how long the party continued, nor the condition of the guests on leaving escape," burbled the *Kansas City Call* with great glee. "Just remember that it happened in Chicago [Rube Foster's city]—and guess the rest!"

But Rube Foster too wanted everyone to recognize the fact that the World Series had reached a climax in his town. He told the local press that he had instructed Jose Mendez to pitch that decisive tenth game—and even called the game for him, while sitting in the Kansas City dugout. Sports editor Frank A. Young's account in the *Chicago Defender* went like this, beginning with Mendez's response to Foster's suggestion that he pitch:

> "If you say so, I do it," [Mendez said] and the Islander awaited Rube's order.
>
> Foster replied: "You go in there, and if you don't know what to throw, look over at me and I'll tell you. Don't put too much on the ball and don't try to throw too hard 'cause it's too cold, but be sure and keep up your nerve. You can do it...."
>
> [A]lthough Mendez got credit for a wonderful victory, he never hurled a ball until he looked at Foster on the bench. It was his knowledge of the Hilldale batters' weaknesses that caused Mendez to win.

It was a wonderful story, the kind Rube Foster made a career of telling. But this one would be his last testament.

Ed Bolden's noontide came a year later. Successfully defending their Eastern League crown by six games over that circuit's new entry, the Harrisburg Giants, the Hilldales again met the Monarchs—and this time routed them five games to one, taking two of the first three in Kansas City and sweeping the last two at home.

Now Bolden's courtiers in the press crowed. The January 7, 1926 edition of the *Pittsburgh Courier* made fun of the losers with this mock eulogy:

"In loving memory of the Kansas City Monarchs, infant prodigy of the National League and only child of J. L. Wilkinson, who held the title of world champions of the diamond until its sudden and violent death at the hands of the clan of Darby, better known as Hilldale, pets of the Eastern League of the baseball war sector. Kansas City departed this life at the tender age of one year."

The 1925 season was noteworthy for a number of reasons. To prevent a replay of the Monarchs' runaway pennant year of 1924, Rube Foster had instituted a split season in the National League, with the half-season winners meeting in a playoff before the World Series. The Monarchs took the first half but finished behind the St. Louis Stars in the second and then just beat them in a seven-game series.

The fast-rising Stars were the talk of blackball. Owned by Richard Kent, another numbers-running black "entrepreneur," the team was managed by Candy Jim Taylor after the fall of his brother C.I.'s Indianapolis ABCs and featured some awesome homegrown players—two of whom would run with the blackball tides until those tides ran no more.

One of these men, at only twenty-two, already had a blackball legacy—a nickname that later generations would regard as the quintessence of blackball élan. This was James Thomas Bell, a slinky five-foot-eleven, 130-pound center fielder with the speed of an ocelot. Born in Mississippi, Bell came to the Stars by way of an amateur St. Louis team in 1922 as a pitcher. After Bell calmly struck out Oscar Charleston in one game, the Stars' manager at the time, the showbiz-minded Big Bill Gatewood, dubbed him "Cool Papa," unwittingly committing the man to the ages.

Switched to a more speed-suitable center field, Cool Papa Bell covered the outfield like windshield wipers. On the basepaths, his winged feet broadened the team's slugging attack into a winning combination of long-ball power and blazing speed—with both of these dimensions aided by a ballpark with some bizarre contours.

Because the St. Louis Stadium, Stars Park, was built so as not to disturb a huge trolley garage in what was to be left field, the left field line extended all of 250 feet, but the center field fence sat a good 500 feet away. Thus, hitters like the aptly named Mule Suttles could clear the short porch while the switch-hitting Cool Papa and the other major homegrown stud, ex-St. Louis Giant shortstop Willie Wells, could smack line drives into the outfield alleys and tear around the bases before the ball could be picked up. Tales of Cool Papa scoring from first base on an ordinary single—even on a *bunt* single, players insisted—became commonplace in the Negro leagues.

In time, many people would also see Wells prevent so many base hits in the field that they would call him the greatest shortstop in creation, or at least the greatest since John Henry Lloyd.

The biggest event of the season, however, occurred not on the field but in a hotel room. In May of 1925, Rube Foster was in Indianapolis to see about reconstituting the ABCs. As he slept in his room, a gas leak left his unconscious form close to asphyxiation when somebody smelled the fumes, broke down the door, and dragged him to safety.

Foster recovered, but he became prone to illness and was unable to play an active role in the 1925 World Series—which proved a financial disaster, producing less than $6,000 in profits and a winning share of just $69 per man for Hilldale, $57.64 for each of the Monarchs.

Now, as players, owners, and the press began lobbying for an end to the World Series Foster had sponsored, Rube was no longer able to fight for blackball's main event. In the summer of 1926, word got around the game that Foster was behaving erratically. The American Giant pitcher Wee Willie Powell swore to author John B. Holway years later that he saw Rube running around on the street outside his home on Michigan Avenue and looking up in the sky for imaginary fly balls to come down. Driving in his roadster one day, Foster struck a woman pedestrian. And another Chicago player, shortstop Bobby Williams, recalled Foster locking himself in the bathroom in his office until someone climbed through the window and talked him into leaving.

Because it was Rube, everyone let him be. But when he began smashing furniture in his home that summer, Foster's wife, Sarah, had to call the police to subdue him. Shortly thereafter, he attacked a friend with an ice pick and was jailed. Appearing before Judge Irving L. Weaver in what was then called Psychopathic

Court, Rube Foster was ruled insane and committed to Kankakee Asylum in that south Chicago suburb.

Ironically, with Foster confined to his hospital bed, the American Giants—led by Rube's half brother Bill, a southpaw with a changeup that froze hitters' legs—won the Negro National League flag in 1926 and 1927, and took home the title both years after whipping the Eastern League champion Bacharach Giants five games to three each year in the World Series.

The victories proved a bittersweet reward. The 1927 Series was the finale of that event, which turned out to be a financial disaster as a result of escalating fan apathy. In the eleven-game series of 1926, a total of only 21,369 people showed up. When no future series were planned after 1927, nobody had the heart to tell Rube Foster.

In 1927, Foster and Ed Bolden suffered similar fates. In the West, few owners anticipated, or hoped for, Foster's return. As Al Monroe recalled, Richard Kent of the St. Louis Stars showed the least respect.

"[Kent] kidded Rube to his face and discussed him to [me] during his absence," Monroe said, "but Rube was wise and knew what was going on."

But Rube could do nothing as the owners quickly elected, without his consent, a new league president, William C. Hueston. A onetime judge in Gary, Indiana, Hueston was now an attorney who had done some pro bono work for the Negro National League. He also had some political connections, having been retained by the postmaster general's office in Washington, D.C., where he now lived. It was Dick Kent who nominated him, and by electing a bland detail man in Hueston, and bypassing another megalomaniac owner, the owners all but renounced Foster's authoritarian rule.

However, living in Washington, miles removed from the league, Hueston did little to help the Negro National League. And that league was in deep trouble. In Chicago, the Carthage of blackball, the American Giants began to unravel with alarming speed.

With Foster ruled incompetent, the club's directors sold the franchise in 1927 to a white businessman from Princeton, Illinois, William E. Trimble. The word in Chicago was that Trimble used this entree mainly to get the lease on Schorling Park, intending to turn it into a dog racing track. When the politicians rejected that idea, Trimble was stuck with a ball team he didn't care about.

Both the ballpark and the ball team fell apart due to neglect. American Giants games became the scene of punk violence that drove fans away in fright. On a broader level, the Negro National League was a matter of hearsay. The black papers, while still functioning as an important power base for the game, carried won-lost records sporadically, if at all, chary of the unreliable game dispatches filed by club officials. No one was quite sure if a playoff occurred in 1928, when the league "office" in Washington reported that the St. Louis Stars had won the first half of the season, the Chicago American Giants the second.

As it happened, 1928 also marked a collapse of the Eastern Colored League. The inevitability of the league's failure was prefaced by Bolden's own crack-up.

As early as 1925, Bolden had seen the omens. The Negro National League was not alone in decline. Once the postwar boom ended in the midtwenties, the black leisure class suffered economic losses. What's more, the early appeal of regular matchups between the elite Eastern League teams no longer seemed exciting.

As fans vanished, Ed Bolden candidly told the *Pittsburgh Courier* that the 1925 season had been "one of the most disastrous years for black teams in the last ten." That season, the Lincoln Giants lost $13,000. In similar debt, the Bacharach Giants were shooed out of their ballpark by police, who padlocked the field until the Giants could pay the rent.

Bolden's marquee team, like Foster's, declined on the field as well as at the gate. The Hilldale Amusement Corporation had to borrow money just to be able to open the season in 1925, 1926, and 1927, and the club experienced a $21,500 loss in the last of those years. In September 1927, as unruly players were turning games into brawls and owners were demanding money every day, Bolden could take no more. He committed himself to a hospital.

A few days later, the Hilldale Amusement Corporation picked a new club president, Charles Freeman. Just as quickly, the Eastern Colored League named a new president, Isaac Nutter, a black man who had purchased the Bacharach Giants from Thomas Jackson. When Bolden did return, in March 1928, he was fully prepared to reassume his duties, but it took a bruising power struggle before

Bolden was reelected by the Hilldale corporation as team president.

In April, he announced the withdrawal of Hilldale from the Eastern Colored League he had founded. "We are through losing money in an impossible league," Bolden told the *Pittsburgh Courier*. "When one man quits this week and then comes back a few weeks later and when one team plays forty home games and another [team] four, then it is time for a halt," he explained— though these realities had not particularly bothered him in years past.

Indeed, it was clear the Bolden had less of a gripe with league logistics than with owners he now wanted to punish for having dismissed him. When the Hilldales played only amateur and semipro teams in the spring and summer of 1928—not coincidentally, making some needed money by holding all their games in Darby and by sharing little of the gate proceeds—the Eastern Colored League simply could not go on without its cornerstone team.

Trying to replace the Hilldales, the Eastern Colored League admitted the Philadelphia Tigers. Organized a year earlier as the Eastern All Stars, the newly named Tigers were owned by one Smitty Lucas, who was described as a "hotel man and cabaret owner"—but was yet another of the numbers men now so common to the black game. When the Tigers failed, however, suddenly everyone knew they had to have Ed Bolden back.

But Nat Strong was another story. The owners of the crippled Eastern Colored League believed there was no longer a reason to fear Bolden's booking partner, nor to go on indirectly lining his pockets with gate kickbacks.

Most of Strong's time was consumed by the white Brooklyn Bushwicks, for whom Strong wanted to gain minor league status. Prowling the corridors at major league owners' meetings, Strong no longer seemed to want to be associated with the black game anyway. Each season, Strong had pulled his Brooklyn Royal Giants out of a number of Eastern League games, and the owners—with the exception of Ed Bolden—regularly pressed for his ouster. As long as Bolden was around, however, Strong had little to fear.

When Bolden removed his team from the Eastern Colored League, Strong was voted out. Soon afterward he folded the Royal Giants. However, he remained an active promoter of Alex

Pompez's New York Cuban Stars. As Ed Bolden was in no way prepared to give up his alliance with this popular team, he listened when, in August 1928, the moribund Eastern Colored League's owners sought Bolden's return through the conduit of the black press.

Bolden's renewed presence was deemed so vital that the Eastern Sportswriters Association, a loose federation of black sports scribes proposed the formation of a new league to supplant the Eastern League in order to ease Bolden's reentry. Pandering to Bolden, the group ran articles in all the eastern papers calling him "the man of the hour" and "the one individual who can work order out of the present chaos."

Properly flattered, Bolden agreed to the new league concept, which looked a lot like the old league concept. Chartered in January 1929, the American Negro League was composed of the holdover Eastern League clubs minus the Brooklyn Royal Giants and with one new franchise, the Homestead Grays of Pittsburgh. And just like the Eastern Colored League, it collapsed, victim of the black economic crash and Bolden's ongoing mistrust not only of his fellow owners but apparently of his own race.

In Darby, the Hilldales were a microcosm of the league's—and all of blackball's—woes. Bolden's crisp, courtly discipline was forgotten as Hilldale players became slothful and practiced the morals of alley cats. During the 1929 season, several players fought each other one night outside a brothel on Fifteenth and Naudain Streets, leaving one with a fractured skull. That same season, a woman fan was shot and killed by her estranged husband during a game at Hilldale Park.

A worse crime to many within blackball was Bolden's ongoing resistance to black employment at Hilldale Park. Although Bolden had presumed to speak for the cause of black opportunity, his attitudes about race were more in line with those of the two white owners of the Baltimore Black Sox, and of course those of Nat Strong.

Bolden refused to hire black stadium workers or, more symbolically, black umpires. In 1925, Bolden had hired a white sportswriter, Bill Dallas, as the Eastern League's supervisor of umpires, and not one black man had umpired a game in Darby since. The usually obsequious *Philadelphia Tribune* blasted this record as "a disgusting and indefensible practice [that is] a reflection upon [Bolden], the ballplayers and the Negro race."

In another editorial on the subject in 1929, the *Tribune* declared:

> It is a reflection on the ability and intelligence of colored people. *Are we still slaves?* Is it possible that colored players are so dumb that they will resent one of their own race umpiring the game? Or is it that the management of Hilldale is so *steeped in racial inferiority that it has no faith in Negroes?* Aside from the economic unfairness of such a position the employment of white umpires at Negro games brands Negroes as inferior. It tells white people in a forceful manner that colored people are unable to even play a ball game without white leadership. It is a detestable mean attitude. There is no excuse for it. [Italics in the original.]

In fairness to Bolden, he was not alone in rejecting black umpires. Rube Foster had never reconciled the problem himself, although the Negro National League did move on the issue when it hired Billy Donaldson in the midtwenties as one of its prime home plate umpires. (A severe, peremptory man, Donaldson was to the administration of the black game what John Henry Lloyd was to its performance.)

For Ed Bolden, time was running out. By 1930, with the American Negro League dead and buried, and with the volatile black press having turned on him, Bolden was ready to quit in Darby and go back to his post office job. Bolden had made some money, and, lost more. One of the sadder moments in the history of blackball occurred during the winter of 1930, when Bolden did not renew the lease of the ballpark he made famous, as the first step toward dissolving the Hilldale team.

As black teams began to fold, the Bacharachs of Atlantic City had followed the Brooklyn Royal Giants out of existence, and the New York Lincoln Giants were next to go down. Trying to buck the tide, three members of the Hilldale Amusement Corporation kept the team in business after Bolden left. Signed to a new lease at Hilldale Park, the club barnstormed through the 1930 season, but inside of a year the Darby dream was over.

On April 5, 1930, sportswriter Randy Dixon wrote in the *Philadelphia Tribune*:

The history of the success of the erstwhile postal clerk reads like a dime best seller. He led a group of mediocre performers through the pitfalls of public opinion, built up a real following and guided the Hilldale Corporation to the heights of Negro baseball. [But] Bolden proved himself a traditional if not typical cullud [sic] man by playing "Uncle Tom" and taking his advantages to the Nordic faction.... He favored the white brethren on all sides.... [m]ade arrangements to take something that had been nurtured by colored people and was a colored institution and bend it in such a manner as to fill the coffers of the Nordic.... [N]ow the man who was once a king is a piker and Ed Bolden is through. We mean THROUGH!

When Rube Foster's wife later told of his dementia, she related how Rube would constantly rave about having to get up from his bed to pitch in the World Series. With the forty-nine-year-old Foster in his fourth year of confinement in Kankakee, Illinois, in 1930, any wistful hope that he might return to baseball had given way to a plaintive plea not to let his memory die.

Foster's staunchest ally in the press, Frank A. Young, wrote in the November 1930 issue of *Abbott's Monthly*:

Today, as this story is written, Foster sits in a hospital fighting to regain his health, which he lost in an effort to put baseball, as played by our own men, on the same plane as that of the major leagues. It is only his stamina that keeps him alive. His former associates and loyal friends hope he will be able to return to his home in Chicago soon to spend the remainder of his days.

In effect, this was the beginning of the revisionist history of Rube Foster. His failures and his hypocrisies, not to mention the cannibalistic urges of his colleagues, were not to be brought up. Instead, paeans would appear like Young's classic overstatement that "Rube Foster's name is written in baseball history so deep that the years cannot erase it. The greatest tribute to the master mind of baseball is what the bleacher fan said: 'After him they ain't no more.'"

If this view seemed confusing, given that Foster's Negro National League was about to collapse, Young had the answer: "Foster left the league just at a time when his services were most needed....The years of toil that Foster put in, burning the midnight oil that there might be a league, is about to become wasted....What Foster built up is going to the rocks and the entire West [of blackball] faces conditions worse than in 1908."

Overlooked was the league's failing condition when Foster left, and the alienation he left behind. The latter was the real point of Young's complaint that "not one of the club owners, nor...the league directors...set aside one sunny day in their home town and played for a benefit game in Foster's honor."

But there would be ceremonial rites and mournful elegies for Rube Foster. When the news came that he had died of a heart attack at age fifty-one on December 9, 1930, all of Chicago mobilized for the kind of valedictory reserved for the town's most illustrious mayors and mobsters. A week later Foster's body was brought to Chicago, where it lay in state for three days as hundreds of people moved through the funeral parlor to view the king in his repose.

In accordance with Foster's wishes, his favorite song, "Rock of Ages," was played on loudspeakers in the hall and outside on the cold street, where mourners lined up around the block. The casket was closed each day at roughly the time that American Giant games concluded.

Though many within blackball shed no tears for him, the Negro National League directors sent a floral wreath of white chrysanthemums, which weighed two hundred pounds and was shaped like a gigantic baseball, with red roses marking the seams. The American Giants' floral arrangement had a baseball diamond of white carnations encircling the initials RF, above which were placed crossed bats and a ball.

Foster's funeral was attended by three thousand people, who heard him deified in the same words that appeared in the *Defender*'s editorial of the following week: Rube Foster "had died a martyr to the game [and was] the most commanding figure baseball had ever known."

The king's final march was a slow, Model-T procession through the snowy streets to a cemetery on the outskirts of town, where he was entombed.

The rub for blackball was that Foster's apotheosis, like his life, did nothing to prevent blackball's widespread failure. But the decade of Rube Foster and Ed Bolden would not conclude without giving birth to two players who would have much to do with blackball's thriving for another decade, and eventually reaching the Promised Land of Rube Foster's idylls.

In the coming days, Satchel Paige and Josh Gibson would create thunder that changed all of baseball forever.

11

An Adventurous and Turbulent Spirit

The 1931 baseball season among the colored clubs of the nation has never had a more dreary time....Baseball at this time needs men with much knowledge of all things connected with the operation of big-time baseball.

—Cumberland Willis Posey, 1931

By 1931, Leroy "Satchel" Paige had become blackball's first major cult hero. Not quite superstar, not quite novice, he was a rather ethereal, word-of-mouth legend who became so without a great many people ever having seen him in the flesh, much less watched him wipe out hitters with the atomic fastball he was reputed to own.

This was so partly because Paige had pitched mostly in the wasteland of southern blackball, where legends were made easily by self-promoting players eager to travel the Turkey Stearnes-Biz Mackey route and be rescued from obscurity by the northern clubs.

For Paige, that route offered a way toward personal survival. Born in a shotgun shack with no plumbing in Mobile, Alabama, in 1906, he seemed to be put on this earth for only one purpose: to throw a horsehide ball harder and truer than any other human. The problem was that his gifts collided with his street survival instincts.

Paige had first picked up a baseball while in a reformatory, where he had been remanded for five years for stealing jewelry.

139

He got his nickname as a young man for stealing satchels from unwary travelers arriving at Mobile's railroad station.

Once he had found a home in baseball, first with the semipro Chattanooga Black Lookouts and then with the Negro National League's Birmingham Black Barons, Paige's unfathomable fastball made blackball people overlook his lack of a functional curveball. But he did pick up an auxiliary pitch from the St. Louis Stars' Plunk Drake that made the fastball look even faster to overmatched hitters—the "Hesitation Pitch." Paige, a six-foot-four, 150-pound string bean with no muscle but plenty of fission in his right arm, would push off the mound and hesitate at the top of the delivery for just a second before completing the throw. The hitters would stride forward to meet a nonexistent pitch, then when the ball did leave his hand, they would be helpless to make contact with Satch's ninety-mile-an-hour fastball as they stood flat-footed, the bat nowhere near cocked.

A born and shameless self-promoter, Paige would make minor headlines simply for the pet names he gave to his various pitches. But whether it was "Long Tom" or the "Trouble Ball" or the "Midnight Rider" or the "Bat Dodger," the result was identical to hitters: The ball came in hard, with a two-foot rise from knee to chest, and almost always on the fine edge of the plate.

Paige's slow gait, his double-whammy, double-pump windups, even his habit of getting to the park at the last minute, if at all, may be construed today as pandering to an Uncle Tom image of how white America saw people of color and how blacks saw themselves in a looking glass warped by the feeble-minded movie roles Hollywood seemed to reserve for African Americans. On the other hand, his act could have been a send-up of that debased sensibility. Whatever it was to the cultural mind set of the twenties and thirties, for Satchel Paige it held one purpose: to make a buck and a name for himself.

In time, that name began showing up in box scores, not in full but as a one-name, nearly pseudononymous mystery. In his first recorded game, on June 27, 1927, Paige started against the St. Louis Stars and hit the first three men he faced. The last, Mitch Murray, chased Paige around the infield with his bat, and when he threw it at Paige, and missed, Satch picked it up and began chasing Murray with it. That set off a melee between the teams, and police in riot gear had to be called to quell the disturbance.

The first professional black player, infielder John "Bud" Fowler, was the star of many white minor league teams. In 1887, he played with the Keokuk, Iowa, team in the Western League.

(Negro League Museum)

Moses Fleetwood Walker became the first black major leaguer in 1884, when he played with the Toledo Club of the American Association.

(National Baseball Library, Cooperstown, N.Y.)

When black pitcher Robert Higgins joined the Syracuse Stars of the International League in 1887, outfielder Harry Simon refused to sit for a team photo with Higgins. As a result, the players posed individually.

(Negro League Museum)

After the color line was drawn by the white majors in 1887, blacks formed their own professional teams. The Philadelphia Giants were owned by white newspaperman Walter Schlichter *(center)* and starred pitcher Andrew "Rube" Foster *(seated, second from right)*.

(Negro League Museum)

The dapper Frank Leland provided the model for black team ownership by making the Chicago Leland Giants a national attraction in the 1910s and 1920s.

(Negro League Museum)

Hall of Famer Rube Foster near the end of his fabled pitching career. The ambitious Foster also owned and managed the Chicago American Giants for three decades and created the Negro National League in 1920.

(National Baseball Library, Cooperstown, N.Y.)

Black infielder Charlie
Grant nearly broke the color
barrier in 1901 when New
York Giants manager John
McGraw tried to pass Grant
off as a Native American
named "Tokohama." When
the ruse came to light,
McGraw released Grant
before the season began.

(James Riley)

Hall of Famer John Henry
Lloyd, pictured during his
days with the Hilldale Club
of Darby, Pennsylvania, is
regarded by some as the
greatest shortstop of all time.

(James Riley)

Ed Bolden *(standing, fourth from left)*, owner of the stylish Hilldale Club of Darby, Pennsylvania, formed the Eastern Colored League in 1923 to challenge Rube Foster's Negro League.

(Negro League Museum)

Although Ed Bolden *(far right)* battled Rube Foster *(second from right)* for Negro League superiority, the two bitter rivals cooperated with each other to establish the Negro World Series in 1924.

(National Baseball Library, Cooperstown, N.Y.)

Hall of Famer James "Cool Papa" Bell began his career with the St. Louis Stars in 1922. He may have been the fastest man ever to play the game.

(James Riley)

Cumberland "Cum" Posey *(second row, third from left)* was called "the outstanding athlete of the Negro race" when he played for the Homestead Grays of Pittsburgh in the 1910s. After Posey became owner of the Grays in 1920, the club won twelve league pennants and three Negro World Series championships.

(Negro League Museum)

The greatest Negro league legends of all: Satchel Paige *(left)* and Josh Gibson. Reputedly, Paige won over 2,000 games and Gibson hit 72 home runs in one season. Gibson was a symbol of strength, but his frailties led to a tragic end.

(Craig Davidson)

Gus Greenlee, racketeer owner of the Pittsburgh Crawfords, hired Paige and Gibson to play for the Crawfords in the mid-1930s. Greenlee formed the second Negro National League in 1933.

(Craig Davidson)

The Pittsburgh Crawfords featured a "murderer's row" of four future
Hall of Famers: Satchel Paige *(second from right)*, Josh Gibson *(far
right)*, Judy Johnson *(far left)*, and manager Oscar Charleston *(second
from left)*. The man in the middle is light-heavyweight champ John
Henry Lewis, who was managed by Gus Greenlee.

(James Riley)

The peripatetic
Satchel Paige wore
the uniform of
many Negro league
teams, including
the New York Black
Yankees.

*(National Baseball
Library, Cooperstown,
N.Y.)*

But even here, the game story identified Paige, with incorrect spelling, only as "Satchell"—and this was how he was known, by variations on that one-word name, for several years. During that time Paige was coveted by so many teams that he made a lucrative cottage industry of leaving them almost as fast as he would agree to a contract, with not the slightest sense of guilt, since the predatory behavior practiced by club owners in the black game had discouraged the concept of player loyalty from day one. With Paige jumping from one team to another for his own benefit, he made it clear that *any* team could have "Satchell," be it semipro, pro, whatever; in time the mere scent of his presence could sell out the house days in advance.

The Paige phenomenon was witnessed by Jimmy Crutchfield, the gritty little outfielder who broke into the Negro National League with Paige's Black Barons team in 1930. Crutchfield would sit speechless as he saw Paige's very name have the effect of a passport all throughout the South—even among whites.

As Crutchfield recalled one such an experience in Alabama, "We were going out to the ballpark, ridin' in cars. And we were speedin'. The cops came up on motorcycles and pulled up aside us and wanted to know where the heck are you guys goin'? We said we were Birmingham baseball players. One cop said, 'You are? Where's Satchel?' We said, 'Satchel is just ahead.' He said, 'Come on,' and they gave us an escort to the ballpark. That's how Satchel stood down there in Alabama."

Suddenly, through baseball and canny self-promotion, a black man had become an authentic celebrity in the South. A still starstruck Crutchfield recalled years later, "We'd be on the field and someone would say, 'Hey, Satchel showed up.' And, boy, it was just like the sun came out from behind the clouds."

Soon, the Black Baron's owner, R. T. Jackson, knew he could not crimp Paige's capitalist meanderings and decided that the next best thing would be to partake of the spoils of Paige's baseball harlotry. Thus, Jackson began to pimp Paige to other teams, renting him out for days or weeks at a time, with the money divided by the two of them.

By 1931, R. T. Jackson leased Paige to his first big northern club, the Baltimore Black Sox. Suddenly, Paige was lost in a new blackball provincialism, as players such as himself were ostracized by more educated, snootier northern players. Shunned as a hick and an interloper, denied starts he felt he deserved, Paige went back to Birmingham—just as that club was about to go out of business along with most of Rube Foster's Negro National League, which was down to six shaky teams.

Now Paige—whose travel routes from here on in would practically draw the outlines of the blackball topography—went to the Nashville Elite Giants, a former Southern League club that had moved into the shriveling Negro National League. Ironically, the Southern League would outlast its patron, the Negro National League, by a year. Before the end of the 1931 season, the Nashville Elite Giants—owned by an affable black numbers man named Tom Wilson—had moved to Cleveland and then back to Nashville. And though Satch found enough time to carry on a secret affair of the heart with Wilson's wife, Bertha, he was in professional limbo, stuck in blackball stagnation while awaiting his big break.

Blackball itself was looking for that same road, even with America as a whole now in the depths of a Depression that blacks had been experiencing since the 1920s. Indeed, because the notion of racial superiority had no meaning in a food line, the communality of equal suffering rendered the black game far less of a racial pariah than a form of good, inexpensive entertainment at a time when it was needed. Thus, men of color now found acceptance among many whites, especially in the dust bowl of the Depression, the blanched heartland of the Midwest.

The future of blackball, and the first wellsprings of baseball democracy, could be found in the corridor running from Minnesota and the Dakotas on down through the farm belt into Oklahoma and Texas. By cultivating these long mercantile routes even during the busiest Negro National League days, J. L. Wilkinson was able to keep his Kansas City Monarchs alive as that league fell apart. By 1931, Wilkinson had to drop out of the dying league and concentrate on playing exclusively in the rural towns.

In the Middle American fairgrounds that spread out before them all summer long, the Monarchs were received as a big league attraction, by virtue of the fact that each county, each town or hamlet had its own "big league" scene. In these pockets of Steinbeckian poverty, the Monarchs were warmly welcomed for the most part, while the Yankees, Cubs, and Cardinals were just names several worlds removed from their lives.

When the Monarchs came through Pittsburg, Kansas, one day, the local paper reported on the festive atmosphere in the town:

...Today the town is in ferment. Broadway, the main street, streams with traffic, all bound north to the fairgrounds. The Fords and Essexes, the Chevies and Darts, the Buicks and Hupmobiles growl along, bumper to bumper, many bearing Missouri, Oklahoma, or Arkansas tags....The players had dressed a block down the street at the Y with its showers and lockers, essential for all the fried chicken, hams, picalilli, cakes, pies, and other edibles the townsmen will present through the day to the Monarchs.

At the fairgrounds, scores of little boys and girls stand shyly on the plot of grass where the bus unloads. (Each one of the 16 Monarchs picks his thralls.) Each one goes marching off toward the field with this little girl carrying his sunglasses, this small Negro boy with his baseball shoes, these blond brothers with his two bats, this barefooted Italian lad with his glove. Frank Duncan resembles a Pied Piper, since it requires a small battalion to carry his vast array of catching equipment. Rogan, the old soldier of the 25th Infantry, who usually marches with quick steps, comes last, accommodating his steps slowly to two tough little Irish kids, who are choked with their good fortune, each holding one of Rogan's hands just like little old sissies.

As an added benefit, J. L. Wilkinson could recoup much of the money he blew in the Negro National League by setting his own terms on these tours. Wilkinson always received at least half the gate, and often made off with 80 or 90 percent. Still, this was hardly a time of financial windfalls. In the late 1920s, Wilkinson had to sell the team's Pullman railroad car and have his players travel by bus. Shucking the natty suits they once wore on the road, by necessity they now wore overalls on the dusty road, and packed fishing poles to catch their meals.

Nor was it a racial wonderland out there. Many of the same people who cheered these talented black men on the field would refuse to serve their food or pump their gas between games. And lodging became so problematical that, like all blackball clubs, the Monarchs eschewed hotels altogether and relied on a loose network of black boardinghouses and private homes on their rounds; if none were available, the players would pitch tents and camp in the woods or even on the ball field on which they would play the next day.

Bravely extending their itinerary into the Deep South at times, the Monarchs were schooled to accept racial indignities from opposing players and the yokels in the stands. But each man had his limits. Once in Texas, infielder Pat Patterson charged into the grandstand and punched a white fan. It was an expensive punch; J. L. Wilkinson fined Patterson $50 for breaking club discipline rules.

While hardships were all in a day's work for the men of blackball, and were easily borne for the chance of a lifetime to play ball for money, Monarch pitcher Chet Brewer—who spent twenty-four seasons playing colored ball—once abridged the endless routine of blackball life into a few sentences.

"We'd just eat and ride and play," Brewer said. "That was the size of it. It wasn't easy street."

Indeed, few of these men were saintly enough to accept being doormats for their cause, at least not in their own world. Many years later, some of the Monarchs were still complaining that while they had to rough it, J. L. Wilkinson never seemed to be there with them in the woods under his own tent; instead, he was able to find the solace of a warm hotel room for himself.

Still, looking back, J. L. Wilkinson's perks were minor compared with his Lincolnesque influence on black baseball. If Rube Foster had made blackball into a profession, Wilkinson made the profession viable. At a time when the Depression was beginning to equalize black and white fortunes, it could be argued that Wilkinson was the sole baseball man with the creative energy to tackle economic realities directly.

In 1929, Wilkinson gambled his and his family's life savings of $100,000 to build baseball's first functional lighting system to facilitate night ball games. For Wilkinson, the main impulse was not the pioneer spirit but the survival of his team. Because working people, black and white, were unable to come to games on weekday afternoons, the Monarchs were primarily a weekend club, and even Sunday games were losing popularity.

To bankroll this crazy new idea, Wilkinson had to cash in his majority stock in the team. Needing to raise more capital, he took in a partner, Thomas Baird, a white billiard parlor owner in Kansas City who had played semipro ball until his leg was mangled in a railroad accident in 1918.

A serious student of baseball and showbiz, J. L. Wilkinson was not the first entrepreneur to consider night ball. One of Thomas Edison's first demonstrations of the electric lightbulb was at an amateur game played at night in 1880. Wilkinson himself had experimented with a gas-lighting system in 1920, and an amateur game in Massachusetts was played under the lights in 1927.

But Wilkinson's new attempt was the most practical one, if not the most sophisticated. He commissioned the Giant Manufacturing Company, of Omaha, to construct a portable system utilizing a gasoline-powered, 100-kilowatt generator with a 250-horsepower motor. Surrounding the stadium on fifty-foot-high stanchions grounded to flatbed trucks, the floodlights consumed fifteen gallons of gas per hour, leaving the outfielders' ears ringing from the din. The beauty of the system was that it was collapsible, allowing easy transit, and also detachable, so that some of the light banks could be attached directly to the stadium roof.

Besides the noise and the power lines snaking through the outfield, the drawback was that the lights made only a marginal difference to visibility. Although Wilkinson's minions in the black press went to work touting the invention when it was ready—the *Kansas City Call* ran a blurb in the June 30, 1930 edition insisting that the lights "made the field as light as day and playing even easier than in the sunlight as it will not reflect in the faces of the players"—the truth was that the batters were terrified as they stepped in to face pitches they saw only as dark gray blobs. Similarly, fielders had to squint and hope a line drive wouldn't cave in their faces.

The first professional night baseball game in history occurred sometime around early March, 1930 in Lawrence, Kansas, though no date or box score survived the occasion. By June, the novelty was receiving widespread attention, not all of it glowing. Even the *Call* dithered a bit with a mid-June story reporting that the lights had caused a fuss in Independence, Kansas, when the glare and the noise kept the animals awake at a nearby zoo. Moreover, the outlines of objects on the field necessitated a new ground rule: two bases for any batted ball that was hit too high to be seen by the fielders.

Mostly, however, night ball was a great success in the heartland, drawing full houses in the cool of evening. When the Monarchs played in Chicago that June, the *Defender* described the first night game in that city as "the most spectacular event in all baseball history." By the end of the 1930 season, the New York Cuban Stars' Alex Pompez had picked up on the idea and installed a similar lighting system at the Cuban's home field in upper Manhattan, Dyckman Oval.

All told, the *Call* was most prescient in its long-view perspective of this new genre of sport. "The Monarchs," said the paper, "will probably do to baseball this year what talkies have done to the movies." Five years later, on May 23, 1935, when the Reds and Cardinals played the first major league night game at Crosley Field in Cincinnati, it was revolutionary to most fans. But to those who'd been watching, it was yesterday's news.

Making money now, the Monarchs had no use for the wheezing Negro National League and dropped out for good in 1931. This loss of black baseball's premier team may as well have been accompanied by the playing of taps for the league, and within a year the circuit that rose and fell with Rube Foster was officially out of business. Not that this denouement was noticed by many people. Indeed, most blackball clubs had by then returned to independent barnstorming as well, under no central governing authority. In the east, in fact, a facsimile of the Monarchs' method was being erected by a team as coldly efficient and dispassionate as its name.

This was the Grays, who played in the smoky province of Homestead, just to the east of Pittsburgh on the bank of the Monongahela River. And while the Grays had seemingly come from out of nowhere to ascend the blackball castes, this ascension was really the culmination of another black Napoleon's thirst for power.

Actually, Cumberland Willis Posey's divine right to shape blackball in his image—or at least to lay claim to that right—predated his birth in 1981. Perhaps no other black family tree in American history had roots that reached so far so early into white loam. Posey's father, the son of slaves, was the first black licensed as a riverboat engineer and eventually worked his way up to become a top hand in the coal, banking, and real estate industries around Pittsburgh; his mother was the first black graduate of Ohio State University, and its first black tenured professor.

The young Cumberland, or Cum, Posey seemed only incidentally an African American. His skin was the color of caramel, his hair was wavy, and with his lantern jaw and serrated teeth the name Cum McPosey would have fit him as well. And yet if Posey ever regarded himself as the fortunate son, when he took to sports he never thought to pass himself off as white.

To be certain, Posey's helpful genetics did breed a definite haughtiness. Along with his family ties and his hue, he was an indelibly gifted athlete, though he carried only 145 pounds on his five-foot-nine frame. And with some doors open to him because of his birth, Posey starred in baseball and basketball and captained the golf team at Penn State University and Holy Ghost College (now Duquesne University). At the same time he was playing semipro baseball and basketball under the pseudonym of Charles W. Cumbert so as to protect his amateur status.

Years later, when Posey could manipulate his own deification in the black press, his early sporting deeds would be recalled in Olympian terms. One such chronicle would trill that Posey had been the "outstanding athlete of the Negro race [and] perhaps the most colorful figure who has ever raced down the sundown [black] sports trail." Cumberland Posey, the article said, was possessed of "an adventurous and turbulent spirit."

In fact, Posey always craved more adventure than on-field gratification could provide. As early as 1911, at age twenty, he was operating a black semipro basketball unit, the Monticellos, which featured Posey and his brother Seward and was regarded as the country's top black basketball team.

Inevitably turning his sights to the evolving idiom of black baseball, Posey played center field for the two-year-old Homestead Grays in 1910. Two years later, with his basketball team in the headlines, Posey began booking the Grays' games. In the meantime, the nature of the Grays changed. Although the team had been created as a spare-time amusement for black steelworkers under the name the Blue Ribbons and then the Murdock Grays, Posey devised a cooperative plan that allowed it to turn pro by having the players share costs and gate receipts.

In 1913, the Grays were said to have won forty-two consecutive games, but were in financial peril because their owners, citing religious reasons, refused to schedule Sunday games. Two years later, a new team owner, Charles Walker, lifted the restriction and also made Cum Posey team captain. In 1918, Posey became manager.

Posey's philosophy in running the team was no different from the viperish instincts of most blackball owners. If he couldn't recruit enough quality players from the local sandlots (two of the most enduring pitchers in the team's history, Charles "Lefty" Williams and Oscar Owens, came this way) he would pilfer them from established clubs.

In the midtwenties, he coaxed the defection of outfielder Vic Harris and shortstop Bobby Williams from Rube Foster's American Giants, third baseman Jap Washington from the Pittsburgh Keystones, pitcher Sam Streeter from the Birmingham Black Barons, and his biggest theft of all, the antediluvian Smokey Joe Williams from the New York Lincoln Giants.

Fifty years old now, Smokey Joe was the only player left in blackball whose career had begun in the 1800s. But the mountainous, hawk-faced pitcher was still hurling his sinking fastball and scaring hitters with his glare. Williams came to Homestead with a trail of some of blackball's most impressive, if unverifiable, statistical achievements—a 41–3 record in 1914, fifteen 20-plus strikeout games, and a 6–4 record against white major league touring teams.

Cum Posey gleaned instant credibility by putting Smokey Joe Williams in a Gray uniform. In 1925, Smoky Joe hurled a no-hitter against a top-notch white semipro team from Akron. Posey increased the Grays' visibility by playing Hilldale, the Baltimore Black Sox, and the New York Lincoln Giants in addition to the usual scheduled fodder ranging from the Homestead Steel Company to the Carnegie Elks Club. The Grays also took the obligatory step of engaging those roving white major league barnstorming aggregations. In one such recorded game, they lost 11–6 to a club featuring Lefty Grove and Heinie Manush, but in another Smokey Joe won a 6–5 match played before nine thousand people at Forbes Field.

In true blackball fashion, Posey began boasting about the team's achievements. In 1925, he claimed the Grays had won 130 of 158 games; in 1926 the Grays allegedly won forty-three in a row, for which Posey grandly presented each of his players with a gold baseball.

By now, Posey had turned over the managing to Vic Harris so as to concentrate on the business end of running the club—he had increased his equity in the team to over 50 percent—and the leverage he had in black baseball became clear through his player acquisitions (two other big catches were the superstar outfielder Oscar Charleston from Hilldale and shortstop John Beckwith from the Baltimore Black Sox in 1927) and by the cavalier way in which he dealt with other owners.

In the late twenties, both the Negro National League and Eastern Colored League were eager to enlist the only profitable team in blackball. But Posey felt disdain for his brethren, seeing them as weak men created to be devoured by strong men such as himself. Posey would not accept sharing power, not when he had stepped directly into it at birth. Like Rube Foster and Ed Bolden before him, Posey had his own newspaper column, in the *Pittsburgh Courier*. But this was more than a ceremonial position—his father had once owned the paper.

Moreover, like Bolden and J. L. Wilkinson, Posey believed power for black men could be achieved through accommodation with white sensibilities. In fact, only a handful of Gray games were played against black teams. Indeed, Posey was accused of threatening white clubs that if they played against other black teams, they would lose dates with the Grays.

For these reasons, people in blackball viewed Posey with distaste. One black reporter, Romeo Dougherty of the *New York Amsterdam News*, wrote in a 1926 column: "They say he [Posey] spends half his time copping or trying to cop players from other teams to help strengthen the Grays.... Posey has been a menace to sport ever since the day the bug of being a big promoter entered his brain."

Even among the Grays, Posey was a curious role model. While he presented a self-portrait of Boy Scout propriety—even card games were prohibited from the Grays' locker room—Posey often behaved more like a gutter rat. Though married, he openly flaunted his womanizing, and even joked about it.

"Cum Posey liked the women. Every town he was in he had a woman," the longtime Gray shortstop Jake Stephens once said.

"He'd say to me, 'You don't know, I might be your father. I used to go to York [Stephens's hometown in Pennsylvania]. I may be your pappy.'"

Sometimes Posey wasn't so genial about it. When one of Cum's paramours broke a date with him and instead went out with Jake Stephens, the gnarly owner issued an ultimatum.

"Stephens," he said, "my ballplayers don't monkey around with my women, or they don't play for me anymore."

Posey also indulged the profligate behavior of his co-owner, Charlie Walker, who seemed to do little but give wild, drunken parties.

This, it surprised few who knew him that when the two Negro leagues wooed him, Posey saw these entreaties as an opening to drive a hard bargain. He suggested that the Grays play two games per month against Negro league teams at Forbes Field, one from each league, as a way to bridge competition between the circuits. But he insisted that the Grays remain independent and refused to give Oscar Charleston back to Hilldale. Quickly, Ed Bolden backed off and the Negro National League lost interest.

But even Cum Posey was lured to the profit potential of a Negro league. When Bolden came to him with his plans for the American Negro League in 1929, Posey misread the blackball currents. Not only was the league gone within months, but the exalted Grays were reduced to also-rans, winning only thirty-four of sixty-three games against league teams.

Undeterred, Posey felt he had gained the right not to pontificate on the ills of organized blackball. In his column in the March 21, 1931 edition of the *Courier*, he assayed the upcoming season—the last call for the Negro National League—as a disaster in the making. The future of the black game, he wrote, "has never had a more dreary outlook."

This nadir in the fortunes of black baseball, in fact, had led to open season on the game's viability. A year before, Candy Jim Taylor, now managing the Negro National League's Memphis Red Sox, wrote a much-talked-about column in the *Kansas City Call* in which he meted out blame for blackball's decline—targeting everyone from owners to players to umpires to the black press.

Cum Posey had many of the same complaints, but unlike most blackball people, who had given up on the viability of a league, Cum had not. As he viewed it, his Grays and J. L. Wilkinson's

Kansas City Monarchs were the only teams that could survive in the absence of a mutually beneficial federation that could ease the cruelties of the Depression. And when Posey postulated the need for "men with much knowledge of all things connected" with big-time baseball operations, blackball people didn't need a scorecard to know whom he meant.

When no one took Posey up on his thinly veiled offer to save the game, Cum concluded that he would have to rescue the black game in spite of itself. This happened during the 1931 season, when the Grays were considered the unofficial colored champions, an honor won on reputation alone. For this season, Posey had put under contract a cornucopia of stars, including the great third baseman Judy Johnson, outfielder Cool Papa Bell, pitcher Bill Foster, and third baseman Jud "Boojum" Wilson.

Wilson, whose nickname apparently derived from the way players described the unique sound made by the wicked line drives he hit was blackball's newest blackguard. A native of Virginia, Wilson first played with the Baltimore Black Sox in 1922 and reportedly hit .471; over the next eight years, he was said to have hit no less than .333 in any year. He lead the Eastern Colored League in stolen bases twice, with a high of 20 in fifty-eight games in 1929.

A baneful sight, Wilson was cast in the image of both Babe Ruth—a left-handed hitter, his torso could barely fit into his extralarge uniform shirt, yet he was spindly-legged and pigeon-toes—and, at least in temperament, John Dillinger. Seemingly looking for a fight all the time, Wilson once reacted to a racial slur by the catcher of a white semipro team by knocking the player cold. When Wilson arrived in Homestead, Pennsylvania, he immediately got into a battle with Jake Stephens, which ended when he grabbed Stephens by his feet and held him out of a sixteenth floor window until Jake apologized.

"For two days I couldn't walk," a still-shuddering Stephens recalled of the incident. "I was so scared. I'd try to walk and my legs would buckle."

In 1931, Boojum stayed right in form, hitting .367, as he joined a muster roll of tough soldiers in Homestead. Only a year before, the old mongoose Smokey Joe Williams had allegedly whiffed 27 men in a 1–0 win over the Kansas City Monarchs when his fastball became invisible in J. L. Wilkinson's murky lights. The Grays' record was recorded at 136–17 that year, and when Posey challenged the dying Lincoln Giants of Pop Lloyd to an end-of-season playoff, they won six of the ten games. In a major coup, several of those games were played at Yankee Stadium. The Lincolns had liberated that slice of white major league turf only months before, on July 10, 1930, for a game against the Baltimore Black Sox before a rousing crowd of twenty thousand.

But it was neither Wilson nor Williams who gave the Grays their gestalt in 1931. All others seemed to recede new before the rising vapor that was Josh Gibson.

While Jud Wilson may have had a Babe Ruth body, Gibson possessed a Ruthian power in his bat. Only nineteen in 1931, Gibson was already blackball's main prodigy and its walking prophesy of creating an even playing field with the white majors. Cum Posey came to tabulate Gibson's home-run totals against all competition not in the teens, a normally high number for black baseball, but in the *tens*—65 in 1930, 72 in 1931. And while these numbers were, and are, impossible to verify, a sufficient number of people saw Gibson hoist enough pitches into the stratosphere that these records seem plausible.

In that "championship" series with the Lincoln Giants alone, Josh sent one skyrocket over the center-field fence at Forbes Field that was estimated to have gone 475 feet—then smoked another shot at Yankee Stadium that kept rising until it smashed into the third tier in left field and fell to rest at the back of the bullpen, about 500 feet away.

More than one Negro leaguer would swear that Josh Gibson sent that ball clear out of Yankee Stadium, something no other human had or has ever done. From that moment on, Gibson would traverse life as the "black Babe Ruth."

For Gibson, however, life at the center of a blackball *Iliad* was a head trip for which he was ill-suited. For one thing, Gibson—a catcher by trade—wasn't really cut in the Ruthian mold. At six-foot-two and 220 pounds, Gibson was huge but compact, not corpulent. His power was economical, not unchained; where Ruth's savage swing could air out the park, Gibson's was a lightning bolt tindered by a snap of his elastic wrists.

Taking a wide, flat-footed stance, Josh needed almost no stride into the pitch, as his power was generated above the waist. Even if fooled by a curveball, he was able to get his hips and arms into the swing. And if he got wood on the ball, it was enough to send it on a slow-rising trajectory toward the next county. Most of Gibson's homers, in fact, were line drives that rose only twenty feet or so off the ground and were still on the rise when cut off by the grandstand behind the fence.

On the more important human level, where Ruth was an overgrown man-child, Gibson was a child brought into adulthood much too soon for his own good. He was born in Georgia, but his father came to work in the coal mines near Pittsburgh during the great black migration, by his teenage years, Josh too worked in the mines, while playing for sandlot teams. Gaining a greater reputation with each cut, he landed on the city's top semipro team, the Crawford Giants. So named because the team originally represented the Crawford Bath House in Pittsburgh's ghetto zone, the Hill District, the Crawfords had become a stepping-stone to the big time when Cum Posey began recruiting their best players for the Grays.

In July 1930, the call came for Josh Gibson, a ninth-grade dropout who had by now had lost his adolescence forever. Although the mythmakers later concocted a wonderful tale about Gibson sitting in the stands as a spectator when Posey called him into the game against the Kansas City Monarchs, had actually been recruited while the Crawfords played a white semipro team from Dormont, Pennsylvania. Soon afterward, he had supplanted Buck Ewing as the Grays' catcher and was drawing headlines in the black papers. These accounts portrayed Gibson as an easygoing kid with the appetite of an elephant and with a ready quip, such as, "A homer a day will boost my pay" and "I don't break bats, I wear them out."

The real Gibson did not resemble this caricature. Away from the ball field, where few eyes followed him, Gibson found no cheers and no idolatry. There, life made him feel small and inadequate, and this torture began that rookie season.

Unbeknownst to his teammates, Gibson had a seventeen-year-old wife just a few months younger than him named Helen Mason. They lived on Bedford Avenue in the Hill District ghetto, and in August 1930 she gave birth to twins, Josh Jr. and Helen Gibson. But his wife went into convulsions during delivery as the result of kidney failure. She lapsed into a coma and died only hours later.

Gibson came away from this tragedy determined to avoid other personal relationships that might end in the same pain. Even his young children felt his coldness. Reared by Helen's mother, they rarely saw Josh, who chose to make baseball a year-round job, spending each winter playing in the Caribbean rather than assuming the role of father in Pittsburgh.

But if the ball field was Gibson's chosen refuge from the betrayals of life, it was only a temporary preserve. Unable to hide from his insecurities, the more balls he smashed out of sight, the more he worried that he would never hit another one. Soon, he believed he had to hit *every* one over the fence, lest he be branded a failure. Later, his neuroses led to strange and reckless behavior, and pitchers knew they could get an edge by playing with Gibson's agonized head. But, for now, the Josh Gibson nobody knew went on wearing out bats, baseballs, and pitchers on a regular basis.

By the spring of 1932, Cum Posey was ready to unveil *his* master plan for a viable Negro league. With great ambition and presumption, Posey called it the East-West League, as he intended the circuit to be all-inclusive of blackball's two fronts. Toward that end, Posey had extended his tentacles into the Midwest. With all traces of both Rube Foster and Tenny Blount gone from Detroit, Posey created the Detroit Wolves, with a puppet front man and a number of transplanted Homestead players, just as Foster had done to put the Detroit Stars in business.

Posey, in fact, merely remodeled Foster's autocracy, practically commanding the enrollment of new, lower-level clubs like the Cleveland Stars, Newark Browns, and Washington Pilots. But Posey didn't know what he was in for when he took in the more established Hilldale Field Club along with the Baltimore Black Sox and the Midwest edition of the Cuban Stars.

While Posey needed the first two of those entrenched teams to ensure lucrative dates in Philadelphia and Baltimore, Hilldale's inclusion meant that blackball was once again giving breath to the great devil himself, the unsinkable Nat Strong.

This time, Strong's empowerment came in a circuitous fashion. Though he had lost nearly all his blackball interests—maintaining only his booking connection to Alex Pompez's New York Cuban Stars—he had formed a business arrangement with a young Philadelphia promoter named Eddie Gottlieb. Although Gottlieb's main property was a semipro basketball team, the South Philadelphia Hebrew All-Stars, or Sphas, in the Strong manner he had amassed title to a baseball field in his city. The usury on Gottlieb's properties amounted to 5 percent of any game and, insidiously, 10 percent whenever a black team played a white team on his premises.

Posey's Grays were powerful enough to strike more favorable terms with Gottlieb in Philadelphia, but no other East-West team could. Hilldale especially felt Gottlieb's pincers. By the time John Drew, a wealthy black Delaware County politician and bus company owner, took over Ed Bolden's controlling interest in the famous team in 1931, he found he could not book his own team's games either in Philadelphia or up in New York because Gottlieb had a reciprocal deal with Strong to split fees on all games between Philadelphia and New York teams.

What's more, Strong had made a major score on his turf when the first new blackball team in New York in decades, the Black Yankees, were formed by the great tap dancer Bill "Bojangles" Robinson in 1931. Through Strong's connections, the Black Yankees made a deal to use Yankee Stadium for selected dates— meaning that Strong was able to collect his 10 percent off the top of some very big crowds.

Cum Posey, of course, wanted those crowds to see the Grays in nonleague games, and thus had to work with both Eddie Gottlieb and Nat Strong. But, as he would learn, doing that was a formula for destruction for the East-West League. John Drew was the first to rebel against kicking back to Gottlieb in Philadelphia and Strong in New York—especially since attendance at Hilldale Park had drastically fallen. On July 18, 1932, a week after only 196 fans showed up one day, Drew folded the club for good.

In the meantime, Posey labored to beat the long odds of economic privation, underfinanced teams, and lack of quality competition. Chaining himself to his office as Foster had, Posey wrote up schedules for the teams, hired umpires, put together a deal with black radio stations to broadcast game results, and even hired an outside agency to compile league statistics.

But by May, the first card in the house quivered as Posey's Detroit Wolves tottered on the edge. Rather than supporting other suffering but more stable teams by disbanding the Wolves and distributing their players, Posey kept pumping funds into the team. By mid-June, when the Wolves disintegrated, all the teams save the Grays were beyond salvation and Posey had to terminate the East-West League.

While this three-month blunder wrecked Cum Posey's bid to become merchant prince of blackball, a few men came out of the debacle as winners. There were Nat Strong and Eddie Gottlieb, who had used the league to play on the same stage as the Homestead Grays. But there was also a baseball dilettante in Pittsburgh named Gus Greenlee who had been watching Posey take his fall and now salivated at the thought of running Posey and his team into the Monongahela River.

The ensuing power struggle between these bitterest of enemies—which would make the Rube Foster-Ed Bolden contretemps seem gentlemanly—would determine blackball's destiny once and for all.

12

Babylon

The banks used to stay open an extra hour or two every evening to
get that numbers money. And everybody knew what was going
on—the chief of police, the burgess, everybody. When the county
was going to come in for a raid, Greenlee would get a notice, and
everybody would close down. There would be no business that day
or night. The police would come in and search, look and look, then
they'd go away, and it would be a month or so before they'd come
back again. Of course, you know that kind of protection, you were
payin' something. The chief of police was in with them.
                            —Walter "Buck" Leonard, first baseman,
                            Homestead Grays, 1934–1950

If William A. "Gus" Greenlee did not bring the black game into
the big league of baseball, he surely introduced it to a higher
level of the underworld. By the time he bought the Pittsburgh
Crawford Giants in 1930, he was intent on constructing a shield
for the numbers business he oversaw in the multiracial ghettos of
the Hill District, a sloping section bordering on downtown Pittsburgh separated by the Ohio River from the more affluent North
Side.

For Greenlee, the sandlot team that had unearthed Josh Gibson
seemed like a propitious front for his real trade, and for a time he
was satisfied to go no further than to hide his numbers money in
the club's account books, busy as he was with fulfilling the
entrepreneurial role in life he had mapped out for himself.

Born in 1897, Greenlee was the son of a masonry contractor,
who built the Marion, North Carolina courthouse. Gus's mother
was the illegitimate daughter of a prominent white man and his

black mistress. Greenlee, whose skin color was more beige than dark brown—and whose hair was a delightful shade of henna— may have figured that, like Cumberland Posey's, his origins carried a certain privilege. One of his brothers became a doctor, another a lawyer. And though Gus had a restless soul and dropped out of college to hop a freight car and come to Pittsburgh in 1916, he had no doubt he too would be eminently successful.

The problem was finding his niche. The young Greenlee worked as a fireman, a cabdriver, and an undertaker. Serving in World War I with the black 367th Regiment, he was wounded in the leg in the battle of St. Mihiel in France. When he reached home, he used his cab to bootleg liquor to gambling dens and brothels around Pittsburgh and Homestead.

Collecting chits, "Big Red" Greenlee—so named for his bright hair and monstrous bulk, spread over six feet, two inches and 220 pounds—was soon able to open his own speakeasy, the Paramount Club, on Wylie Avenue on the Hill. Gus used his newfound influence to persuade top dance bands and singers to play the club. But he went over the line by catering too openly to a biracial crowd; when word got around that black men were consorting with white women, the authorities suspended his liquor license.

Promising to tone down the bawdier aspects of the club, Gus got back his license, and soon branched out into promoting dance bands for other clubs. By the early thirties, he had two more clubs, the Sunset Cafe and the Crawford Grille, the hottest nightspot in town. With its doors open all hours of the day in spite of local blue laws, Greenlee was the embodiment of the phenomenon that saw black men involved in vice to achieve power and respect—and to become prime movers of a new, high-tone black society dependent solely on its own means for sustenance.

Although this was a lifestyle that had rubbed off from the vice underworld governed by men of Italian, Irish, and Jewish descent in New York and Chicago, the netherworld that congealed around the African-American racketeers retained its independence. In a kind of nonaggression pact, a man like Gus Greenlee paid his respects to the white mob, but when he was on his own turf he had no need to kiss anyone else's ring. Indeed, in order to extend their power, vice lords, black and white, came to see Greenlee for aid and to pledge that they would leave Gus's numbers domain alone.

The hoi polloi—newspaper columnists, society crawlers, judges, police bigwigs, the theater crowd, and both straight and crooked polticians—paid their homage to Greenlee. A night's visit to the Grille could reward a visitor with an extraordinary bill of fare: from mouth-burning drinks and juicy bear meat on the menu to Duke Ellington on stage for the after-dinner show. Like other ghetto numbers men, Greenlee kept his "business" out of the conversation. To all, and especially to Gus, the numbers, and the money they drained from the pockets of indigent black working people, were a mere formality, a means to provide the finest black entertainment.

Gus's success was due in large measure to his character. He provided an instant font of mystery and romance. Rumors abounded that rivals for power who did not accommodate him could be found at the bottom of the Monongahela River, as he was said to have connections to the highest families of the mob.

Yet, while Gus enjoyed the fear these tales inspired, he also considered himself a benefactor to the poor. When the Steel City Bank, the only bank on The Hill, collapsed in 1925, Greenlee in effect became the district's bank, making numerous interest-free loans to small black businesses and large social causes. People who came to him in need left with money in their wallets.

Around The Hill, no one saw Big Red—with his panatela stuck in his mouth and his garrulous laugh resonating through the Grille—as a sinister force or an exploiter of his own people. However, Greenlee was not a political, or even a race-conscious, man. His in crowd consisted of white ward heelers and corrupt politicians who had a hand in the numbers rackets. One of his more notable cronies was Art Rooney, who ran the numbers game on the white North Side before he bought a team of his own, the Pittsburgh Steelers, to play in the seminal National Football League. Gus's most important ally was State Senator James Coyne, a Republican from Allegheny County.

Moreover, for all of Greenlee's largesse, he ran his business with a mechanic's eye for detail. Operating through a web of accountants, Gus kept his assets hidden. When he and his numbers henchman—a ghetto shark named William "Woogie" Harris— would visit Gus's bank to conduct business, the bank would close down until the transactions were computed. This was indicative of the wink-and-nod arrangement Greenlee had with the authorities. Trying to keep up the appearance of law and order, Gus was fined

$100 every so often for gambling, but few city tax officers dared question his daily take of around $25,000.

Greenlee's interest in black baseball grew out of that watchful gaze over his business. Initially, Gus knew little about baseball, or any other game outside of the numbers racket. But when the promoters of the Crawford Giants ran out of money, Greenlee agreed to make another charitable contribution, and bought the club. The first game under Gus's aegis explained why: The Crawford Giants took the field wearing uniforms emblazoned Coyne For Commissioner.

But obsessions quickly took over Greenlee, and as soon as he learned of Cum Posey's money tree in Homestead, he threw himself into the Crawford Giants, which happened to provide a respectable shelter for the numbers money. When Gus had begun to take his daily strolls through the Grille, he'd noticed that black ballplayers were among the club's most popular habitués. Seeing them treated as stars on the order of Duke Ellington or Cab Calloway, Greenlee realized that he had another entertainment asset at his disposal and more VIPs to join his crowd.

Midway through the 1930 season, Greenlee put the Crawford Giants on full salary and began challenging Posey's sovereignty. Easily sliding into the role of blackball magnate, he waved a fat bankroll in the direction of established Negro leaguers like shortstop Bobby Williams—who came in to manage the new pro club—pitcher Sam Streeter, outfielder Jimmy Crutchfield, and shortstop Chester Williams. The Crawford Giants made their home grounds at Ammon Field on Bedford and Wylie Avenues. Most satisfyingly for Gus, this was the only place to watch baseball on The Hill, since Posey's Grays had no home games other than the selected dates they could arrange at Forbes Field.

The growing local action at Ammon brought in crowds of fans, gamblers, and Greenlee's celebrity pals, including the glitterati from the Crawford Grille. Indeed, the ballpark became a social scene in itself. Even though gambling was prevalent, there was a palpable sense that rowdyism and vulgar language at the park would soil the black race now that black baseball was a matter of race pride, and it was generally avoided.

Cum Posey and his Grays thus could not hope to deal with the Crawford Giants, or Crawfords, as they became known, by ignoring them. Given the Crawfords' rise and the partying going on at Ammon Field, the *Pittsburgh Courier* began to press hard for the two teams to meet on the field. Goaded by Greenlee, Posey finally scheduled the historic first contest between the Crawfords and the Homestead Grays for July 14, 1930 at Forbes Field.

This game brought activity on The Hill to a standstill. With the betting action furious and fans of both clubs chanting in football style, the Crawfords failed to get one hit off the Grays' Oscar Owens for five innings. But spitballer Harry Kincannon was baffling the Homestead hitters in turn. Going into the ninth inning the Grays held a 3–2 lead. The Crawfords had two men on base with two outs when Charlie Hughes ripped a liner into left-center field. Vic Harris ran about a mile and a half and speared it with a running, lunging catch to end the game, giving Posey's Grays the victory.

When the teams met again at Forbes Field in June 1931, the Crawfords suffered a devastating defeat, losing 9–0. But this disaster only made Gus Greenlee maniacal about cutting Cum Posey down to size. No longer a sports illiterate, Big Red now fancied himself the greatest sports promoter in Pittsburgh, having broadened his horizons to include ownership of both the Crawfords and future black light-heavyweight champion John Henry Lewis.

Gus was not a silent owner. While converting the Crawfords into his own team, Greenlee had begun to weed out most of the pre-Greenlee Crawfords and replaced them with other seasoned blackball players, including infielders John Henry "Pistol" Russell and Walter "Rev" Cannady, the aging but still potent Judy Johnson, and pitcher-catcher Ted Radcliffe.

By July 1931, owning a priceless if somewhat yellowing Who's Who of blackball's first Negro league generation, Greenlee acquired the vanguard of the second generation. It happened in early August of 1931, when Satchel Paige put on a Crawford uniform.

Paige's first game with the team that cemented his leading-man role in blackball came on August 6, 1931 in the season's return match with the Grays at Forbes Field. Paige did not start the game, but relieved Harry Kincannon in the fourth inning with the Crawfords holding an 8–7 lead. As Paige recalled many years later, "When I kicked up [my] foot and threw that first one, the crowd screamed. I kept kicking that foot up in the sky, twisting like a pretzel, pushing and throwing."

Scalding the Grays' bats with the "Trouble Ball," Paige pitched a shutout for five innings. According to the Crawfords' center fielder, Harold "Hooks" Tinker, "The Grays hardly hit a foul ball off Satchel. He was throwin' aspirin tablets." When the Crawfords broke open the game late and won 11–7, the victory went to Paige, and so did the headlines. The *Courier* called his outing "masterful and sensational," sparking the kind of combustible prose with which the black press would treat Satchel Paige over the next decade and a half.

For Gus Greenlee, the marriage with Paige was essential—and maddening from the beginning. In what would be a taste of things to come, Gus had to chase the rolling stone pitcher all over the map, from one boondock game to another, before finally getting Satch's marker on a Crawford contract—an act that, Greenlee would find out, meant very little to Paige.

Gus had to pay Paige a salary of $300 per month, or $3,600 a year. (By comparison, the top big league salary in 1932 was Babe Ruth's $52,000—after the Babe was forced to take a Depression-mandated pay cut from $75,000. This sum though, was around five times more than most other major league star players received. Paige's salary was the equivalent of the amount given to the big league's lowliest players.) But with Satch in the fold, Greenlee had much reason to celebrate his team and himself. Late in 1931, Greenlee anticipated impending glories by committing $100,000 to construct an impressive new ballpark for the Crawfords on Bedford Avenue. It would be the completely black-owned Greenlee Field.

But not even Gus Greenlee would have dared to fantasize that when Greenlee Field was opened on April 30, 1932, the pitcher-catcher battery on that heady day would be no less than the two most marketable icons in all of blackball: Satchel Paige and Josh Gibson.

As with Paige, persuading Gibson to join the new order was a matter of money: an investment of $200 a month, a good $100 more than what Cum Posey had been paying Josh. Unfortunately, getting him into a Crawfords uniform did not prove so simple.

As it happened, Gibson had re-signed with the Grays the day before Greenlee offered his contract. The naive Gibson had no qualms about signing his second contract in as many days, but Posey was irate about it. First Posey tried to reason with Gibson, calmly maintaining in his *Courier* column that Gibson was "very young" and had been "poorly advised," an apparent allusion to pitcher Roy Williams, who had just jumped from the Grays to the Crawfords and was known to be a close friend of Josh's.

When Gibson refused to change his mind, Posey tried to get tough with him. If Gibson did not return to the Grays, Posey vowed, "he will not play in Pittsburgh." Posey went on, "Today, baseball is a business. It is time an example was made of a few players [who have] signed obligations, but will jump to any club for a few dollars more."

Posey, of course, made no mention of his role in perpetuating the custom of team-jumping. That may have played some part in Posey's not taking the matter to court when Gibson held firm. Posey could only try to hector Gus Greenlee in his column. But Greenlee was moving far ahead of Posey, and the opening of Greenlee Field witnessed Gus at his loftiest.

This high-water mark in black sports entrepreneurship occurred when the Crawfords opened their 1932 season in a game against Bojangles Robinson's New York Black Yankees. Attendees included the mayor of Pittsburgh, the city council, and all the county commissioners. *Courier* editor Robert Vann dedicated the stadium, whereupon Gus made his entrance in a red convertible. Surrounded by a marching band, he received a standing ovation from the capacity crowd of six thousand. Clad in a white silk suit and tie, Gus walked to the pitching mound and threw out the first pitch.

That the Crawfords lost the game that followed was of little significance. Satchel Paige was matched strike for strike by Jesse "Mountain" Hubbard, a man who carried sandpaper in his back pocket to scuff the ball. With the game scoreless in the ninth, the Black Yankees scratched out a run on an infield hit. But the game was not over until Josh Gibson came up in the last of the ninth and sent a shot screaming to dead center that Clint Thomas caught against the fence for the last out.

Not to be outdone by anyone—not Posey, not J. L. Wilkinson—Greenlee installed a $6,000 permanent lighting system at Greenlee Field. Big Gus was spending all kinds of money to make his name in the black game, which only months before had seemed to be gasping its last breath. Greenlee's revival show would be condemned by some on the white side of the game as the stage upon which blackball entered its Babylon, but on the black side no one except Cum Posey begrudged Greenlee his laurels as the preserver of blackball.

For a coarse man, Greenlee was melding sport and culture in a way black baseball had not experienced before. And it was certainly indicative of Posey's nature, and of his own agenda, that he refused to enter into any alliance with Greenlee, even though the black game—and especially Posey's team—would have benefited by it.

In that season of 1932, Posey—whose Grays played mostly to small crowds—watched in horror as some hundred and twenty thousand people paid their way into Greenlee Field. Greenlee, a mobster with a mother wit, got around the Pennsylvania curfew laws that halted night games after 10 P.M. by *starting* some games at 12:01 A.M. That neat ploy drew large crowds. At other games, the Crawfords held raffles, the way Ed Bolden had at Hilldale games, with door prizes ranging from a season ticket to a Ford sedan.

But rather than share in this pool of promotional ideas, Posey would have nothing to do with Greenlee, both on business and alleged ethical grounds. Choosing not to put Greenlee's tough-guy act to the test by personally vilifying him, Posey took the safer route of deceit. When Gus petitioned for entry into Posey's short-lived East-West League, Posey agreed, but only under certain conditions. Posey would not only draw up the Crawfords' schedule and determine their roster, but his brother, Seward Posey, would become the team's manager, since he had helped book Crawford games the year before, when the club was struggling.

These terms were clearly meant to drive Greenlee away, and they did. But when the East-West League collapsed, it was Gus Greenlee and not Cumberland Posey who owned a winning hand. Though Gus became dangerously overextended—despite his various coups, Greenlee lost around $16,000 in 1932—it was worth that much and more for his to see Cum Posey in free fall.

The Grays, too, were spitting up debt, forcing Posey to schedule games against the Crawfords in order to share in the huge hate receipts always generated by the rivalry. Clinging to their honor, the Grays won ten of nineteen games between the clubs in 1932. But Posey was hardly in a position to claim victory. Because he had lost so many players to Greenlee, while others quit because he could not pay them, Posey was having trouble even getting nine men on the field at once. Games were canceled, the rent couldn't be paid at Forbes Field, and Gray players were said to be calling Gus Greenlee asking to come aboard. The Crawfords could now brag about those white big league All-Star teams coming to play them—and about beating those white teams. In October 1932, for example, the Crawfords took five of six games from a barnstorming unit fronted by the great Cub slugger Hack Wilson.

And, in the lowest blow of all to Posey, it was Gus Greenlee's turn to make noise about superintending a new Negro league.

In bidding to become the latest blackball owner to pick up the fallen bough of Rube Foster, Greenlee was following the Foster tutorial almost to a T. To spread the gospel of the Crawfords, Gus took his team on the same missionary tour as the American Giants had made from 1910 to 1920.

Beginning in April of the 1932 season, the Crawfords climbed into their new $10,000 Mack bus with a top cruising speed of sixty miles per hour and vacuum booster brakes and—sometimes with Gus himself at the wheel—rolled over seventeen thousand miles through the Deep South and back to Pittsburgh, playing ninety-four games in 109 days through July 21. Greenlee could gloat that his team had won every series except two, losing once to the Black Yankees and once to the Grays.

To the extended family of black man that stretched from northern steel towns to dirt-poor southern farmland, the Crawfords were an epic poem come to life. Here were mythic warriors straight from the pages of the black weeklies—Satchel Paige, Josh Gibson, Cool Papa Bell, Judy Johnson, Oscar Charleston....As with the old American Giants, when they came out on the field, their uniforms were as bright as their beaming obsidian faces. And in those places, where time seemed to be on hold, the clock would move just a little with the promise of baseball.

Gus Greenlee had also learned the Foster technique of inveigling the black press, and used it to co-opt Cum Posey's influence. This was a must, since Posey regularly derided him now in his *Courier* column as a shameless numbers man unfit to own a ball team. It was Posey, in fact, who revealed how Gus had cultivated good press notices for himself by moving part of his gambling operations into the same building in which the West Penn News Service was based.

As Posey pointed out, West Penn, a black news syndication service, had run a series of articles in 1932 that were very flattering to Greenlee and hostile to Posey, charging that Cum was trying to dominate black baseball. The author of the articles, John L. Clark, had had a remarkable change of heart about Greenlee. Only months before, when Clark worked for the black *Pittsburgh American*, he was writing a series about the city's numbers rackets which would have incriminated Greenlee. Then Gus hired Clark away and put him on the Crawford payroll, and the reporter began writing pro-Greenlee pieces for West Penn.

Although Posey tried to use this sequence of events to compromise both Greenlee and Clark, he became furious when Clark soon thereafter began to write for the *Courier*. And Clark wasn't the only pro-Greenlee voice at the paper Posey's father had once owned. Another, sportswriter Rollo Wilson, wrote in 1932 that the Crawfords "have taken the play away from the Grays and no longer do Smoky City fans consider Cum Posey's bunch the penultimate [sic] in baseball."

Thus positioned, and cushioned, Greenlee was ready to support Foster's notion of a Negro league, but with crucial differences designed to avoid Foster's failure. For one thing, the new prominence of blackball within the black social set, and the rise of all-black movies and big bands, meant that the time was ripe to disown the hypocrisies of blackball owners who preached racial "purity" while relying on white patronage.

A black league, as Greenlee saw it, ought to be black in more than roster only. There had to be a black economic foundation and black capitalization at the gate for the game to be taken seriously as a form of self-determination. Greenlee did not resent or mean to exclude white fans, whose continued goodwill, he knew, would prove critical. Rather, he said, black fans were failing to live up the real meaning of the words "Negro league" by not committing to blackball in big cities outside of Pittsburgh.

Just as disturbing to those pushing a new blackball structure was this premise's corollary: the flow of black fans into major league ballparks. Taking note of rising black turnout at big league games in Philadelphia, the *Philadelphia Tribune* criticized "colored adorers of the Athletics" and "blind and cringing Negroes" who would turn their backs on the black game. In the World Series that year, between the Yankees and Cubs, it was estimated that one-fifth of the thirty thousand fans who attended the second game at Yankee Stadium were black.

Now was not the time for such charitable support of the white game, Greenlee believed. Gus wanted the promise of all that black capital to be a reward for white big league teams, an inducement for on-field integration not a license for continued segregation. Thus, blackball teams had to become a public trust within the ghetto, with real money spent for marketing and social causes that could create an overall identity beyond the baseball diamond, and lure black fans to black games.

Similarly, the charade of verbally respecting player contracts while acting in the reverse manner had to end, he maintained. There had to be uniform rules of conduct, with league fines for player rowdyism, an old disease that had grown out of control. In the savage pit of blackball, the line between aggression and assault was nearly invisible, and the players carried the scars to prove it. Where once white players slid into bases with spikes aimed at black men like Fleet Walker, now it was Negro leaguers who routinely tried to take each other out that way. In 1931, Judy Johnson's pants were cut to shreds by the Baltimore Black Sox's aptly named Crush Holloway on a collision at third base.

"We had more trouble in the Negro leagues than playing with white boys," Johnson once said. "My leg's all cut up."

Such gratuitous violence was infectious. Even a respected player-manager, the Grays' Vic Harris, punched out an umpire named Jimmie Ahern in 1932, leading some umpires to carry pistols in their back pockets. (Ahern filed assault-and-battery charges against Harris, but the charges were later dropped.)

By Greenlee's reckoning, the man to lead the refinement of blackball was Gus Greenlee. And Big Red certainly had the elevation to carry out his plan. Greenlee was able to get the attention of the Chicago American Giants and the reformed Detroit Stars, the split-season winners of the last Negro National League season in 1932, and sell them on the need to continue that league under new management.

Yet, even here, for all of Greenlee's pretensions, the owners of these two teams demonstrated that one component of blackball would not change with the times. Both the Chicago and Detroit clubs had passed into white hands, and it was a sour irony that the grand old team of Rube Foster could not have survived if not for the mercies of a Chicago flower shop and mortuary owner named Robert Cole, who had purchased the club from the lamentable William Trimble in 1932. That Cole was hardly an improvement on Trimble soon became evident. Trying to save money, Cole wanted to take the team off salary and pass the hat at the ballpark to pay them. Cole offered the team's manager, Willie Wells, a bribe if he would encourage the players to accept the plan, but Wells was so offended he quit the team on the spot and went to play for the New York Black Yankees.

What's more, Greenlee faced the same obstacle as Cum Posey had, when he found he could not book games in either Philadelphia or New York without the express agreement of Eddie Gottlieb and Nat Strong. Rather than deal with these famous devils, Greenlee chose to leave out those crucial markets from his plans, forcing his to offer league membership to Posey's suffering but still marketable Homestead Grays.

In no position to refuse, a proud Cum Posey gave his pledge, though with no small degree of condescension. "Regardless of opinions concerning the owners of the clubs," he wrote in his column, in obvious reference to Greenlee, "it [the new Negro National League] is helping the Negro Race morally and financially."

Yet Posey had not the slightest intention of perpetuating Greenlee's status, only of buying time for his ailing team. Even as he signed up with Greenlee, Posey was looking for ways to embarrass him.

If Gus was wary of this unlikely alliance, he was too pumped up by seeing the pieces of his baseball fantasy falling into place to care about the possible pitfalls. In February 1933, Greenlee and delegates of six other teams met at the Crawford Grille to ratify the constitution of the National Organization of Professional Baseball Clubs. However, the absence of one team in particular meant that Greenlee had failed to obtain a most important piece for his league: the Kansas City Monarchs.

Blazing those egalitarian trails of the Midwest, the Monarchs now had their fingerprints in nearly every baseball-related activity west of the Mississippi. With their games booked by the canny Tom

Baird, the Monarchs had, for example, struck up a partnership with a money machine called the House of David.

Running in the same bizarre ethnic derby as Eddie Gottlieb's South Philadelphia Hebrew All-Stars, the House of David team represented the religious colony of the same name in Benton Harbor, Michigan. Formed in 1903, the team—its players distinguished by long beards that wrapped around their faces when they ran after fly balls—did in the beginning spread the word of the shepherd king of Israel. But by the thirties the gospel was profit. Their fans were by and large rabid gamblers, and their players increasingly *goyish*.

Cutting into this action, Tom Baird arranged for the Monarchs to play and share fees with the House of David in contests throughout the summer. These games proved so popular that the Jewish baseball team eventually split into several versions, giving rise to entities with names more suited to ethnic restaurants: the Original House of David, the Kansas City House of David, and the Mexican House of David. Later, there would even be a decidedly oxymoronic *Colored* House of David. In 1932, Baird signed the great female Olympic champion Mildred "Babe" Didrikson to play second base with the House of David to pump up the gate.

By that same year, the Monarchs themselves had split, amoebalike, into several mutations, including a number of "traveling" teams featuring would-be and had-been Monarchs unable to make the big club. When the Monarchs advertised their appearance in a town, the locals didn't know which Monarchs they would see, and it didn't seem to matter. Baird and J. L. Wilkinson would have needed an adding machine to ring up the profits of all the permutations of Monarch and House of David games. Often, the income derived from just the House of David games—which included rental of the lighting system—allowed Wilkinson to save on expense and travel costs by delaying the Monarch's season until midsummer.

In the manner of a mob godfather, Wilkinson imperiously carved up the Midwest at his whim, by doing business with favored local promoters eager to partake of the Monarchs' largesse. One, Ray Dean, was given the Iowa turf, and performed so well that he eventually was given the bookings of the House of David, which let Tom Baird concentrate on Monarch business.

Another money spigot for the Monarchs was the California

Winter League. This four-team conference based in Los Angeles was a warm-winter opportunity for big leaguers in search of an offseason paycheck. The league's promoter, Joe Pirrone, was progressive enough to welcome black players—not to play side by side with whites, even though most of the conferences squads were padded with minor leaguers and ragtag sandlotters, but to perform on their own segregated team. The black entry was variously known as the Los Angeles Stars or the Los Angeles White Sox, and by the late twenties these teams would essentially be the Monarchs in different uniforms.

Paid $50 per month plus expenses, the black players also earned a notoriety among Hollywood movie types, who had caught on to the hip esprit of black baseball and attended the games in large numbers. But just as Hollywood refused to broaden the dim-witted, lazy roles given to black actors, Joe Pirrone, who played for one of the white teams each year, was not keen to preside over a league championed by blacks. Although the Monarchs-Stars-White Sox routed unmotivated big leaguers regularly each winter, Joe Pirrone would often cancel the scheduled title game, fully knowing what the outcome would be.

Yet these wonderful athletes were making some important gains, since they could bring their talents closer to the *au fait* white world than they would otherwise have been able to get. When Satchel Paige joined the Monarch sojourners and pitched in the California Winter League in 1932, he beat the Joe Pirrone All Stars 8–1 in his first outing, yielding 5 hits and fanning 11—including the Dodgers' Babe Herman all four times he came to bat. Later, Paige struck out 22 hitters in another game. And even though Paige correctly regarded his "big league" victims as factory-second's players, with each of these wins the Paige cult expanded more deeply into socially acceptable circles.

Despite his far-flung baseball interests, J. L. Wilkinson did not want to hook up with a new Rube Foster. While Wilkinson had dealt reluctantly with Tenny Blount and Richard Kent in the old Negro National League, the egomaniacal Gus Greenlee—and, to a lesser degree, Tom Wilson, who brought his numbers front, the Nashville Elite Giants, into the league in the early spring of 1933—posed a potential public relations catastrophe. Indeed, Wilkinson, whose own ego matched the territory he had annexed, was already planning to raid the new league's teams on the dubious and self-righteous grounds that their players would be better off rescued from that budding quagmire.

And so, for now, Greenlee had to be satisfied opening the maiden season of the second Negro National League—the name to which the league officially answered—with a team lineup filled out by lightweight clubs like the Columbus Bluebirds, the re-organized Indianapolis ABCs and the Detroit Stars. Holding court as pontifically as Rube Foster and Ed Bolden had, Greenlee had himself anointed president and decreed the election of Tom Wilson as vice president and the penurious Robert Cole as league treasurer.

Promising austerity to match the times, Greenlee's inaugural address was a refreshing change from the airy megalomania of Foster. Said the man who mere months before knew not a whit about baseball, the year of 1933 "was a crucial time for the game. One thing is certain—there will be no big salaries for any of the players this season." Greenlee's plans included slashing ticket prices to make the game palatable to black fans, which the new Negro National League desperately needed to prove itself.

But Greenlee's best idea of all—which he cribbed from the majors—would come a few months later with the establishment of the Negro league's all-star game. Christened the East-West Game, it was to be played in July of that year at Comiskey Park in Chicago, one month after and in the same locale as the first-ever major league game of its kind. Just as that game, which featured a Babe Ruth home run, helped to redefine baseball's glamour in the hollows of the Depression, the blackball edition helped cement the black game as worthy of such a showcase.

For the black community, it meant quite more. With its partici-pants chosen by the votes of black people on ballots distributed by black newspapers—unlike the big league method, in which the sportswriters chose the players—this event plugged into the hot-button urgency of enfranchisement, as well as the everyday heroism of the successful black man.

In Black America circa 1933, such an event was a divine gift.

13

The New Negro

Do you consider Amos 'n Andy a reflection on your race? Are you Amos or are you Andy? Do you know any other race of people who would allow themselves to be so exploited?
                                        —*Pittsburgh Courier*, 1931

The social leap forward of blackball was indicative of something larger in the black culture, a state of mind that explained both the race chauvinism of Gus Greenlee and the sudden fervor among urban blacks to frequent major league ballparks.

The first wave of black nationalism since the abolitionists had emerged in the midtwenties. Taking the lead of Sinclair Lewis and Theodore Dreiser, whose works reflected the rise of social consciousness in the late 1920s, black authors eschewed subservient sensibilities and began writing defiantly about the black condition. Coalescing around the neon-lit vitality of upper Manhattan, the Harlem Renaissance nurtured the acrid writings of Claude McKay, who sounded the mood of the times in poems like "The Lynching," "If We Must Die," and "To the White Fiends," and the poignant, cheeky verses of Langston Hughes works like *The Ways of White Folks* and *The Weary Blues*. The growing sense of identity, however, was best expressed by the title of Alain Locke's volume of essays *The New Negro*.

This hard-bitten idealism fueled not only the Harlem Renaissance writer's colony but the proliferation of all forms of black art. By the thirties, Harlem not only had its poets, but the dance bands of Fletcher Henderson and Charlie Johnson; Chicago had Luis

Russell and Louis Armstrong, Baltimore had Chick Webb, Washington had Duke Ellington. The "New Negro" showed up in the art gallery as well, in the paintings of Hughie Lee Smith, Charles Seabred, and Romare Bearden.

And, of course, he also showed up in black sports. African Americans could take immense pride not just in Satchel Paige and Josh Gibson but in the breakthrough mainstream popularity of Joe Louis. Louis was the polar opposite of Jack Johnson, and his hushed, dignified reign as heavyweight champion caused no one to yell for a "Great White Hope," a fact appreciated by black opinion leaders. Between 1933 and 1938, Louis's name appeared on the front page of the *Chicago Defender* more than anyone else's—three times as often as Ethiopian emperor Haile Selassie's!

In the years to come, the Joe Louis saga would carry a host of less-than-rosy metaphorical lessons for the cause—including Louis's manipulation at the hands of white promoters that left him penniless. But, in 1933, four years before taking the title, Joe Louis—and, to a lesser degree, Gus Greenlee's boy John Henry Lewis—put black men on an even footing with white men in pro boxing.

This achievement and recognition offered tremendous implications for black baseball, and it was no small portent that Gus Greenlee made room for Joe Louis to be associated with blackball. For years Greenlee tried to arrange for Louis to buy a Negro league team, and while it never came to pass, Louis was a regular at Crawfords contests and even appeared as an umpire in a few games. Another important association involved Bojangles Robinson and Louis Armstrong. Emulating Robinson's ownership of the Black Yankees, Satchmo bought a semipro Negro baseball team in New Orleans, the Smart Nine, placing him in the blackball orbit.

By the mid-thirties, blackball, even with all of its class and geography-based schisms, had a tradition that fit comfortably into the larger American baseball tradition. Indeed, given the Chicago Black Sox gambling scandals and the crude history of Cap Anson and Ty Cobb, who could have blamed the blackball burghers for seeing their game as *superior* to the whites' at a similar stage of development? As it was, there were more college graduates, per capita, in the black game than in the majors. Academic-minded men like Kansas City's George Sweatt taught school in the offseason, while Baltimore's Laymon Yokely pitched sporadically for his Livingston College team even while playing in the Negro leagues.

As a stratum, the men of blackball were expected to be a cut above the white players in order to strike a rough equivalence. Thus, those in and around the game could be hard on their own when nagging reminders of old minstrel stereotypes appeared. People in the black game felt mortified that a part of blackball tended by white men in the Nat Strong mold had not progressed one inch from the marketing strategies of the Page Fence Giants. More mortifying still was the fact that this buffoonery was a moneymaker on the barnstorming trails and even in the ghetto.

Teams practicing the rituals of self-mockery included the Havana Red Sox. Operated by Syd Pollock, a white sports promoter from North Tarrytown, New York, their act was an update of the old Cuban Giants goof. Few if any of the players were actually Cubans, and all acted more like jungle creatures as they toured the same Midwest alleyways as the Monarch and House of David collectives.

To do so, Pollock had to come before the godfather of prairie baseball, J. L. Wilkinson, for consent to play the same trails. Wilkinson linked Pollock up with another favored promoter, Abe Saperstein of Chicago, who himself had been permitted to operate a Colored House of David basketball team to be the regular barnstorming opposition of Saperstein's major property, the Harlem Globetrotters.

Founded in 1926, the Globetrotters played their games nowhere near Harlem but used the name to establish a race identification with the "Globetrotters" concept originated by Wilkinson's All Nations teams. Going far beyond Wilkinson's tasteful showbiz inclinations with the All Nations, Saperstein molded magnificent black athletes into the worst white assumptions of how Negroes behaved. Some Globetrotters bulged their eyes and cackled, some shuffled along, and all performed some distinct trick with the ball, either dribbling it between their legs or stuffing it under their shirts when the shot was supposed to go up. If this was the overriding image of black men for many in the American Midwest, at least the Monarchs were a counterbalance of dignity and class. But when Saperstein did take his team literally globe-trotting in the late thirties, it was the only was that much of the world came to know African Americans.

With the appearance of Abe Saperstein and Syd Pollock and their creations in the early thirties, observers in the black press believed that far too many Americans—including black Americans—were being inured to these stereotypes promoted on ball fields and hard courts. While Pollock's Havana Red Sox were described by condescending white sportswriters in such terms as "fun makers" and lauded for their "witty sayings and repartee" with fans, black scribes were in no mood for such left-handed flattery. Ira Lewis of the *Pittsburgh Courier*, for example, blasted Pollock's club as a "monkey team" and "a collection of chattering jackasses."

Yet these idiot life-forms held dear by many whites not eager to change their conceptions about the black race, were not going to go away. Nor did many black fans, holding the same assumptions, want to see them disappear.

Still, all these various endeavors were part of a growing black assimilation. The brilliant W. E. B. Du Bois called it the evolving "twoness" of being black in America: that is, being black and being American. And the particular assimilation of black baseball surely was twoness in microcosm, which is why black spectators faced such a dilemma. Black leaders wanted them to support the National Pastime, in which they had increasing equity, but at what point would this patronage of the white game be at the expense of the black game?

These kinds of moral and economic dilemmas would only worsen as blackball edged closer to whiteball. But if Gus Greenlee or any of his confreres understood this massive contradiction in their existence, they ignored it as the second Negro National League charged ahead.

Not that the first months of the league didn't experience uncertainty. From the start, it was clear that the Columbus Blue Birds could not survive, and Greenlee's dreams of a uniform schedule fell victim to the same stadium-availability problems and prohibitive travel expenses that had bedeviled past Negro leagues. Even so, Greenlee had obtained prime coverage in the black papers, with standings published weekly. In late June, the *Pittsburgh Courier* ran a comprehensive statistics chart displaying the top four hitters of each team. Club by club, the top hitters were Oscar Charleston (Pittsburgh, .450), Dennis Gilchrist (Columbus,

.500), Clarence "Spoony" Palm (Detroit, .371), George McAllister (Homestead, .323), Sam Bankhead (Nashville, .400), Fred "Tex" Burnett (Baltimore, .525), and Turkey Stearnes (Chicago, .287).

The first marquee game for the league took place in mid-July, when the Crawfords and American Giants met in a doubleheader at Greenlee Field to decide the first-half championship. Needing to win both games, Oscar Charleston, now the Crawfords' player-manager, gambled by holding back Satchel Paige for the potential clincher and starting Bertram Hunter in the opener. The strategy looked good when Hunter beat Bill Foster 3–2. But with the flag on the line, the Crawfords suffered defeat when the American Giants strafed Paige for nine hits and he was beaten by Sug Cornelius, 5–3.

But a bigger jolt to Greenlee came when Cum Posey found the means to bloody his hated rival's nose. Mired in fourth place, Posey had no compunction about seeing how far he could bend league rules. Just after the second half began, Posey brazenly raided the Detroit Stars—a team he resented for having taken the territory left by Posey's deceased Detroit Wolves—and took two players for the Grays.

At once Gus called a meeting of owners and engineered the suspension of the Grays. Because Posey's action was so blatant, he may have forced a confrontation in order to expose Greenlee's hypocrisies in dealing with the scourges of Posey's East-West League, Nat Strong and Eddie Gottlieb. In any case, his deed done, Posey refused to return the two players and officially pulled out of the league, taking his barely alive team back to independent ball.

Posey, however, knew that he would have to deal with Gus Greenlee sometime again, when the stakes would be high for both men.

As trying as the Posey matter was, the big doings that surrounded the inaugural East-West Game provided another victory for Gus Greenlee, who booked the black all-star game in conjunction only with the *Chicago Defender* and the *Pittsburgh Courier*. While essentially a clone of the majors' event, the East-West Game had a special impact on blackball. Despite all efforts to mimic the white big league rubrics of intraleague rivalries, pennant races, and playoff games—or possibly because these efforts had been crippled by fratricide among Negro league teams—the strength of the black game consisted of its transcendent players.

Knowing this, Greenlee did not restrict fan voting to players in the Negro National League, but rather to "East" and "West" players. All major black newspapers carried write-in ballots. Yet because the *Courier* and *Defender* were by far the most widely read, the ballots favored players of the heavily covered Crawfords and American Giants.

As the September 8 game neared, an avalanche of over a million and a half ballots arrived at the papers' offices. The big surprise was that the voting trends showed a poignant sentimentality for traditional icons. Rewarded for their long, hard labors, the top vote-getters were aging heroes like Turkey Stearnes (the leader with 59,904), Oscar Charleston (runner up with 43,793), Bill Foster, Boojum Wilson, Biz Mackey, Vic Harris, Judy Johnson, Newt Allen, Frank Duncan, Willie Wells, Mule Suttles, Cool Papa Bell, Alec Radcliff, and Lefty Streeter—with touted newcomers like Satchel Paige, Josh Gibson, and Sam Bankhead a notch below.

Even before the first pitch was thrown, the event had grown in significance. Awaiting the game, sports editor William G. Nunn of the *Courier* proclaimed, "They made me proud that I'm a Negro, and tonight I'm singing a new song!"

Although attendance for the game was limited by gray, rainy weather, around twenty thousand fans came to Comiskey Park and saw Bill Foster go the route and beat Lefty Streeter in the West's 11–7 win (in effect, an American Giants win over the Crawfords), with the Babe Ruth role played by Mule Suttles, who blasted a long home run.

But as William Nunn noted in his postgame story, the particulars were dwarfed by the broader significance of the East-West Game.

"We saw a baseball epic unfold itself on this historic field this afternoon," Nunn wrote. "No diamond masterpiece was this game! No baseball classic! Those words are relegated into the limbo of forgotten things." Instead, Nunn saw the event as symbolic of "the titanic struggle for [freedom]."

For Gus Greenlee and the other owners, there was much significance, too, in the profits that were were divided up. One-third, or around $3,000 each, went to Gus Greenlee, Robert Cole, and Tom Wilson, the National League brain trust who had posted bond for the operating costs and down payment at Comiskey Park. Another $2,500 went to the park's owners, the Chicago White Sox. The players received only travel expenses. At this stage in black-ball history, none of them openly complained; just playing was reward enough.

Except for the White Sox share, all the money from the East-West Game was transferred into black hands. An auxiliary benefit was that one hundred and fifty blacks were hired as vendors, ticket-takers, and ushers. All in all, it was not a bad day for blackball.

Ironically, the East-West contest seemed to take the wind out of the Negro National League season; confirming the reality that the game's gallery of players reflected the best in black baseball, the game for many became the shining and climactic moment of the year. In its aftermath, attendance dwindled throughout the league. Consequently, Gus Greenlee did not carry out plans for a playoff, though his decision was not made until the Crawfords had rallied to win the second-half title by sweeping a thrilling dou-bleheader against the Nashville Elite Giants on the last day of the season.

This twin bill, played in Cleveland's big league stadium, League Park, on October 1, seemed to Gus to be an unmatched event. In the first game, Satchel Paige blew a two-run ninth-inning lead. Then, with the game deadlocked in the twelfth, Cool Papa Bell lined a shot up the alley in left-center and flew around the bases like a tornado, finally sliding home with an inside-the-park homer that won the game 4–3. Cool Papa's "flying spikes marked 'finis' to as great a diamond struggle as we've seen," wrote William G. Nunn in the *Courier*.

When the Crawfords took the nightcap, Greenlee believed no more proof was needed to crown his boys as the league's first champions, which he declared them two months later. Gus left no room for Robert Cole, whose American Giants had won the first half, to challenge the decision; again, Greenlee's word was law. Besides, Gus had not formed this circuit to play a World Series; he did it to prove that black businessmen could make a profit in baseball, as that would be the most effective lever in prying open the majors' closed door.

What Greenlee did not realize was that such dictatorial inside games could make a joke out of baseball. In coming years, similar machinations would determine other alleged flag-winners. And Greenlee only made things worse when, responding to criticism of his unilateral decisions, he named as the first league commissioner Rollo Wilson, his *Courier* mouthpiece.

Still, the Negro National League was here to stay for a while, and when it began the 1934 season, it was stronger, having placed two new teams in big markets, the Philadelphia Stars and Newark Dodgers. Unfortunately, in order to create the Stars, Greenlee had to broaden the role of Eddie Gottlieb.

Demonstrating how rapidly things could change in blackball, the formation of the Stars marked the return of Ed Bolden to the game. But this time Bolden served only as a figurehead; Gottlieb was really the man behind the club. Expanding his ownership interests into baseball, Gottlieb had created a horsehide version of his ethnic basketball team, the South Philadelphia Hebrew All-Stars.

Eager to get a black team into Philadelphia, Gus Greenlee patronized Gottlieb by not only sending the Crawfords to play the Sphas in July 1933, but ensured Gottlieb a huge crowd by guaranteeing that Satchel Paige and Josh Gibson would appear. In what turned out to be an electrifying game, Gibson got three hits and Paige pitched the final two innings and received credit for the victory when the Crawfords scored two runs in the ninth to win 5–2.

Soon afterwards, Gottlieb bankrolled the black Philadelphia Stars. For appearance's sake, he enlisted Bolden to purchase a minor interest, allowing Bolden to assume the guise of majority owner. Indeed, when the Stars first began play as an independent club, the black press often referred to the team as the "Bolden Stars." Free of league restrictions on player raiding, the Philadelphia Stars reeled in proven Negro league players such as catcher Biz Mackey, third baseman Boojum Wilson, shortstop Dick Lundy, and outfielder Rap Dixon. A major attraction from the start, the Stars crashed Gus Greenlee and Robert Cole's private party at the East-West Game, when all of these players were elected by the fans for spots on the East squad. The next season, the Stars acceded to Greenlee's request and joined the Negro National League.

And while all of this activity elevated Ed Bolden again, the truth was that Bolden was now a mere wraith of the man who had challenged and helped bring down Rube Foster, an ironic payoff for his race-neutral policies that had kept Nat Strong in business. But, living in peace now as a frontman with no real power, Ed Bolden would be a part of blackball for the rest of his, and its, life.

For Gus Greenlee, the 1934 season was kingdom come. Feeding off a Satchel Paige at the peak of his career, Gus rang up gargantuan crowds and headlines all season long. With a perfect sense of timing, in the promotion of both the Negro National League and himself, Satch went to the mound on July 4 against the Homestead Grays. He gave up a walk in the first inning to Buck Leonard—and then retired every other hitter, in order, but for one who reached base on an error. Striking out eight of the first nine Grays, and 12 over six innings, Paige threw fire past the last two hitters—to total 17 strikeouts in all—and walked off with a 4–0 victory. Not again, at least officially, would any Negro league hurler strike out as many as 17 men (nor had any white major leaguer except Dizzy Dean done so up until then).

Buck Leonard, the great-hitting first baseman, was so stunned by Paige's high-rising heat on that July 4 that he asked the home plate umpire to inspect the ball in one of his at-bat appearances, to make sure that it was of this earth.

"You may as well throw 'em all out," Satch ragged him from the mound. "'Cause they're all gonna jump like that!"

Greenlee's problem was that Paige would fail to remain with the Crawfords long enough for his team to hit its stride. Satch would appear on Sundays; then, as soon as he left the mound, he'd be off to the next gig he had rustled up with whatever team had come up with the cash.

To be sure, the new league solidarity and loyalty oaths meant nothing to Paige. He was still going his own way, still keeping miles apart from his teammates, literally and figuratively, giving Greenlee no choice but to go the R. T. Jackson route and cater to Paige's whims and avarice. Gus now arranged the outside gigs, not just to split fees with Satch but to keep him on a leash, however long.

In fact, Gus had no objection to making the profit margin higher by allowing Paige to take Josh Gibson with him at times.

Gus even had placards made up for them to take on their travels—Satchel Paige, Guaranteed to Strike Out the First Nine Men, they would read, with the addendum (as if needed); Josh Gibson, Guaranteed to Hit Three Home Runs.

No archive exists than can verify the matching of deed to vow. Nor does it matter if Paige and Gibson ever fulfilled those promises. The crowds came to ballparks across America just to see them play. Paige, of course, knew he could do what he wished. On the road, *he* would choose his place of lodging, whether it be a white-only hotel or a black rooming house. The white promoters needed him so badly they would accommodate him at almost any cost.

Paige's constant absences, approved by Greenlee, cost the owner big houses and league victories. The beneficiaries of Paige's leave-taking were the American Giants, who again coasted to the first-half title in 1934, which frustrated Greenlee further when he saw the ease with which Paige beat the American Giants 3–0 on a five-hitter in Chicago in the second half. That game prompted the *Chicago Defender* to file a half-serious request with Greenlee.

"When the Craws left the city no one was sorry," the paper said. "Truth of it is we hope they never come back here, and, if so, our plea to Greenlee is please, please leave Satchel Paige at home."

Home, though, could be anyplace at any time. In August, with the second East-West Game coming up, Greenlee grew worried that Paige—who easily outpolled everyone in the fan voting this time around—would miss the event for some half-baked semipro game. That kind of snub, Greenlee realized, would be right in line with Paige's blasé disregard for Negro league formalities. Everything the man had done vaunted his view of himself that he was bigger than the black game, which upset the other Crawfords, especially since they also envied Paige for the money he earned.

But Negro leaguers, thick-skinned by nature, could ultimately accept Paige's extravagances. His narcissism was tempered by an ingratiating wit and the lack of a hard-edged arrogance. It was difficult to hold a grudge against a man who brought so many fans to those Sunday games that Gus Greenlee and the other owners could afford to pass around bonuses to the players.

Still, many did brood about what they perceived as Paige's greed, since there was so little money to go around. Late in the season, a highly jaundiced item ran—unsigned—in the *Courier* that had obviously been fed to the paper by anonymous players and owners. It read:

> Satchel is a great pitcher, but he can't be used as an example of colored baseball players. Satchel was picked up by Gus Greenlee when all the other owners were disgusted with him. Gus exploited Satchel throughout the United States and forgot all about such men as Gibson, [Leroy] Matlock, Bell, Charleston, [Bill] Perkins, the men who made the Pittsburgh Crawfords.

Moreover, the old feeling among some northern-bred players that Paige was something of a boorish clod persisted. Many years later, Jake Stephens, the tough little Gray shortstop, bared his own grievances against Paige to author John B. Holway in a book entitled *Black Diamonds*.

"Satchel and...those southern boys lived a different life than we lived," Stephens said. "We didn't even much associate with them off the ball field, because they were what you'd call clowns. They didn't dress the way we dressed, they didn't have the same mannerisms, the same speech.

"And you have this other problem with the southern boys. They've never been used to making money. Give them a hundred and fifty a month, first thing you know they go all haywire, living on top of the world, walking in the restaurant with their baseball jackets on that say, 'Pittsburgh Crawfords.' The older fellows, we had neckties on when we went to dinner, I mean because that's how you're supposed to do. You're a gentleman, you're a big-timer."

It was Jake Stephen's studied, and priggish, opinion that Satchel Paige is "the most overrated ballplayer ever God put breath into" and a man who should have had to "carry bats and balls [for] fellows like Jud Wilson and Oscar Charleston."

With this kind of static always playing out against the whistle of Paige's fastball, Gus Greenlee probably figured that Paige's frequent absences from the Crawfords actually eased tensions. And in fact, Greenlee and the Crawford players tolerated him as long as he played in the really big games. It is doubtful that Satch understood that even this much was required of him. His most brilliant moments occurred when he played for other teams.

For example, in August 1934, Greenlee consented to the wishes of J. L. Wilkinson and Tom Baird to "borrow" Paige for one week to pitch in the annual *Denver Post* baseball tournament. In another milestone for Wilkinson, this was the first time that this twenty-four-team national tourney—a small-time rite of summer that was important to purists of baseball below the big league level and to gamblers looking for action—had permitted the entry of black teams, in the form of the Monarchs and the Colored House of David. Wilkinson wanted Paige, but not for the Monarchs. Rather, looking ahead to a title contest that would yield him a portion of both the winning and losing shares, Wilkinson assigned Paige to the Colored House team.

Greenlee not only saw the profit potential for Paige and himself, he also wanted to placate Wilkinson, who he still hoped would join the Negro National League. Gus was especially eager to be nice to Wilkinson now, since J.L. had not long before complained about the East-West Game—when six Monarchs went to Chicago to play on the West squad, yet not one had got into the contest. And so Gus gave him Paige and Satch's personal caddy, catcher Bill Perkins (it was Perkins, not Josh Gibson, to whom Paige most often threw his fastballs while playing with the Crawfords).

While Wilkinson was pleased, things didn't go exactly as he'd expected in Denver. All J.L. had in mind was a decent opponent for the powerful Monarchs, but Paige upset the calculations. Donning an ersatz red beard during the tournament, he was both a howl and unhittable—and after three wins in five days, he beat the Monarchs, striking out 12 in a 2–1 Colored House victory.

Still, like Paige—who received a cut from the top of the gate as well as a portion of the $7,500 awarded the winning team—Wilkinson and Baird came out way ahead, taking half the winning share and all of the $2,500 losing share. Furthermore, with the promoters having taken two black teams to the championship game of an integrated national tournament—certainly a historic first—the notion of integrated baseball was no longer just an implausible fable.

Holding to his unspoken bargain with Greenlee, Paige returned east and made his way to Chicago for the 1935 East-West Game—which must have shocked Gus, since, taking no chances, he'd had to name someone else as the East's starting pitcher, Philadelphia's

Stuart "Slim" Jones, a long and lanky carbon copy of Paige. Owner of a molten fastball, Jones was also a hard-living, heavy-boozing night crawler.

However, as happened whenever Satchel Paige appeared in a ballpark, he inevitably became the main attraction. And though he spent the first five innings in the bullpen, when he was called on to relieve Harry Kincannon in the sixth with the game scoreless, a current of energy ran through Comiskey Park. As the *Pittsburgh Courier*'s sports editor Chester I. Washington, wrote of Paige's entrance before thirty thousand fans:

> Pandemonium reigned in the West's cheering section. An instant later, a hush fell upon the crowd as the mighty Satchell [sic] Paige, prize "money" pitcher of the East, leisurely ambled across the field toward the pitcher's box. It was a dramatic moment. Displaying his picturesque double windup and nonchalant manner, Satchell started shooting 'em across the plate.

In rapid-fire order, Paige struck out Alec Radcliff, then quelled the bestial Turkey Stearnes and Mule Suttles on easy fly balls. In the bottom of the inning, Cool Papa Bell singled and stole second and, with two outs, when Boojum Wilson topped a grounder to second and beat the throw to first, Cool Papa came all the way around to score. Paige did the rest, shutting the West down on only one hit over the final innings.

Though Paige had pitched better and certainly more complete games, he'd probably never pitched one that did more for the Negro leagues. With delirious abandon, the black press, which had gathered en masse in Chicago for the game, covered it in windrows of hyperbole—Chester Washington, summing up his game story, called it "the mightiest and most colorful drama of bats and balls in all diamond history." More consequentially, now came the first signs that black baseball was beginning to catch the attention of important members of the white sporting press.

In the white *Chicago Times*, sportswriter Marvin McCarthy waxed just as enthusiastic as Chester Washington, even though, significantly, McCarthy mentioned only one of the players by name—Paige, whom he dubbed "Black Matty," comparing Satch with the great white pitcher Christy Mathewson. In part, McCarthy's story read:

He stoops to toy with the rosin bag—picks up the old apple. He mounts the bag, faces third—turns a sorrowful but burning eye toward the plate, nods a nod that Hitler would give his eye for—turns his gaze back to the runner on second—raises two bony arms high toward heaven, lets them sink slowly to his chest. Seconds pass like hours.

The batter fidgets in his box. Suddenly that long right arm shoots back and forward like the piston on a Century engine doing 90. All you can see is something like a thin line of pipe smoke. There's an explosion like a gun shot in the catcher's glove. "Strike!" howls the dusky umpire.... Thereafter the great Satchel Paige had 'em striking out like a labor union leader.... The long, lean lanky [Paige] is truly the black Mathewson.

Some black writers regarded this brand of crossover coverage as no more than condescension—a theory given credence by the fact that no voice in the white press sought to end the majors' color line. One of the most influential of the black journalistic *cognoscenti*, Dan Burley of the Associated Negro Press—whose stories were often ripped from the wire and run as written in the black papers—attacked McCarthy's seemingly glowing paean to Paige and the East-West Game.

"White sports scribes are in a quandary as to how to take the presentation of honest-to-goodness baseball as played in the [East-West] classic," Burley seethed. "Some writers see a chance [to] burlesque Negroes in the game.... Marvin McCarthy, in his burlesque conceptions of the game, got a jump on the rest of the white scribes. He was SURPRISED himself that Negroes could play that kind of baseball, but tried to cover it up with a narration a la Roy Cohen." (This reference was to the author of popular detective novels of the thirties that featured stereotypical black characters with names like Florian Sappey and Epic Peters.)

Dan Burley and others could also not abide the fact that the same manner of crude bombast and hype was a staple of sports coverage in the black papers; in these dispatches, every other week seemed to herald the "greatest game ever played," and every climactic play was prefaced by the bromide that a great hush had fallen over the crowd. In truth, neither black nor white sportswriters knew how to cover African-American athletes with any degree of sophistication, and surely not with the dignity they deserved.

Still, acknowledgment by the white power structure, whether within baseball itself or in the media, exponentially increased the possibility that blackball would have to be reckoned with. Indeed, in 1934, the signs were so promising for the fate of the Negro National League that nothing seemed capable of stunting it. The league was even strong enough now to withstand the evaporation of its two top pitching attractions.

One was the Philadelphia Stars' Slim Jones, the Satchel Paige clone who had won 25 games that season, including two of the three against Paige, and had won the Negro National League title-clinching game against the Chicago American Giants in the league playoffs. Tragically, Jones was never quite whole after that awesome season of 1934. His pitching arm and his body decayed by escalating alcoholism, Jones never won more than four games in any of the next four seasons. Finally, during the winter of 1939, unable to afford an overcoat, he collapsed on a freezing Philadelphia street and froze to death at age twenty-five.

Less tragic, but more precipitous, was the departure of Paige himself.

14

Hearing the Call

> Let bygones be bygones, and let's get together and make some money.
>
> —Tom Wilson, Negro National League
> vice president, October 3, 1936

As the 1934 Negro National League season neared an end, Satchel Paige's wanderlust had taken him to the woodsy terrain of the Dakotas, a tier so remote that J. L. Wilkinson had bypassed it on the routes he claimed for the Kansas City Monarchs. Yet this lapland of crystal lakes, fur trappers, and Native American reservations echoed the acceptance of multi-racial baseball occurring in the heartlands lying to the south.

This was not a new development, either. As far back as the 1890s, Bud Fowler—the first known black pro ballplayer and founder of the Page Fence Giants—had played on a South Dakota team with Walter Ball, the pitching ace of Frank Leland's Chicago Union Giants. In the years thereafter, a team in Waseca, Minnesota, won a state tournament with three black players, and the Sioux Falls (South Dakota) Canaries had integrated the National Baseball Congress tournament in Wichita, Kansas, with a black player named Jake Collins in the mid-1920s.

But it was probably John Donaldson, the great Monarch pitcher of the 1910s and '20s who cleared the way for later Negro leaguers to play up North. Operating like Satchel Paige—that is, playing with any teams in the area that offered up cash—Donaldson gained such a cachet locally that the original House of David team was formed around him in Sioux City.

187

For Paige himself, the immediate precursor was Ted Radcliffe, his old running buddy from the streets of Mobile. Radcliffe had joined the Pittsburgh Crawfords in 1934 and quickly gained a measure of notoriety when he caught Paige in the first game of a doubleheader at Yankee Stadium—then pitched and won the second game. Seeing Radcliffe perform this feat, Damon Runyon, the famous New York newspaperman and lionizer of small-time high-rollers, dubbed him "Double Duty," cutting Radcliffe an identity that would stick with him for life.

Midway through the 1934 season, Radcliffe walked out on Gus Greenlee and took an offer to play with an integrated semipro team in Jamestown, North Dakota. Already in Jamestown were Negro leaguers like Chicago American Giant second baseman Red Haley, St. Louis Star catcher Quincy Trouppe, and freelancing Monarch pitcher Chet Brewer, whose names drew strong competition on the barnstorming trails, including one team that featured well-known white major leaguers Jimmie Foxx, Jimmy Dykes, and Tommy Bridges. The Jamestown team was so strong that it beat the big league boys throughout the Dakotas and in Canada.

Then, seduced by Ted Radcliffe's tales from the woods, Satchel Paige jumped the Pittsburgh Crawfords in September and finished the season with Jamestown's big rival, an integrated team in Bismarck, North Dakota—which made an offer he could hardly refuse: $400 for a month's work and an automobile off the lot of the Bismarck team's owner, a used-car dealer named Neil Orr Churchill.

For Gus Greenlee, this was a tolerable defection, since the season was about over. What's more, Paige kept his promise to return in time to play for a Negro league all-star club against a major league squad fronted by the redoubtable Dizzy Dean. This series of games in mid-October was likely the biggest challenge ever to blackball's manhood. Though Dean was the only bona fide big leaguer on the white side, the specter of a man like Dean—a thirty-game winner for the World Series champion St. Louis Cardinals that season—leveling the playing field so that black men could step onto it with him provided a shot of credibility to every Negro leaguer.

The irony of these games of fellowship was that they never would have happened if not for the enlightened graces of Dean, a white man from Lucas, Arkansas. Dean's motivations may have had something to do with fairness and justice, but probably had as much to do with the money that could be gleaned from the cult reputation of Satchel Paige, Josh Gibson, Oscar Charleston, Slim Jones, Bullet Joe Rogan, and Vic Harris. Dean once confided that he made more on these tours with black men than he had winning the World Series—and the black men who made the cash register ring for Dean could reap similar rewards, pulling in as much as $1,200 themselves for two weeks' work.

Though historians have made much of it, the fact that the Negro team won a majority of the games in the series meant little in light of the puny level of talent on Dean's team—and did even less for the cause of baseball integration, since the white press generally ignored the games. These events, as with all other games pitting black versus white, were for the money, a fact understood by everyone involved. For a social movement to develop around games like these, the Negro leagues were going to have to prove they could endure on their own.

And so, with no pretensions, only a hungry appetite for cash and respect, the games began with Slim Jones beating Dean in Philadelphia's Shibe Park. Then Paige—a near-negative image of Dean, as both men were all arms and legs and both could talk from sunup to sundown without anyone really knowing what they were talking about—beat Diz in Cleveland, striking out thirteen. Satch then saved one game for Jones as a relief pitcher at Forbes Field, striking out the side in the ninth.

The punctuation mark, or marks, though, may have been supplied by Josh Gibson. Standing in against Dean in a game played in York, Pennsylvania, Gibson crashed a two-run homer in the first inning, then a solo blast in the second. Dean, who clearly had not been throwing his big league stuff in these games, nonetheless had seen enough. Removing himself from the mound, he played the rest of the game in right field.

Gus Greenlee, petrified at the thought that Paige might be on his way again, tried to buy Satch's loyalty with benevolence. When Paige married Janet Howard, a waitress at the Crawford Grille, in the fall of 1935, Greenlee hosted a reception at the Grille that lasted all night and boasted three big bands and a tap-dancing show by Bojangles Robinson, who was Satch's best man. Gus also paid for the honeymoon in Los Angeles, which coincided with the California Winter League season, from which Greenlee made sure he would profit.

Rather than cede the California turf to J. L. Wilkinson's Monarch's, Greenlee and Tom Wilson, the Nashville Elite Giant owner and Negro National League secretary, put together their own traveling club for Joe Pirrone's league. The only black team to be admitted that season, they were called the Philadelphia Giants, and drew the services of stars like Mule Suttles, Cool Papa Bell, and Turkey Stearnes. But it was Satchel Paige who commanded the attention.

In fact, this California Winter League session turned into Paige-versus-Dean redux, since Diz took his all-star barnstorming unit to play as an entry in the league that winter. When the two great pitchers met again in early November, the event attracted eighteen thousand people to the minor league park Wrigley Field. It also attracted a much better Dean team than before, Diz beefing up the club with proven players like Dolf Camilli, Frank Demaree, Wally Berger, and Dizzy's brother and Cardinal pitching mate Paul Dean. And Dizzy himself was now determined to beat Satchel Paige.

That the white major's best pitcher and the black majors' best pitcher were practically indistinguishable but for their skin color was as obvious as the flaming fastballs that cut through the Los Angeles smog that day. They matched each other strike for strike. Wally Berger recalled the eeriness of seeing two men who "were about the same size and both pitched the very same with the same speed—about ninety miles an hour." Berger, an outfielder for the Boston Braves, was the only big league hitter to get to Paige, banging out a double and a triple.

"He got one down a little too low and I hit it off the center-field fence," he said of his two-bagger. "As I was running, he followed me to second and yelled, 'How'd you hit that one?'"

At one point, Paige even made good on the old vow of his barnstorming gigs, by striking out three big league hitters—Camilli, Demaree, and Gene Lillard—on nine straight pitches.

Satch and Diz looked like they could mow down hitters forever, until Dean cracked first and the Philadelphia Giants scratched out a run in the thirteenth inning. When it was all over, Dean had struck out fifteen and Paige seventeen.

Paige would stream out of this game with an air of invincibility (he did not lose a single game in the California League that year, while winning six, as the Giants were awarded the league title without a playoff game). Back in Pittsburgh, Gus Greenlee preened not just because of the Giants' success but because he believed he had Paige committed to the Crawfords. Inasmuch as he had gotten Paige's marker on a new contract, he did. But *how* Gus had managed to do so would cost him.

During Paige's wedding reception at the Crawford Grille, Gus had shoved the contract—for the same $350-per-month salary as the year before, despite Paige's litany of triumphs—under a very drunk Satch, who scribbled on it, not knowing what he was signing (or probably, at that moment, his own name). When Paige's head cleared and he realized what Gus had done to him, he immediately walked, accepting another offer from Neil Orr Churchill in Bismarck, North Dakota.

Nor was Paige the only one to accept an offer from Churchill. That spring, Churchill had gone on a spending frenzy and lured to his formerly all-white Bismarck team almost all the black players from the Jamestown, North Dakota, team that had caught the public's attention the year before. After Paige signed, Satch induced the defection of a Crawford teammate, pitcher Barney Morris. With this array of blackball talent, the Bismarcks, as they were called, steamrolled greenhorn opponents throughout the summer in the northern corridor and Canada. Then they ripped through the state tournament in Wichita, Kansas. After beating semipro teams with ruggedly all-American names like the Wichita Watermen and the Denver Fuelers, the Bismarcks put their money pitcher, Satchel Paige, on the mound in the title game against the Haliburton Cementers of Duncan, Oklahoma. Somehow, the Duncan boys got nine hits off Satch, but he fanned fourteen and drove in the winning run himself in the Bismarcks' unexpectedly tight 2–1 victory.

Next came the same *Denver Post* tournament Paige had monopolized the year before—and, with a sense of sublime symmetry, Paige closed out the series by defeating the same Colored House of David team with which he had slain the Kansas City Monarchs back then, winning 2–0.

Paige had become very rich—his cut of the gate plus his winning-player share amounted to well over $3,000 just for the two tournaments alone—and very publicized. Now his pulling out an old riff could evoke national headlines. During a game in McPherson, Kansas, Paige, ahead 14–0, waved all his fielders off the field and into the dugout except for his catcher while he pitched the ninth inning and proceeded to strike out the side. This timeworn Satchel gag was treated as a revelation in the press. The *Baltimore Afro-American* reported that Paige "had entered the hall of fame...by calling in the infield and outfield of his team...in their game with the white Kansas nine."

The problem for Paige now was that he was the equivalent of a man without a country. With Bismarck having reached the crest of the small-time baseball world, Neil Churchill had reasons to jettison his star. The most urgent came about when Bismarck town fathers heard tales of Paige's entertaining white women in his trailer on the edge of town. Cheering Paige on the mound as the team went for the town's first championship of any kind was one thing; offering up their daughters to a black man's bed was another.

During the season, Churchill had succeeded in keeping secret Paige's visit to the Mayo Clinic for the treatment of gonorrhea. Now, Churchill, whose used-car business depended on his town's goodwill, was one step away from a major scandal. Indeed, years later, Ted Radcliffe, who had shared that notorious trailer with Paige, spoke a fitting epitaph to that wild season in the Dakotas.

"It's amazing," Radcliffe said, "that we all got outta that place alive."

His reputation saved, Neil Orr Churchill became Bismarck's mayor in 1939. Satchel Paige, on the other hand, was cast adrift in the blackball sea. Not only was he in violation of his Crawford contract, but Gus Greenlee had him banned from the Negro National League. What's more, Greenlee had no reason to lift the ban, since he was doing quite nicely without Paige.

With Paige absent, the Pittsburgh Crawfords caught fire. They won twenty-six of thirty-two games to take the first-half title by seven games over Tom Wilson's Elite Giants, which had briefly relocated to Columbus, Ohio, for the 1935 season. Greenlee had begun to claim other victories as well. Without the credibility of league membership and competition, Cum Posey's Homestead Grays had been relegated to almost the same status as the church and industrial league teams they played in the sticks. By 1935, a humbled Posey had to petition for reentry to the league.

Greenlee also won a round against J. L. Wilkinson. Because of Posey's raid on the Detroit Stars, Wilkinson, believing that Greenlee was a lion with no fangs, breached their gentleman's agreement. Midway through the 1934 season, J.L. had gone directly into Gus's lion's den and come away with no less than Cool Papa Bell and Bertram Hunter from the Crawfords. With money to spare, he then lifted Sam Bankhead from the Elite Giants and Turkey Stearnes from the Chicago American Giants.

For Greenlee, the timing of these thefts was particularly galling, and he made points playing the victim. The *Chicago Defender*, once sworn to uphold Rube Foster's honor against eastern slickers like Gus Greenlee, was now allied with Gus in the Negro National League and in the East-West Game promotion. The black newspaper attacked Wilkinson for "waiting until the flag race is hottest and in many cases undecided" before "grabbing players" from competing teams.

Even Wilkinson's friends seemed hard-pressed to defend him. The *Kansas City Call*, avoiding the main issue, simply reminded it readers that Wilkinson had "stayed in baseball during these stressful times for the sake of the men" who were now making a living in black baseball. In the *Call's* view, the game owed one to J. L. Wilkinson.

Gus Greenlee, however, paid out more money to the players, ensuring league loyalty, and by the start of the 1935 season all the wanderers had returned to the league—with Greenlee receiving a bonus when Sam Bankhead joined the Crawfords and hit .336 for the season.

While the chastened J. L. Wilkinson maintained his wary distance from Greenlee, Cum Posey had come to believe that he had to outdo Gus. This, when Posey brought the Homestead Grays back into the league, he brought in a Gus Greenlee of his own. He chose as his co-owner Rufus "Sonnyman" Jackson, the numbers king of Homestead and the kind of ghetto symbol Posey had cursed as a blackball pariah in years past.

Though Jackson owned a legitimate business—supplying jukeboxes to nightclubs in Pittsburgh, including Greenlee's—and his own club, the Skyrocket Cafe, his presence made the once-square Grays seem fit for Greenlee's society of scoundrels. And while Sonnyman spoke Gus's language of the gutter in league meetings, Posey would be free to concentrate on the pure arts of baseball—until, that is, Greenlee's power base could be eroded. Then, Cum Posey would strike.

For now, Gus appeared to be untouchable. His team had reached such mighty heights that Greenlee decided that any Crawford players elected by the fans to the 1935 East-West Game would play on the *West* squad, so as to open up the East team to players overlooked in the voting. Since this put Josh Gibson, Oscar Charleston, Cool Papa Bell, Jimmy Crutchfield, and Chester Williams in the same lineup as the cream of the Chicago American Giants—Willie Wells, Mule Suttles, Alec Radcliff, Turkey Stearnes, Sug Cornelius, and Ted Trent—the West team that took the field at Comiskey Park on August 11, 1935 may have been the most spectacular lineup of Negro league talent ever assembled.

And yet, as so often happens when a mismatch is expected, the game held several surprises. The East team was distinguished by grizzled Philadelphia Stars like Biz Mackey, Dick Seay, and Boojum Wilson, and by two New York Cubans of major historical note: Luis Tiant and Martin Dihigo. Both of these native Cubans actually spent more time playing in sugar plantation–lined fields in the Caribbean and Central America than in the Negro leagues, but their periodic stints with the New York Cubans drew thousands of Hispanics to league games in New York's Dyckman Oval and Yankee Stadium, a crucial fan base for blackball. (Much later, the pool of Latin players that made it into the white majors would include Tiant's son, Luis Tiant Jr.)

By trade, both Tiant and Dihigo worked as pitchers, but Dihigo was so gifted that he could handle any position on the field with equal brilliance. In this East-West Game, he started in center field and ended on the mound, and also stole a base. The East was ahead 2–0 in the first inning and led 4–0 in the fifth, but the West's "Dream Team" battled back to tie the contest in the ninth inning. The East then tallied four more in the top of the tenth— only to see the West tie it again with four in the bottom of the inning.

For once, the "greatest game ever" embellishments of the black press just might have been justified. The *Pittsburgh Courier*'s sports editor, William G. Nunn, in his game story, captured the game's thrilling resolution and eventual hero:

"For the West, Mule Suttles at bat!"
That's the resonant voice of the announcer, speaking through the new public address system of the park.
"T-H-E M-U-L-E!"
Reverberating through the reaches of this historic ballpark and bounding and rebounding through the packed stands comes the chant of some 25,000 frenzied spectators.

They're yelling for blood! They're yelling for their idol, the bronzed Babe Ruth of colored baseball to come through.

It's more than a call! It's a chant! It's a prayer! Surely, that superb slugger out there, pitting his eyes against the blinding speed-ball of one of the greatest all-around ballplayers ever to tear up turf with pitching spikes, has heard the call! But let us show you the picture in its entirety....

Cool Papa Bell had worked Dihigo...into a hole and had strolled to first base. [Sammy] Hughes went out, Dihigo to [Ray] Dandridge on a perfect sacrifice as bell blurred the other way scooting to the mid-way station.

Chester Williams was called out on strikes after vehemently insisting that one of Dihigo's blazing speedballs had hit him.

Josh Gibson...who had connected for two doubles and two singles in five trips to the plate, was purposely shunted.

And that's the picture as the announcer's voice, rather hoarse from detailing eleven innings of superb competition, announced: "For the West, Suttles at bat."

Dihigo, his uniform dripping with perspiration, wiped the sweat out of his eyes, and shot a fast ball across the plate. Ball one, said Umpire [John] Craig.

Again, came that blinding fastball, letter high and splitting the plate....Suttles stepped out of the batter's box, dried his sweating palms in the dust around home plate, tugged on his cap, and moved back into position. He looked dangerous as he wangled his big, black club around. But so did Dihigo, who was giving it his all.

Once again came that smooth motion, that reflex action of the arm, and then!—a blur seeming to catapult towards the plate.

Suttles threw his mighty body into motion. His foot moved forward. His huge shoulder muscles bunched. Came a swish through the air, a crack as of a rifle, and like a projectile hurled from a cannon, the ball started its meteoric flight. On a line it went. It was headed towards right center. Bell and Gibson were away with the crack of the bat. But so was [Paul] Arnold, center fielder of the East team, and [Alejandro] Oms, dependable and dangerous Cuban star, who patrolled the right garden. No one thought the ball could carry into the stands....

The ball continued on its course and the packed stands rose to their feet. Was it going to be caught? Was it going to hit the stands?

No, folks! That ball, ticketed by Mule Suttles, CLEARED the distant fence in far away right center, landing 475 feet from home plate. It was a herculean swat. One of the greatest in baseball. As cheering momentarily hushed in the greatest tribute an athlete can ever receive, we in the press box heard it strike the back of a seat with a resounding thud, and then go bounding merrily on its way.

And then...pandemonium broke loose. Suttles completed his trip home, the third-base line filled with playmates anxious to draw him to their breasts. Over the stands came a surging mass of humanity.

Wrote the *Call*:

Not since the celebration following the news that the armistice had been signed [ending] the bloody conflict known as the World War has Chicago seen its citizenry go stark mad for a few minutes. Score cards were torn up and hurled into the air. Men tossed away their summer straw hats and women screamed.

Less maniacally, but of no small importance, the *New York Times* made room inside its sports section for a one-line mention of the game, and the paper of record would go on doing so for future games. The East-West Game was more than a showcase now; it had graduated to being *news*.

For Gus Greenlee, the beat went on when the Pittsburgh Crawfords met the New York Cubans for the Negro National League crown, though Dihigo's team made the Crawfords' season a struggle. After soaring to the first-half title, the Crawfords had watched the Cubans race past them to take the second half, even with all the Crawfords' guns. Josh Gibson led the league in home runs with 13 in forty-nine recorded games. Gibson also displayed rare speed for a man his size. He was first in stolen bases with 8, twice as many as Cool Papa Bell was credited with. Greenlee also found a superb replacement for Satchel Paige in Leroy Matlock, a junkballer with pinpoint control who went 19–0 over the season.

But the other team had Martin Dihigo as player-manager, and it was nearly enough. Behind Dihigo and a rookie American pitcher, Johnny Taylor, the Cubans won the first two games of the best-of-seven playoff. The Crawfords' Leroy Matlock won game three benefitting from a clutch Gibson triple, but Dihigo won the next as the Cubans went up three to one. The Crawfords' veteran pitcher Roosevelt Davis won game five, but a weary Matlock fell behind 5–2 in the eighth inning of game six.

Now, in the critical moment of the series, Martin Dihigo miscalculated. Although Johnny Taylor was pitching well, Dihigo took out the youngster and put himself in to pitch with two men on. But Oscar Charleston hit Dihigo's first pitch out of the yard to tie the game. Unnerved, Dihigo then gave up a double to Pat Patterson and Matlock reached first base on an error. Facing the old warrior Judy Johnson, Dihigo went to 3–2 on the count, then Johnson lined a base hit up the middle to drive home what would be the winning run, 6–5.

The seventh game was just as tense. The Crawfords were again behind, 7–5 in the eighth, when Josh Gibson slammed a homer off Luis Tiant to draw to within one run. Then Oscar Charleston drove another pitch out of the park to tie the game. In the ninth, Cool Papa Bell singled, stole second, and—in a typical Cool Papa piece of work—came all the way around to score when an infield grounder was bobbled.

This time, Gus Greenlee didn't have to contrive a champion-ship. His team had earned it.

In his bliss, Gus was big enough to forgive Satchel Paige once Paige swallowed his pride and made himself available to the Pittsburgh Crawfords again. Actually, the reconciliation was the result of mutual need.

Although Paige had been taken in by J. L. Wilkinson at the end of the 1935 season, Wilkinson made it clear that it was a one-shot deal; Satch would throw a couple of games for the Monarchs against the American Giants in exchange for a percentage of the gate. When that gig ended, Paige sought some way to get back into the league that had banned him. Fortunately, Tom Wilson provided the opening when he formed another postseason Negro all-star team under the all-purpose name of the Philadelphia Giants to play again against the Dizzy Dean All-Stars.

Paige immediately accepted Wilson's invitation—which had obviously been cleared with Gus Greenlee—to join the squad, then hurried to York, Pennsylvania. In his first game against Dean, who was fast becoming his personal foil, Paige pitched a 3–0 shutout, all the runs coming on Josh Gibson's tremendous homer off Dean in the first inning. Then Paige beat Dean again by the same score at Forbes Field, aided by a Boojum Wilson homer.

The next tour of duty for the Philadelphia Giants was Joe Pirrone's California Winter League, and Satch again complied with the assignment. But he detoured from the winter season just long enough to create some more folklore. At the behest of northern California promoter Johnny Burton, Paige formed his own team, the Satchel Paige All-Stars, to face a white major league club of Bay Area natives, including Ernie Lombardi, Augie Galan, Cookie Lavagetto, and Gus Suhr—and a certain minor leaguer about to join the New York Yankees, Joseph Paul DeMaggio.

With his big league unveiling still months away, DiMaggio may have faced the best pitcher he would ever hit against in that February 7, 1935 game in Oakland. Because the Paige team was mainly composed of local black sandlotters, Satchel had to bear down hard. Giving up only three hits, he struck out Suhr three times and Lavagetto twice on the way to twelve strikeouts over nine innings, at which time the game was tied 1–1. Then, in the last of the tenth, with two outs and Dick Bartell on third base,

DiMaggio stepped in as dusk was dropping over the field. Barely able to see Paige's fastball, DiMaggio chopped a high bouncer that ticked off Satch's glove and dribbled toward the second baseman, whose throw to first was beaten by DiMaggio as the winning run scored.

DiMaggio earned a lot of mileage from this scratch hit, and so did the Paige legend. For years, the story circulated that DiMaggio was so thrilled to beat Paige, even with a cheap hit, that he pronounced himself ready to play in New York. Another story, a true one, was that a Yankee scout wired the big club a report that read "DiMaggio All We Hoped He'd Be: Hit Satch One For Four."

While such public spectacles had convinced Paige that he was bigger than the black game—and maybe the white one—Satch, like Cum Posey, realized that he needed the bunting of the Negro National League to place his deeds in context. League affiliation was the basis now for top competition and money—and even J. L. Wilkinson was ready to admit that. In fact, Wilkinson used his temporary relationship with Paige to barter an agreement with Gus Greenlee, once Satch signaled his willingness to return to the Crawfords and Gus agreed to lift the ban against him.

Because Greenlee believed Wilkinson might want to make a bid to re-sign Paige in 1936, Gus gave J. L. an inducement not to do so: Negro National League recognition for a league of western and southern Negro clubs that Wilkinson was planning to have ready for 1937. Promising Wilkinson interleague competition with the older circuit and a possible resumption of the Negro World Series—which had last been played in 1927—Greenlee envisioned the new Negro American League as the western division of the Negro National League and both leagues as the ultimate order of the blackball world.

Actually, Greenlee was open to just about any condition, even splitting his authority with Wilkinson, to get Paige back. Beyond the obvious Paige mystique, Gus could see that his Crawfords were in trouble when the 1936 season began. For one thing, Leroy Matlock seemed to have lost his stuff, and indeed would fall from 19–0 the year before to 3–2. For another, Greenlee's steady debts were mounting to intolerable levels; even though the Crawfords had won the league title, Paige's absence had cost Greenlee at the gate, and the year's losses ran to over $10,000.

Ironically, as his league became more and more viable, running it turned into a horrendous chore for Gus; losses on league expenses were several thousand dollars in 1935. All this bad economic news only mocked Greenlee's attempts to become a big-time sports promoter. When he bankrolled John Henry Lewis's drive to the light-heavyweight championship that he won in October 1935, Gus had a hard time explaining to the league where his priorities lay.

For the first time, the other owners began questioning Green-lee. There was talk behind his back that Gus was taking too much off the top of the East-West Game. Greenlee's treasurer, the Chicago American Giants' miserly owner Robert Cole, was accused of failing to account for certain league funds. Not used to such disrespect, Gus angrily fired back that the owners were not paying their league dues and threatened to eject the deadbeats.

"Up to now I have been a congenial fellow," Greenlee said, then warned, "You'll see fighting Greenlee equipped with everything neeeded to win" any showdown with rebel owners.

Greenlee was convinced that Satchel Paige would become a panacea for his troubles—and maybe even a lever by which to profit from the white major leagues, who he believed might hire Negro league stars. Paige's stirring performance in Oakland had unleashed rumors that several white big league clubs might offer tryouts to black players. The black *Oakland Tribune* also reported the Paige was being considered to pitch for a team of white minor league all-stars in a game against a major league touring team a week later. It never happened, and Paige himself dismissed any charade of a major league audition, saying sagely:

"This business of tryin' us out at the tail end of the season makes me laugh. If they wanted to try out colored ballplayers they'd take them to training camps, same as the white boys....No sir, I'm not giving up any of my money just to make some owner look good-hearted."

And yet such rumors led the blackball owners to ponder contingency plans—not to hasten integration but to hold it hostage to their own self-interests. Invoking proprietary rights, Gus Greenlee had no intention of allowing men like Paige and Josh Gibson to be taken from him. If the white big leagues were going to include blacks, the plan he had in mind was to offer lower-level players first, as a way to open up bidding for the big-name stars.

With these fantasies parading before him, Greenlee re-signed Satchel Paige, at a nominal pay increase and with the usual understanding that other teams could rent the pitcher for games throughout the season.

Acting like the model citizen, Paige showed up for most games on time and, his Crawford identification intact, earned the most votes among pitchers for the August East-West Game, his 4,919 second overall only to Josh Gibson's 5,187. Nonetheless, Gus was so nervous that Satch would fail to appear that he chose the struggling Leroy Matlock as the East's starter, Crawford players having returned to the East squad. Matlock earned the win in a 10–2 rout before around thirty thousand fans at Comiskey Park, as Paige mopped up with three flawless innings.

With Paige around for the big Sunday league games and winning seven of nine games in his return season, the Crawfords rebounded from second place in the first half of the year to finish with a league-best 20–9 record in the second half—which again afforded Greenlee the excuse to suspend any playoff with the first-half champion Washington Elite Giants and have his puppet commissioner, Rollo Wilson, certify his Pittsburgh team as 1936 league champions. And, Tom Wilson of the Washington team, actually favored the move, since his Elite Giants had dropped into the cellar in the second half. Both Wilson and Greenlee had lost interest in league affairs anyway once the directors of the *Denver Post* tournament agreed to the entrance of a black team other than the Monarchs and House of David in that year's tourney.

The team that emerged, called the Negro All-Stars, had Paige, Gibson, Cool Papa Bell, Gray first baseman Buck Leonard, and a talented trio of Elite Giants—third baseman Felton Snow, outfielder "Wild Bill" Wright, and second baseman Sammy Hughes. Managed by Tom Wilson, they swept the Denver field in seven straight wipeout games to claim the $5,000 first prize. Gibson hit four home runs and Paige won three games, the last a 7–0, eighteen-strikeout monster against an absurdly overmatched semipro team from Borger, Texas.

In fact, the Borger players came into the game with such cold fear that the team, in a baseball first, had ordered plastic helmets to wear while batting against Paige, not quite confident they could survive his fastball if it got away from him. They needn't have worried: One of the Negro stars, Monarch pitcher Jack Marshall, swore that Paige "never threw a ball higher than the belt line" during the game.

The Negro All-Stars concluded their sojourn in the Midwest, playing a white major league All-Star team headed by Rogers Hornsby, who was playing out his Hall of Fame career as player-manager of the St. Louis Browns. The real attraction of this series, however, wasn't the aging "Rajah" but the first matchup between Paige and a seventeen-year-old pitching sensation named Bob Feller.

In Des Moines, the two flamethrowers melted the tall plains grass; over the first three innings, Feller struck out eight and Paige seven, with each yielding just one hit before giving way to other pitchers. The Negro team pulled out a late win, but, more important, though few knew it yet, those unforgettable three innings were a seed that would in time help to sow baseball's racial reformation.

For the time being, however, the only reformation that could be felt occurred within blackball's own borders, one that broadened and bridged the two geographical sectors of the game.

The first matter of importance was the admission of the New York Black Yankees into the Negro National League late in 1936. While this made the New York market and Yankee Stadium property of the league, Gus Greenlee had to make some unpleasant accommodations.

The Black Yankees were no longer owned by the beloved Bojangles Robinson. When in 1932 the team became too big for the tap dancer to handle, he sold his controlling interest to James "Soldier Boy" Semler, a Harlem numbers runner who almost single-handedly ran this glamorous blackball franchise into the ground.

Looking no further than the next game, Semler ignored budding younger players in favor the big-name has-beens; in short order he phased out salaries and paid players according to the gate they drew. By mutual agreement, when the Black Yankees played Negro National League teams, the winning team would take 60 percent. Semler's boys won so few of these contests that one Black Yankee of the era, shortstop Othello "Chico" Renfroe, recalled that, at the rare times the team had a chance to win, "The [baserunner] would be sliding home with the winning run, and Semler would be out there at home plate sliding with him."

Though Gus Greenlee, Tom Wilson, and all the league's owners had to keep on amicable terms with Semler to get a share of those lucrative Yankee Stadium dates, they assumed that Semler had no respect for other teams, nor for his own players. Despite regularly cheating his players, when several jumped the team and went to the New York Cubans and the Brooklyn Eagles in 1936, Semler sued to get them back. To some in blackball, this was not unlike a plantation owner recovering runaway slaves.

Still, by 1937, keeping the league in New York was highly desirable for Greenlee—though, for Gus, the decision had really been made a couple of years earlier. That was when blackball's favorite whipping boy, Nathaniel Colvin Strong, made his final exit.

When Nat Strong died of a heart attack at age sixty-one on January 10, 1935, blackball consigned him to perdition. Writing about Strong six years earlier in the *New York Amsterdam News*, the old blackball warhorse, Sol White, said of him: "There is not a man in the country who has made as much money from colored ballplaying as Nat Strong, and yet he is the least interested in its welfare." That may as well have been Strong's obituary.

Although Strong was connected to the Negro National League, as long as he was alive the league refused full membership to the Black Yankees, which would have placed Strong in the league's inner sanctum. At least nominally, however, Strong's influence continued after his death, when his second-in-command, William J. Leuschner, retained Strong's minority interest in the Black Yankees and took over the operation of Nat Strong Baseball Enterprises. This booking agency that ran the breadth of so much blackball history was still the largest client in New York's World Building and continued to profit from nearly every game featuring black teams east of the Hudson River. But Bill Leuschner was a caretaker, not a mover, and so blackball could, with a little stretch, mark the passing of Nat Strong as a day of liberation.

Despite the demon's passing, the new Negro American League, like the ongoing Negro National League, was rife with white influence peddlers. When the league came into existence in the spring of 1937, it stood as a self-tribute to the two venerable teams of the Midwest, the Kansas City Monarchs and the Chicago American Giants. For the Giants, it was a rebirth as well, since the club changed hands from the reviled Robert Cole to a black

Chicagoan and former owner of the Memphis Red Sox, Dr. J. B. Martin, and shifted from the eastern-skewed National League to its appropriate geographical conference.

This restructuring, part of the Gus Greenlee–J. L. Wilkinson nonaggression pact of 1936, made the natural rivalry of these two great teams the focal point of the new league. Almost as filler, the league's second tier was made up of two intrepid former Negro Southern League teams that had survived Jim Crow—the Birmingham Black Barons and Memphis Red Sox—the wobbly and at times nonexistent Detroit Stars and St. Louis Stars, and new clubs with little chance of survival, the Cincinnati Tigers and Indianapolis Athletics.

As usual, J. L. Wilkinson opted to keep his guiding hand hidden. His official capacity in the official league ruling body was vice president. The league president, however, was his handpicked front man, Horace G. Hull, the assistant to J. B. Martin, and the commissioner was a puppet from way back—Major R. R. Jackson, Frank Leland's bobo with the Chicago Unions, who was now in his eighties.

But as much as anyone else, the man who was empowered by the Negro American League was Abe Saperstein. The Chicago promoter's currying of favor with Wilkinson had paid off. While Saperstein was not given a cut of league games in Chicago, nonleague games remained under his control, including those contests that brought to Chicago the Pittsburgh Crawfords or the Homestead Grays. This meant that when the American Giants played a nonleague opponent, Saperstein would receive a 5 percent commission. He found an even bigger plum in the East-West Game. Beginning with the 1937 game, Saperstein, as official booking agent for the match, would take a 5 percent commission there as well.

For all its grand designs, the Negro American League was at it inception clearly a junior member of the blackball hierarchy, an adjunct to the Negro National League—but only until Gus Greenlee was betrayed once again by Satchel Paige.

Satchel Paige nearly wrecked the Negro leagues in 1937 when he led a walkout of Negro leaguers to play in the Dominican Republic. Paige *(left)* persuaded nine players from the Pittsburgh Crawfords to come with him, including Josh Gibson *(center)* and catcher Bill Perkins.

(National Baseball Library, Cooperstown, N.Y.)

SATCH' TELLS HIS STORY

Satchel Paige, telling 48,000 fans that he did not advice against the use of Negro ball players on major league teams.

Always at the center of controversy, Satchel Paige addresses the crowd at the 1941 East-West Game to deny he had spoken out against major league integration.

(Carnegie Library of Pittsburgh)

Satchel Paige showed that blacks belonged in the white majors by beating Dizzy Dean *(center)* in several exhibition games and handling big league hitters like the Washington Senators' Cecil Travis *(left).*

(James Riley)

Some of the most influential Negro league leaders were white men such as Kansas City Monarchs co-owners J. L. Wilkinson *(right)* and Tom Baird *(left),* seen here with C. A. Franklin, editor of the *Kansas City Call.* Wilkinson brought night games to the Negro leagues five years before the white majors began playing under the lights.

(Kansas City Call)

The turbulent Effa Manley. Although her husband, Abe, owned the Newark Eagles, Effa ran the team and regularly clashed with the other Negro league owners.

(Craig Davidson)

Although the Negro leagues strove for a dignified image, teams like the Zulus remained popular through the years by catering to negative stereotypes of blacks. Zulu players wore jungle war paint and grass skirts.

(Kansas City Call)

A rare group shot of Negro league movers and shakers, taken before a game at Yankee Stadium in 1939. In the top row are Baltimore owner and Negro National League commissioner Tom Wilson, New York Yankees owner James Semler, and New York Cubans owner Alex Pompez *(left to right, directly behind trophy)*. Kneeling at center are Baltimore catcher Roy Campanella *(wearing gear)*, ex-Black Yankees owner Bill "Bojangles" Robinson, and newspaperman Ches Washington *(left to right, grouped around trophy)*.

(Baltimore Afro-American)

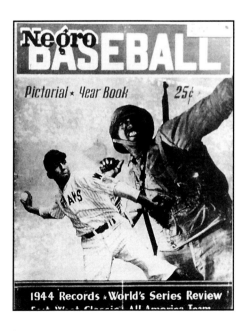

Black periodicals made the point that black heroism abroad in World War II rendered baseball segregation indefensible at home.

First baseman Walter "Buck" Leonard, who played with the Homestead Grays from 1933 to 1950, was the third Negro league player to enter the Hall of Fame, after Satchel Paige and Josh Gibson.

(National Baseball Library, Cooperstown, N.Y.)

Jackie Robinson, pictured with the Kansas City Monarchs in 1945. By season's end, he was signed by the Brooklyn Dodgers and groomed to cross baseball's color line.

(Jackie Robinson Foundation)

Jackie Robinson, shown here in a photo from the seventies, would be eternally linked with the man who signed him to a major league contract, Brooklyn Dodgers chief executive Branch Rickey. In April 1947, Robinson broke into the Dodgers' lineup and won the National League's Rookie of the Year award.

(Jackie Robinson Foundation)

The Negro leagues' last hurrah was a 1946 barnstorming tour between the Satchel Paige All-Stars and a white big league all-star team headed by Cleveland Indians pitcher Bob Feller. Paige *(in doorway of plane)* earned a larger salary in his prime than most white major leaguers.

(National Baseball Library, Cooperstown, N.Y.)

Cleveland Indians owner Bill Veeck took a chance signing the forty-two-year-old Paige in 1948—and Old Satch repaid the favor by winning six of seven games, drawing record crowds, and helping the Tribe win the world championship that year.

(National Baseball Library, Cooperstown, N.Y.)

Paige *(left)* also helped calm the nerves of a young, uptight Larry Doby, the Newark Eagles outfielder who became the first black to play in the American League in 1947.

(H. V. Pat Reilly)

Some great Negro leaguers didn't get the chance to play in the white majors, including Hall of Fame third baseman Ray Dandridge, who got no further than playing in the minors with the Minneapolis Millers in the early 1950s.

(National Baseball Library, Cooperstown, N.Y.)

The last Negro league team, the Clowns, endured through the mid-1960s, playing mostly for laughs. Managed by the great Negro leaguer Oscar Charleston *(center),* the Clowns featured a player known as King Tut *(left)* and female second base-man Connie Morgan.

(National Baseball Library, Cooperstown, N.Y.)

The day that turned all Negro leaguers into "second-class immortals": Satchel Paige enters the Hall of Fame on August 1, 1971, greeted by baseball commission-er Bowie Kuhn.

(National Baseball Library, Cooperstown, N.Y.)

15

Early Evening Quarrel

This thing [the subject of white booking agents] is bigger than any of us here. It isn't just a question of my team or your team winning, or of who'll make money next season or who won't. This matter has developed into a race issue.
—Newark Eagle owner Effa Manley, 1940.

Even before the 1937 season began, Gus Greenlee's problems had become epidemic. On The Hill, the numbers racket had turned from a money tree to a bramble bush. As in most big cities, a new breed of clean-government politicians had moved out the old clubhouse crowd in Pittsburgh, and Greenlee's gaming operations were caught in the thorns.

The periodic for-show raids of the past were replaced by genuine, and regular, busts of betting games at the Crawford Grille. Where once Gus had been tipped off before a raid, now the word on the street was that the cops had enlisted an employee of the Grille as an informer. If so, it may have meant that Greenlee was so preoccupied with baseball that he was letting his guard down in his primary business.

Racketeers now began to consider giving up the action. Indeed, the inner-city system had changed, because the inner city itself had. As income and education had risen, middle-class paragons of home and family had begun to clash with seedy underground hustlers. Even back in the late twenties, black cultural tastemakers had turned against black authors of pulp fiction. One reviewer labeled Langston Hughes a "sewer dweller" and the "poet low-rate" of Harlem because of his "obsession for the more degenerate elements" of black city living. Suddenly, lower-class blacks weren't pariahs only of white American but of their own race a notch above them on the social ladder.

For the old purveyors of the vice trade, the game was to become legitimate. Thus, Tom Wilson, who by the time he'd moved the Elite Giants to their most secure home, Baltimore, in 1938, had completely divested himself of his rackets practice and was running the team with undivided attention.

Morality and cultural trends aside, the simple fact was that fewer bets were being made, and payoffs on winning numbers could bankrupt a rackets boss. The scuttlebutt was that Greenlee had to pay off on some staggering wagers in 1936, causing him to cut his losses any way he could. Unfortunately, his initial attempts to do so succeeded only in mortally offending two of the most important players in the black game.

During the championship season of 1936, both Josh Gibson and Cool Papa Bell became convinced that Greenlee was treating them like peons. Years later, Bell told John Holway in *Voices From the Great Blackball Baseball Leagues* that although he outhit Gibson that season, "they [Crawford management] said, 'Don't you send out any statistics [to the newspapers] about what you're doing.' The secretary of the Crawfords wanted to tell the truth but they fired him. They didn't want to rate me over Josh or Satchel Paige, because I'd ask for more salary.

"I stole 175 bases that year [in league and nonleague games] but they only gave me credit for 91. The last game I played I got five hits out of six [at-bats], stole five bases. But they didn't take the score book out there that day and I didn't get credit."

Gibson felt no more respected, because even though Greenlee wanted to pad Josh's numbers for the public, he didn't seem eager to pad Gibson's pocket. Josh was so frustrated by Greenlee's refusal to augment his $250-a-month salary that he jumped the Crawfords and played the last few weeks of the 1936 season with his original team, Cum Posey's Homestead Grays. Unfazed, Greenlee listed Gibson on the Crawfords' 1937 roster. But when Gus still refused to give him a raise, Josh went home and held out.

Now Greenlee's flacks in the black press went after Gibson. John L. Clark, whom Gus made the league's secretary, was no different from "Commissioner" Rollo Wilson; neither man refrained from acting as Greenlee mouthpieces in their *Courier* columns for the sake of ethics. In 1935, Clark wrote an article that offered the absurd argument that Gibson—the leading vote-getter in the East-West Game balloting the year before—was "not the kind of asset that more colorful and less capable players might be [because] he has not developed that 'it' which pulls cash customers through the turnstiles although he has been publicized as much as Satchel Paige."

With such public insults swirling around Gibson, Ed Bolden and Cum Posey moved in to make offers for his services. Posey offered giving Greenlee $2,500 in cash, plus catcher Pepper Bassett and third baseman Henry Spearman, in exchange for Gibson and the ageless Judy Johnson, making this the biggest player transaction that had ever been proposed in Negro ball. Though the black papers played up the deal, linking Gibson and Johnson as "Punch 'n' Judy," Johnson, offended that Greenlee was about to ship him out, promptly retired.

Meanwhile, as Opening Day neared, Gibson continued what was the then most famous holdout in blackball history. As nerves frayed in Greenlee's camp, Gibson was derided by John L. Clark in the *Courier* as a "perpetual holdout."

Gibson's inner turmoil and increasingly heavy drinking habits and curfew violations—heretofore a private blackball matter— were revealed to the public, though without specifics, as Clark wrote euphemistically that a "complex temperament had been developing [within Gibson] in the past year...[and] had engrossed him."

What Greenlee hoped to accomplish by this subtle insult was to shame the insecure Gibson into giving up his fight for respect and autonomy. But, soon convinced that Gibson would never back down, Gus had to make the trade for Bassett and Spearman and $2,500, and even persuaded July Johnson to briefly come out of retirement so that the deal could go through. This made a very ironic beneficiary of Cum Posey, who got back the prodigal "black Babe Ruth."

Trying to put a good face on this serious privation, Greenlee began to boost Pepper Bassett's talents. Bassett was no more than a workmanlike catcher, but he had the inspiration to promote himself by catching some exhibition games while sitting in a rocking chair. Now, Greenlee had a multicolored rocker built for Bassett to do the same thing in selected nonleague games. Gus also swore that Bassett "can knock a gnat off a dwarf's ear at a hundred yards."

Bassett did his part in 1937 by hitting .444 to earn the starting catcher position in that season's East-West Game. And Greenlee made sure everyone would notice Bassett by not even allowing Gibson or Biz Mackey to get into the game. Bassett then went 0-for-3 in the East's 7–2 victory. But Gus could not alter the reality of a season ruined before it ever began. No sooner was Gibson gone, in fact, than another cataclysm arrived that would reduce Greenlee's power to rubble.

When Satchel Paige came to the Crawfords' April spring training camp in New Orleans, he walked into a thicket of swarthy men in white suits and Panama hats who were waiting for him. As it turned out, these men were emissaries of sundry banana republic leaders in the tropics, and they were making big-money offers to Negro league stars.

The tropical countries had heretofore conducted their seasons in the winter in order to draw black and white major leaguers looking as much for a paid vacation in the sun as for serious baseball. Now the baseball powers in Cuba, Puerto Rico, and Mexico would expand their leagues into summer, and into direct competition with the American baseball season. And while this excluded the white big leaguers—for now—the black big leaguers were under no similar compunctions to stay at home.

Greenlee felt this incursion in March, when Martin Dihigo, acting as an agent for the Cuban league, signed Spoony Palm of the Black Yankees, Showboat Thomas of the New York Cubans, and Bill Perkins and Thad Christopher of the Crawfords. Greenlee succeeded, by court order, in getting back his men, but he was not able to stem a far more serious hemorrhage when Paige violated his contract and signed to play summer ball in the Dominican Republic for the astonishing sum of $6,000.

That was only step one, however, in what became a wave of defections. Paige also was hired as an agent of Los Dragones, the team from Ciudad Trujillo, the capital of Santo Domingo that, at the time, had been renamed to honor the island country's dictator-president, Rafael Leónidas Trujillo, who also owned Los Dragones. Paige was given a cache of American dollars to induce other Crawfords to play for the team as well. Within days, he had gotten no fewer than five of them—Cool Papa Bell, Leroy Matlock, Sam

Bankhead, Harry Williams, and Herman Andrews—to make the expedition, at $3,000 a man.

Greenlee was caught completely off-balance by this quick and devastating strike. He tried desperately to reverse the tide, again by filing court orders and claiming that the fleeing players were "under indictment." But neither Gus nor the U.S. court system carried any muster with Rafael Trujillo, who had come to power in 1930 by taking control of the once-American-financed National Guard and then nationalized all of the country's American-owned sugar and rum businesses. But while Trujillo ruled by the bayonet and the firing squad, he was a man who understood that the opiate of baseball could do much more for his image among the Dominican masses if his name was made synonymous with the country's best team.

Since this strategy had obvious risks—losing carried the brand of shame, and the Dominicans wouldn't stand for fixed games— Trujillo was prepared to spare none of his blood money to build a winner. In addition to the Americans—who in a few weeks included Josh Gibson, who'd also been persuaded by Paige to join Los Dragones—the Trujillo team imported Puerto Rico's best player, Petrucho Cepeda (father of future big leaguer Orlando Cepeda) and Cuba's Lazaro Salazar, who only a month before had, with Martin Dihigo, been recruiting many of the same men for their own country's baseball league. The team also included the Dominican Republic's most heralded players, Enrique Lantigua and Amable Sonlley Alvarado.

But Trujillo's political opponents—those who were still standing—were using the same methods as the dictator's to boost themselves and thereby be in position to replace Trujillo once *la revolución* came. The two other Dominican League clubs, in San Pedro de Macorís and Santiago de los Caballeros, were owned by such Trujillo opponents, and they had lured Negro league headliners. San Pedro came up with Chet Brewer, Pat Patterson, Showboat Thomas, Spoony Palm, Johnny Taylor, Clyde Spearman, and the Crawfords Bertram Hunter and Thad Christopher—as well as the two magnificent Cubans, Luis Tiant and Martin Dihigo. Santiago had Spoon Carter and George Scales.

Obviously, this was a full-scale contretemps for Gus Greenlee, whose leadership had already been under fire. Gus failed in the courts to force the defectors to return. Early that season, he had a

Dominican consular employee arrested during a game at Greenlee Field and detained without cause when Gus suspected him of trying to sign players. Then, on May 1, Greenlee had his newest puppet league commissioner, New York City civil servant Ferdinand Q. Morton, issue an ultimatum: The defecting players must return to their league teams or face dire consequences. Greenlee's own prepared statement enumerating the penalties was released a few days later:

> The men who have sacrificed their time and money to develop [black] baseball, will not allow any one player or any group of players to wreck the league. These men must realize that the league is far larger and more powerful than they are. They left without notice, after they had been signed to contracts to play with league clubs. If they fail to report to their clubs by Saturday, May 15, they will be banned from organized baseball for one year and fined.
>
> Furthermore, no league club will play in ANY PARK where outlaw ball-players appear.... An agreement has already been entered with Major Robert Jackson, [commissioner] of the Negro American League and our organization to enforce the suspension of these players. When they return to the States, they will have nowhere to play.
>
> In addition to the suspension placed against these men, our league is contemplating immediate action against Martin Dihigo...and Salazar, to bar them from organized baseball in the United States for life.

The most bitter condemnation, however, was reserved for the real ringleader of the raids, Satchel Paige. The *Courier*, spreading Greenlee's bile, blasted Paige as a man who "proved again that he is about as undependable as a pair of second-hand suspenders. Satch, along with (the other jumpers) should be barred...until they learn to regard a contract as more than a mere scrap of paper."

When no one heard from Paige, the headlines on the front sports pages of the premier black papers carried the news in the largest possible type that the black game had exiled its number one attraction.

"League Ban Hits Paige" was the banner in the *Baltimore Afro-American*.

"Satchell Paige Will Be Banned From N.N. League" tolled in both the *Pittsburgh Courier* and *Kansas City Call*.

The headlines surely spoke of Gus Greenlee's command and sure-handed response to crisis. And yet, for Gus, the unkind truth was that while the defections damaged several teams in both leagues, by far the largest hole was left in the Crawfords—a fact which did not disturb blackball's other owners. While the Crawfords were riding high, Greenlee's authority had been inviolate. But now they were mortally wounded, and staggered through a season of hell, finishing next to last in the first half of the Negro National League season with an 11–16 record (standings were not recorded in the second half), just one-half game ahead of James Semler's pitiful Black Yankees. Besides Pepper Bassett, only two other Crawfords appeared in the 1937 East-West Game.

During this difficult season for Gus, the anti-Greenlee forces in the league grew stronger and more vocal. And, of course, Cum Posey gained the most altitude. Having constructed another superb team, Posey and his Grays—led by Vic Harris, Buck Leonard, and pitcher Edsell Walker—easily weathered the absence of Josh Gibson and roared off to win both the first- and second-half league titles, obviating any playoff and making Posey a major player in blackball again.

Riding the crest, Posey collected enough chits to win election as the Negro National League's secretary, a feat that was accompanied by Gray co-owner Sonnyman Jackson's election to the league's board of directors. Posey also broadened his team's purview, cutting a deal with the white major league Senators to use D.C.'s Griffith Stadium for a number of Gray games. That meant that the Grays, who continued to schedule some games at Forbes Field, were the only black team with access to two big league parks.

Moreover, even though Posey lost money in 1937 (along with every other league team), he was working independently of Gus Greenlee to form a power bloc to serve his personal ambitions. This opportunity fell into Posey's lap when Greenlee, seeking some peg on which to hang his ebbing power and distract attention from the Dominican Repbulic disaster, suddenly began campaigning *against* the influence of white promoters he had allowed into the league, specifically Eddie Gottlieb. Vowing to "shake off the sinister influence of the great booking agents of the East," Greenlee promised, "There will be a reorganization and the Negro National League will be placed on a solid foundation in 1938."

These words, hypocritical as they were, provided an opening to Posey, who now did a little haggling of his own, allying himself with Gottlieb and Bill Leuschner—the very men he had once scorned for destroying his East-West League. Only two years earlier, Posey, in a fury, had written in his *Pittsburgh Courier* column that the white agents were "forces stretch(ing) out like an octopus" and that "they will attempt to ensnare the various club owners by devious methods (that) have one objective, the destruction of the league." And when the Black Yankees were admitted into the circuit, Posey branded the team "one of the tools by which these forces hope to crush organized Negro Baseball just when (it) is strongest, and thus crush it for all time."

But now Posey was one the tentacles of the octopus. And out of this expedient and squeamish alliance came a Greenlee-proof majority coalition: Posey, Semler, Gottlieb, and Abraham Manley. The last, the owner of the Newark Eagles, had entered the league in 1935 when that team played first in Brooklyn and then bought out and merged with the Newark Dodgers the following year. In a six-team league, with Greenlee and Tom Wilson yoked, Manley's swing vote was critical to Posey—and it went to him, after Cum maneuvered to have Manley elected league vice president, ousting Wilson, in 1936, and then treasurer in 1937.

Midway through that 1937 season, the new majority zeroed in on President Gus Greenlee. More and more, league meetings became unbearably tense as the Posey faction tried to undercut Greenlee by objecting to every one of his motions. Finally, by July, with Gus mortally wounded by the mass defections to the Dominican Republic, he was voted out of office.

Tom Wilson became the compromise choice as the new president, mostly because of his calming, mediative skills among men who—beyond the Greenlee issue—could hardly agree on anything. But Wilson was up against more than he could possibly mediate. The *Courier* reported that one league conclave degenerated into such a free-for-all that "every view put forward by any member appeared to be a challenge to the other members."

In fact, Posey's majority rule proved tenuous because the Newark ownership did not act as a rubber stamp. The Eagles' course of independence was not due to Abe Manley but to his mercurial wife, Effa. Clearly, the league patriarchs would have preferred Abe Manley to do the talking for his club. Short, cigar-chewing, and chummy, Abe Manley was comfortable in any pool hall—which would be the last place anyone would find Effa Manley, whose tall, refined primness told of a long day in the beauty parlor. But as decorous as she was, Effa was not satisfied being any man's decoration.

In Effa Manley, the men of the Negro leagues had on their hands a prefeminist terror who broached not only racial but sexual barriers without the slightest tremor. Long before there was a Marge Schott in baseball, Effa Manley created much more of a fuss in black baseball, the difference being that Effa made sense when she spoke.

Officially, the Newark club was run by Abe Manley, a man who easily met the seemingly mandatory Negro league requirement of running a numbers racket. Manley did his running in Camden, New Jersey, near Philadelphia, though by the midtwenties he had left the Camden numbers behind after white mobsters moved into his territory and made their point by firebombing Manley's Rest-A-While nightclub. Manley moved to Harlem, where he continued in the numbers but also invested successfully in real estate.

Manley met Effa Brooks at the 1932 World Series at Yankee Stadium and the following year they married, when he was forty-eight and she thirty-three. In 1935, Manley formed the Brooklyn Eagles and was able to schedule dates at Ebbets Field when the Dodgers were out of town. For Abe, this was fantasy fulfillment, the chance to be able to sit in a big league dugout in his business suit and pretend he was Rube Foster. For Effa, ownership of a black ball team was far more: the machinery to further a cause, one she had been living all her life, almost as if by compulsion.

There was irony in this woman's obsession. In an era when some blacks dreamed of passing for white, Effa Manley was in fact a white woman passing for black. Born in Philadelphia, she was the illegitimate daughter of a white seamstress who cuckolded her black husband by having an affair with the white man for whom she worked. This union produced Effa—and provoked a lawsuit for alienation of affection by the husband, leading to a $10,000 settlement that may well have been a legal first: a black man winning legal satisfaction from a white man's adulterous affair with his woman.

Despite her bloodline, and the fact that she was raised by her white parents, Effa grew up with six mulatto siblings and gravitated to the black point of view. Rather than getting by by virtue of her white skin, she enjoyed the challenge of getting by in the black world, posing as a light skinned black. Taking up residence in Harlem in the twenties, she met and married Abe and then became visible for her civil rights work with the NAACP and the Citizens' League for Fair Play, which conducted boycotts of white-owned stores that refused to hire blacks. Her one-on-one meeting with the owner of Blumstein's Department Store was credited with the hiring of fifteen blacks there in 1935.

As did many black leaders, Effa perceived the strong metaphoric bridge black baseball provided the civil rights movement—and the literal one, given the job opportunities it offered on the field and in the stands and the front office. Thus, while Abe was the juice man of the team, she called the shots on and off the field.

Effa prevailed upon her husband to make a first-class operation of the Brooklyn Eagles, and he did. Gaining entry to the Negro National League, he hired the steady hand of blackball veteran Ben Taylor to manage the club and paid flattering salaries to sign primarily homegrown area talent. When word of Manley's salaries spread, several of James Semler's New York Black Yankees walked across town; Semler got most of them back by court order, but one he didn't was the superb outfielder Clarence "Fats" Jenkins. Abe also took the Eagles to Jacksonville, Florida, for spring training, and their Opening Day game against the Homestead Grays at Ebbets Field in 1935 drew New York Mayor Fiorello La Guardia, who threw out the first ball, and coverage in the white New York press.

But the meager appearance of only three thousand fans that day underscored the problem for the Manleys in Brooklyn. Although Nat Strong was by now in his grave, Brooklyn remained his landmark. And so while Manley dealt directly with the Brooklyn Dodgers for Ebbets Field dates, competition with Negro National League teams allied with Eddie Gottlieb and Bill Leuschner was nonexistent, as were games with Strong's Bushwicks and other local white semipro teams. Just as disconcerting, black fans in Brooklyn were far more interested in the white-staffed Dodgers.

These were realities the Manleys could not fight, and in 1936 they took a new route. Annexing the cellar-dwelling Newark Dodgers, they bought out that club's owner, Charles Tyler, a chicken farmer who operated a bar and grill called the Chicken Shack and whose team only laid eggs.

The Manleys kept only three of the Dodger players when they moved the Eagles to Newark, two mortal and one heaven-sent— third baseman Ray Dandridge. A squat, bowlegged man who may have been the equal of any third baseman who ever lived, Dandridge covered the position like a spreading pool of oil, sliding left or right with no apparent effort to dig out hot grounders, then slinging the ball to first without taking as much as a half-step. Dandridge also was a tough out at the plate, hitting .354 in 1936 and .404 in 1937, and .335 over eight Negro league seasons.

Because the Eagles played at Ruppert Stadium, home of the Yankees' Newark Bear farm team, Abe and Effa now had made connections with both the Brooklyn Dodgers and the Yankees. And as their team began to solidify as a powerful franchise, running second to the Grays in 1937, they—or rather Effa, who attended league meetings in place of her husband—became a prime player in the new organizational shakeout of the Negro National League.

That would have happened regardless of Gus Greenlee. But once Greenlee had been voted down to the status of a mere owner, Effa began to crusade for a more perfect blackball model to reflect a more perfect cause. The black race, she insisted in 1936, "does not know its own strength, and when it begins to realize what really fine things the race is capable of doing it will show rapid progress."

Then, at a January 1937 league meeting, this brash woman rose and stunned the men's club of blackball owners by condemning them. According to a dispatch in the *Courier,* "Mrs. Manley, who is rapidly learning the business end of the baseball game, addressed the members and in no uncertain terms expressed her disapproval of the way the members conducted league business." In Effa's view, "[A] wonderful future [is] possible for Negro baseball if [it is] conducted in a businesslike manner," rather than victimized by the chaos and petty one-upmanship of the day.

If the other owners were not quite prepared to deal with a woman with such chutzpah, the black press was more than eager to see a shake-up of the old guard, who had only played musical chairs when Greenlee was deposed. After years of seeing crude blowhards making a mess of a good thing, Frank A. Young, the *Chicago Defender's* longtime sports editor, wrote to Effa in 1940, "I find you very gracious, very ladylike, and knowing more baseball than some of the so-called baseball experts, who have been in the game for years."

Effa's credibility turned upside down one attitude of black society that had not changed with the conversion to middle-class life—just as in white society, the meltdown of sexism was years behind the racial revolution. In Effa Manley, there was more than just culture clash—there was sexual anxiety. While Cum Posey knew the rules had now changed, to him and his brethren those rules mainly concerned etiquette. After one owner used profanity at a league meeting, for example, Posey called Effa to apologize for this indelicacy.

But the Effa phenomenon cut much more deeply into the male ego. First of all, demonstrably, Effa was not an ornament; she was whip-smart and cocksure. Monte Irvin, who joined the Eagles' outfield in 1938 and played there until the white majors called him a decade later, correctly understood the owners' unease. Irvin told author James Overmyer, "The Negro league owners were all going in their own directions—nobody had any intelligence but her. They were jealous of her looks, jealous of her money, just naturally resentful."

Effa saw what many of them refused to comprehend. Among Effa's complaints were the continual problem of imbalanced schedules and the league's temporizing in naming a nonowner with a business head as league president or commissioner. Another complaint arose when Effa did an audit of the league's finances in 1937 and found that the teams had spent only a combined $175,000 for their operations. Effa ventured that Negro baseball deserved more, as befit what she correctly termed a "multimillion-dollar operation."

But her main complaint went right to the heart of the black game's shamefaced wedlock with white booking agents. For this crusade, which was part and parcel of her wish for full black control of the Negro leagues, Effa cited her husband as her moral compass. Writing of the "tentacle-like grip" of the booking agents in her memoirs years later, Effa recalled that "Abe had been waging a one-man war against the booking agents from the first day he entered the picture. Abe always tooks the unwavering position that league teams should do their own booking." But while Abe rarely crossed swords with the other league gentlemen on this touchy issue, Effa drew hers quickly.

Effa's campaign ran counter to Cum Posey's plan that would return him to power. And, as he listened to her with bewildered wonder, it must have occurred to Posey that, in having given Effa Manley such bite, her teeth marks might someday be found on his own throat.

Undoubtedly, Effa enjoyed being the center of attention, in part because she knew she was a public relations boon to blackball. In 1938, she won more attention for her team and the black game than most players had ever done when the white *New York Post* ran a photo of her with one high-heeled foot on the top dugout step, wearing an Eagle jacket and cap as she beamed across the field.

For Effa, this pose was not an affectation. Often, she was said to have overruled her manager's calls by flashing signals to the players from her box seat in the stands. One story, probably apocryphal, had it that an Eagle catcher looked toward Mrs. Manley a little too late and was knocked cold when the pitch struck his head.

Talk about the league was that Effa's player moves went beyond the field and the clubhouse, with much of the gossip centering on pitcher Terris McDuffie, who came to the team in 1936 and soon was the ace of the staff. On one memorable day, McDuffie pitched a complete game, winning against the Black Yankees on July 4, 1938—then came into the nightcap with one out in the first inning and hurled eight and two-third innings to earn his second victory within about five hours.

A self-promoter in the Satchel Paige mold, McDuffie modestly called himself the Great McDuffie, and in 1934 the white *New Jersey Herald-News* introduced him to crossover fans as "Negro baseball's Dizzy Dean" and "an eccentric star." And yet among many Negro leaguers, McDuffie was a man not to venerate but to desecrate. Strutting peacocklike around the field, he lorded it over teammates and opponents, secure in the knowledge that he had Effa Manley on his side—in the most literal sense.

Apparently, civil rights and baseball could consume only so much of Mrs. Manley's passions. In her memoirs, written late in her life, she told of spending stolen hours in the company of unnamed young black ballplayers. But those around the blackball scene didn't have to read the book to know that Terris McDuffie was one ballplayer who knew his way around Effa's bedroom. Whether Abe Manley ever suspected his wife's unfaithfulness provided endless gossip for the team. But a strong clue came during a team bus ride to Homestead during the early summer of 1938. Abe was overheard by the team's traveling secretary, Eric Illidge, mumbling that when the team got home, "I'm going to trade that son of a bitch McDuffie." A few weeks later, the Great McDuffie—with or without Effa's approval—was traded to the Black Yankees for pitcher Jimmy "Slim" Johnson.

The fact that a good but not exceptional player like Terris McDuffie had earned mention in the same sentence as Dizzy Dean in the white press was indicative of the regenerative powers of black baseball. Even though the most celebrated of Negro leaguers had left their teams in the lurch by sailing to the tropics, it took no time for a new coterie to replace them as fan favorites.

In its ever-continuing evolution, old became young again as soon as new names did passable imitations of Satchel Paige or Josh Gibson or Sam Bankhead. In the late thirties, those names included Dandridge, Homestead's great first baseman Buck Leonard, and the Black Yankee pitcher Barney Brown—as well as the players in the West given broader exposure by the Negro American League, such as the Monarchs' ox-strong outfielder Willard Brown and Indianapolis's lithe first baseman Ted Strong, who displayed the same amount of raw talent playing basketball in the off-season with Abe Saperstein's Harlem Globetrotters.

This development could not have escaped the attention of the men who had sailed away to a fortune in what they believed was a Caribbean paradise. By the early fall, at the end of the baseball season in the Dominican Republic, almost to a man they were dying to get out of the country, which had turned into a Devil's Island for them.

From the start, it was evident that Rafael Trujillo's expectations of a championship ball team came at the cost of freedom and sanity. To keep the players focused on baseball and only baseball, *el jefe* removed all distractions. Day and night, the African Americans on Trujillo's Los Dragones team were escorted by uniformed, rifle-toting soldiers to and from their hotel and the ball field, with no detours allowed to the local nightspots.

Understanding neither the language nor the customs, the players had no idea that this was Trujillo's way of protecting them from harm and dissipation. Indeed, the Latinos on the team believed the *americanos* were being coddled, while they had to fend for themselves and live in squalor.

For the Trujillo team, the most trying moments came before and during the championship series against San Pedro de Macorís. The night before the event got under way, Chet Brewer, the great Monarch pitcher who had pitched for the Santiago team, came to Ciudad Trujillo to watch the series.

"We went by where the ballplayers liked to socialize," Brewer recalled. "We were lookin' for Satchel and them and we couldn't find them. So a little kid on the street, he said, '*Esta en la cárcel*'—that they was in *jail*! Trujillo had put them in jail…so they wouldn't rouse around."

The next day, Los Dragones were let out, only to take the field between soldiers with bayonets. Trujillo's men were lined up along the first-base stands, his rival's troops along the opposite stands. With the two people's armies glaring at one another, the game had the dark and sinister undertones of a Graham Greene novel, with everyone expecting at some point to be caught in a cross fire. Worse, the addled Satchel Paige and Leroy Matlock lost the first two games and Los Dragones went down three games to none before storming back with three straight wins to set up the biggest game ever to be played in the tropics.

Now, Paige—who would be inhaling antacid tablets all game long to calm his churning stomach—went out to the pitcher's mound fully expecting to win or die. "I had it fixed with Mr. Trujillo's polices," Paige wrote in his memoirs. "If we win, their whole army is gonna run out and escort us from the place. If we lose, there is nothin' to do but consider myself and my boys as passed over Jordan."

A jittery Satch fell behind 5–4 in the seventh, at which point, he later swore, "You could see Trujillo lining up his army. They began to look like a firing squad." Though this nightmare scenario was surely all in his imagination, it served to inspire him and his teammates. In the home seventh, Paige singled and Sam Bankhead hit one over the fence to move the team ahead 6–5. Satch then ended the contest with two shutout innings.

Their work done, the Americans raced back to the hotel, packed up, and jammed into taxicabs to take them to the dock to catch the first boat back to the States—with the lone exception of Paige. Although for years Paige would tell horror stories about the Dominican experience, he actually stayed behind on the island, pitching exhibition games rather than having to beg to get his job back in the Negro National League.

Later Paige alienated himself from blackball and at the same time asked for redemption. "I would be willing to go to South America and live in the jungles rather than go back to the league and play ball like I did for ten years," he told the press. And in the next breath: "I am pretty sure that when I get back to America I will not be a stranger to the Negro National League. Likewise I find it hard to believe that the people back home would turn their backs on me, simply because I wanted to earn more money. If I was such a bad fellow, why did such men as Josh Gibson, Matlock, Bankhead, and Cool Papa Bell and others follow me?"

For all of the rebel players, and for the owners they had jilted, reconciliation proved a touchy issue. Though each side wanted to pick up where they'd left off the preceding spring, faces had to be saved and egos needed to be soothed, not to mention the "lifetime" bans decreed by Gus Greenlee and endorsed by all the owners. Consequently, when the players returned to American soil in the fall of 1937, they bided their time by forming their own touring all-star team, which they called the Trujillo All-Stars as a way of cashing in on their notoriety as fugitives and international champions.

Shortly thereafter, this vehicle provided Paige with yet another way to reenter the Negro leagues—and to get even with Gus Greenlee one last time.

16

Showdown at High Noon

In the major leagues it has been the policy to cleverly ease troublesome players out of baseball and it looks as if the colored owners are going to do the same thing with (Satchel) Paige. Many express regrets that such an outstanding star should prove so hard to handle but point out that both sides probably feel they are right and that it would be dangerous to compromise.

—*Newark Herald News,* May 14, 1939

The expatriate Negro leaguers playing with the Trujillo All-Stars need not have worried that the lifetime ban levied against them would ruin their careers. Within weeks of their return, Tom Wilson and J. L. Wilkinson were already finding ways to ease the bans in small increments.

Because Wilkinson still monopolized the Midwest turf on which the All-Stars hoped to barnstorm, he sent the word to his favored promoters, Ray Dean and Abe Saperstein, to book the team's games throughout the late summer of 1937. Through this largesse, the All-Stars—who at once became known in the press and to the fans as the Satchel Paige All-Stars as soon as Paige joined them on his return—gained entry to the *Denver Post* tournament, which they won going away.

The next stage in the reconciliation process was Tom Wilson's decision to schedule an important matchup between the Paige team and another of Wilson's Negro league touring aggregations. Actually, the Paige All-Stars received far more publicity and drew bigger crowds than the Negro leagues' own postseason sideshow—a series of games between the Negro National League–winning

Homestead Grays and a squad composed of players from the Negro American League champion Kansas City Monarchs and second-place Chicago American Giants.

By the time the Wilson-made game took place on September 20 at New York's Polo Grounds, it was the only game that seemed to matter. It quickly earned a place in that pantheon of blackball contests reported by the black press as the "greatest game ever played." Before a boisterous crowd of around 22,500, the New York Cubans' Johnny Taylor matched scoreless innings with Paige, giving up not a single hit as the drama heightened.

Then, in the eighth, the Philadelphia Stars' Jim West clubbed a two-run homer off Paige. In the top of the ninth, Taylor retired George Scales, Spoony Palm, and Cool Papa Bell to preserve a spellbinding no-hitter.

With these games providing the footbridge, the rebel players walked back to their league teams in time for the 1938 season. Having dropped all their lawsuits against the players, both leagues assessed a nominal fine of one week's salary against each of the players. Josh Gibson didn't even suffer that much of a loss. Late the previous summer, Cum Posey had rushed him back into the Grays' lineup, making the astonishing claim that he had given Josh permission to jump to the tropics.

While this rapprochement was taking place, the biggest marquee attraction in the black game was, as usual, going his own way. Gus Greenlee fully anticipated rehiring Satchel Paige to facilitate his dreams of regaining blackball power. However, Gus, in his usual fashion, struck with a crude sense of vengeance. Negotiating long-distance through the black papers in the spring of 1938, Greenlee offered Paige a salary of $350 a month, a pay *cut* of almost 50 percent from his last Crawford contract.

"I wouldn't throw ice cubes for that kind of money," was Paige's reply.

Apparently having learned nothing from his suicidal efforts to discredit Josh Gibson in the black papers, Greenlee now waged an offensive to tear down Paige's reputation. Imposing standards that amounted to censorship, Gus prevailed upon Cum Posey to send out a directive to black sportswriters who might cover Paige instructing them "not to print unfavorable league publicity unless assured of the facts" by the league office.

A few days later the *Courier's* Wendell Smith wrote a searing indictment of Paige, who he maintained "is not the pitcher he once was. He is getting older and his famous fastball has slowed to the point where batters can distinguish between a pea and a bullet. There was a time when they couldn't see it."

Not only that, but, reminiscent of John Clark's recent diatribe against Gibson, Smith accused Paige of not being able to think straight. Smith wrote on April 16: "Considering the number of games he would be required to pitch, $450 a month [sic] is more than a fair offer. It is even better than some of the [white] major league pitchers.... His stubborn attitude is getting him nowhere."

Unfortunately, this attack occurred only months after Paige had won his most flattering encomium yet—in the *white* press. In a column in the September 24, 1938 edition of the *Chicago Tribune*, Dizzy Dean, Satch's old comrade in interracial capitalism, reflected back on his classic exhibitions against Paige and etched Satch's features into a Mount Rushmore of pitching immortals. Dean wrote:

> A bunch of fellows get in a barber session the other day and they start to arguefy about the best pitcher they ever see. Some says Lefty Grove and Lefty Gomez and Walter Johnson and old Pete Alexander and Dazzy Vance. And they mention Lonnie Warneke and Van Mungo and Carl Hubbell and Johnny Corridon tells us about Matty and he sure must of been great and some of the boys even say Old Diz is the best they ever see.
>
> But I see them fellows but Matty and Johnson and I know who's the best pitcher I ever see and it's old Satchel Paige, that big lanky colored boy. Say, Old Diz is pretty fast...and you know my fast ball looks like a change of pace alongside that little bullet old Satchel shoots up to the plate. And I really know something about it because for four, five years I tour around at the end of the season with all-star teams and I see plenty of Old Satch.
>
> He sure is a pistol. It's too bad those colored boys don't play in the big leagues because they sure got some great ball players. Anyway, that skinny old Satchel Paige with those long arms is my idea of the pitcher with the greatest stuff I ever saw.

In the past, Dean's motivations for such facile overstatement regarding black ballplayers could have been querstioned as pure gate hype, since black players were kept at a safe distance from white players' jobs. But now, even if integration wasn't yet seen as inevitable, discussion of it was serious and no longer idle fancy. Thus, for all his huckstering, Dean's words were an important emolument for the cause, and the black press printed them with abandon. The *Chicago Defender,* for example, reprinted the column with the headline "Diz Says Paige Is Best Pitcher in Baseball."

Becoming accustomed to these blandishments, Paige was hardly intimidated by the Negro leagues' coarse attempts to deflate him. Knowing that a snap of his fingers could command an audience with any black sportswriter, he relished the league's opprobrium, as it only sustained his resentment of all authority, black or white.

Wallowing in his outlaw status, he resolved never to play for Greenlee again, nor for any other team that wasn't prepared to meet the only offer he insisted he would accept—$3,000 a month. And just so nobody missed this news, Satch rigged his own press campaign.

On April 23, the *Courier*—demonstrating that the black press had far too many voices and points of view to blindly fall in behind any league office's marching orders—carried a long and congenial feature on Paige. The paper reported that the great pitcher was hanging out in Harlem's Woodside Hotel with the Mills Brothers and "wore a brand new gray tailor-made Easter suit and light hat and said he was having a fine time learning to do the Boogie-Woogie."

With Paige dancing on Gus Greenlee's head, Gus knew he was again beaten by the monster he had created when he brought Paige to Pittsburgh so many heartaches ago. And so by the end of April, with the season a month old, Gus began looking for a graceful way out of his never-ending Satchel Paige dilemma.

He found one in Newark. Despite Paige's outlandish asking price, Abe and Effa Manley were actually willing to pay this kind of money to acquire his services for the Eagles. Only three years before, in fact, the Manleys had offered Greenlee a flat payment of $5,000 for Paige, which would have dwarfed the $2,500 bounty Cum Posey paid Greenlee, along with two players, to get Josh Gibson back to Homestead.

In 1935, Greenlee had immediately turned down the Manleys' offer, since Satch was bringing in that much money in gate receipts on one good Sunday. Now, with Abe and Effa stockpiling the Eagles with Negro League veterans—their so-called Million-Dollar Infield of 1937 (Ray Dandridge, Willie Wells, Dick Seay, and Mule Suttles) seemed to have a million years of experience—the Manleys indicated that the offer for Paige was still on the table. Gus took the money and considered himself lucky to get even a cent for blackball's problem child.

As usual, Paige had his own agenda to satisfy before he would go to Newark, one that was radical even for him. In weighing the pros and cons, Satch was tempted not only by Abe Manley's money but also by Effa Manley's carnal urges, which were common knowledge around the black game.

His own marriage notwithstanding, Paige was eager to dally in the same way Terris McDuffie had in his days with the Eagles—and in the same way Satch himself had in his own affair of the heart with Tom Wilson's wife back in Nashville. Laying out this precondition in correspondence with Effa, he did not get the response he hoped for. Indeed, not only did she not take him up on the raunchy offer, she didn't even take it seriously.

Regarding Paige's wish that Effa become his "sideline girlfriend," as she gently put it in her memoirs many years later, Effa recalled that "I didn't know what to say, so I just threw it [Paige's letter] away."

If Effa ever confided any of this nutty scenario to Abe, he surely reacted differently than he had in the matter of Terris McDuffie. While Paige delayed making his decision, Abe sought to protect his new would-be investment. In May, he obtained a limited court injunction that forbade Paige from playing for any other team in New York or New Jersey.

But by the time Manley asked a sheriff to serve the injunction, Paige was beyond anyone's reach. Without having stopped to pitch a single league game, Paige was now hurling for the Mexican League, another Latin challenge to America's monopoly on summer baseball. Paid the stunning sum of $2,000 a month, Paige joined Cool Papa Bell and scattered other Negro leaguers in the high Sierras.

Out $5,000 once Paige refused to report to Newark, Greenlee once again had the Negro National League "ban" Satchel Paige "forever from baseball." But for Greenlee, this old song was a dirge suited for his own funeral. Finished as a power broker, Gus spent the 1938 season, another long and losing one, readying his own farewell to blackball.

Throughout the season, Gus sold off his best players to other teams, trying to take whatever profit he could from the carcass of the once-proud Crawfords. He hired Jesse Owens, the black Olympic track hero, to boost laggard ticket sales by staging pregame exhibitions in which Owens would run against racehorses on the field. By the end of the season he had made Owens a part owner of the club. Then, following the season, Greenlee closed Greenlee Field rather than pay for its upkeep, leaving the team with no home and Gus's name an obscenity even among his longtime yes-men.

One, John L. Clark, who was also the Crawfords' secretary, now used his *Courier* column not to butter up Greenlee but to skewer him, primarily for allowing Greenlee Field to have risen and fallen as a blackball lesson in failure. Taking note of Greenlee's curious record of having employed more whites than blacks at the park, Clark surmised that blacks had consciously stayed away from the place in recent years because of that incongruity.

In his column in the December 10, 1938 issue of the *Courier*, Clark condemned Greenlee for having failed to operate Greenlee Field with what Clark called "a purer racial interest." Without invoking Greenlee's name, Clark's blistering column saw the closing of the park as an apocalypse for the city's black community. He wrote:

> [S]ince there was no single individual, or group of individuals, blessed with that foresight, that courage to be a part of the thing and correct the faults, it is safe to say that Pittsburgh is no place to attempt big things for Negroes. . . . Greenlee Field joins the list of banks, industries and other enterprises which should not be again attempted in this city for the next 100 years.

No longer in the business of face-saving, and seemingly out of fight after being thoroughly pummeled, Greenlee tamely replied in a bylined *Courier* column on March 23, 1939 that his decision to close the park came "[a]fter a careful study of the baseball outlook, and in a review of my experience and losses of the past seven years." And, shockingly, he seemed to endorse Clark's overly pessimistic verdict about the future of black sports in Pittsburgh: "We can no longer plan for the day when important industrial conditions will appear and make more profitable athletics in this section....Perhaps new blood will bring new ideas and new weapons."

With this clear, and weary, signal of his intentions, Greenlee took the final steps out the blackball door. Seeing his exit coming, the Negro National League owners, as a backhanded tribute, named Greenlee "honorory president," a sop that Gus didn't need or want. On April 8, he threw the title back in the owners' faces, saying his resignation "will serve the best interests of all concerned."

He then sold off his majority interest in the Crawfords to his younger brother, Charles Greenlee, who in turn sold the team— the onetime epicenter of black cosmopolitan society—to a group of white businessmen in Toledo, though the team never played a single game there before folding in May 1939.

Gus Greenlee, meanwhile, stole away to the Crawford Grille to ponder his next move—and a track record of failure. Only two months before Gus's exile from blackball, his boy John Henry Lewis had been given a shot to fight Joe Louis for the heavyweight title. John Henry was knocked down three times and then counted out at 2:29 of round one. Adding tragedy to failure, the day before the fight Gus's other younger brother, Jack, was killed in a car crash. And the day after the bout, Lewis had to retire from boxing with an eye injury.

But if life had turned sour for Greenlee, it was worse for the black Pittsburgh baseball fans. John Clark was right: Having been partly forsaken by Cum Posey and completely abandoned by Gus Greenlee, Pittsburgh would not again be a major player in the sport or the cause of black baseball.

In his idleness, Gus Greenlee no doubt rued the times he had allowed Cum Posey back into the Negro National League. Now, with Greenlee and the Crawfords a fading memory, the Grays had the field to themselves, and would win the league title every single season from 1938 until 1945, a ramrod steadiness that was nearly matched by J. L. Wilkinson's Kansas City Monarchs in the Negro American League.

That circuit seemed more and more not so much a league as a

revolving phalanx of inferior clubs meant to be crushed under the Monarchs' wheels. This crowd now included the Negro American League's answer to the Crawfords' dying glory, the Chicago American Giants, whose dynasty was heading for the scrap pile by the late thirties. The Monarchs' domination was propitiously timely, saving the league from possible disaster following a 1938 season that had played like a freak show.

In the league's inaugural season of 1937, the Monarchs and American Giants had predictably had the field to themselves, finishing one-two before the Monarchs took four out of five games in the playoffs to win the league crown. But then the two legendary teams were beaten out by two presumed doormats, the Memphis Red Sox and Atlanta Black Crackers, who won the two halves of the 1938 season and moved into the playoffs, a circumstance that seemed to bewilder no one more than the playoff teams themselves.

Although a seven-game championship series was set, the Red Sox and Black Crackers clashed over scheduling, expenses, gate-splitting, and almost everything else. After Memphis won the first two games, the bickering became so bitter that Major R.R. Jackson, the elderly league commissioner, halted the madness. He declared the series a "no contest" and ended the season right there.

The Monarchs, by winning the next four league pennants, established an effective counterbalance to the Grays' grade-A professionalism. The Negro leagues needed this sense of tribal unity in order to appear no different from the white major league family and its structure. Rube Foster had that sense of unity when he first publicly fantasized about a meaningful Negro league organization in the 1910s. As such, it now also made necessary, and compelling, the resurrection of the Negro League World Series, which had been last played in 1927.

A certain cautious presumption began to again germinate within the black game that a just and honorable fate awaited it, even with all the harebrained bumbling in high places. However, this age of reason would not be ushered in until Satchel Paige had very nearly transformed the peaceful symbiosis between leagues into Armageddon.

Toiling away for the Agrario club of the Mexican League—at, as noted, the remarkable salary of $2,000 a month—Paige's once-rubber arm dried like a fig in the thin alkaline air of Mexico City.

Feeling a strange sensation of stiffness, then soreness, Paige tried to heal himself by throwing harder. But he was thirty-two, and the years of laughing at the concept of physical conditioning while roaming the bars at night now became his undoing. The pain spread to his right shoulder, and soon he was unable to lift that precious wand to belt level.

Still, refusing to admit what that pain meant, and hearing the catcalls of the aficionados after each disappointing outing, when Satch took the mound in a game against Club Azules on September 5, 1938, in Mexico City, matched up against the great Cuban Martin Dihigo in a game that excited all of Mexico, it was a matter of macho pride for him. And even though each pitch was pure torture, Paige massaged the corners of the plate, not with his usual heat but with a farrago of junkballs, something he'd never had to do before. Finally, in the seventh, the hitters stopped looking for the fastball that never came which had left them helpless to hit the bloop curves that went by. Waiting him out, timing their swings to the slow stuff, they loaded the bases on a hit and two walks. Then, trying to go with heat, Satch threw a wild pitch that scored a run.

Still, he retired the side with no further damage done, allowing himself to walk off the mound with heroic dignity. He removed himself from the game, whereupon his team tied the score, getting Satch off the hook, although Dihigo won the game with a homer in the ninth.

But, now, Paige had to look into a murky future. Doctors examined him and told him he would probably never be able to pitch again. And when he returned home that fall, this time it was not so easy to get around his second lifetime ban. With rumors of his injury circulating, the Negro leagues suddenly wanted to part of the excesses they had endured when he was healthy.

Inquiring about possible coaching or managing jobs around the Negro National League, he was met with indifference, one seemingly designed to make Paige atone for his past sins. "Negro baseball was closing in on me tight," he wrote in his 1961 autobiography. "They wouldn't even take me for my name." That was because his name had become synonymous both with outrageous behavior and an era of Negro league folderol that was deemed inappropriate by those who increasingly saw the black game as a cause. Indeed, as if reflecting the new reign of supremacy by the businesslike Homestead Grays, the senior Negro league was fast acquiring a stodgy, self-important mustiness.

The similar reign by the Kansas City Monarchs in the Negro American League, on the other hand, reflected the J. L. Wilkinson school of inspired gimmickry. Through Wilkinson, promoters like Abe Saperstein and Syd Pollock had become empowered. These two white booking agents seemed more contemptible to many blackball purists than Eddie Gottlieb and Bill Leuschner, because they didn't merely control teams and property rights but took the Wilkinson protocols of showbiz baseball to new lows of racial indignity. By the late thirties, both Saperstein and Pollock had interests in two teams that had become infamous in most blackball quarters but fabulously successful at the gate—which once more imposed the prickly conundrum of having to live with these loathsome forms.

Successors of Pollock's Havana Red Sox, the Clowns (sometimes called the Ethiopian Clowns) and the Zulus had methodologies that were nearly identical and a pipeline between them for players to shuttle from one team to the other. Playing throughout the Midwest, the incubator of so many progressive baseball trends, these teams seemingly tried to top each other in screeching, shuffle-footed behavior. The Clowns took the field employing such jungle anonyms as "Wahoo," "Tarzan," "Monkee," and "Selassie" (after the Ethiopian leader). The Zulus appeared wearing grass skirts and made up in *whiteface*.

For obvious reasons, Saperstein and Pollock were not eager to clarify their ownership roles with these teams. Hidden by the clubs' shadowy directory of officers, Pollock maintained that he was only the general manager of the Clowns and that in fact the owner of record was a black man, Hunter Campbell.

But this explanation did nothing to ease the growing discontent about the ascendancy of Pollock and Saperstein, who had the greater influence. Even J. L. Wilkinson began to distance himself from the Chicago promoter. When both leagues' owners agreed before the 1940 East-West Game to strip Saperstein of his $1,500 promotional fee, Wilkinson did not stand in the way.

Still, Wilkinson saw Satchel Paige not as a symbol of bad taste but of the blackball heritage of hard-won heroism. Paige was a man who had paid dues on mounds from one end of the continent to the other, spreading the word, even if too often the word was

"I" or "me." And so, in the spring of 1939, Wilkinson took a calculated gamble that Paige's name was still nonpareil at the box office.

The gamble earned Wilkinson a fortune. Because of Paige's still-undetermined arm injury, Wilkinson had limited his appearances to the Monarch's traveling team, composed of mediocre players not good enough to play for the big club. At the start, Satch did no more than stand in the coaching box or maybe turn in an inning at first base. And yet just the chance to see the skinny icon-desperado standing erect drew thousands of people to rickety little ball yards on hot Sunday afternoons in the plains.

Gradually, as Satchel's arm recovered, newspaper reports told of his striking out hitters with his old frequency. J. L. Wilkinson was astonished that his second-rate team—known, inevitably, as the Satchel Paige All-Stars—was outearning the Monarchs. Though locating this club's whereabouts could be difficult, the black press still bowed to Paige's name and drawing power. Even thousands of miles away in Pittsburgh, an upcoming game in Milwaukee between Paige's team and the lamentable Clowns during the summer of 1939 merited the two-column headline "Satch Paige and His All Star 9 to Play Clowns."

But now Wilkinson found himself in a bind. He wanted to promote Paige to the Monarchs for the Negro American League season, but doing so would fly in the face of the Negro National League–mandated ban on the great pitcher. Wilkinson, thinking he had found a loophole in the seeming desire of the Negro National League's masters to purge Paige from their memory, asked in early May 1939 for the league's permission to sign Paige to the traveling team, and got it with no trouble, since, as the black *Newark Herald News* reported, "hardly an owner was willing to be troubled with the eccentric hurler."

But the owners were not through ostracizing Paige. In the month that passed, the Negro papers began to balance their affirmative trackings of Paige's games with nasty comments provided by league owners. Cum Posey bade his own farewell to Paige in his *Courier* column, likening Satch to "a child who has been brought up wrong."

In what read like part eulogy and part reproof, Posey's column clearly set into motion a historical revision of Paige. While Posey called him "a phenomenal and well-publicized [pitcher]," it was with inverse logic that Posey ignored Paige's drawing power, insisting instead, "No colored club drew enough...to pay him a salary commensurate with his ability."

Posey ventured that, in the last analysis, "Negro baseball has been very good to Paige" but "his unreliability...kept him from being a really valuable asset to any team. Personally, we never considered Paige as good a player as [Smokey] Joe Williams, Dick Redding, or Jesse Hubbard in their prime." And: "[S]ome owners are genuinely glad to have him leave."

J. L. Wilkinson regarded these tacit postmortems as an attempt by the owners to unconditionally discharge themselves from all commitments regarding Paige. But when Satch played winter ball after the season in Puerto Rico and won that league's most valuable player award by throwing some awesome games, Wilkinson's plans to bring Paige to the Monarchs hit a snag. Now, it seemed, Paige wasn't considered a derelict after all. On the contrary, in the spring of 1940, the rights to his services was suddenly a hot issue.

Abe and Effa Manley, who had let Paige slide out of the league with no dissent only a year ago, now acted as though the last twelve months had never happened. With Paige apparently mended, they casually mailed him a Newark Eagle contract, believing they still owned him by dint of their attempted deal with the Crawfords, a strange rationale since the deal was not consummated. And now that the Crawfords were defunct, the Manleys wanted to have their Satchel and their $5,000, too. Moving to turn rationale into reality, Effa prematurely issued a statement in early May claiming that Paige was "about to arrive" in Newark.

In fact, Paige had not amended his original precondition for coming to the Eagles, which was to make Effa Manley a notch on his bedpost. Without knowing of the heavy-breathing particulars, the *Baltimore Afro-American* nonetheless unwittingly nearly gave them away in a vague item stating that "Mrs. Manley was very insistent about what she would have and would not have before they could reach even the basis for an agreement."

When Effa would *not* have any of what he proposed, Paige went back to the Paige All-Stars, pending elevation to the Monarchs. His amorous negotiations aside, Paige used the occasion to once again tear into the Negro National League, explaining during this war-nervous period that he had left the league in the first place because of its elements of "Hitlerism," and correctly pointing out that when he'd needed work, no one in the league had given him any.

It must have pleased Paige to no end that his latest walkout was plunging the Negro league into a crisis. It also had to do his ego good to realize that, though a reprobate, he now stood as an essential commodity in the Negro league inventory, one that was now shrinking because of another foreign incursion.

Early in the 1940 season, nearly two dozen black players defected to the summer Mexican League—and the Manleys were rocked, losing the incomparable Ray Dandridge in 1939 and both Willie Wells and Leon Day in 1940. The Grays would lose Josh Gibson to Mexico for most of the 1940 and 1941 seasons, causing Cum Posey's co-owner, Sunnyman Jackson—in Gus Greenlee's paranoid style—to eject a Mexican consulate employee named A. J. Guina from the park during a Grays game at Forbes Field.

Writing of this incident in the *Courier,* Wendell Smith reported that Jackson "detected Guina's Latin accent and became suspicious. He asked the diplomat if he were Mexican, and when he found his suspicions were correct, proceeded to escort Guina out of the park....After a heated argument outside the park, the Mexican called the police and Jackson was taken to the station." Charges against Jackson, however, were dropped.

Obviously, the team that owned Satchel Paige during this latest threat to blackball's security stood to become the hub of Negro league attention. And this prospect far outweighed the hyprocrisy of making a messiah out of a man most owners despised—as well as the irony of the peripatetic Paige saving the black game from other mercenary men.

The Manleys, who were nothing but shameless in their renewed pursuit of Paige, soon found themselves swept up in a game of bluff and dare, with dire potential.

In late June 1940, when the two Negro leagues called a joint meeting to deal with the Paige problem, the owners gathered in Harlem's Woodside Hotel—coincidentally, one of Satch's favorite hangouts—under what the *Afro's* sports editor, Art Carter, described as "war clouds which threaten to disrupt the [Negro National League] schedule...and probably lead to a split in the loop." Carter added that because of the "stormy issue over the ownership of Satchel Paige, recalcitrant pitcher, fireworks are slated to boom."

The Manleys held the dynamite and the matches. Prior to the meeting, they had obtained promissory votes from the New York Cuban Stars and New York Black Yankees. If the Eagles withdrew from the league over this issue, those two teams would go as well, a development that Carter predicted might "throw the league into complete discord."

After two days of wrangling, the Manleys realized they could not get Paige and began to look for a way out that would benefit them. Abe Manley then announced that he had signed Buster "Bus" Clarkson and Spoon Carter from the roster of the Toledo Crawfords, who had switched over to the Negro American League after Gus Greenlee's former team went west. In so doing, Abe made the point that what was good for J. L. Wilkinson's rooster in flaunting interleague agreements was good for Abe Manley's hen.

This spiteful feint effectively held the talks hostage. At first, National and American Negro League presidents Tom Wilson and J. B. Martin tried to use moral logic and force to end the stalemate. They jointly ruled that Paige could not be compelled to play in Newark for the Manleys and that even though the Toledo Crawfords were about to dissolve, Clarkson and Carter had to go back to Toledo.

But the Manleys stood their ground, and with the cracks in the Negro National League now visible, Wilson and Martin agreed to settle the crisis by acceding to the Manleys' extortion. Clarkson and Carter were told to pack for the trip east and the Woodside Conference ended with nerves so frayed that blackball-watchers had to wonder if the Negro leagues had learned anything about fraternity in the last four decades.

17

Stormy Petrel

Colored America's share in the war effort will determine its share in the peace that follows.
——Masthead of the *Baltimore Afro-American*, 1942

Abe and Effa Manley were now ready to take on the man who was impeding them from their primary aim of making blackball a totally black game. This, of course, meant that Cum Posey's neck was now squarely on the block. Ironically, the Manleys might not have moved against Posey had not he been weakened by Abe and Effa's failure to keep Satchel Paige in the Negro National League.

As could have been predicted, Paige's activities with the Paige All-Stars quickly became the linchpin of the Negro league scene. In this resurrection of his legend, Paige also won some important crossover notices in the tabernacles of the mainstream white press. The summer of 1940 brought graphic Paige profiles in *Time* magazine and the *Saturday Evening Post;* a year later, another appeared in *Life*.

Benevolent exposure such as this was worth a mint in public relations value to the black game as a whole, despite the habitual racial stereotyping and condescension employed by white writers in these still-unfamiliar sorties into the black culture. To *Time*, for example, he was "large, dark Leroy (Satchelfoots) Paige," a man who, the news magazine related erroneously, "owes his nickname ...to his size 12 shoes" and "got strong by shouldering 200-lb. blocks of ice. Last week his old ice-wagon employer recalled his prodigious appetite: 'That boy et mo' than the hosses.'"

In the *Post,* writer Ted Shane gazed at the obscure netherworld of the Negro leagues. His take, fully intended to be laudatory, read like this:

> Their baseball is to white baseball as the Harlem stomp is to the sedate ballroom waltz. They whip the ball around without looking where it lands, and woe to the receiver if he isn't there instinctively. They play faster, seem to enjoy it more than white players.... [They] play way back on the grass and rush up on a ball like tumblers. They think it a weakness to catch a ball with two hands, and enjoy amazing dives into the bag to out foot runners. Players clown a lot, go into dance steps, argue noisily and funnily....
>
> Some are positive magicians at bunting...."We plays for home-run bunts," Oscar Charleston, a great player and now manager...says. Charleston could also hit, I'm told. "Once Charleston, he start to bunt, decided to cross up the infield instead—hit the ball so hard he bus' the ball to pieces—the covah flyin' one way—the pieces the other," a licorice enthusiast thrills.
>
> Paige, always the showman...would crank his apelike arms a half dozen times, uncrank them, lean back till he almost lay on the ground, bring that huge left foot up till it almost kicked out a cloud, then would suddenly shoot the ball from somewhere out of this one-man melee.
>
> "You cain't see nothin' but dat foot," complained his league victims. "It hides the ball park and Satch, too! Sometimes you don' know the ball's been pitched till it plunks behind you!"

Within the blackball culture, these farcical accounts caused some consternation, not for their dubious content but because the leaders of the Negro National League regarded the real winner in this publicity geyser neither blackball nor even Satchel Paige, but J. L. Wilkinson.

With Wilkinson a partner with Paige in per-game gate receipts, the owner delayed bringing Satch to the Kansas City Monarchs, not wanting to disrupt the Monarchs' team chemistry or the Paige All-Stars' moneymaking march. Wilkinson, meanwhile, received more than enough helpful publicity when Paige was identified in

Time not as the leader of the Satchel Paige All-Stars but rather as a member of "the Travelers, a roving division of the Kansas City Monarchs."

Finally, in late September 1940, Wilkinson believed the time was right for Paige to don the Monarch uniform. In a seamless transition, Satch's first start for the club drew ten thousand fans in Chicago for a game against the American Giants; his next one brought twelve thousand to the park in Detroit.

Though it probably took some getting used to, Wilkinson realized that the Kansas City Monarchs had for all intents metamorphosed into the Paige All-Stars. And while this change would cause some internal problems among some veteran Monarchs—especially longtime pitching aces like Hilton Smith and Chet Brewer, whose own stars were suddenly dimmed by Paige's—J. L. Wilkinson was already mapping plans to transform the Monarchs beyond recognition. By the early forties, the Monarchs—who had come from the marrow of the Midwest—were more of an eastern team, traveling frequently to play heavily touted games in Yankee Stadium against eastern clubs that would have to take less of the gate than usual just for the privilege of playing them.

Fearing just such an erosion of Negro National League prestige, Abe and Effa Manley could tolerate no more of the league's inertia. On February 4, 1940, at the annual owners meeting—held, revealingly, in the Philadelphia offices of Eddie Gottlieb—Effa stunned the room when she rose to demand that Tom Wilson be removed as league president.

This demand was consistent with Effa's old complaint that the league should have a nonowner as its president. Her choice for the job was Dr. Cilian P. Powell, the publisher of the black *Amsterdam News.* But picking on Wilson was actually a backdoor way to get at both Posey and the Manleys' real target: Eddie Gottlieb. The ubiquitous Art Carter, filing yet another *Afro* report on a league meeting filled with rancor, explained Effa's game plan:

> In a fiery speech, Mrs. Manley insisted that her reasons
> for seeking dismissal of Wilson were based on the league
> president's approval of an agreement whereby Gottlieb,
> as a private booking agent, collects 10 percent on
> promotion of games in Yankee Stadium, the loop's most
> profitable promotions. She assumed the position that

the league was a colored organization and that she
wanted to see all of the money kept within the group.

Effa touched a nerve by addressing this long-simmering issue,
and the arguments grew heated. Hearing the pro-Gottlieb faction—Posey, Wilson, and Ed Bolden—offer their rationales, Effa
became somewhat unrecognizable as the gentlewoman to whom
Posey had once apologized for the ungenteel language at another
owners meeting. Her temper flaring, Effa called Posey a "hand-
kerchief head"—which is the parlance of the times was a slur on
the order of "Uncle Tom."

Posey was stung, maybe more so because the slur had come
from a woman. According to the *Amsterdam News*'s coverage, Effa
"hurled epithets at Cum Posey [who] left the meeting in a huff,
vowing that he would never return as long as Mrs. Manley was the
Newark Eagles' representative."

Or, as it turned out, at least until she would stop haranguing
everyone about Eddie Gottlieb. As it was, Effa won vital support
for her case. By the time a vote could be taken on the Wilson
question—the Gottlieb question, really—Posey could do no better
than to fend off defeat with a 3–3 deadlock (the Manley coalition
with the New York Black Yankees and New York Cubans having
held), which allowed the old guard to table the issue and keep
Wilson in the presidency. Still, the whole business embarrassed
Posey considerably.

Unable to get Effa Manley's effrontery off his mind, Posey once
more trained his newspaper column on an enemy. On February
17, he charged with great moral outrage that Effa "took advantage
of her sex in the deliberations." Going on, Posey groused that "we
have never heard so much senseless chatter and baying at the
moon as was done by one party."

Insisting that the matter of the white agents had never bothered
anyone in the league until Effa made it into "a race issue," Posey
tried to brand her a hypocrite.

"We wonder," he wrote, "if the Negro scribes who [attended the
meeting] and heard the irrational outburst concerning race pride
know that the Newark Eagles pay a publicity man [Jerry Kessler]
$50 a week, and this publicity man is a white man?"

Ultimately, Posey wanted it to be known that Effa Manley's
performance in Philadelphia was "a disgusting exhibition."

Tom Wilson was also roiled, and he too made his case in the press. In a letter to black sports editors, Wilson called Effa's suggestions "idiotic." Suddenly no longer in his usual conciliatory mood, Wilson sniffed that "it does not make sense to have a woman who positively does not know the first thing about baseball, tell experienced men how to conduct their business."

But these attempts to diminish Effa Manley and her views proved unsuccessful. As Posey himself had noted in his column, her remarks in Philadelphia came before "a prepared crowd of New York sportswriters." PR savvy as she was, the black press was already partial to her, and fully aware that her sex was advantageous to newspaper sales.

The 1940 meeting served to make Effa, after Satchel Paige, the prime cause celebre in blackball in the early forties. When the *Afro* ran a group picture of the league's owners after the meeting, it cropped and enlarged her photo and placed it alone next to the group shot—atop a caption trumpeting her as the "Stormy Petrel" of the league. From now on, Effa Manley was more Carrie Nation than society matron.

Most fascinating about all this commotion over Eddie Gottlieb and Abe Saperstein was Effa Manley's privately held belief that the pro-Gottlieb faction's reasoning about the white agents actually made some sense. As Posey explained in that February 17 column, Gottlieb had used his influence to cut the fee Negro league clubs paid to rent Yankee Stadium from $3,500 to $1,000 per game, thus saving the league around $10,000 in 1939. While Gottlieb had collected $1,100 in booking fees for those Yankee Stadium dates, league teams involved in the games reaped about $16,000 in profit.

By contrast, when Jim Semler tried to circumvent Gottlieb and promoted three Negro league doubleheaders at Randall's Island Stadium, which sat on an island in the East River, the profits totaled $12 per team.

Effa Manley was familiar with the arithmetic. Years later, she candidly recalled her ambivalence about the perpetual quandary of racial symbolism versus sound capitalism. Personally, she said, "I thought those other men [the booking agents] had experience but when I saw what [Abe's] attitude was, I didn't pursue it any further. He was probably right, but I was thinking about the financial result."

What's more, Effa could not have been very comfortable with her two allies on league issues, James Semler and Alex Pompez. The hopelessly inept Semler was bad enough, but while both men came out of the underworld, Semler seemed like an altar boy next to Pompez, the longtime owner of the New York Cubans.

Unmistakeable in his white silk suits and pockets full of Havana cigars, Pompez had lately taken to dropping from sight for long periods while he ran from the law. Among all the numbers men who felt a tightening noose around their necks, Pompez's situation seemed them most dire. During the early thirties, Pompez once estimated that his operation grossed some $8,000 per day—a figure that at once caught the attention of the Dutch Schultz mob that ruled New York's vice trade.

As Pompez recalled, he was visited one day by Schultz himself, with the proverbial unrefusable offer. Putting his gun on a table in front of Pompez, Dutch told Alex he was going to join the syndicate, and that if he didn't, "You are going to be the first nigger I am going to make an example of in Harlem."

These charming details came to light when New York District Attorney Tom Dewey pursued the Schultz mob and its pawns in the city's political machine. But before Dewey could get to Schultz, the mob did, gunning him down in 1935. When Pompez heard about this development, he decided it was a good time to take a yearlong vacation in Europe.

When he returned late in 1937, Pompez hid out from both the mob and Dewey, living in the basement of Newark Eagle second baseman Dick Seay. He then fled to Mexico, where he was apprehended after a shoot-out and extradited back to New York, having agreed to turn state's evidence in 1938 against a corrupt New York politician named James J. Hines.

For cooperating, Pompez was allowed to plea-bargain and was given two years' probation on misdemeanor charges. Yet neither Pompez's history nor his status as a convicted felon concerned his fellow blackball owners, who were after all not so different from him. Not only was the affable Pompez allowed to oversee the New York Cubans, he was *rewarded* when the Cubans were given entry into the Negro National League in 1939. Thereafter, he stood as one of the black game's most esteemed gentlemen.

Pompez was also of inestimable value to Effa Manley in her power struggle with Cum Posey and Eddie Gottlieb. While

Pompez had allied himself with Nat Strong, and had a working relationship with Gottlieb and Bill Leuschner, he had little to lose in turning his allegiance to the Manleys. Since his long absence from the Cubans, the team had its lease to Dyckman Oval and needed the popular Eagles as a local rival if he was going to recoup his losses while the Cubans played strictly as a road team. Thus, for Pompez, regular appearances in Ruppert Stadium were far more important than the occasional appearance in Yankee Stadium.

But for the Gottlieb issue, Effa might just as easily have put her outrage to work against a man like Pompez—who she considered a very different breed from Abe and the other numbers runners in the black game. But Gottlieb was the issue, and once she was committed to Abe's position, Effa could not equivocate. By 1941, she had started to make men quake and walls move. Indeed, when the two Negro leagues took away Abe Saperstein's $1,100 promotional fee at the 1940 East-West Game, it could be construed as a halfway gesture designed to defuse the issue and get her off their backs.

By the early forties, the East-West Game had become a stormy issue in itself, and in need of some serious updating in the area of player compensation. Reflecting their growing professionalism, those men chosen by the fans to play in the game no longer considered participation in the event to be its own reward.

In the week before the 1940 game, when it became clear the owners were still not going to pay a cent above incidental expenses—claiming that the players salaries covered the East-West Game—player grumbling led the owners to attempt to mollify them by giving each of them a gold Elgin wristwatch.

But this did not close the rupture. In 1941, it was evident months before the July 27 game that the return of Satchel Paige to the contest after a five-year absence would sell out the game for the first time. On game day, 50,256 fans came to Comiskey Park, several hundred more than the official seating capacity and over twice the turnout for the previous year's game. And with the owners as usual due to carve up nearly all the profits, the players watched the mounting gate sales the week before the game and again grumbled, this time louder.

The West squad, particularly incensed by Paige's side arrangement with the game's promoters to be given a cut of the gate, took what was then a radical step for pro ballplayers. Days before the game, they threatened to boycott the contest unless they were paid in cash. Unable to justify not doing so, the owners in both leagues handed out $50 to each All-Star.

Not that this sum went far. The Newark Eagle outfielder Monte Irvin, who played in that East-West Game and four others, recalled that the $50 "usually lasted one night. When you got home you might be broke, but you had enough memories to last a lifetime."

The Negro leagues could thank the heavens that Gus Greenlee, for all his shortcomings, had pushed the East-West Game to fruition. By now, the game was easily the most identifiable and durable of blackball totems. As Irvin described the giddy scene surrounding the event in 1941, it was an idyll:

> Count Basie had written a song called *"Goin' to Chicago Blues,"* and a singer named Jimmy Rushing had made it into a very popular record that year. They were playing it on the radio during our train ride, and everybody in our car was singing, *"Goin' to Chicago, sorry that I can't take you."* Goin' to Chicago. I couldn't wait.
>
> We finally pulled in late Friday night and checked into the Grand Hotel. The whole scene was festive and fun. People like Basie, Ella Fitzgerald, and Billie Holiday would always make it their business to be in town for the East-West Game, and we'd be sure to check them out at the jazz clubs. You didn't go to Chicago to sleep. By comparison, I found out later, the big league All-Star Game wasn't nearly as much fun....
>
> The 1941 game was played on a scorching Sunday afternoon. Still there must have been fifty-two thousand people there....At the time, Comiskey Park held only fifty thousand people, but you could always do business with the fire department, so they'd let people sit in the aisles....
>
> There were a few whites scattered throughout the stadium, but mostly it was blacks of all backgrounds, all shapes and sizes, men and women and children. Black

people used to *love* baseball. I wish I knew what happened to that love for the game. Maybe it's becoming an economic thing—but people had to scrape by in the old days, too.

The East-West Games were a joyful experience. They put red, white, and blue banners up all over the park, and a jazz band would play between innings. People would come from all over the country to be part of this spectacle. The games were good. The players were great. If you could have picked one all-star team from the two squads, it surely could have rivaled any white major league all-star team of the time. That team would have been as good as any all-star team that's ever played.

Although Satchel Paige was billed as the West's starter, a minor arm injury put him in the bullpen at game's start. But the fans had come to see him pitch, and Satch knew it. "Satch was the center of attention," Irvin said. "As we stood around the batting cage, he'd say, 'Fellas, the East-West Game belongs to me. I don't have to pitch but two or three innings, so I'm gonna be *very* stingy today. In fact, I'm givin' up nothin'! When I get around to the Grand Hotel tonight, I'll buy you a beer. But today, nothin'! Zero!'"

When he did pitch, it was in the eighth inning and the East had the game in hand, leading 8–1 behind a Buck Leonard home run. In fact, up to then, it seemed the game—attended by a good many white sportswriters and white big league scouts—would go down mostly as a harbinger of the new blackball vanguard. While Paige had swamped everyone in the fan voting, the destiny of the black game now fully belonged to its most important generation—those young, strong players of the early and midforties. Men like Irvin, the stumpy Baltimore Elite Giant catcher Roy Campanella, Homestead center fielder Jerry Benjamin, and two exciting Kansas City Monarchs—left fielder Willard Brown and second baseman William "Bunny" Serrell.

And the 1941 East-West Game seemed to belong to Dave Barnhill, the superb pitcher of the New York Cubans who pitched brilliantly and gave way to the mandated Paige appearance late in the game. Satch's contribution was a mere two-inning mop-up. But the black press—now firmly committed to riding Paige's stallion, as long as it rode straight into a blackball heyday—covered Satch's meaningless stint with awe. "Satchel Gives Crowd Greatest Thrill!" the *Defender* splashed on sports page one.

Long forgotten now were the Gus Greenlee-Cum Posey-Wendell Smith jeremiads against Paige, replaced as they were obsequious prose similar to the *Chicago Defender's* comment about Satchel Paige on that day: "There's a certain grace, a deliberate calm, an uncanny relaxation, plus a great pitching head and a whip-cracking arm, which still knows how to get his fast one up there with the speed of lightning.... The man who is today the most colorful figure in baseball may be in the afternoon of his...dazzling career, but today he's as great a pitcher as there is in the country...and that takes 'em all in!"

What is more, Paige seemed to take this role as the Negro leagues' angel of redemption to heart; he never again walked out on a contract, and now placed personal conquests in the context of blackball progress. And those conquests were becoming epochal. On October 5, 1941, J. L. Wilkinson booked a game in St. Louis's Sportsman's Park between the Monarchs and a white major league All-Star team fronted by a now-mature Bob Feller, who with the Cleveland Indians had become arguably baseball's best and hardest-throwing pitcher.

Up until now, Sportsman's Park had a segregated seating policy. As the *Kansas City Call* reported, the stadium had an "unsavory reputation [as] the only major league park in the country where Negroes are relegated to the bleachers and pavilion and denied grandstand seats." At first, the park's managers indicated they would not alter this policy for the Monarch game, but when ticket sales soared they threw open the grandstand to blacks; in the end, twenty thousand black and white fans mingled without incident and saw a fabulous game—won by Feller's team when hometown hero Stan Musial smashed a Paige fastball over the pavilion for a 4–3 victory.

With more and more symbolic racial barriers falling before the inspired determination of black baseball, Cum Posey and his ruling bloc knew that the blackness of the game was nothing to trifle with. By now, the old bugaboo of white umpires handling Negro league games had been resolved, as the two leagues had begun to hire former black ballplayers as umpires.

And now, Posey moved closer to the Effa Manley bloc on the never-ending issue of white booking agents. In December 1941, Posey sent a letter to Effa examining ways in which the Negro National League might schedule five dates at Yankee Stadium independently of Eddie Gottlieb and Bill Leuschner. Laying down exactly who was boss, Posey assured her that the league's president, Tom Wilson, "would go along the way the rest of the league wanted it done," though that really meant what Posey wanted done.

Not that Gottlieb and Leuschner were going to retire quietly. Still possessing the weapons of their trade, they tried to punish Effa Manley for her crusade by withholding attractive dates at Yankee Stadium from the Eagles. But the Manleys had weapons, too—on the field. So long as the Eagles grew in stature, the promoters needed the team.

In fact, at the end of the 1941 season, an item in the *Pittsburgh Courier* carried the improbable news that "the feuding Manleys and Gottlieb have figuratively kissed and made up." If so, it was probably primarily due to the pledge of peace taken by all parties in the Negro leagues after the next great defining event in the evolution of blackball. That event occurred on the terrible morning of December 7, 1941.

If the blackball fathers in 1918 had drawn the high-minded if fallible conclusion that the sacrifices of black and white men in combat would automatically result in mutual gain on the home front, their successors a generation later would not be so naive. From the moment the embers began to burn at Pearl Harbor, black society in general vowed that it would not be shut out of the American war effort and its palpable unifying effects at home.

White men of intolerance had to know as well that past betrayals could not be repeated this time. Even before Pearl Harbor, the gathering war effort was obliged to include African Americans by an amendment to the Selective Service Act that stated, "There shall be no discrimination against any person on account of race or color" by the removal of unwritten regulations kept black GIs confined to the kitchen or latrine.

No one knew whether these liberation edicts would correspond to reality in base camps and on the battlefield. Nevertheless, blacks enlisted in enormous numbers. (They served in segregated units, integrated regiments not having been mandated on grounds that it would be destructive to morale.) By midwar, over a hundred and seventy thousand black men and women were in uniform, and the Negro leagues were well represented. Newark lost pitcher Max Manning from 1943 to 1945, Monte Irvin in 1944, and Leon Day and outfielder Larry Doby from 1944 to 1945. Kansas City lost pitcher Connie Johnson from 1943 to 1945 and both out-fielder Willard Brown—the Negro American League leader in hits and home runs for three straight seasons—and the great first baseman Buck O'Neil from 1944 to 1945. The Black Yankees' second baseman Dick Seay and Baltimore's third baseman Sammy Hughes were gone from 1943 to 1945. Homestead's third base-man Howard Easterling missed the 1944 and 1945 season.

One black player, in fact, was more important to the war effort than almost anyone knew. Quincy Trouppe was playing in Mexico when he was drafted, but was granted an exemption as part of an agreement between the U.S. and Mexican governments to transfer eighty thousand Mexican workers to U.S. defense plants.

The white major leagues were nearly debilitated by the war. Though President Franklin Roosevelt directed that the game continue to be played, in the interests of nationalism, it went on without practically any of its elite players. Compelled by public opinion to enlist in the service so as not to flaunt privilege and class, 25-game winner Bob Feller and the Senators' .359 hitter Cecil Travis went to war in 1942; the next year, so did Joe DiMaggio, Ted Williams, Bob Lemon, Johnny Mize, and Enos Slaughter, all future Hall of Famers and all gone for the next three seasons. Red Ruffing was lost for the next two years, Luke Appling and Billy Herman were gone for 1944, and Duke Snider, Stan Musial, and Bobby Doerr missed 1945.

Given the state of the white majors these stars left behind—in which teams accepted as big league material a one-armed out-fielder and a one-legged pitcher, among other odds and ends—it was not subversive that the men of the Negro leagues, and their fans, began to contemplate gains black Americans could make because of the war. For those who looked, there simply was no way of overlooking the odd inversion of the two baseball worlds during the war years; while the white game was barely recognizable, with many teams replacing war-fighting players with men classified as 4-F—the St. Louis Browns rose from the cellar to win the American League pennant in 1944 primarily because they fielded the most effective of the 4-F baseball class—the black game reached a plateau.

Joe Louis had proven with one frightful punch to Max Schmeling that African-American sports idols could become superb patriotic symbols. But even less modest men like Satchel Paige could be synonymous with God and country in the black community. Accordingly, black fans drew closer to the Negro leagues as a source of pride. Millions of blacks working in defense plants and making good money packed league games in every city. In retrospect, this movement would ultimately toss segregation off its axis.

The black press made that dual march across two battlefields its cause. The *Afro's* masthead rally cry that "Colored America's share in the war effort will determine its share in the peace that follows" was only the most mannered. By contrast, the *Defender* made the case with far more fire—"Remember Pearl Harbor and Sikeston too," cried the paper's editorial page, the latter in reference to a ghastly lynching in that Missouri town in 1941, an acrid reminder that blacks had more than one war to win.

Within black baseball there was a similar doughtiness, since it was obvious bigots could not sustain white big league canards about the ability gap between the races. No longer could underwhelming performances by white all-stars in games against blacks be written off to the whites' indifference to these contests; during the war, whiteball was so depleted that an aging, sore-armed Dizzy Dean was trotted out as the only serviceable big name in the latest round of these matchups played for war charities.

One game, for the Navy Relief Fund, pitted the Dean All-Stars and the Kansas City Monarchs at Wrigley Field in 1942, marking the first time a black team had played in this ivy-walled baseball shrine. When the Monarchs won 3–1 behind Satchel Paige and Hilton Smith, and Dean could barely retire the side in one inning of work, black sportswriters fumed that the only way blacks could play in Wrigley Field was to *lower* themselves to meet current whiteball standards.

Frank A. Young, the longtime *Defender* sports editor, wrote with a blunt pen rarely seen in the days when blacks dared not claim superiority over white big leaguers. Young declared that the large biracial crowd at Wrigley, "proved once and for all that America's baseball fandom want to see a ball game regardless of race, color or creed of the performers. And while the White Sox were taking a 14 to 9 licking [at] Comiskey Park, here was Satchel Paige, Hilton Smith and the Monarchs performing in big league style but denied the right to play in the big leagues because of their color."

Young went on. "Maybe the front office at Wrigley Field will sit up and take notice. The best part of the crowd...was not white. These brown American fans are baseball-hungry but they are sick and tired of paying their hard-earned money to see second rate performers because the performers must necessarily be white according to Judge Landis, high mogul of organized baseball and the various prejudiced owners."

The large black turnout during wartime for Negro league games—a dream come to fruition for those in blackball who had fretted about black fans' divided baseball loyalties—dramatically boosted the fortunes of many men who had recently been viewed as lepers. Abe Saperstein, for example, survived not only the enmity of blackball owners but wartime travel restrictions and deprivations. In 1942, Saperstein formed a new Negro circuit, the Negro Midwest League, a minor league similar to the erstwhile Negro Southern League, and earned new leverage by developing players for the black majors.

Only a year later, Saperstein, back again in the power structure, persuaded the Negro American League to relocate the Cincinnati Buckeyes to Cleveland so that Saperstein's reviled Ethiopian Clowns could have the Cincinnati market, as Abe preferred. In 1943, Saperstein would be granted permission to purchase an interest in the Birmingham Black Barons, whose owner of record was black funeral parlor proprietor Tom Hayes. In time, Saperstein would also purchase Rube Foster's legacy, the Chicago American Giants.

The biggest wartime fortune, though, would be amassed by Satchel Paige. Despite his new image as a paragon of American virtue, Satch was not averse to a little wartime profiteering. Primed as the main attraction of the 1942 East-West Game, Paige drove his usual bargain for a cut of the gate—but now, he demanded an advance.

J. L. Wilkinson was used to giving Paige favors. He had recently begun chartering a DC-3 airplane to ferry Paige to and from games, a luxury enjoyed by no other player in America. But Wilkinson was not eager to ask the two league presidents to make a special dispensation for Paige to receive an advance, which might alienate the other players, and so he gave $800 of his own money to Paige.

Given his éclat—which he could measure by the roughly $40,000 he earned yearly in the early 1940s, more than any *white* player of the time—Paige was inevitably sought out by the white press for comment on the issue of big league integration. Interviewed by the Associated Press shortly before the East-West Game, Paige implied that the time and the conditions weren't right for a mandated end to the color line. Alluding to "unharmonious problems," he worried about playing "not only in the South, where the colored boys wouldn't be able to stay and travel with the teams in spring training, but in the North, where they couldn't stay or eat with them in many places."

He added, "All the nice statements in the world from both sides aren't going to knock out Jim Crow."

These were reasonable concerns. However, Paige had his personal agenda: His income would drop if he joined the white majors, and he remained embittered about rumored big league tryouts that never occurred. In truth, he seemed like the worst possible spokesman for the black game at a time of delicate public discourse about integration. Indeed, Paige's remarks supported the rationalizations of many white obstructionists, and were given much weight at the same time that designated Negro league spokesmen were publicly floating trial balloons about integration in the white majors—with proper protections for what they considered the black game's rights in any detente.

At about the same time that Paige spoke out, the Homestead Grays' popular manager, Vic Harris, also expressed his qualms, but in a way the black owners endorsed. "If they take over our best boys," Harris told the *Afro,* "we will be but a hollow shell of what we are today. No, let us build up our own league and...then challenge the best white team in the majors and play them."

This, of course, was precisely how the blackball lords always preferred to deal with integration: never equivocating about the justness of the overall goal, but staking a claim to their presumed rights by proposing to hold back their prime products and then offering them for big bucks when the demand existed. Even back in 1938, the *Afro* carried this admonition by Art Carter:

[I]t's all right to keep up the fight for colored boys to enter the big white leagues, but the job would be so much simpler if we'd clean out our own setup first and start putting out real ball clubs, with efficient methods...start ballyhooing our own players and putting on big-time games in a big-time way, drawing in thousands of spectators in key cities through the East and then see how quickly those race bars would come down. MONEY TALKS in any man's language.

In 1942, the *Afro*'s Ric Roberts concurred, pointing out the harsh truth that "regular big-league baseball requires an economy that the colored people and their resources simply cannot match. The NNL and NAL are largely week-end and night ball groups that freelance during weekdays. As long as they must depend for the most part on colored pocketbooks [they] will remain horse and buggy leagues."

While those comments provided ammunition to white big league diehards, blackball supporters knew they told a cruel truth. Paradoxically, while black fans had become a large economic force, the Negro league clubs lagged behind them in the quality of their operations. Realizing that those fans, more than the black players themselves, were what white major league owners were most interested in, a Solomon-like Cum Posey pleaded for all deliberate speed on integration.

"Negro baseball owners have had a very hard time building up Negro baseball into a paying business," he wrote in his *Courier* column. "We are going to continue building [it] up....If we get our clubs so that they can play for a real world's championship, we will play it. If some clubs of the white major leagues wish our players we will sell them. We have a business and we are going to attempt to protect it the same way as any other Negro or white businessman.

"In the meantime, we would advise all Negro players to do all in our power to improve their playing, so if the chance ever does come to join a major league club, they will be ready."

As Posey saw it, several Negro leaguers were ready to play in the white majors. Satchel Paige, Josh Gibson, Roy Campanella, Ray Dandridge, and San Bankhead were the best candidates. But Posey's delusions about a phased-in era of good-faith dealing between the black and white leagues got no further in the white big leagues than broad, nonbinding statements of advocacy by such white big league owners as the Washington Senators' Clark Griffith. In 1938, Griffith went on record as saying, "There are few big league magnates who are not aware of the fact that the time is not far off when colored players will take their places beside those of other races in the major leagues."

Offering similar verbal bouquets in the late thirties were National League President Ford Frick and Chicago Cub owner Phil Wrigley, both of whom said that integration was "inevitable." Yet if Clark Griffith put himself in the forefront of change, the most he offered was to suggest that some kind of "championship" game between the black and white major leagues might somehow be arranged someday.

Griffith's tap-dancing around the issue was understandable. As the owner of Griffith Stadium, at which Posey's Grays played most of their home games, Griffith had every reason to be a friendly landlord, since, like the New York Yankee owners, he was collecting a considerable sum of money in rental and concession fees, on a par with Eddie Gottlieb and Abe Saperstein. In 1942, the Yankees pocketed around $100,000 on blackball games at Yankee Stadium, and Griffith was not far behind.

The white game's official position was postulated by Kenesaw Mountain Landis. The grim-faced and now-antiquated commissioner insisted in 1942 that "there is no rule, formal or informal, no understanding, subterranean or otherwise, against hiring Negro players."

This comment was big news in the black press. The *Afro* reacted to it with the optimistic headline "Landis Clears Way for Owners to Hire Colored." However, the *Courier* felt there was reason to be skeptical. "Was The Judge Jiving?" the paper asked. Indeed, the record of the past few years did not support Landis's claim. That same year, 1942, black civil right leaders were allowed to address a major league meeting, and offered proposals to advance integration. But Landis, ignoring pleas by several owners to debate the issue, tabled the motions and sniffed, "What's next on the agenda?"

This was only the latest in a series of called bluffs that saw white big league clubs back down from lip-service liberalism. Back in 1937, with the Pittsburgh Pirates in a tight pennant race, the

Pittsburgh Courier's Chester Washington had sent a telegram to the Pirates' manager, Pie Traynor. Since "your club needs players," the wire read, "[I] have answers to your prayers right here in Pittsburgh"—and avouched that Josh Gibson, Buck Leonard, Satchel Paige, and Cool Papa Bell were "all available at reasonable figures."

Traynor didn't bother to reply, but after the Pirates finished a close second in the race, rumors circulated that the club's owner, William Benswanger, was about to sign Josh Gibson and Buck Leonard for the 1939 season. He did not, and years later Benswanger attempted to blame Cum Posey for it. "I tried more than once to buy Josh Gibson," he said, but insisted that Posey ordered him to "lay off," reasoning that, in Benswanger's opinion, "It would start a movement that would eventually break up the Negro leagues."

This explanation seemed disingenuous, since the white owners did not care about black owners' concerns, nor the state of the Negro leagues. Indeed, Wendell Smith accused Benswanger of "unmitigated story-telling." Still, Benswanger let it be known, "If [the race question] came to an issue, I'd vote for Negro players....I know there are many problems connected with the question, but after all, somebody has to make the first move."

But there was no vote, and no first move—least of all not by Benswanger, when given another chance. In 1943, the owner was persuaded by the Communist Party *Daily Worker's* sports editor, Nat Low, to give tryouts to Baltimore's Roy Campanella and the Cubans' pitcher Dave Barnhill. As Campanella recalled the experience, Benswanger immediately dissuaded the players by telling them that the pay would be too low and a long tenure would be required in the minors. The two men were not scared off, but Benswanger canceled the tryouts, citing unnamed "pressures."

Similar hustles were felt by other Negro leaguers. Also in 1943, Baltimore pitcher Nate Moreland and a young former all-American football player from the University of Southern California named Jackie Robinson requested a tryout at the Chicago White Sox spring training camp in Pasadena, California. The stocky but fleet Robinson especially impressed the club's manager, Jimmy Dykes, who commented that Robinson was "worth fifty thousand dollars of anybody's money. He stole everything but my infielders' gloves." But Dykes, too, passed, prompting Moreland to bitterly comment, "I can play in Mexico, but I have to fight for America, where I can't play."

By the end of the year, the optimism in the black press had collapsed. The *Afro,* which had taken Judge Landis at his word, published the headline "Hopes for Colored Players in Major Leagues Fade With Waning '42 Season."

The weekly *Sporting News* was notable for its color-blind coverage when it and baseball were both young. Now the paper—which proudly called itself "The Bible of Baseball"—joined the conservative obstructionists who claimed a rush to integration would be reckless. In its August 6, 1942 edition, publisher J. G. Taylor Spink, in an editorial titled "No Good From Race Issue," labored to make the pressure, and not the cause, the issue.

Spink wrote that both black and white baseball executives "prefer to draw their own talents from their own ranks and both groups know their crowd psychology and do not care to run the risk of damaging their own game." Those who would do so, he said, were surely "agitators, ever ready to seize an issue that would redound to their profit and self-aggrandizement," instead of "looking at the question from the broader point of view or for the ultimate good of either race," or even considering the "tragic possibilities" that would occur should interracial strife spill over to the field.

Spink concluded that the "agitators" had better stop "mak[ing] an issue of a question which both sides would prefer to be left alone."

J. G. Taylor Spink did more than act as a spokesman for white big league resistance. He constructed the platform for the big league reactionaries of both colors to rest their case, at least for as long as they could get away with it.

18

Let Nature Take Its Course

[By] 1944, we in organized Negro baseball could see quite plainly the...handwriting on the wall. The gathering storm of inevitable baseball integration was approaching rapidly, ever more relentlessly.

—Effa Manley

Despite the black efforts to integrate baseball, white owners seemed determined to wait out the war and then welcome their big stars back to an unaltered game.

Though few on the side of obstruction openly spoke of it, about a third of white big league players came from the South, a fact that Satchel Paige had alluded to in citing "unharmonious problems" awaiting blacks in the white game. As well, a number of players were avowed members of the Ku Klux Klan.

In 1938 New York Yankees outfielder Jake Powell—a policeman in Ohio during the offseason—told a radio interviewer in Chicago that he took "pleasure beating up on niggers and then throwing them in jail." Judge Landis, whose office received thousands of letters by outraged blacks, suspended Powell for ten days, and the Yankees had Powell make the rounds of bars in Harlem to apologize personally to black fans.

Powell—who ironically often played in barnstorming games against blacks—nonetheless was met with verbal abuse by black fans at white big league games, and was the target of thrown bottles. A petition drive to extend Powell's suspension to one year brought six thousand signatures, and a black boycott of Ruppert's Bear, manufactured by Yankee owner Col. Jacob Ruppert, was proposed. But even though Frank A. Young wrote in the *Defender* that the Powell remark fanned racial emotions in Chicago higher than they'd been at any time since the city's race riots of 1919, Landis let the matter slide.

Most white players, and owners, were not guilty of racism, only timidity. All enjoyed the benefits of baseball's sweet life, and did not seek any change that would upset the system. Again, Paige had put his finger on the crux of baseball's economic sight lines when he mentioned the potential problems in the South. White major league teams had established important business arrangements with southern towns to use their stadium facilities for spring training, and often to install farm teams during the season. Sensitive to local customs and Jim Crow laws precluding integration, the clubs chose not to disturb them.

The owners also chose not to consider that they might have had the moral authority to change old customs, using as an inducement the economic welfare their ball clubs brought to satellite cities; threatening to walk away from these towns might have been one of the most potent weapons against Jim Crow, but not one club used it until much later on.

But even in the North, economic reality resided in the great euphemism of "property values." Behaving no differently than any other white neighborhood warily trying to wall itself off from would-be black neighbors, the owners told themselves their investments would be diluted as black players devalued the field and black attendees, en masse, scared away the white fans who regularly filled the stands.

What's more, baseball seemed to want to impose these rules on the minor leagues, fearful that the farm teams might turn out to be a proving ground for workable integration. In 1941, a Western League promoter, E. Lee Keyser, made a handshake deal with Satchel Paige to play for a team in that white minor league. But the deal was rescinded—reportedly when the news reached Judge Landis.

Landis must have felt like he was defending the Alamo once the white press began to pick up on the integration theme. In the late thirties, some prominent white journalists attacked Landis for his antediluvian views. Among them was Westbrook Pegler, who commented about the Jake Powell incident that "Powell got his cue from the very men whose hired disciplinarian [meaning Landis] had benched him for an idle remark." Baseball, Pegler bluntly wrote, treated "Negroes as Adolf Hitler treats the Jews."

The *New York Post* also attacked Landis, for "smug hypocrisy" in his handling of the Powell matter. That several white club owners had chastised Powell, the *Post* editorialized, did no more than allow them to "calmly proceed with their own economic boycott against this minority people."

Even before the Powell storm, Pegler, Jimmy Powers of the *New York Daily News*, Shirley Povich of the *Washington Post,* and John Kieran of the *New York Times* wrote about the folly of baseball's apartheid. Pegler was the most direct, excoriating the game's "silly unwritten law that bars dark Babe Ruths and Deans from the fame and fortune they deserve." But the *Boston Herald*'s Bill Cunningham may have offered the most ingenious and compelling logic: "Let's give them a chance—let 'em up here and let's see if they can hit."

In 1941, when *Time* profiled Satchel Paige, the magazine put in its own brief pitch for integration, though its cautious prose could not be confused with Pegler's:

> The owners and managers say that their Southern players and their visits to Southern training camps would make trouble if Negroes were on the team. But many a shepherd of a limping major league club has made no secret of his yearning to trade more than a couple of buttsprung outfielders for colored players the calibre of Satchelfoots Paige.

Still, as long as the cause was obscured by the advances of Nat Law's *Daily Worker,* it could be stalled with the smoke-screen raised by J. G. Taylor Spink, who referred to integration activists as "social-minded drum beaters." Wendell Smith, in fact, reflected in 1947 that "the Communists did more to delay the entrance of Negroes in big league baseball than any other single factor."

Meanwhile, Negro baseball chugged on, living some of its most splendid moments, with Stachel Paige, predictably the protagonist in many of them. But the Negro league owners knew that real success at this pivotal time required them to get tough and bring back many of the players who had defected to Mexico. Josh Gibson was a prime example.

In 1941, Gibson, who could be as shameless about contracts as Paige, quit the Homestead Grays only days after signing a new deal with Cum Posey for $500 a month. Taking an $800-a-month offer from the Mexican League's Vera Cruz team, Gibson joined a lineup that included Negro leaguers Willie Wells, Leroy Matlock, and Ray Dandridge.

Back in Pittsburgh, Posey again used his *Courier* column to attack Gibson's defection, writing that "We are the fall guy once more as we were in 1932 [when] Gibson signed a contract with the Grays, then used his contract to get more money from the Pittsburgh Crawfords." But Posey went further this time. He sued Gibson for "any losses the Grays incur through his leaving." Placing damages at $10,000, Posey asked the court to award him the deed to Gibson's home in the Hill.

Posey's bid failed, and Josh Gibson led Vera Cruz to the Mexican championship and was named the league's MVP. But Gibson did tell Posey he would return to the Homestead Grays in 1942, whereupon Posey dropped the lawsuit and paid Gibson a Satchel Paige-like salary of $1,500 a month. What Posey could not have known at this point was that when Gibson came back home he would be in declining health, his mind and his body self-destructing.

Abe and Effa Manley also turned to the courts to try and reclaim their decamped players, with mixed results. Explaining her case, Effa sent a letter to league presidents Tom Wilson and J. B. Martin, stating that "for the large amount of money I have invested, all I really have for that money is the ball players." Thus, when shortstop Lenny Pearson was about to join Dandridge, Wells, and Leon Day in Mexico for the 1941 season, she employed Harlem attorney Richard E. Carey to take legal recourse.

Carey first asked the State Department to hold up Pearson's passport, claiming fraud, since Pearson had been advanced a part of his salary. Pearson then decided not to go to Mexico after all. The following year, when Pearson was again close to a Mexican deal, Carey wrote to the player's draft board, attempting to have his military status upgraded to 1-A. Pearson again stayed put.

This success led Effa to try the draft-board strategy with Ray Dandridge and to recommend to J. B. Martin that the two leagues should use it as well. Dandridge, however, not only refused to accede to the threat, but Effa was forced to back down when Maj. P. E. Schwehm, New Jersey's military commandant, said that, under law, "no action can be taken…to make [ballplayers] stay in essential industry." Such action, he added with an irony that must have made Effa blanch, "might be definitely misconstrued, particularly because of [Dandridge's] color."

And so, while other players trickled back and forth across the border, Satchel Paige kept the black game firmly anchored. At the 1942 East-West Game—the one he overshadowed with his remarks that seemed to oppose baseball integration—he turned to melodrama.

Though the fans had given Paige eighty thousand more votes than any other player, Satch did not start the game. When the contest began, he wasn't even in Comiskey Park, and didn't arrive until the second inning. He's apparently worked out a scenario befitting a great showman, because when he was called in as a relief pitcher in the seventh inning of a 2–2 game, he bypassed the mound and walked directly to the dugout, where an open microphone was waiting for him. Taking it in hand, he stretched its cord to home plate and, before 45,179 people, delivered his soliloquy.

"Ladies and gentlemen," he began, "I would like to take this opportunity to deny a statement which the daily papers credited to me. I want you to know that I did not say anything against the use of Negro players in the big leagues. A reporter came to me and asked me what I thought about playing on major league teams. I told him I though it was all right. He said, 'Satchel, do you think white players would play with the colored?' I told him I thought they would, but that if they wouldn't it might be a good idea to put a complete team in the majors."

While he did not really clarify himself, he did with this clipped peroration end the controversy. He put down the microphone, went out to the mound to thunderous cheers—and blew the game, giving up three runs and taking the loss in the East's 5–2 victory.

Paige fared better a few weeks later in what would be the last storied performance of his blackball life, or lives. Fittingly, it happened when the two leagues finally revived the Negro League World Series. In fact, this series would be the absolute crest of blackball's own many lives. Matching the two most stalwart teams in the black game's history, the Kansas City Monarchs and

Homestead Grays, blackball's legend and promise would never again reach the heights it did in those seven games.

Opening on September 8 under the arc lights of Griffith Stadium, Paige gave the Monarchs an edge. He retired the first ten batters and went on to beat the Grays 8–0. Then, coming on in relief of Hilton Smith in game two, Paige had a 2–0 lead in the seventh when he gave up a base hit to Jerry Benjamin. Now, with a man on and two out, Paige's inner voice told him the time was ideal to give blackball its all-time climactic rush.

Buck O'Neil, the great Monarch first baseman, was the first to find out what Paige wanted to do. When Satch called him over to the mound, he told Buck that he was going to intentionally walk the next two hitters, Howard Easterling and Buck Leonard, so that he could pitch to Josh Gibson with the bases loaded—thereby making all of blackball history a prelude to this one time at-bat. O'Neil could hardly believe he heard right.

"Aw, man." he told Satch. "You gotta be crazy!"

But the Monarchs' manager, Frank Duncan, could read Paige's mind. When he came to the mound to see what the fuss was about, and learned the plan, he reassured O'Neil.

"Listen, Buck," he said. "You know all these people we got in this ballpark? They came out to see Satchel and Josh. So whatever he wanna do, let him do it."

Actually, there were some serious baseball factors that had led to Paige's derring-do. For one thing, he had almost always handled Josh well, being able to mess with his head and disrupt the big man's concentration, and Gibson was 0-for-7 in the series so far. For another, Josh Gibson was a deeply troubled behemoth.

Gibson's recent excursion to Mexico may not have been worth $800 a month, considering the toll it took on him. Already drinking far too much, both he and Vera Cruz teammate Sam Bankhead openly guzzled case after case of *cerveza* in the dugout during and between games. Although booze could not keep him off the field or quiet his bat, while in Mexico he began to toy with a new, more perilous high: heroin.

The genesis of this desperate turn in his life was Gibson's crumbling relationship with his common-law wife, a woman named Hattie. A stern, rather humorless woman, she had kept his self-abusive tendencies from lurching out of control. But when they separated in the early forties, Josh began an adulterous affair with a Washington, D.C. woman named Grace Fournier, whose husband was stationed overseas during the war.

The antithesis of Hattie Gibson, Grace was a heavy drinker herself, and she and Josh were rarely seen without both smelling of liquor. Worse, Grace was a known narcotics user; during games, she would sit in the stands chain-smoking furiously and shivering, even on hot days, with a heavy blanker pulled over herself and her knees tucked under her chin. And while no one knew exactly why, early in the 1942 season it was all too clear that something was wrong with Josh.

He was tired all the time now, and complained of feeling ill. People around the Homestead Grays said he looked nervous and depressed, and at times seemed to be in a stupor. Once gregarious, he grew more and more sullen and withdrawn. Most shockingly, the lean, hard Gibson had become a fat man, his 225 pounds seemingly all in his belly. The load made it hard for him to squat behind the plate and get up again. He did his catching while standing in a crouch, slightly bent at the knees.

Cum Posey and Gray manager Vic Harris became alarmed at his behavior. Harris once found Gibson in the bullpen during a game, knocking back brews. But because Josh could tear the hide off a ball even with glazed eyes and swaying at the plate, no real disciplinary action was taken against him; nor was there any great concern for his health on the part of his manager and his owner. Harris simply kept Josh out of the lineup when he was too sloshed, mainly to keep from hurting himself. A day later, Josh's head would clear and everyone would act like nothing happened. Indeed, Gibson reportedly hit .323 in league games in 1942, with a league-high 11 home runs in forty games; a year later, his average was said to be no less than .521, with 14 homers, both league highs.

Satchel Paige probably was aware of some, if not all, of Gibson's problems. And while Josh could be a tough out even if he was unconscious, after playing a seamless season in two countries he was in need of a long rest. And so Paige figured now—in game two of the rejuvenated Negro World Series—was the best time to get under Josh's skin. As Buck O'Neil recalled it, as he has a thousand or so times through the years at Negro league reunions, "Satch was talkin' to him. 'Hey, Josh, you remember back when we were playin' wid the Crawfords and you said you was the best hitter in the world and I said I was the best pitcher? I told you then, I said one day we were gonna meet and we'll see what's what.' And Josh said, "Yeah, Satchel, I remember that...."'

"First Satch says, 'All right, Josh, I'm gonna throw you some fastballs'—and Josh says, 'Show me what you got' But now right before he winds up he says, 'Now listen, I'm gonna throw you a fastball letter high'—and, *boom,* it's strike one; Josh didn't move the bat. Satch gets the ball back and says, 'And now I'm gonna throw you one a little faster and belt high'—and, *boom,* strike two. Josh didn't move the bat.

'Now everybody's standin' and goin' crazy. And Satch looks in at Josh and says, 'Okay, now I got you oh and two, and in this league I'm supposed to knock you down. But I'm not gonna throw smoke at yo' yolk—I'm gonna throw a pea at yo' knee'—and, *boom,* strike three; Josh didn't move the bat. And Satch walks off the mound and the crowd is yellin' and screamin' and he walks by me and he says real slow, 'You know what, Buck? Nobody hits Satchel's fastball.'

"Josh didn't know if Satch was jivin' or he was gonna do what he say. Josh never did make up his mind, so he just stood there."

Actually, O'Neill got some of the small details wrong—a not uncommon occurrence when surviving Negro leaguers get together to tell magnificent stories and lies about old times. According to the *Afro*'s game story, Gibson did in fact swing, fouling off the first two pitches and then "whiffing" on the third. But the only detail that matters was the one announced by the *Afro* headline: "Satch Fans Josh Gibson With Three on Bases." In the blackball warp, it was as mythically perfect as Babe Ruth "calling his shot" in the 1932 World Series.

This historic deed filed away, Paige could not afford to fail in the rest of the series. After Hilton Smith started for the Monarchs and won game three, 8–4, Paige took the ball for game four, which was played in Yankee Stadium according to the normal blackball preference of going where the big gate was, even if it meant going to New York in the middle of a World Series between Pittsburgh and Kansas City. Satch won 9–3.

Game five, with the Monarchs a win away from the title, was in Kansas City's Ruppert Park, and Paige demanded the ball yet again. This time, though, the Grays got to him; staving off their doom, they took him down to a 4–1 defeat. But this game really began when the last out was made. Because Cum Posey happened to have signed four new players on the eve of the game—three Newark Eagles, including pitcher Leon Day and the Philadelphia Stars' Bus Clarkson—J. L. Wilkinson lodged a protest with both leagues after the loss, on grounds that Posey had used "ringers."

Posey insisted that Tom Baird, the Monarchs' co-owner and general manager, had agreed to the last-minute signings, in exchange for certain "demands." Baird said he agreed to no such thing, and the game was voided, though it stood as one more example of Negro league tomfoolery.

Paige was slated to start again in the replayed fifth game. But when it began in Philadelphia's Shibe park, he was paying a $20 traffic ticket in Lancaster, Pennsylvania, having been pulled off the road by a state trooper for speeding en route to the ballpark. But as soon as he put on his uniform, Frank Duncan, with the Monarchs down 5–4 in the third inning, rushed him to the mound—just in time, if fate had cooperated, to face Josh Gibson in a rematch of their epic confrontation.

However, Josh, his body aching, had come out of the game in the top of the inning. Satch struck out his overmatched replacement. Robert Gatson, then allowed only two Grays to reach base, both on walks, over the rest of the game, winning 9–5 and making the Monarchs the world's colored champions at a time when it actually mattered to carry that designation. Paige, at thirty-six, with his baffling array of pitches, was now a complete pitcher.

But if Paige believed his whim was still blackball's command, he soon learned otherwise. Prior to the 1944 East-West Game, acting expressly to co-opt Paige's bargaining leverage—and any that the other All-Stars might have—the owners in both leagues relieved the fans of their well-exercised voting power and chose the East-West Game participants themselves. Thus Paige could not successfully make any exorbitant demands on J. L. Wilkinson.

This was a risky move, given the symbolic power of black suffrage in any form. Commissioners J. B. Martin and Tom Wilson insisted the new rule was not made to avoid the sentiment of the fans, but to reward unsung but deserving players. At the same time, Martin and Wilson had the good sense to divert any player dissent by arranging the first serious pay scale for the game: $200 per player, $300 per manager, and a pool of $300 per club to be split by players not chosen for the East-West Game.

Although these figures were much less than the owners' shares, the money-starved players eagerly accepted the terms—all, of course, save one. But Paige, who could no longer justify his avarice by pointing to the will of the fans, had to know he had been outfoxed when his usual demand for a cut of the gate and an advance was rejected by Negro American League Commissioner J. B. Martin. Paige then tried to bluff in order to cast himself in a better light. On the day before the 1944 East-West Game, Paige said that unless *all* the proceeds from the contest went to the Army-Navy Relief Fund, "I'm gonna lead a walkout and they won't have any East-West Game."

By now, this annual event had reached the point where no man could tarnish it. The East-West game outdrew the white All-Star Game in 1938, 1942, and 1943, and would do so again in 1946 and 1947. In 1943, 46,327 fans—a quarter of them white—had come to Comiskey Park, compared with the 29,589 who attended the white big league game at Forbes Field. J. B. Martin, fully aware that the East-West Game was bigger than Satchel Paige, called his bluff, declaring Paige ineligible for the 1944 year's game. And while Paige won some sympathy in the black press, which misconstrued his cynical proposal as a patriotic gesture, soon afterward his reckless habits were recognized as pure avarice.

That 1944 East-West Game, in fact, marked the end of Satchel Paige's Negro league reign as icon and thorn. Although he remained as a part-time pitcher with the Kansas City Monarchs, he spent most of the next several seasons on the barnstorming trails, toiling for semipro teams that would offer substantial sums for three innings of diffident work. Out of spite, he avoided all future East-West Games, but his absence was less and less conspicuous with each passing year.

When Paige did take a turn with the Monarchs, his indifference on the mound drew little tolerance, but vicious criticism, from blackball aficionados, who now expected no-nonsense professionalism. In 1945, Paige was scheduled to pitch before a large crowd in Forbes Field, but pulled out, claiming a sore arm. The *Courier* lambasted him for making "suckers of the fans....He made 'em turn out, and then crane their necks like a flock of kangaroos looking for him [even though] they had paid their hard-earned dough to see him pitch....

"He's the 'Great Satchel,' the man who has received more than any other player in the history of Negro ball for doing less."

In the past, excellent pitchers like Hilton Smith and Booker McDaniel had suffered the indignity of pretending to be Satchel Paige in certain games when Paige was billed to pitch but neglected to show up, or else being called on to relieve him after his requisite three innings of work. Now, Smith and McDaniel refused to carry on the charade. Yet, though Satchel did little to encourage it, the Paige legend continued. For Smith in particular, it mocked his wounded ego.

"I won a hundred and sixty-one games and lost twenty-two, but most people never heard of me; they've only heard of Satchel," Smith said in the 1980s. Smith expressed some common misgivings about Paige, giving voice to the private sentiments of other Negro leaguers who never spoke ill of him, keeping the faith these men shared about maintaining a united front.

"I took my baseball seriously," he said. "I just went out there to do a job. But Satch was an 'attraction'; he could produce and so he'd clown a lot." Of being a stand-in for Paige for so many years, Smith said quietly, "I guess it really hurt me...but there wasn't anything I could do about it."

While it was too late for Hilton Smith to crawl out from under the Paige shadow—an arm injury ended his career in the midforties—the black game could offer many new attractions, both players and teams. The 1942 Negro World Series, in fact, was the last time the two patriarchal franchises, the Monarchs and the Grays, would meet for a title.

Cum Posey's team took the next two championships, beating the Birmingham Black Barons both times. And, in 1945, the year of military victory, the Cleveland Buckeyes—owned by black numbers man Ernie Wright and led by player-manager Quincy Trouppe; outfielder San Jethroe, the league leader in hitting and stolen bases; and pitcher George Jefferson—rose from the second-tier of the Negro American league to win both halves of the league schedule, then ran the Grays off the field four straight in the Negro World Series, the last two games by scores of 4–0 and 5–0.

All of black baseball rode out the war years in high style. Just before the war, having operated at a loss for seven straight years, the Negro National league's cash flow was down to $159.23, and team dues were rarely being paid. But from 1942 to 1945, every team cleared at least $25,000 in profits each year, and J. L. Wilkinson routinely collected $100,000. In 1942, the teams had spent a combined $500,000 on operating expenses, compared with the pittance of $175,000 that Effa Manley had complained about in the late thirties—and the leagues still came out ahead when blackball rang up its first $2 million season in gate receipts.

But as the Negro league owners dreamed about their stake in baseball's coming democracy, a new name in the ranks would rise to the surface and upset all the calculations, in both the black and white games.

The cataclysmic events that would deliver baseball into its modern age would take the game completely by surprise. Indeed, the cycle of dashed hopes and broken promises seemed never-ending. In 1944, Bill Veeck Jr., the rakehell son of former Chicago Cub president Bill Veeck, tried to purchase the debt-ridden, doormat Philadelphia Phillies. Veeck put together a group of investors, made an attractive offer for the team, and came to an agreement with the club's owner, Gerry Nugent.

However, the deal fell through—along with big league integration—after Veeck (acting "out of respect for Judge Landis," he later said) informed the commissioner of his intention to bring black ballplayers to the Phillies, starting immediately. Veeck reflected, "With Satchel Paige, Roy Campanella, Monte Irvin, and countless others...I had not the slightest doubt that in 1944, a war year, the Phillies would have leaped from seventh place to the pennant."

But the very morning after he met with Landis, Veeck was stunned to hear that Gerry Nugent had sold the club to the National League, and that league president Ford Frick had awarded the franchise to a man named William Cox, whose offer was approximately one-half of Veeck's. According to Veeck, Landis was surely behind this betrayal and had even taken a bow for preventing Veeck from "contaminating the league." (Exactly what William Cox brought to the league was seen in his first year as an owner, when a red-faced Landis banned Cox for betting on his team's games.)

Cold-blooded though it was, when Kenesaw Mountain Landis died of a heart attack just after the 1944 season, opponents of the color line took hope that the long night of segregation would soon end. The new commissioner, the effervescent A. B. "Happy" Chandler, had come to prominence as the governor of Kentucky and had upheld the state's policy of separate schools for black children. But Chandler began his new job repeating the right bromides about integration, and, unlike Landis, vowed to make it happen.

"If a black boy can make it on Okinawa and Guadalcanal, hell, he can make it in baseball," Chandler told the *Pittsburgh Courier*'s Ric Roberts, adding, "Once I tell you something, brother, I never change. You can count on me."

The problem was that the pliant Chandler appeared to be less in charge of the game than were some of its powerful executives. New York Yankee president Larry MacPhail—an adamant race obstructionist—seemed to regard himself as the de facto commissioner, with veto power over the race issue. In March 1945, at the urging of the *Afro*'s Sam Lacy, the white majors erected an advisory panel, the Major League Committee on Baseball Integration. Its members included Philadelphia court magistrate and Pennsylvania state athletic commissioner Joseph P. Rainey—Effa Manley's candidate for Negro National League president in 1942, and a future president of the NAACP—and the two most influential white team executives: Larry MacPhail and Branch Rickey.

Few knew it at the time, but the latter two men were the main forces at work during this precarious time for baseball integration—although the major revelation would have been that Branch Rickey was going to break the logjam.

A former mediocre catcher with the St. Louis Browns, and manager and then general manager for the St. Louis Cardinals in the twenties, Branch Wesley Rickey was an original, even if nobody could quite figure out what made him tick. Born on an Ohio farm, he was a devout and overly pious man who even as team president refused to attend Sunday games. A stickler for prim and priggish rites of politeness, Rickey required that people address him as "Mr. Rickey." But as Branch Rickey ascended the baseball ladder, this brusque man with bushy eyebrows and a dramatic flair in speech and manner became famous for some decidedly unchristian traits—such as ruthlessness, self-aggrandizement, and a lack of concern for league rules when he felt they should be bent.

Many people have attempted through the years to explain Rickey's hybrid nature. *Time* once called him a crossbreed of Phineas T. Barnum and Billy Sunday. But the best one-word description of Branch Rickey came from *New York Star* sportswriter Tom Meany. Borrowing from John Gunther's description of Mahatma Gandhi—whom Gunther called "a combination of God, your father, and a Tammany Hall leader"—Meany branded Rickey, for eternity, as "the Mahatma."

Rickey was also an undisputed baseball savant, and his instructions to players at his "baseball camps" about the correct way to hit, slide, and run the bases became standard lore throughout the game. Rickey practically drew the blueprint for major league farm systems and scouting operations, and the $100,000 salary, plus stock options, the Dodgers gave him to come to the Brooklyn front office in 1942 made him better paid than any two of the game's highest-paid players combined.

It was, and still is, unclear if Rickey had any hard, inbred principles about race. In coming years, he was only too happy to ascend the pedestal built for him as baseball's great liberator. "I don't mean to be a crusader," Rickey disclaimed modestly in 1945, then went on with sweeping nobility, "My only purpose is to be fair to all people and my selfish objective is to win baseball games....

"The greatest untapped reservoir of raw material in the history of the game is the black race. The Negroes will make us winners for years to come. And for that I will happily bear being called a bleeding heart and a do-gooder and all that humanitarian rot."

Another time, Rickey solemnly avowed: "I couldn't face my God much longer knowing that His black creatures are held separate and distinct from His white creatures in the game that has given me all I own."

If Rickey wanted to mine that "reservoir of raw material" he spoke of, however, his way of going about it seemed not very different from that of any other white executive. In March 1945, just seven months before he announced Jackie Robinson's signing, Rickey's Dodgers were working out at the team's wartime spring training camp at Bear Mountain, New York. With no advance word, Joe Bostic, sports editor of the black New York newspaper

People's Voice, showed up with two veteran Negro league players—
Philadelphia Star pitcher Terris McDuffie and New York Cuban
outfielder Dave "Showboat" Thomas—and boldly demanded
tryouts for them. As Bostic recalled, Rickey's reaction was to go
"berserk almost, with fury," for being put on the spot.

Rickey finally allowed the tryouts, but like Chester Washington's
experience with Bill Benswanger in Pittsburgh, the expedition was
cursed. If Terris McDuffie, Effa Manley's erstwhile paramour, had
passed his prime at age thirty-four—he compiled no better than a
5–6 record in 1944—Thomas at thirty-nine was positively moldy.
Bostic himself admitted many years later to author Jules Tygiel, in
Baseballs Great Experiment: Jackie Robinson and His Legacy, that his
main aim was to create a scene that would serve as the "psychological breaking of the conspiracy of silence" in baseball.

Most observers took the affair for the publicity stunt it was, and
the fact that a photographer from the Communist Party's *Daily
Worker* came along with Bostic to Bear Mountain made for an easy
dismissal. But while the reason for Rickey's sputtering rage would
soon be understood, at the time it appeared to be no more than
another white response to integration.

Indeed, only a week later, a different black sportswriter, Wendell Smith, arranged another tryout for three black players, this
time with the Boston Red Sox. These players were far more
worthy than McDuffie and Thomas, since Jackie Robinson, about
to join up with the Kansas City Monarchs that season, was one of
them, along with the Cleveland Buckeyes' Sam Jethroe and the
Philadelphia Stars second baseman Marvin Williams. But this
tryout, too, proved a futile exercise. The manager of the Sox, Joe
Cronin—who was not even present for the sham tryout—freely
admitted years later that it was a waste of time, since "We all
thought that because of the times it was good to have separate
[black and white] leagues."

Among white owners, Larry MacPhail confirmed that view.
Although MacPhail was once a baseball visionary—as general
manager of the Cincinnati Reds, he brought night ball to the white
majors in 1935—he was now a rigid conservative. Not incidentally, of course, his New York Yankee employers were handsomely
enriched by those huge audiences at Yankee Stadium for Negro
league games. Through MacPhail's stalling, the Major League

Committee on Baseball Integration never held a session, and with MacPhail feeling the heat on the race issue, he wrote with alarm to Commissioner Chandler that baseball had a "problem" all right, but it was not denial of human rights as much as the imposition of Negroes being forced into its ranks.

MacPhail noted that the situation was becoming "increasingly serious and acute," and stressed, "we can't stick our heads in the sand and ignore the problem. If we do, we will have colored players in the minor leagues in 1945 and in the major leagues shortly thereafter."

MacPhail was remarkably prescient, though when he wrote those words he, like everyone else, was in the dark about Branch Rickey's clandestine activities to crack the color barrier. Not that there hadn't been some clues about Rickey. In retrospect, the near seizure he had when Joe Bostic showed up at Bear Mountain with two black ballplayers occurred because Bostic threatened to expose Rickey's plans before he himself was ready to do so. Sam Lacy later received another clue when the reporter complained to Rickey about MacPhail's obstruction. "Well, Sam," Rickey told him, "maybe we'll forget about Mr. MacPhail. Maybe we'll just give up on him and let nature take its course."

Only a few weeks into the 1945 season, Rickey tantalizingly said he had an announcement to make about blacks and baseball. But, far from signing a black player to a contract, Rickey revealed that he had formed a team to play in the United States League, an all-black circuit being formed by black and white businessmen that was scheduled to begin the season in May.

The establishment of this Negro league was a mystery and conundrum to everybody on both sides of the color line—no doubt just as Branch Rickey had planned it. As Rickey himself defined the new league, it would sharply differ from the two extant Negro leagues: Contracts would be standardized, schedules made uniform, rowdyism curbed, and ownership held to a higher class of people.

Rickey lent the Dodgers' name and a fraction of the club's resources to the league's Brooklyn Brown Dodgers, who would have the use of Ebbets Field when the white Dodgers were on the road. But Rickey would commit to no loftier ideal than speculating that the U.S. League might possibly wiggle into the organized baseball structure someday, and he allowed only that some of the league's better players could conceivably find their way onto white major league rosters.

This very scheme had in fact been bandied about before in white big league circles. The plan was that under the guise of "cleaning up" the black game, either by buying an existing team or creating a new league, white owners could recruit the black game's most promising talent. Rickey had come close to openly embracing that plan when he'd decried the two Negro leagues for being "in the zone of a racket," by which he'd meant to lampoon shady black owners, and, ironically, blackball's reliance on white booking agents as overlords, whose existence—as Effa Manley feared would happen—furnished the proof that the entrenched black owners deserved neither recognition nor rights as legitimate businessmen.

The initial reaction to the new league was vast cynicism, and even anger, on both sides of the divide. In the black press, which had become increasingly militant about the issue, sentiment ran high that this was yet another cynical white attempt to gain profits generated by black players. In the *Defender*, Frank A. Young attacked Rickey for "assum[ing] the role of an Abraham Lincoln in Negro baseball," and took a stand against "hav[ing] any major league owners running any segregated leagues for us."

Taking note of the team nicknames in the new league—which in addition to the Brown Dodgers also included the (Chicago) Brown Bombers—Young pointedly remonstrated, "We have enough 'black' this and 'brown' that...and we don't need any more."

To Rickey's white critics, the move smacked of opportunism, designed to play to the hopes and pocketbooks of black fans in Brooklyn—a suspicion held as well by many Negro league people, who believed that Rickey primarily wanted to loosen those fans' loyalties to Negro league games at Yankee Stadium and bring them to his borough. This body of opinion believed that playing the race card was the worst kind of pandering.

Small wonder, then, that Rickey wanted his other racial initiatives to remain a secret. Even the apparently trivial business of the U.S. League was chancy, since Rickey, like all the white executives, took very seriously and potential risk of alienating white fans and southern white players, of whom the Dodgers had many.

Actually, it was two years before, in 1943, that Rickey had decided to investigate the possibility of including black players in the Dodgers' future, a decision made somewhat easier by the club's fall from contention and the need to rebuild the team. When Rickey obtained the approval of the Dodger owners and the team's board of directors to proceed with his covert plans, such was the delicacy of even this germ of an idea that all concerned swore themselves to secrecy, not even telling their own families about it. And Rickey told only a handful of his front office staff. His son, Branch Rickey Jr., the club's farm director, beseeched his father not to go forward, fearing that Dodger scouting missions in the South would face hostility if the plans were ever made public.

The Mahatma ignored him. He sent his scouts throughout the United States, Puerto Rico, Mexico, and Cuba to bird-dog black players for the United States League, with the understanding that the scouts were to do it as surreptitiously as possible. The reports they sent back to Rickey covered the entire range of blackball, from evergreens like Satchel Paige, Josh Gibson, and Buck Leonard, to young veterans like Baltimore Elite Giant catcher Roy Campanella, Cleveland Buckeye outfielder Sam Jethroe, and Birmingham Black Baron outfielder Piper Davis, to youngbloods with presence and maturity.

As the search continued, Rickey narrowed the list down to Campanella, rookie Newark Eagle pitcher Don Newcombe, and Kansas City Monarch shortstop Jackie Robinson.

All three men had the background and character virtues that Rickey was looking for. Campanella, at twenty-four, was the son of an African-American mother and Italian father, and though he was the most closely associated with the dread Negro leagues—having already played nine seasons with Tom Wilson's Elite Giants—"Campy" had grown up playing baseball on integrated teams, which could ease his entry to white big league life.

The nineteen-year-old Newcombe was a huge right-hander with a torrid fastball, and while he was tough and wily for his years, Rickey knew he would need more time to grow into the manhood necessary to withstand the enormous pressures of the big leagues. That left Rickey with the oldest, least tainted by a blackball connection, and the most suited by intelligence and temperament to walk the minefields with grace and a cool head—and to understand why he had to do so. Possessed of all these qualities, twenty-six-year-old Jack Roosevelt Robinson was the chosen son.

Robinson was Dodger scout Clyde Sukeforth's man. Sukeforth, a former major league player, scouted him all during the spring and summer of 1945 as Robinson traveled with the Kansas City Monarchs. Finally, by late August of 1945, Rickey advised Sukeforth of the biggest decision any baseball man had ever made, and sent the scout to Chicago to meet up with Robinson before a Monarch game at Comiskey Park. Sukeforth told Robinson that Rickey was about to offer him a Dodger contract, but that Rickey wanted to meet with him personally in Brooklyn.

Late that afternoon, player and scout boarded a train for New York. Their trip must have passed in a surreal fog of anticipation and angst. For this was a journey not only across land but through a new portal of history, one that would not end in Flatbush.

19

A Good Democratic Shock

I'm ready to take the chance. Maybe I'm doing something for my race.
—Jackie Robinson, *The Sporting News*, November 1, 1945

Every time I see the Dodgers get beat I say they don't deserve to win for what they did to Negro baseball.
—Effa Manley, 1978

Although Branch Rickey labored for long months choosing his pilgrim, it seems inconceivable in hindsight that any African-American ballplayer but Jackie Robinson could possibly have been considered. By every empirical or intuitive measure, Robinson not only qualified for the role Rickey chose for him—he seemed to be born expressly for challenging hoary rituals with uncommon dignity and valor.

All his young adult life, Robinson had to live with crude constraints placed on his burgeoning athletic abilities. Born in Georgia and raised in Pasadena, California, Robinson's two years at UCLA in the early forties were a major portent of where he was headed; the school's first four-letter man, he excelled in just about every sport ever invented, including "nonblack" ones like golf and swimming.

Robinson's blood surely carried the tonic of greatness—his older brother, Mack, was a member of the triumphant U.S. track-and-field team in the 1936 Olympics in Berlin, and placed second

273

to Jesse Owens in the 200-meter dash. But when Mack returned home, the only job he could find was as a janitor. Similarly, despite Jackie's conquests at UCLA—which earned him the sobriquet of "the Jim Thorpe of his race"—when he had to drop out of school to help support his indigent mother, the celebrated all-American halfback could be found running the ball for the Los Angeles Bulldogs, a semipro barnstorming team.

Robinson's most serious preparation for the white big league thresher came when he was drafted into the U.S. Army in 1942. Stationed at Fort Riley, Kansas, Robinson was stunned to learn that, in spite of his education and high intelligence scores, he was rejected for entry to officers candidate school. Undeterred, he took his case to Joe Louis, who was also stationed at Fort Riley; within days, the Department of War reversed the decision and Robinson earned promotion to lieutenant.

In Fort Riley's racial climate, black GIs could play football with white GIs on the base, but not baseball. Although Robinson was asked to play on the camp's gridiron team, he refused, even when ordered to play by the camp colonel, in order to protest the baseball prohibition. When Robinson was named morale officer for black soldiers at the camp, he tried to increase seating for blacks in the segregated PX and got into a heated argument with a white officer who said he didn't want his wife "sitting next to a nigger." Regarded as a troublemaker, Robinson was eventually transferred to Fort Hood, Texas.

There, as military racism blended with the Jim Crow locale, Robinson got himself into serious trouble. Boarding a bus outside camp, he was told by the driver to move to the back, "where the colored people belong." He resisted, was arrested by military police, and was brought before a court martial in July 1944. Robinson defended himself eloquently, pointing out that the army had recently prohibited segregation in its ranks. The charges were dropped, and Robinson won an honorable discharge.

These qualities—fierce, righteous anger and the presence of mind to win over enemies with his intellect—impressed Branch Rickey, far more even than Robinson's exploits on the field with the Kansas City Monarchs. Brought onto that team by Hilton Smith during one of the Monarchs' sojourns to the California Winter League, Jackie was a thoroughly competent infielder and hitter—he hit a reported .345 with 5 home runs and 13 stolen bases in 1945 and was the starting shortstop for the West in that year's East-West Game—but was constantly bothered by a sore shoulder.

If Rickey and Clyde Sukeforth, the Dodgers' scout, had consulted the Monarch players or coaches about Robinson, which they did not care to do, they would have heard that he was no giant among these men. Having already experienced mainstream adulation while at UCLA, Robinson did not allow himself to fit into the brotherhood-in-misery Negro league mind-set. By his surly isolation from his teammates and complaints about playing conditions, he made it clear that blackball was no more appropriate for him than the Los Angeles Bulldogs had been.

On the Monarchs, the feeling of loathing was quite mutual. Few players tried to get close to Robinson, and all resented the fact that J. L. Wilkinson, attempting to replace Satchel Paige as the drawing card, immediately instructed manager Frank Duncan to play the attractive Jackie Robinson at shortstop—replacing Jesse Williams, an all-star at the position who was probably the most popular Monarch. Robinson, a religious man who neither drank nor smoked, nonetheless displayed flashes of temper on and off the field that upset his teammates. To Branch Rickey, though, Robinson's alienation from the team and the Negro leagues in general was all to the good.

Robinson's meeting with Rickey in the latter's office on August 28, 1945 has become one of sports' most famous one-act dramas. In part this legend was due to Robinson himself, who portrayed himself in the 1950 movie of his life, *The Jackie Robinson Story*, imbuing the meeting scene with the stuff of legend. The celluloid Rickey gets right in Robinson's face, screaming at him the sort of verbal epithets Jackie would hear from day one in the white game, trying to provoke him. When Robinson asks, "Mr. Rickey, do you want a ballplayer who's afraid to fight back?" Rickey rages, "I want a player with guts enough *not* to fight back!" Rickey then poses the possibility that a white player might come sliding into Robinson with spikes up and a fist aimed at his cheek.

"Well, Mr. Rickey," Robinson replies smartly, "I've got another cheek."

According to Clyde Sukeforth, who was a witness to the meeting, the movie version was accurate. As the scout related the tense atmosphere of the meeting to author Jules Tygiel, Rickey "was so engrossed in Robinson...he didn't hear a damn word I said." Beginning his game of baiting Robinson, Rickey at first "stared at [Robinson] as if he were trying to get inside the man. And Jack stared right back at him."

For Robinson, this three-hour audition was his finest moment, since he later admitted in his memoirs that Rickey's hard and unrelenting gaze made him feel "almost naked," and that the Mahatma's playacting "was so convincing that I found myself chain-gripping my fingers behind my back." But when Robinson stood up to Rickey's barrage and clearly demonstrated that upon encountering the inevitable virulent acts of racism he would be able to keep his head cool, Rickey knew he had picked the right man to integrate America's National Pastime.

The contract details were more mundane. Robinson would receive a salary of $600 a month with the Montreal Royals, and a $3,500 signing bonus. This was $200 more than Jackie had been making with the Monarchs, but the money was deemed irrelevant by Rickey. Indeed, for the Mahatma, the most significant contract language was the stipulation that from here on in Robinson had no "written or moral obligation" to any other club—meaning that Robinson was not only free and clear of any further liability with the Monarchs, but that the Monarchs were due not one penny in compensation from the Dodgers. By the inclusion of this clause, precedent was set that would raze the Negro leagues as a functioning commercial enterprise.

After Robinson signed the contract, Rickey handed him a copy of Italian philosopher Giovanni Papini's book *The Life of Christ*. He then instructed Jackie to study the passage entitled "Nonresistance" and sent him on his way to Kansas City—with Robinson sworn to keep the liaison a secret to all but his wife and his mother. Other details remained to be settled before Rickey would deem the time right to go public.

The last thing Rickey wanted was a premature announcement that would make the event seem precipitous. Furthermore, sensing the worst, Rickey preferred that player contracts for 1946 be sent out and signed before the Jackie Robinson bomb exploded in Brooklyn. For the time being, Robinson's isolation in the Negro leagues proved an added benefit as Jackie wasn't close enough to anyone to spill the secret. Although no one knew it was an omen, Robinson and the Kansas City Monarchs continued to go their separate ways. And Rickey could carry on with his interest in the

United States League, one that was now purely diversionary.

In Rickeyan fashion, he carried on the elaborate U.S. League ruse in full gear. Not scrimping on costs, he had hired the great Negro league autocrat Oscar Charleston to manage the Brown Dodgers, and made certain to tout the team and the league to the New York sporting press. But, unknown to Rickey's fellow U.S. League guardians, in perpetuating this con, Rickey was plotting nothing less than the destruction of blackball in its entirety.

Rickey even had his own Judas. Negro league people could see through Rickey's tirade about "cleaning up" the black game once the U.S. League was up and running. Indeed, Rickey had no objection that the owner of the Pittsburgh team—the new Pittsburgh Crawfords—was an old stalwart of blackball corruption.

With Rickey providing the entree, Gus Greenlee was back in town.

In Gus Greenlee, Branch Rickey may not have had a man of virtue, but for Rickey's purposes Greenlee was something better: a man thirsting for vengeance against the existing Negro leagues. For Gus, his old brethren, the owners, were ingrates who took his league and his team away from him after he had gone to the wall for all of them. By being taken into Branch Rickey's confidence—or so he believed—Gus was sure he had found the road back to glory.

If the U.S. League was Rickey's Trojan Horse, it was also Greenlee's mule with which to kick Cum Posey in the pants. In fact, the new league owed its life more to Gus's vengeance than to Rickey's pragmatism. In 1940, with Greenlee a year in exile, Gus had tried to reenter the Negro National League's high council with a new idea—to stock a reconstituted Crawfords not with proven players but, as in the team's embryonic days, with sandlot stars. Posey, luxuriating in his hard-won resurgence to power, brushed off Gus's entreaty, then did so again in 1941, 1942, and 1943. Giving up his crusade to get back into the Negro leagues, Greenlee threatened to "wipe out" the men he damned for "ruining" his grand old league.

At the 1944 East-West Game, Greenlee could be found in the shadows, working as a provocateur, egging on the players to demand more money from the owners and fueling walkout speculation. Gus hoped to tear apart the two leagues. When that failed, he launched the U.S. League and began doing what he had done in the past to build the legendary Crawford teams—in the proud tradition of blackball, he raided the two leagues' clubs.

Branch Rickey's indulgences fortified a determined Gus Greenlee. When Rickey became a participant, the U.S. League had begun to congeal. Soon eight teams came into existence, with an assortment of black and white owners. As it happened, few marquee-name players joined the league. Besides Oscar Charleston, the only bona-fide name was Bingo DeMoss, whose resumé stretched back to the days of Topeka Jack Johnson and C. I. Taylor. DeMoss went to the Chicago Brown Bombers as manager. Despite the lack of glamour, press attention was assured because of Rickey's association, and the league began play on schedule in May 1945—and immediately started drowning in debt.

Rickey stayed with the U.S. League until rigor mortis began to set in. By then, in midsummer of 1945, nearing closure on the Jackie Robinson exercise, he withdrew from an active role. It was obvious the Brooklyn Brown Dodgers would not return for the 1946 season, if one took place. Gus Greenlee now knew that Rickey had deserted him. If Gus planned to hack away at his old enemies, he would be using an axe without a handle. Gus continued operating the circuit, but by the end of the 1946 season, when the U.S. League went out of business, it is doubtful that anyone in baseball even knew it was still around.

Branch Rickey, meanwhile, was amazingly successful in keeping the Robinson signing a secret. Indeed, he might have been able to put off the announcement until after New Year's Day of 1946 had not politicians discovered the salability of baseball integration as a campaign issue.

Prodded by civil rights groups, the Fair Employment Practices Act (FEPA) was passed by the New York State Legislature in 1945. This followed by months the passage of the Quinn-Ives Act banning discrimination in hiring. The latter statute empowered a committee to investigate violations of the law, and one of the committee's targets was baseball. In the early fall of 1945, it issued a public call for the three New York teams to end discrimination in hiring black players. At the same time, Mayor Fiorello La Guardia made a grandstand play of his own with the formation of the Mayor's Commission on Baseball. Originally, both Branch Rickey and Larry MacPhail were members, but they dropped out, for opposite reasons, when La Guardia pressed for a report announcing that "baseball will shortly begin signing Negro players."

For Rickey, the idea that political pressure, and not his meticulous planning, would be credited as the force that liberated baseball was galling and unacceptable—not just to his vanity but, he felt, to the cause as well. Thus, Rickey hurriedly modified his plans. On October 22, he called Robinson and told him to catch a flight to Montreal. The next day, it fell to Hector Racine, president of the International League's Montreal Royals, to make the fateful announcement of Jackie Robinson's signing with the Dodger organization.

Racine had called together the local press by saying no more than that he had something "very important" to tell them. But no one could have foreseen the nature of this news. When Racine brought Jackie Robinson into the room, it was likely the last time Robinson had any degree of anonymity for the rest of his life, and that lasted only a few minutes before Racine told the two dozen reporters assembled that Robinson had been signed to a contract. "We are signing this boy," said Racine to a perfectly stunned room, "because we think of him primarily as a ballplayer," and because "we think it a point of fairness."

Branch Rickey was not in Montreal that day; trying still to downplay the story—as he would for the next six months, or right up until Robinson put on a Brooklyn uniform—the Mahatma sent to the press conference his son, Branch Jr., the Dodgers' farm director who had so vehemently opposed the move.

Now, however, Branch Jr. took the floor and pronounced the new Dodger farmhand "a fine type of young man," "intelligent," and "college-bred"—all code words designed to soothe the baseball establishment. Though Rickey Jr. acknowledged that Robinson would face hellish attacks in the South and from some players throughout the white game, the young executive made it clear that the clock was running out on intolerance. Choosing an apt metaphor, he said that any player who quit the game rather than change with the times would be left behind to work "in a cotton mill."

Robinson, as was his style, faced the occasion with a regal bearing and a fetching wit. "I am some sort of guinea pig," he said easily. "But, hopefully, I'm going to be the best guinea pig that ever lived, both on the field and off." In an interview with Wendell Smith for the November 3 edition of the *Pittsburgh Courier*, Robinson accepted the heavy vestment of race empowerment. "I will not forget that I am representative of a whole race of people who are pulling for me."

With the secret now out, the reaction to the Robinson signing in the press, black and white, reflected the general sentiment on both sides of the game. While the white papers barely reacted to what many white Americans regarded as simply having been inevitable, the Negro papers rang in a bacchanalia of excitement.

The *Amsterdam News*, already looking ahead, described the signing as "just a drop of water in the drought that keeps faith alive in American institutions." NAACP president Roy Wilkins, in his syndicated newspaper column, envisioned a Robinson in a uniform made more of sackcloth than flannel, and the man more apostle than ballplayer.

"The millions who read box scores very likely have never heard of George Washington Carver," Wilkins wrote. "But Jackie Robinson, if he makes the grade, will be doing missionary work with these people that Carver could never do. He will be saying to them that his people should have their rights, should have jobs, decent hours and education, freedom from insult, and equality of opportunity to achieve."

In its editorial in the November 3 issue, the black *Michigan Chronical* declared, "Southern white boys who may be shocked will recover in due time...a good democratic shock in the right place might do them a lot of good."

Branch Rickey also came in for his share of praise in the black press. One such tribute came from the usually sardonic Dan Burley, who in the December 1945 issue of *The Crisis* provided Rickey with a new nickname—the "John Brown of baseball." Burley lionized Rickey as a "deeply religious man with the fire of a crusader burning in his breast." The *Courier* concurred, exclaiming that Rickey "stood up and defied a baseball world he knew would be rebellious" and "was motivated by a firm conviction within that he was doing the right thing."

Other voices, however, were not so sure that Rickey's motivations were pristine. The timing of the Robinson announcement— coming in the maelstrom of the Mayor's Commission, the Quinn-

Ives Act, and FEPA—suggested to some that Rickey had been forced to act. This deduction overlooked the complete failure to act on the race issue by Larry MacPhail's Yankees and the New York Giants. And yet it allowed people like MacPhail himself to posture against change, claiming he would not be pressured or descent to the level of a vulgar publicity stunt.

Longtime integration foes played heavily on these sophisms. J. G. Taylor Spink, trying immediately to dampen any bandwagon effect that might develop to sign black players, cautioned in the November 1 edition of the *Sporting News* that the response to Robinson's breaking the segregation barrier was "out of proportion to the actual value of the story." He branded the signing a "legalistic move" rather than a moral or practical one. Spink declared that "the racial problem in baseball was as far from a satisfactory solution as ever."

What's more, even Rickey found use for the fiction that the devil and not his conscience made him do it. When Rickey explained to Dodger players at spring training in 1946 why he had signed Robinson, he had to confront some players' discontent over the signing, most vocally expressed by southern Dodgers like Dixie Walker, Bobby Bragan, and Kirby Higbe. He shrunk from his picaresque public stance and cited the Quinn-Ives Act as a contributing factor.

Rickey was also faulted with the claim that Robinson simply was not good enough to merit such attention. When Robinson went to Montreal, he was dogged by predictions of failure from numerous white baseball "experts" who had seen little of him on the field. Bob Feller, who had barnstormed over the previous winter with his own major league All-Star team and played against a Negro team fronted by Robinson—and cut short the series of games between the teams when Robinson demanded more money than Feller was willing to give him—offered no support. Feller said Robinson had "football shoulders" and "couldn't hit an inside pitch to save his neck." While Feller maintained that "I hope he makes good," he concluded, "I don't think he will."

Reading these quotes, Robinson was almost amused. Pointing out that he had faced Feller in exactly two games, he noted, "If you lined up ten of us [black players], I'll bet he couldn't pick me out of the bunch."

Still, whatever the spirit in which the comments were offered, they were not made only by whites. Many Negro leaguers shared in private these evaluations of Robinson's qualifications. Years later, Homestead's Buck Leonard admitted that the general feeling around blackball about Robinson was not kind. "We thought we had other ballplayers who were better," he said. There was even some talk that Jackie may have been chosen because he would have the best chance of *failing*, thereby staining the name of all black players and stopping the experiment in its tracks.

In truth, most of the opinion about who deserved the promotion was woefully out of touch on both sides of the game. Here, in 1946, was J. G. Taylor Spink, in "The Bible of Baseball," promulgating the preposterous claim that there was "not a single Negro player with major league capabilities." The fact that a Bob Feller could adjudge Satchel Paige and Josh Gibson as the only Negroes qualified for the white majors was absurd enough; it reflected more pathetically on blackball that these two icons—one over forty, the other crumbling by the day—were still being offered up as better candidates than Robinson by no less than Cum Posey and J. L. Wilkinson.

For his part, Paige handled such effusive praise with common sense, realizing that white hard-liners may have been using him merely to denigrate Robinson. Although he could not help feeling hurt that he was overlooked, and while he too was unconvinced about Robinson's talents, Paige's public response was uncharacteristically that of the good company man, lest he say something that might destroy the opportunity for Robinson and all men of color.

"They didn't make a mistake in signing Robinson," Paige said. "He's a number one professional player. They couldn't have picked a better man." He also called Robinson "the greatest colored player I've ever seen."

Paige also understood why Branch Rickey peremptorily eliminated for consideration Paige and an entire generation of Negro leaguers. Speaking with a sassiness that was common to him but which would have been foreign to Jackie Robinson, Satch— proving why he would have been about the worst choice for such a mission—ruminated, "They'd have to put me right in the majors, and that might have caused a revolution because the high-priced white boys up there wouldn't have had a chance to get used to the idea that way."

In the interregnum of Robinson's minor league season, few fans beyond those who read the pages of the black newspapers were aware a revolution was occurring. While the baseball world awaited Robinson's entrance, Rickey quietly signed four more Negro league players in the spring of 1946, with a fraction of the Robinson fanfare.

First, late in January, he hired a twenty-two-year-old pitcher, John Wright, who had gone a reported 25–4 for Homestead in 1943 before serving two years in the U.S. Navy. A pleasant and low-key man, it was clear from the start that the Louisiana-born Wright had gotten the nod mainly to provide companionship for Robinson in Montreal, and to serve as a calming influence if needed.

Next, in early March, the Baltimore Elites' Roy Campanella and the Newark Eagles' Don Newcombe got their calls from Branch Rickey and were dispatched to the Dodgers' Double-A team in Nashua, New Hampshire, in the New England League—after the club's other farm teams in the South and border states refused to take on black players. But at least Campanella and Newcombe had a home team in the United States. That Robinson and Wright did not led the *Chicago Defender* to note dryly that "America, supposedly the cradle of democracy, is forced to send its first two Negroes in baseball to Canada in order for them to be accepted." The paper might have added that their promotions required the new black minor leaguers, with the sole exception of Robinson, to take a pay cut from their Negro league salaries.

Most black and white owners, in the meantime, remained on their respective treadmills, with no apparent sense of the change that was in the air. In the first confounding days following the Robinson signing, an irate Tom Baird, co-owner of the Kansas City Monarchs, interrupted blackball's public euphoria by threatening to protest to Commissioner Chandler and file suit against Rickey for spiriting away his shortstop.

"We won't take it lying down," Baird said. "Robinson signed a contract with us [in 1946] and I feel he is our property." Later, Baird added, "I have been informed that Mr. Rickey is a very religious man. If such is true, it appears that his religion runs toward the almighty dollar."

Rickey, of course, had his reasons for not having taken the considerate route of purchasing Robinson's contract in advance or at least compensating the Monarchs after the fact. Beyond his simple penury and his contempt for the Negro leagues as "rackets," Rickey knew that negotiation with the black team might well wreck his conspiracy of secrecy; he also could not see how Robinson's $400-a-month arrangement with the Monarchs, which Jackie insisted was a handshake agreement, constituted a standard baseball contract.

On this point, Rickey was technically correct. Despite all of the blackball attempts through the years to standardize contracts and circumscribe team-jumping, the cheapening of team loyalties by players and owners—which had doomed any inclusion of a reserve clause going back to the Frank Leland era—made Negro league contracts mere salary chits. (Only in 1946, after the first wave of players were looted from their rosters, did the Negro league teams adopt the white major league contract language verbatim, hoping this would lend some sort of credibility to their covenants.)

On a larger scale, Rickey doubted that the black game had any legitimate sanctioning authority at all. In an interview with Wendell Smith, he described the Negro leagues as just "a booking agents' paradise. They are not leagues and have no right to expect organized baseball to respect them."

Even so, Rickey might have been on shaky legal ground—he was not concerned with the moral ground—and the other white owners fretted for a time that Tom Baird's lawsuit might in the end wipe out the reserve clause if Robinson's Monarch pact was found to be legal. If Rickey had in fact "liberated" black players by making them all free agents, they why were not white players just as free? However, Rickey and whiteball's contract sanctity escaped legal scrutiny—at least for now, and for three more decades— when the Mahatma's new friends in the black press defended his actions. Every major Negro paper attacked Baird, in verbiage that must have scalded the conscience of the white Monarch co-owner and his equally white partner, J. L. Wilkinson. The *Defender* evoked powerful guilt imagery in calling Baird "as selfish as any plantation owner" for standing in the way of Robinson's crusade. The *Courier* urged Baird to stop "hamper[ing] those who have made a step forward," noting that while Baird had a legal and moral case, the Robinson signing "transcended everything else at this particular time."

Faced with this criticism, Baird immediately took back his

threats, and Wilkinson felt compelled to state that while he believed the Dodgers "owe us some kind of consideration...we will not protest to Commissioner Chandler. I am very glad to see Jackie get this chance, and I'm sure he'll make good."

Effa Manley too must have felt like she was on the griddle. When Rickey took Don Newcombe from the Newark Eagles, she said nothing publicly, but pleaded with Rickey in a series of letters for compensation—only to be ignored. Later, she happened to run into Rickey at a Negro league game, and told him, "I hope you're not going to grab any more of our players. You know, Mr. Rickey, we could make trouble for you in the Newcombe transaction if we wanted to." But when word of her threats got out, several black sportswriters persuaded her to do nothing.

In an effort to do *something* that might protect their imagined rights, the black owners lodged a gentle grievance with Happy Chandler, stressing that while they were "glad to see our players get the opportunity to play in white baseball, [we] are simply protesting the way it was done"—and beseeched the commissioner to rule that white owners deal with black owners and not directly with players.

The blackball commissioners, Tom Wilson and J. B. Martin, met with Chandler and petitioned for the realization of an old blackball pipe dream: recognition as either major or minor leagues within organized baseball. Chandler responded only with condescension and outright insult—he would be glad to extend this recognition, he said, but only when "you can come to me with a clean bill of health" as "fair and honest" and "clean out the gamblers."

For their trouble, Wilson and Martin suffered opprobrium in the black press, which seemed to be turning on blackball more and more with each passing day. Branch Rickey had used virtually the same terminology in scolding the Negro leagues to "clean up" their act, but when Wilson and Martin reacted to Chandler's dismissive declaration by agreeing with it, Wendell Smith attacked them in the *Pittsburgh Courier* for "whimpering before Chandler" and for selling out principle for a pat on the head—although Smith himself would have preferred not that the Negro leagues simply go away.

"All they cared about," Smith wrote, "was the perpetuation of the slave trade they had developed....[They] will shout to the high heavens that racial progress comes first and baseball next. But actually the preservation of their shaky, littered, infested, segregated baseball domicile comes first, last and always."

In retrospect, it was at this volatile stage, when the black press no longer had any use for blackball—its semblance of racial pride having mutated over time into an emblem of servility and narrow business interests—that the Negro leagues began to die. Wendell Smith particularly seemed to be a one-man Inquisition. Rickey had put Smith on the Dodger payroll to follow Robinson on a regular basis and file propitious stories for his *Courier* readers from white minor league outposts; now, the onetime blackball flack began looking from afar at Negro league business with a sneering, snobbish disdain.

Blackball was by now a can't-win game. Still, those in the ranks of the Negro leagues couldn't read the portents, not even on March 28, 1946—the day Cum Posey died.

In the days after the Robinson announcement, Posey had grown depressed over the future of the black game he had guided for decades—not so much because of Branch Rickey's maneuvers as because of the Negro league owners' impulses to water down any effective central authority. Ironically, Posey had come to share his old foil Effa Manley's renewed insistence on a stronger Negro National League czar than Tom Wilson. But even with Posey's support, Effa did not get her candidates elected. The last time she tried, she put forward the name of the veteran black Chicago sportswriter Al Monroe.

Posey, his influence waning and his health failing, could see an era of blackball disintegrating before his eyes. Exhausted after years of infighting, Posey was diagnosed with terminal cancer. Now a dying man, in the fall of 1945 Posey learned more about the sham of Negro league loyalties when Eddie Gottlieb turned on him. Gottlieb, trying to grab more power, tried to move Wilson out as Negro National League president but for a weaker leader to be his puppet, a white copromoter named Frank Forbes. Posey, for all his conceits, could never have been branded a slave trader, and he was needed now more than ever if the Negro leagues were to have a future in the modern baseball democracy. After years of making alibis for the white promoters, Posey now wanted blackball to stand on its own, without the booking agents to prop it up.

Finding little support from most of the other owners—who, blinded by profit, were loath to cut the lifelines of Gottlieb and Abe Saperstein—Posey knew he and Wilson's day was over. On November 19, 1945, Posey sent a melancholy letter to Wilson, bemoaning that "We are getting so much hell, which we don't deserve, as we have built the League and did not hurt anybody while we were building it.... We both took office together and we will go out together but only because of illness."

Cum Posey was right. He and Tom Wilson did leave together. In 1946, Wilson, who was amenable to stepping aside for a leader of substance and vision, was so disgusted after being deposed as league president by Gottlieb's flunky that he sold the Baltimore Elite Giants to black businessman Richard Powell and had infinitely more fun running a dog track and nightclub back in Nashville. But in May of 1947, he followed Cum Posey into the grave after suffering a heart attack.

With the presidency made purely titular and captive to Eddie Gottlieb—who moved himself into the office of Negro National League secretary—the black press attacked the most convenient Negro league pariah since Nat Strong. Writing in the *Courier*, Wendell Smith began to pound on Gottlieb, whom he derided as "Brother Eddie." Smith had to tread carefully over the minefield of anti-Semitism that had become part of the angriest black denunciations of Gottlieb and Abe Saperstein—just as it had against Strong, who in 1921 had been branded "the Hebrew Menace" in one black paper. Using heavy sarcasm as his weapon of choice, Smith attacked not Gottlieb's faith but for a highly selective sense of fellowship with blacks. In a column on February 8, 1947, he traced Gottlieb's rise in the form of a parable:

> Not too many years ago, a character by the name of Eddie Gottlieb was sauntering around the streets of Philadelphia, posing as a promoter. He had his office in his hip pocket and nothing in his head but some ideas about exploiting Negroes in sports. In those days he was a very humble character and the sports mob classed him as...a man free of prejudice. That's the way it usually is with guys who see a chance to "move in" and "take over" in such cases. They establish themselves as liberals first.... That's the way it was with "Brother Eddie." He

became the Negro's friend.... He knew how tough it was to get along because other people had been booting his people around for thousands of years, too....

So "Brother Eddie" got in good. He became a fixture in Negro baseball. He made piles and piles of dough as an owner of the Philadelphia [Hebrew] Stars...Then somebody organized the Basketball Association of America, a league of the pro court world. "Brother Eddie"—our friend—was named the coach and manager of the Philadelphia Warriors, an entry in this new league. That's where he showed his true colors, however. "Brother Eddie" is running that team now, but has forgotten his old friends. He refuses to give them a chance to play on his team. He contends that he can't find a Negro good enough. He hasn't tried to find one, of course, and we all know that.

"Brother Eddie" has...disrobed as a liberal. Today he's a prejudiced, biased man. He's a traitor of sorts in the world of sports. He will have nothing to do with Negro basketball players in the winter months. When baseball season starts, however, "Brother Eddie" will be back with us. He'll be operating his Philadelphia Stars and raking in the dough of Negro baseball fans.

By now, however, Wendell Smith and nearly all of the other influential black journalists had no delusions that they could save blackball from its own devices. And while they had cause to forsake a game they believed was about to be made extinct by social realities and internal suffocation, their abandonment was in many ways cruelly insensitive to the black game's traditions, not to mention its employees still out there on the field. In the end, any hope that blackball could somehow evolve with the new baseball democracy as some sort of minor league feeder, and die out with dignity and order, was dashed not only by the white establishment, but by many in the black establishment as well.

Years later, that uncomfortable fact—which for years was overlooked in most Negro league studies—would become all too stark to men like Wendell Smith who had helped send the Negro leagues down the river. And they would live with intense private guilt the rest of their days.

White hard-liners certainly had no intention of giving in to social realities in 1946—not easily, anyway. Both Branch Rickey and Happy Chandler alleged that in that year white big league owners voted 15–1, with Rickey casting the only nay ballot, in a secret session to condemn Rickey's racial moves, and endorsed a written statement reading "However well intentioned, the use of Negro players would hazard all the physical properties of baseball." (If Chandler's allegation is true, he for one did little or nothing to change minds or upbraid the recalcitrants. Neither did he make any public comment, later explaining rather weakly that he took no action because "the press didn't know about" the whole matter.)

Still, the Jackie Robinson test case continued. In his second at-bat with the Montreal Royals on April 18, 1946, Robinson smashed a three-run home run; later on in the game, he bunted for a hit, singled for another, and stole two bases—a performance that Joe Bostic wrote in *People's Voice* was a "cudgel for Democracy." Bostic was already convinced that "an unassuming but superlative Negro boy [had] ascended the heights of excellence to prove the rightness of the experiment."

That much became apparent as Robinson walked unbowed through a thicket of provincial racism, particularly in the South, where some Royal games were canceled in Florida, Georgia, and Virginia when the Montreal team refused to bench Robinson and John Wright. These cancellations showed that, in some places, things had not changed in the decades since white teams with Fleet Walker and Bud Fowler had faced the same resistance and ultimatums. However, in most places life was different indeed. Over the 1946 season, *The Crisis* noted in October, Robinson had been responsible for at least fifty thousand additional paid admissions in the International League.

Those numbers, of course, were almost as important to Branch Rickey as Robinson's league-leading .349 batting average and 113 runs scored, and second-highest 40 stolen bases, as he took the Royals to the league championship and victory in the Little World Series, the minor leagues' title round, against the Louisville Colonels. (Ironically, the normally calm and collected John Wright was unable to stand the pressure and was released from the team in midseason, to be replaced briefly by the veteran Homestead Gray pitcher Roy Partlow, who was also released; both men were then re-signed by the Dodgers and sent to the lower minors.)

At the same time, in Nashua, Roy Campanella was doing nearly as wonderfully as Robinson. In fact, Campanella's .290 average, 13 homers, and 96 RBIs, and his savvy work behind the plate, led some to speculate for a time that Campy, not Robinson, might make it to Brooklyn first in 1947. Campanella also wrote a neat little footnote into the record books when, in mid-July, Walter Alston was ejected from a game and handed the lineup card to Campy—making him the first African-American manager in white baseball history, if only for one day. At season's end, however, Robinson made Branch Rickey's decision easy. Rickey now determined that while Robinson would begin spring training in 1947 with Montreal, he would begin the new season in Brooklyn.

Riding these expectations, Robinson formed an offseason Negro league touring team, that included Roy Campanella and Buck Leonard. And yet, as big-time as Jackie had become to people on both sides of the color line, there was an even bigger name that transcended race barriers. The *big* money on the autumn barnstorming circuit wasn't attracted by the Jackie Robinson All-Stars, but by the umpteenth version of the Satchel Paige All-Stars, which played against a white big league All-Star team headed by Paige's old crony Bob Feller. Quickly, these contests escalated into a coast-to-coast extravaganza in which the two squads traveled by DC-3 airplanes between sold-out houses.

Played around the same time as the World Series of both whiteball and blackball, the three-week Paige-Feller series was heavily publicized, and in the cities on the tour came close to obscuring the official championship matches between the St. Louis Cardinals and Boston Red Sox and Paige's Kansas City Monarchs and Newark Eagles. Satch, in fact, could barely be bothered with the Monarchs' latest title run. After winning the first game of the series in relief, he came into the second and fourth games and was knocked all over the ballpark in two Monarch losses. Clearly indifferent to the series, Paige took a walk, not showing up for the final three games, the last two of which the Eagles won to capture Abe and Effa Manley's first championship.

The players on the Feller team, who included Mickey Vernon, Johnny Sain, Phil Rizzuto, Bob Lemon, and eventually Stan Musial, were paid salaries ranging from $1,700 to $6,000 which for some was almost half of their yearly pay; Musial, joining up halfway through the tour, took home $3,000—more than his winning World Series share. With the exception of Paige, who by arrangement with Feller pitched for his usual cut of the gate, the Negro league stars—the likes of Hilton Smith, Buck O'Neil, Quincy Trouppe, Philadelphia Star outfielder Gene Benson, and Monarch outfielder Hank Thompson—were allowed far less by Feller, who controlled the paychecks. Yet, for most, it was more than they had ever earned playing ball.

The white race-obstructionist establishment felt it benefited from the perpetuation of these ongoing spectacles of black-versus-white. These series were the antitheses of the drive toward big league integration; moreover, the resurrection of the clownish, forty-year-old Paige fed the cause of the white hard-liners. To those fearful of Jackie Robinson's success, a man like Satchel Paige became a kind of Anti-Robinson, as a paradigm of the typical old-pro Negro leaguer who would be cast aside by integration and who would be jobless once integration destroyed blackball. Feigning empathy, hard-liners like J. G. Taylor Spink and Larry MacPhail reiterated their advice that each side of the game be left undisturbed.

Such counterfeit pity, however, did hard-liners on either end little good. If only on a subconscious level, the Paige-Feller caravan made inevitable the deluge that would follow Robinson. Ironically, Paige, by beating Feller in their head-to-head contests, achieved a new career as a white big league pitcher, and the Paige team's hitting star, Hank Thompson, by blasting several long home runs against Feller, became a prize catch for the white majors.

In fact, every glittering achievement within the context of the Negro leagues only seemed to predicate blackball's coming fall. This included even the East-West Game, which kept on churning out profits for the owners and seemed to be an unflinching symbol of continuity; not only did the Comiskey Park game pull in over forty-five thousand people in 1946, but a second East-West contest was played in Griffith Stadium in Washington, drawing sixteen thousand. But, by now, the only real relevance of the event was to provide a talent showcase for white big league scouts to see—virtually every black player signed by whiteball teams over the next half-decade had performed at one time or another in an East-West Game. The Negro leaguers themselves would come to view the game not for its effect on racial pride but for its effect on their chances to escape from the Negro leagues.

The last sad omen of the requiem of the Negro leagues was the most horrid of all. And yet, as an allegory of fate requited and fate cursed, the last stanza in the Ballad of Josh Gibson could not have been more fitting.

Actually, the end was written for Gibson as far back as New Year's Day 1943. Bothered by stabbing headaches the last weeks of the 1942 season, Josh assumed they were merely from his constant hangovers, but on that January 1 he blacked out and fell into a six-hour-coma. Ten days later, when he left Pittsburgh's St. Francis Hospital, Gibson's doctors publicly said the problem had been caused by exhaustion, and little more was made of it.

Considering that Gibson was always being advised by doctors and his managers to rest—advice which he invariably ignored—it seemed to be a plausible diagnosis. Especially since Gibson went right on wearing out the ball at the plate. He hit a reported .526 in 1943, and if anything his home runs seemed to be getting longer; that season, he smashed three into the Griffith Stadium bleachers in one game, the last a 460-foot screamer.

The following year, 1944, Gibson's bloated body became noticeably drained, though age and carousing were assumed to be the cause of his loss of power. While Gibson could still give the ball a long ride now and then, he was the largest and portliest singles hitter in baseball, taking the ball deep only fourteen times over the next two seasons. But because he led the league with a reported .393 average in 1945, many simply believed that, at thirty-four, Gibson had made a smart adjustment in his game—if not his ruinous lifestyle.

Thanks to Cum Posey's careful management of news regarding him, Gibson's Teflon reputation faced almost no scrutiny in the black press. Because no more than oblique references about Gibson's obsessions with alcohol and hard drugs ever appeared in the black papers, the meager coverage of blackball's stars in the white press never mentioned such dark matters. In 1943, when *Time* followed up on its breakthrough piece about Satchel Paige with a similar profile on Gibson, the author obviously had no idea there was anything to the man beyond the humble Gibson façade. Making him out to be a safer kind of icon than the mercurial Paige, the magazine reported that Gibson was "no gaudy eccentric. [Unlike Paige] he drives no cerise roadster, makes no startling statements about a strict diet of fried food, and he receives no $40,000 a year salary."

Periodically, the black papers would carry a throwaway item about Gibson missing games while begin given a "rest"—which in truth usually occurred when Gibson was too drunk to lace up his spikes. But no one reported, even if they knew it, that a good many of Gibson's rest stops were spent in sanitariums under observation, after Posey began to believe that Josh was losing his mind.

Even so, these hospital visits were designed more to settle Josh down—or "boil him out," as the Gray players took to calling it, in order to get him back onto the field—rather than to cure his mental tortures or to get him off heroin. To Posey, a man looking to preserve his profits, having Josh Gibson on the field, even under heavy sedation and barely able to stand up, was better than not having him at all. Posey even arranged for Gibson to be let out of his padded room for weekends, accompanied by two hospital attendants, who would rush him back to his bed right after the games.

The pitiful sight of blackball's Babe Ruth—the very metaphor of the quiet dignity and strength of its players—being led around like a drugged grizzly bear in a circus was actually an apt metaphor for the Negro league's decline and fall. But few knew of it, and Josh still retained enough self-respect to keep secret what was to him the most pitiful truth—that when he had blacked out in 1943, it was due not to exhaustion but to a brain tumor that doctors said was terminal.

Not once did Gibson let on, and, despite his travails, when he was on the ball field he was able to summon all his energies to give a passable imitation of the old, indestructible Josh. The problem was, Gibson had become a genuine public menace. Josh couldn't seem to go into a bar without causing a tumult that necessitated police intervention. Often the cops would take him straight to St. Francis Hospital for his boiling-out session, in a straitjacket—though once when he awakened from sedation, he simply tore the thing off his body with a massive shrug. Another time, before the cops could subdue him, he broke free and ripped the axle off the police paddy wagon with his bare hands.

In 1945, when Gibson missed the East-West Game, Cum Posey offered the explanation that Josh had been suspended for violating "training rules" and the matter was left at that. In truth,

Gibson had not been able to find his way to Chicago. By now, it was his teammate Sam Bankhead's job to keep tabs on him, and Sam never knew when he would have to get up in the middle of the night and pull Josh out of some gutter. On one such midnight run, he found Josh on a hotel ledge six floors up, swearing he was going to jump.

"Go ahead and jump. See if I care," said Bankhead, who knew how to puncture Josh's self-pity whenever Gibson threatened to kill himself. Josh came inside. But Bankhead too was helping to kill Gibson. Probably the heaviest drinker in blackball, Bankhead thought nothing of draining shot after shot with Josh in barrooms all around the league.

Still, in the end, and over time, Josh Gibson succeeded in killing himself. While he had ruled out any brain surgery, fearing he would live out his life as something for a clay pot, it was only a matter of counting the hours before his boozing and shooting up produced the same effect.

The fall and winter of 1946, when Gibson played in the Puerto Rican League, would turn out to be his last innings as a ballplayer, and they were none too attractive. One day he was arrested when he was found wandering, nude and in a daze, through the streets of San Juan. When the *policía* asked him just what he was doing, he said he was on his way to the airport. Instead of jail, he was put in a local sanitarium. Upon release, he was not allowed to play ball and was sent back home to Pittsburgh.

Suffering more raging headaches, dizzy spells, and seizures, he seemed to be preparing himself for the end. He made a belated attempt to recover the family life he had long left behind. For years, Josh's mother-in-law, Elizabeth Mason, with whom his twin son and daughter lived, had clamored for him to pay some kind of child support, often barging into the ballpark to demand money from him. Despite her efforts, the children grew up in deep poverty. Now, Josh tried to strike a relationship with Josh Jr. He took to sleeping in the same bed as the boy, but refused to help financially, and the rapprochement failed.

Josh also terminated his calamitous affair with Grace Fournier, the woman who many suspected had hooked him on dope—or rather, Grace ended the relationship, when her soldier husband returned from overseas. But Gibson could not reverse his slide, and his refuge all through his last winter wasn't the ballfield but the taverns of Pittsburgh. It was that winter, of course, that the anticipation about Jackie Robinson joining the Dodgers ran high, and Josh's depressions deepened with the realization that he had missed—or blown—what might have been his calling.

By the turn of another new year, ravaged now as well by bronchitis and high blood pressure, he could no longer care for himself, and moved into his mother's house on Strauss Street on Pittsburgh's North Side. A few weeks later, he awoke feeling in good spirits and popped over to Gus Greenlee's Crawford Grille for a few drinks. The next day, Sunday, January 19, he went to see a movie at the Garden Theater and fell unconscious in his seat. Josh's doctor, Earl Simms, was called and had him taken to his mother's home. Josh did not come around, and the doctor injected him with medication and left with Josh in a deep sleep.

At 1:30 A.M. that morning, with his sister, Annie Mahaffey, and his younger brother, Jerry, at his bed, Josh Gibson died of what was called a stroke.

Gibson's funeral at the Macedonia Baptist Church drew hundreds of mourners, and his death—which came as a great shock to many who thought they knew him well but didn't know him at all—was cause for anguish and heartache, and even a revisionist theory that Gibson had died of a heart broken by white baseball's failure to promote him.

But Gibson's demise was not simply overwhelming personal tragedy sharpened by the egregious paradox of a great athlete cut down in the prime of life. Neither was it merely a statement about life's harsh whimsies that Josh Gibson—who in his final season was making $1,700 a month playing ball—died without leaving enough money for his family to afford a gravestone. Whether any or even some of the mourners who buried him in Allegheny Cemetery that day realized it, the timing of Gibson's exit—coupled as it was with Jackie Robinson's entrance—placed the day in a higher context. As would become apparent soon enough, these funeral rites were also for the Negro leagues.

20

Darkness Comes

[Jackie] Robinson owes his enduring niche in history to factors that are so much more significant than his ability to field and hit a ball [but] there have been a number of Negro players, denied the calendar break that favored Robinson, who would have had the right to point to him and say, "There, but for the meanness and ignorance of man, go I."
—Joe Williams, *New York World-Telegram & Sun*, February 1957

Once in a while I get a kick out of thinking that my name was mentioned as one of the stars of the East-West Game and little things like that. I don't know whether I'd feel better if I had a million dollars [but] I can say I contributed something [to baseball].
—Jimmy Crutchfield, 1971

With their foundation stripped, the Negro leagues collapsed almost immediately after Branch Rickey's delicate maneuvers went forward with perfect precision in Brooklyn. Jackie Robinson's painless insertion at first base (he would be switched later, permanently, to second) in the Dodgers' lineup on that strangely matter-of-fact afternoon of April 15, 1947, set the tone for a revolution that in time not even the most insistent integration holdout could deny had been just and necessary.

Robinson, of course, with his almost cosmic sense of self-commitment and elegance, made the case moot for Rickey and the integration movement. Robinson's test came not so much on Opening Day or any other game as it did when player resistance first broke out in early May. Mired in an 0-for-20 batting slump,

Robinson came into Philadelphia for a series against the Phillies and was showered with what the *Afro* called a "display of unsportsmanly conduct [by] the Phillies, who proved the first team to 'ride' the new Dodger. With their manager, Ben Chapman, playing a major role in the jockeying, the [Phillies] jeered and catcalled from the bench throughout the series."

This display, though, must have been a salve for Robinson's bat, as he broke out of his slump and led the Dodgers to a three-game sweep. Two weeks later, a more serious danger arose when the story broke that Dodger outfielder Carl Furillo and pitcher Ed Head had tried to get several St. Louis Cardinal players, including All-Stars Terry Moore and Mary Marion, to go along with the idea of a player strike protesting Robinson's elevation.

National League president Ford Frick at once threatened swift retribution. Any player carrying through on what Frick called this "complete madness" would be suspended, he said. "And I don't care if it wrecks the National League for five years," Frick added, pledging that the league "will go down the line with Robinson, whatever the consequences. This is the United States of America and one citizen has as much right to play as another."

Frick, who turned out to be more of a leader on integration than the posturing Happy Chandler, had experienced a remarkable conversion. A onetime sportswriter, Frick had declared in the early 1940s that the public "has not been educated to the point where they will accept [black players]," and added that "colored people did not have a chance to play during slavery, and so were late developing proficiency."

But Frick, like most judicious baseball men, could recognize the benefits Jackie Robinson brought to the game. For one thing, as embodied by Robinson, the canon of fairness could no longer be brushed off as the sloganeering of agitators. More pertinently to the owners, the real fear of the white establishment—property values tumbling when black fans took white seats—was quickly eased when Robinson drew legions of black fans not only to Ebbets Field, where attendance in 1947 shot up by 400 percent, but to stadiums all around the league, without the core of white attendance being affected much at all.

Now, black *plus* white was workable baseball math, and a powerful subliminal message. In the April 19 issue of the *Courier*, in the newspaper's coverage of Robinson's debut, the first page of the sports section featured a three-photo sequence ranging across the top of the page. It depicted interracial crowd scenes at Ebbets Field that first week of the season. The banner headline was "Jackie Robinson Packing 'Em In."

An ebullient Wendell Smith reported that while the unreconstructed Georgia racist Dixie Walker was being booed by the fans, Robinson "has been cheered and hailed in every ballgame and there is no doubt that the fans are more sentimental about him than their once-beloved Dixie." Smith wrote that Robinson "might easily dislodge Dixie Walker as the 'Peepul's Choice' in Brooklyn." In May, it was reported that Robinson was receiving so much fan mail that Branch Rickey's staff had to answer letters for him.

One may put aside the hysterics of the Negro press, which lost any tempering sense of objectivity when covering the Robinson story. The *Courier* even gave Robinson his own bylined column, ghosted by Wendell Smith. Robinson's undeniable appeal to the general public made it obvious that southerners like Dixie Walker were rapidly becoming the dinosaurs of the game; Walker probably realized this fact himself, since as things turned out he made every effort to be helpful to Robinson during the season, as did Carl Furillo. And Ben Chapman, after the bad publicity of the catcalling incident in Philadelphia, took pains to pose for pictures with Robinson later on. The working metaphor for that strange and monumental summer, in fact, was the warm and sincere friendship between Robinson and Kentuckian Pee Wee Reese, the splendid Dodger shortstop.

Robinson's fight was not really over. For years he would face death threats and scattered fan abuse. But the race issue was essentially clinched long before he put up his final numbers—a .297 average, 29 steals, 125 runs scored—which won him Rookie of the Year honors and drove the Dodgers to the pennant. If a benchmark is needed to stamp Robinson's official acceptance, it was probably the cover story he merited in the September 22, 1947, issue of *Time* magazine.

It seemed almost incidental that the same season witnessed another momentous tilting of the baseball landscape. Bill Veeck had rebounded from his aborted attempt to buy the Philadelphia Phillies in 1944 to purchase the Cleveland Indians a year later. He was now in position to fulfill his original desire of enfranchising black baseball players.

On July 5, Veeck made headlines by signing twenty-two-year-old Newark Eagle second baseman Larry Doby to an Indian contract. Only twenty-seven himself, Veeck had no generational bond to the canards of racism; explaining his incentive in signing Doby, Veeck later said that "all my life I have been fighting against the status quo, against the tyranny of fossilized majority rule."

What's more, Veeck was a devotee of Negro league baseball, and had been in the stands when Satchel Paige beat Dizzy Dean in Los Angeles in 1936. Paige, in fact, had been Veeck's first choice to bring to Cleveland, even with his age and iconoclastic habits. But with the Indians rebuilding their club, Veeck worried about being accused of a publicity stunt to hype the gate.

Instead, well aware of Doby's talents—through early July, Doby was leading the Negro National League in hitting and home runs, with a reputed .458 average and 13 homers—Veeck turned his sights to the Newark outfielder. Doby had also caught Branch Rickey's eye, but Rickey willingly eased off so that Veeck could integrate the American League. Effa Manley, who had been burned when Rickey took Don Newcombe, knew for some time that Doby was a hot property, and had tried to protect herself by offering Doby for sale, in vain, to the New York Yankees for $100,000. And while Veeck was not about to pay that kind of money for Doby, neither did he take the Rickey route and stiff the Eagles—though to Effa, Veeck's largesse of $10,000 was insulting nonetheless.

"You know, if Larry Doby were white, and a free agent," she told Veeck, "you'd give him a hundred thousand dollars to sign as a bonus."

But Effa, admitting that "I'm in no position to be bargaining with you," accepted the stipend, partly because Veeck said he would give her another $5,000 should Doby complete thirty days in Cleveland and partly because her complaining had once again drawn the ire of black sportswriters. She now wanted to "get the Negro papers off my back," she said.

For Doby, all this came with such suddenness that he could scarcely comprehend that he had gone from the Negro leagues to the white big leagues in the space of one day. Up until now, Doby's background had read like a lower-case Jackie Robinson story. Born in South Carolina, he'd moved to Paterson, New Jersey, then commanded attention as a four-letter man in high school and won a scholarship to Long Island University. Doby also served during the war, in the navy. But the similarities with Robinson ended once Doby made his white big league debut only hours after signing and struck out in his first at-bat.

Doby, who had none of Robinson's white-hot inner flame, was an eerily quite and timid man, and was prone to accept things as they came; he once said that as a young man, he was "unconscious of racism." Consequently, he was unprepared for the continual tension that went with the territory he'd staked out. Although Cleveland fans were generally supportive of Doby, Veeck's office was bombarded with twenty thousand menacing letters that first year, and for spring training the following year Veeck moved the Indians' base from Florida to Tucson, Arizona. Doby was so chary of provoking racial emotions that if the man ahead of him hit a home run, he would wait to shake hands with him until both were out of sight in the dugout. With every epithet hurled from the stands, or sour look from a teammate, Doby retreated further.

In a rut from day one, Doby saw action mainly as a pinch hitter and notched only five hits in thirty at-bats, a .151 average. Even Jackie Robinson, from across the leagues, seemed disappointed in Doby. In his *Courier* column, Robinson advised that the coiled Doby not "try so hard that he'll lose his effectiveness" and said that comparisons between them were inappropriate. He added, "There's enough pressure on him without worrying if he's doing as good as I am."

Robinson had license for such presumption. His ego swelling as his wondrous tour de force continued, Jackie was now a one-man movement, which is why practically nobody noticed the downer of a racial experiment that played out in St. Louis in 1947. Here, in the big league town that had been the last to integrate the grandstand in the ballpark shared by the city's two major league teams, the American League's Browns signed two Negro leaguers at once, Monarch outfielders Willard Brown and Hank Thompson, and also reserved a thirty-day option on the Birmingham Black Baron outfielder Piper Davis.

From the outset, it was apparent that the Browns' owner, Richard Muckerman, had made the move for all the wrong reasons. Unlike Bill Veeck, who had refrained from bringing Satchel Paige to Cleveland that year because it might have been perceived as a novelty act, Muckerman all but admitted that the last-place Browns were looking to the two black players to put people in the park. Muckerman put little study into the choices. Though Brown and Thompson were above-average Negro leaguers—and Brown had developed a folk hero following for belting some tape-measure home runs—Brown was past thirty and a flawed player, and the twenty-one-year-old Thompson, although talented and a former war hero, was also a surly man with a police record and a drinking problem, and carried a gun.

In his first game, Thompson went 0-for-4. In his first game, Brown hit into two double plays. It didn't get much better the rest of the season for Brown, who hit .179. And while Thompson was hitting a respectable .256, neither man moved fans—black or white—to come to Sportsman's Park. That, more than anything else, got each of them an outright release on August 23. Probably the best candidate of the three, Piper Davis, a slick outfielder who also played in the offseason with the Harlem Globetrotters, was offered a minor league contract but turned it down.

At this point, even though Jackie Robinson had made integration a fact, if was by no means a sure thing that the revolution was at hand. To most white owners, the new strategy seemed to be to treat Robinson as the fulfillment of the quota, in toto. And if few fans noticed the failure of the three black American Leaguers—as well as that of the second black National Leaguer, pitcher Dan Bankhead (brother of Homestead's Sam), who after Rickey took him from the Memphis Red Sox on August 25 was ineffective in three games and was quietly sent down to the minors—the owners no doubt wanted these cases to show that Robinson was indeed an anomaly.

The pooh-bahs of the Negro leagues may have been secretly hoping the same thing—or at least that the halting progress of integration would mean that the Negro leagues would retain some viability as an incubator of future Robinsons. In this delusion, as it was expressed by the *Defender*, "Negro fans [will] want to see the players whom the major league scouts were watching. So [will] white fans." But beyond the scouts, whites could not have cared less about the arcane elements of a league that was failing when

Robinson fled it. Neither did it help that Robinson continued to speak and write unkindly about blackball, most acutely in a bylined *Ebony* magazine attack in May 1948, entitled "What's Wrong With the Negro Leagues?" In the piece, he found little reason to wish the leagues well.

Robinson's refusal to drop his old grudge against the Negro leagues for having made him feel uncomfortable in 1945 was small-minded. Although Robinson had pledged to Wendell Smith that he would be a black man first and a ballplayer second, he was unable to do what Satchel Paige had done in shilling for Robinson—sublimate pique in favor of a little helpful propaganda. If black fans needed a license to shut their eyes to the Negro leagues, Robinsons's article provided it.

Actually, Robinson didn't have to say much for this abandonment to proceed. Right from the start of the 1947 season, wherever Jackie went was where black fans went to see him play. In New York and Newark, this meant Ebbets Field; in the other National League cities, it was the closest place the league schedule took the Dodgers, be it Philadelphia, Pittsburgh, St. Louis, Chicago, or Cincinnati. After this uplifting experience, few fans had the desire or the money to return to the hash of Negro ball. And if they did, Negro league coverage in the black papers ended the idea.

In 1947, for example, the *Courier* ran a story about a black businessman named Sam Jackson who had organized a group of five thousand fans to attend Robinson's first game against the Pirates in Forbes Field. Jackson told the paper, "Anyone with the least bit of racial pride should join us and show Mr. Rickey we are grateful." This, then, was the new priority: Black economic power was to be shifted to the white game, in hopes of forcing white teams to, as Jackson said, "realize how much money [they] are missing by refusing to sign Negro players."

The defection of fans from Negro league games to National League games—i.e., Robinson—did not immediately translate into mass signings of black players by white teams. In 1948, only Branch Rickey and Bill Veeck made integration moves again—Rickey with the expected promotion of Roy Campanella to the Dodgers, Veeck with the completely unexpected elevation of Satchel Paige to the Indians. But these two moves were of critical importance. Campanella, in easing so naturally into the lineup, made it seem like he had belonged there years before, effectively snuffing the fable that Robinson was somehow a rare and singular creature.

Paige was important in the opposite way. Veeck had correctly perceived that, with the Indians now in contention for the pennant and already drawing huge crowds early in the season, Satch would be judged on his still-crackling arm, not on his legend and his antics. Signed on July 7 by Veeck, who extended J. L. Wilkinson the courtesy of a $5,000 payment, Paige became that summer's hot sports story. Drawing sellout-plus houses routinely around the American League (the Tribe drew a club- and league-record 2.7 million at home, in no small measure because of Paige), "Old Satch" promptly earned more respect for the Negro game over that one summer than several generations of black players had achieved on the field over the preceding three decades. Here was the greatest sporting legend since Babe Ruth being seen by the masses for the first time at age forty-two—Veeck squeezed every drop out of the age gag, implying that Paige may really have been over fifty—and the sympathy and respect he engendered stoked the notion that justice had surely been denied him and men like him.

This was Satchel Paige in clover, humiliating major league hitters half his age and still having time for the old riffs, like the "Hesitation Pitch," which, with Paige's momentary pause at the top of his delivery, so dumbfounded hitters and umpires that league president Will Harridge eventually ruled the pitch illegal with men on base. It was also Bill Veeck at his most impish. When Veeck signed Paige, J. G. Taylor Spink used every one of his spurious arguments against integration to attack the owner; by early August, after Paige had turned in a number of impressive games, most recently a three-hit shutout against the Chicago White Sox, and had drawn over two hundred thousand people in his last three starts, Veeck sent a cheeky wire to Spink that read:

PAIGE PITCHING—NO RUNS, THREE HITS. DEF-INITELY IN LINE FOR THE SPORTING NEWS ROOKIE OF THE YEAR AWARD.

Although the Paige media fireball, which won him a profile in *Life* magazine, burned out by late August, and the Indians went down the stretch run with a strong four-man rotation that excluded Satch, he was instrumental in the Tribe's pennant-winning season. He went 6–1, with a 2.48 ERA, 45 strikeouts and 2 shutouts, and even had a couple of base hits. And while he was limited to a token, one-game mop-up appearance in Cleveland's World Series victory over the Boston Braves, he had the satisfaction of knowing that after all those years on the outside and then being nearly forgotten in the Jackie Robinson show, history would record that Satchel Paige was the first black pitcher to ever take the hill in the World Series.

To others aware of the irony of it all, the real rush may have come when J. G. Taylor Spink actually took Bill Veeck's advice and named Paige as *The Sporting News*'s Rookie of the Year. Satch, though, was unimpressed.

"I declined the position," Paige said later. "I wasn't sure what year the gentlemen [*sic*] had in mind."

But these niceties were peripheral to the real meaning of Paige's big league reckoning. Actually, there were several meanings. One was to validate not only Paige's long past but that of blackball itself—if Paige could go 6–1 as an old wheelhorse, it must have occurred to many, what kind of holy terror must he have been as a colt? Furthermore, it helped the Indians, who drew those 2.7 million people through the turnstiles. Arguably the two biggest attractions in the game now were two African Americans of totally different stripes: Jackie Robinson with his growling but contained sense of righteous indignation, and Satchel Paige with his puckish sense of the absurd.

A good many upwardly mobile blacks—most notably the black sportswriters, but also Jackie Robinson—detested Paige's clownish character and his flippant refusal to comply with the white game's norms of conduct. Even now, with the whole world watching, he was no more reliable than before in getting to the park on time and curtailing his drinking and philandering nightlife. But while these black people shuddered at what they considered Paige's regressive ways, the more subtle point could be made that Paige proved invaluable to the cause as a human face with human flaws. For whites, it was a rather comforting thought that not all great black players were so politically charged as Jackie Robinson. Baseball would be able to look to Satchel Paige for reassurance that transition to integration need have neither a hard nor a bland face.

Certainly, Larry Doby benefited by Paige's two seasons in Cleveland; though he didn't care for Paige personally and related little to his Negro league legacies, the pressure and attention that was delivered unto Paige allowed Doby to quietly flourish, and he became a .301 hitter in 1948. He would go on to play thirteen productive seasons with the Indians and White Sox. Doby also managed the White Sox in 1978, though he would run afoul of the law when he left the game. Doby's development proved to be a vital stepping-stone as well. In its May 1949 issue, *Ebony* magazine pointed out, "Although Robinson pioneered in the majors, probably Doby has been a more important factor in sending club owners into the chase for Negro talent." Doby, the magazine said, "demonstrated convincingly that a Negro player, given the right opportunity, encouragement, and direction, can attain baseball heights."

Doby probably never saw himself as a missionary. However, after he did so well against American League pitching in 1948, many major league teams made their first incursions into the new age. Boston Brave owner Lou Perini credited Doby's example in explaining his decision to bring "a delegation of Negro players" to the Braves' spring training camp the following year. Other clubs began heavily scouting Negro league games, which increasingly seemed to exist only for the consumption of the white scouts. By 1948, there were sixteen blacks in the white minors, though most played either in the Dodger or Indian chains.

To be sure, beginning with the 1948 season, the Negro leagues had gravitated from the illusion of becoming wards of big league integration to the sad necessity of trying to sell off as many players as they could just to keep money coming in. The falloff in attendance was their undoing. Reflecting league-wide losses, the Newark Eagles in 1947 slid from a hundred and twenty thousand paid admissions to fifty-seven thousand—translating into a $22,000 deficit for the Manleys. Now, with blackball in ruins, the owners began feverishly cutting player salaries—and instituted baseball's first salary cap—forcing some Negro leaguers to play out their careers in the Mexican League. For the lucky few of them, salvation came in the form of the white majors.

Among these chosen was Monte Irvin, the gifted Eagle outfielder whom Branch Rickey had considered the man to break the color line until he was called into military service. Effa Manley, who had been badly offended when Bill Veeck paid $10,000 for Larry Doby, reportedly began shopping Irvin around in 1947. He was making a top salary, by blackball standards, of $5,000 a year and draining the Manleys' finances. Her asking price went as low as $1,000, but she got no takers. Then, when the Eagles began to ebb as a contending team after Alex Pompez's New York Cubans swept a late-season doubleheader in 1947 to take the Negro National League crown, the Manleys tried to sell the club.

As the 1948 season wound down, and attendance dropped even more precipitously, Effa publicly called on Newark's black fans to come to Ruppert Stadium as a matter of racial conscience, a plea that did not sit well with black sportswriters, who had by now requisitioned the black conscience for use in the integration battle. The *Kansas City Call*, in a somewhat irrational editorial, scolded Effa as if she were standing in the way of integration. "The day of loyalty to jim crow…is fast passing away," the paper said. "Sister, haven't you heard the news? Democracy is a-coming fast."

Seeing no way to reply to such bile, Effa unhappily announced that the final game of the season "will be the last for this year and probably the last one for the Newark Eagles forever." Noting the Eagles' end, the *Courier*'s Jack Saunders began readying the Negro leagues' coffin. "[W]hen a team like the Newark Eagles, with plenty of money behind it, is the first to cry quits, it looks bad—very bad," he wrote. "For if the Eagles cannot stand the gaff of empty seats, what is to happen to the New York Cubans, Baltimore Elites, New York Black Yankees and Homestead Grays?"

Saunders' prophesy quickly came to bear. After the 1948 season, the Black Yankees went out of business and the Homestead Grays pulled out of the league and concentrated on barnstorming. The Grays had taken the 1948 Negro World Series in five games against the Birmingham Black Barons, but won their twelfth pennant and third World Series in near-total obscurity, since few black papers covered the league races or the series—which, not coincidentally, was the last Negro World Series ever to be played.

Effa now made a deal to sell the Eagles to black Memphis businessman W. H. Young, who planned to move them to Houston. However, when she learned that Branch Rickey had signed Monte Irvin and intended to ship him to the Dodgers' St. Paul team in the American Association, she decided she would not leave the game with the taste of another insult; putting the deal with Young on hold, she filed protests with Commissioner Happy Chandler, National League president Ford Frick, minor league commissioner George Trautman, and American Association president Bruce Dudley.

Rickey, who by now was more sensitive to the contract-sanctity issue, backed off, releasing Irvin from the Dodger stable. Effa then held off on the final sale of the Eagles while again shopping Irvin to the other white New York teams. The Yankees said no, but Giant owner Horace Stoneham agreed to pay $5,000. Though this was only half the sum that had irritated Effa in the Larry Doby signing, she took it. Within a week, she had finalized the Eagles' sale and left the game—bewailing the corrosion of the blackball soul. She censured everyone from Rickey to the black press to black fans for having forgotten the most basic lesson of the black game's existence. She told *The Sporting News* in October, "The Negro leagues were born of prejudice. Now, the whole matter is so involved, with prejudices inside prejudices, and in some places a total lack of sincerity."

Although Effa then offered herself as a roving ambassador of the remnants of the Negro leagues, her attack brought ridicule and derision from black sportswriters. Sam Lacy complained that Effa "still blames everyone but those who are really responsible for the present plight of Negro baseball," meaning the owners. Predictably, Wendell Smith's comments proved the most caustic. Smith wrote that Effa's complaints were no more than "weepings," the kind that "gave [Negro league] meetings an atmosphere of moistness."

Effa's biggest failing, he went on, was that "she refused to recognize that nothing was killing Negro baseball but Democracy....When men like Rickey and Veeck decided to put some Democracy in baseball, it meant that the lush days for owners of Negro league teams were over."

And so it came to pass. After that 1948 season, with the Eagles, Grays, and Black Yankees out of the loop, the Negro National League disbanded, its sixteen-year-old experiment—twenty-six years, if Rube Foster's league of the same name is grafted on to the Gus Greenlee-Cum Posey circuit—to endure in memory as the cornerstone of the blackball heritage.

Now, with the gravestone in place, the league's surviving teams had to scramble for shelter in order to evade the fate of the Homestead Grays after going back to independent ball and barnstorming. For a time the Grays were managed by the widows of Cum Posey and Sonnyman Jackson. Then, in 1949, the two women gave the club to Posey's brother, Seward "See" Posey. But a year later See Posey fell ill, and with the Grays having lost $30,000 that season, he folded the fabled team just before he died.

By the spring of 1949, the New York Cubans, Baltimore Elite Giants, and Philadelphia Stars joined a revamped Negro American League, playing in an Eastern Division rounded out by the Indianapolis Clowns and Louisville Buckeyes. The cadaver of the Newark Eagles, now in Houston with only a handful of the Manleys' roster, went into the Western Division of the league, which housed the still-breathing godheads of the halcyon days: the Kansas City Monarchs and Chicago American Giants, as well as the Memphis Red Sox and Birmingham Black Barons.

No longer, however, were there delusions of a long blackball stride across the emerging new landscape of baseball. Like their players, these teams weren't there to lead the integration cause, but merely to hold on to the very tip of its tail. In the process, even the most urban teams tried to copy the Monarchs' longtime method of operation, which was to make their way out into the tall grass of the Midwest barnstorming pastures—doomed as the barnstorming game was, now that the new invention of television was limiting the baseball universe to the white big leagues.

The Monarchs' decline signaled how futile it was to carry on. J. L. Wilkinson, who was seventy-four in 1948, was in poor health and had cataracts in both eyes. His imminent death, coming so soon after Cum Posey's in 1946, would elevate blackball's body count to too high a point. With the end near, Wilkinson sold his interest in the club to Tom Baird, whereupon Baird had to slash salaries in half, to an average of about $200 a month. But, as with the other owners, Baird's real mission was to sell whatever players he could to white major league teams, who at once trucked them off to various minor league affiliates.

After the 1948 season, Baird peddled two Monarchs to the New York Giants, pitcher Ford Smith and Hank Thompson, whose second stint in the white game began, along with the careers of Monte Irvin and Smith, on the Giants' Triple-A farm club in Jersey City. In 1949, Baird sold four more players to the white minors: shortstop Gene Baker, pitcher Booker McDaniel, catcher Earl Taborn, and pitcher Robert Thurman, the last two of whom were given minor league contracts with the New York Yankees' Triple-A team in Newark.

This hectic shuttling from blackball to lower-level whiteball was common across the Negro league map in the late forties. The Yankees, who were constantly under fire for lagging on hiring black players, signed three Negro leaguers to minor league deals: Birmingham shortstop Artie Wilson, Homestead outfielder Luis Angel Marquez, and Philadelphia outfielder Frank Austin. Now that Larry MacPhail had retired from baseball, there was speculation that the Yankees, the most venerated team in all the majors, would outdo Branch Rickey's commitment to integration.

Of the new black minor leaguers, the prospects looked best for Ray Dandridge. In 1949, the New York Giants signed the great bowlegged Eagle third baseman along with the New York Cubans' pitcher Dave Barnhill and sent them to their Minneapolis farm club in the American Association. At the time, Dandridge was at least thirty-six, but told the Giants he was twenty-nine, and nobody doubted it when he went on a 28-game hitting streak. He finished the season with a .364 average, second best in the American Association, and the reasonable expectation was the Dandridge and numerous other blacks were about to take their place on white major league rosters.

Instead, as if by some new stratagem of resistance, most of these men were left rotting on the farm; as the new decade of the 1950s arrived, their only movement was from one bush league team to another. The onetime Yankee prospect Bob Thurman, who had ravaged International League pitching, won trips to three other league teams before he finally got a shot to play with the Cincinnati Reds in 1954 as a thirty-three-year-old pinch hitter. Piper Davis wasn't even that lucky. Signed by the Boston Red Sox in 1950, he would play in four different minor leagues in eight years, then pass out of baseball without ever reaching the majors.

Ray Dandridge, who followed up his magnificent rookie season in Minneapolis by hitting .311 and winning the American Association's Most Valuable Player award in 1950, continued to scald bush league pitching for several years—all the while yearning desperately to, as he said years later, "put my foot in major league ball." It never came to pass. The Giants, who had called up Monte Irvin

1949 and Hank Thompson in 1950 and seemed to want to keep to a one-a-year quota, had the choice in 1951 between Dandridge and his young roommate in Minneapolis—a smooth outfielder named Willie Mays, who had been purchased for $5,000 from the Birmingham Black Barons early that season. Mays got the call, and Dandridge—who was so popular in Minneapolis that the minor league club may have asked the Giants not to move him— had lost his last chance. Still angry many years later, Dandridge approached Horace Stoneham at an old-timers game.

"You had the chance to sell my contract," he berated the Giants' owner. "You had the chance to bring me up and you wouldn't do it. You could have called me up for one week! I could have said I hit in the major leagues."

In the end, men like Dandridge fell victim to what almost certainly was a conspiracy by white owners to hold integration to a trickle. Philadelphia general manager Art Ehlers told the *Courier* in 1953 that "the major leagues were reluctant, and the men who were ready became overage and lost their opportunity."

If this smelled like collusion, Happy Chandler apparently didn't mind the scent. Neither did Ford Frick, who replaced the hapless Chandler in 1951. Frick came into the commissioner's office charged with representing owners' interests, and retained little of the firebrand spirit he'd showed in running interference for Jackie Robinson in 1947.

For the lords of white baseball, moving toward democracy with all deliberate speed was the appropriate velocity, caught as the game was in an American culture getting accustomed grudgingly, if at all, to the doctrine of pluralism.

Even Branch Rickey, when he left the Dodgers to become the chairman of the board of the Pittsburgh Pirates in 1951, fell into the new big league comfort zone. The Great Liberator would sign a host of blacks, but promoted no men of color to the big club, with the conspicuous exception of Roberto Clemente, a phenomenal Puerto Rican outfielder whom he drafted from the Dodgers' organization in 1954 and called up the year after.

Still, the trickle was constant and cumulative. Significantly, a good many of the blacks who were tapped for the white majors rang up some major achievements, including Roy Campanella's Most Valuable Player awards in 1951, 1953, and 1955. Blacks also captured, with startling regularity, the National League Rookie of the Year award. In 1949, Don Newcombe finally got to Brooklyn, and won the trophy with a 17–8 record. In 1950, it was taken by Sam Jethroe, late of the Cleveland Buckeyes, who went to the Boston Braves and hit .273, with a league-leading 35 steals.

That same year, outfielder Luke Easter, who had gone from the Homestead Grays to the Cleveland Indians only to hit .222 in 1949, redeemed himself with a 28-homer, 107-RBI campaign. Monte Irvin hit .299 in 1951. But, like Ray Dandridge in Minneapolis, he was overshadowed by Willie Mays, who hit .274 with 20 homers and won Rookie of the Year honors.

Hank Thompson, in his second stay in the white majors, was called up to the Giants late in the 1951 season. He helped propel them to the pennant by hitting eight home runs down that famous stretch run against the Dodgers that climaxed with Bobby Thomson's "shot heard 'round the world." Hank Thompson would go on to a five-year run in the white majors—no small feat considering that he had shot a man dead in a barroom argument in 1948. The Giants supported Thompson, aiding him in his successful defense of justifiable homicide before sending him to the minors.

Satchel Paige also returned to the white major leagues in 1951, at age forty-five or thereabouts, when Bill Veeck bought the moribund St. Louis Browns. Pitching for this floating wreckage of a team, the ageless Paige would turn in some of his finest work on the mound and pitch in the All Star-Game in 1953, his last full year in the white majors.

As a sidebar to this sequence of small but important gains, a few other splendid old Negro leaguers enjoyed a taste of the big time as well—Quincy Trouppe with Cleveland, and Bus Clarkson with the Boston Braves. Indeed, the delectable irony about the new black influx was that, outside of Willie Mays, the black Rookie of the Year winners were old by baseball standards. The last two ex-blackballers to win the award, pitcher Joe Black in 1952 and second baseman Junior Gilliam in 1953—both in service to the Dodgers—had been true rookies almost a decade earlier while they were breaking in with the Baltimore Elite Giants, Black in 1943 and Gilliam in 1945.

In the last wheeze of Negro league life, the shakeout of players and teams would not be complete until blackball had given life to the careers of the men who needed a break the most—those who came from the ball fields of the South. Because the nexus of minor league teams below the Mason-Dixon line was so entrenched, meaningful integration in the South was still years away, and blacks reared in the segregated South had almost no chance to be signed on their own to play for these clubs. One such player was a young shortstop from Mobile, Alabama, named Henry Aaron.

In 1952, Aaron weighed in at a scrawny 150 pounds, was knock-kneed, and, though he hit right-handed, kept his left hand over his right on the bat. This unorthodox "cross-handed" style was effective because of Aaron's amazingly pliable wrists, but when he joined the Indianapolis Clowns, his manager, Buster Haywood, put an end to it, which probably moved Aaron's career beyond the short term. Batting in the conventional style, he hit cleanup and was credited with a league-leading .463 average in 1952. (Aaron, incidentally, disowns this figure as typical Negro league record-keeping fiction; a late-season slump, he has said, actually put him well under .400.)

The Clowns changed Aaron in another respect, at least temporarily. Even five years after the coming of Jackie Robinson, the team's *shtick* was unchanged; hamming it up, acting out a vision of Negroes otherwise last seen in minstrel shows, the Clowns defiantly mocked the now-strengthened cause—with the same justification as in the twenties, that people still paid to see Negroes perform as, well, clowns. Syd Pollock still owned the team, Abe Saperstein was still boking them around the Midwest, and the players were still hung with nicknames regarded as appropriate to their race. In 1952, these names included "King Tut" and "Spec Bebop." Hank Aaron went by the name of "Pork Chops."

But Syd Pollock was under no delusions that he could get along without the alms of the white big leagues. Although the Clowns won the Negro American League title in 1952, the circuit was down to six teams in varying stages of economic decay. For Pollock, the solution was clear as soon as Aaron began tearing up league pitching. By early April, Pollock had persuaded the Boston Braves to take out a thirty-day option on Pork Chops Aaron. Then, in late June, Pollock had to choose between bids from the Braves and the New York Giants. Pollock took the Braves' $10,000—thereby ending the chance that Hank Aaron and Willie Mays might have played together in the same outfield.

In late June, Aaron was sent to the Braves' Jacksonville, Florida, team in the Triple-A South Atlantic, or Sally League, where he compiled 22 homers and 125 RBIs and won the Most Valuable Player award. In 1954, Aaron broke in with the newly relocated Milwaukee Braves and hit .280. Twenty-three seasons later, Aaron ended his career as baseball's all-time home-run king, with 755 of them, and as the game's last link to the Negro leagues.

With players like Aaron and Mays gone from blackball almost as soon as they arrived, all that some black teams could really do to try and put people in the park was to send in the clowns, or whatever else would play to the public. These circus attractions included the appearance in the lineup of midgets and even white players who, in a strange and roundabout mutation of Jim Crow, were forbidden to play by local authorities in the South. Pollock, borrowing a gimmick that went back to J. L. Wilkinson's All Nations, employed not one but three black women players: Tony Stone, Connie Morgan, and Mamie "Peanut" Johnson. Stone was good enough at second base that Tom Baird purchased her contract so she could play in the Monarchs' infield in 1954.

But Baird realized that such gimmickry was not going to reverse blackball's coma, and having long since turned the grand old Monarchs into a virtual lawn sale for big league browsers, he now made some serious pocket money selling off players like catcher Elston Howard, who became the first black Yankee in 1955, and pitcher Connie Johnson to the Baltimore Orioles. His biggest score, though, was the sale of shortstop Ernie Banks to the Chicago Cubs in 1953 for $20,000. Two years later he sent George Altman and Lou Johnson to the Cubs, who also hired Buck O'Neil as a coach and scout.

Baird's final sale was himself. In 1955, when the Athletics moved from Philadelphia to Kansas City, Baird sold the Monarchs. The Athletics then hired him as a scout—the same path taken by Alex Pompez, whose extraordinary reformation from gangster to nobleman was complete when he closed down the New York Cubans and took a job as a scout for the New York Giants. Among Pompez's first signings was Orlando Cepeda, son of the great Puerto Rican slugger Petrucho.

Negro League players advanced no further into the white baseball sacrarium. Instead, as the Negro leagues' influence wasted away, blackball's own congregation grew smaller and smaller. In what seemed like a symbolic effacement, a fire burned the Crawford Grille to the ground in 1951. Gus Greenlee had been battling a government indictment for failure to pay income taxes and the fire may have sapped his legendary pugnacity. On July 7, 1952, he was dead. Only a year later, Abe Manley passed away.

Tom Baird's successor, black Kansas City businessman Ted Rasberry, took up the unenviable chore of keeping blackball alive when there was no clear reason why it should continue to exist. Rasberry's lone ally was J. B. Martin, who held the dual role of commissioner and president of the Negro American League even after Martin's Chicago American Giants stopped playing in 1953. Rasberry and Martin succeeded in bringing two teams—from Mobile, Alabama, and New Orleans—into the league in 1957. But by then the black game's most bankable attraction, the Clowns, had gone the barnstorming route under new ownership. From 1958 on, there was not trace of league activity.

Blackball's last miscalculation came in 1957, when the Los Angeles Dodgers offered the tottering Negro American League a chance to become subsidized by the club. J. B. Martin, nattering about keeping an "open market" in what had become almost nonexistent player sales, turned down the Dodgers' offer. The white majors gravitated more and more into signing black players out of high school or off the sandlot. While Martin waited for Ford Frick to subsidize his circuit for all of baseball to utilize, the league and the black game withered and died.

All that was left in the New Frontier of the sixties were the Monarchs, the Clowns, and the wraith of the East-West Game. Even with no league and no East or West teams in sight, Martin scrounged up enough money to stage a pallid facsimile of blackball's onetime jewel until 1963; then, disappearing crowds in Chicago forced the East-West Game—which was being played between essentially barnstorming semipros—to Kansas City, where the final contest was attended by a few thousand fans lured by curiosity or long memories.

Ted Rasberry held out with the Monarchs until 1965, leaving the legacy of a thousand or so people from Fleet Walker and Octavius Catto to Rube Foster and Cum Posey and Satchel Paige and Josh Gibson in the hands of Edward Hamman, Syd Pollock's successor as overseer of the Clowns. Hamman, however, seemed to be attuned to an entirely different black sporting ethos.

"We are all show now. We clown, clown, clown," Hamman said. "[We] are the Harlem Globetrotters of baseball."

The Clowns did not honor the blackball tradition—they desecrated it. The club made it through year and after until the early eighties, though by then the act had gone beyond the embarrassing into the simply weird. While their last owner, Dave Clark, advertised the Clowns as kind of curio, the absolute final connection to the race struggle in the game, few blacks cared to patronize this farcical team. The Clowns actually contained more white than black players; Clark would send team photos to newspapers with black faces pasted on the white players' bodies. For baseball historians, this furnished a most ironic demise to blackball. With whites pretending to be black, the American game had come full circle since black men had had to pose as Cubans for E. B. Lamar in the 1880s in order to be employed as ballplayers.

A far more virtuous laurel to blackball began as an idle thought in sportswriter Jimmy Cannon's column in 1938 that the greatest Negro league players deserved to be considered for inclusion in baseball's Hall of Fame. Then, after the 1956 season, Jackie Robinson retired from the game, and with his entry into the Hall assured, it occurred to many baseball opinion leaders that an awkward public relations problem lay ahead—namely that racial detente would not be complete until reparations were made to those warriors left along the ruins of the color barrier.

Now, the idea of giving the baseball sacraments to the best of these victims resurfaced, first in a *Sporting News* editorial by, of all people, J. G. Taylor Spink. In the September 26, 1956 issue, Spink made the case for Satchel Paige. Under the headline "Paige Merits Place in Hall of Fame," Spink wrote with sound logic and a dose of twenty-twenty hindsight:

> There is no danger that the Negro race will not eventually be represented at Cooperstown. Jackie Robinson is only the first of a long line of candidates.... But Robinson and his contemporaries are eligible under the rules. It would be an ironic comment on our sense of justice if one who meets the requirements...were barred on the technicality that he did not spend ten years in the

majors. [Paige would] have spent ten or maybe 20 or 30—if baseball people hadn't discovered the true meaning of democracy belated[ly].

In February 1957, Joe Williams of the *New York World-Telegram & Sun* picked up on the cause, pointing out that while "the distinction of being the first Negro to break the color line must always belong to Robinson...this does not mean...that he was the best of all Negro players....To canonize Old Satch [in the Hall of Fame] would be at least a symbolic gesture, a ritualistic concession that, for far too many years the Great American Pastime was anything but American."

The problem was that, beyond eligibility rules, the shrine at Cooperstown carried an overblown symbolism for baseball traditionalists.

The Hall of Fame was more than a testimonial to baseball's greatest players, it objectified the unbroken chain of traditional baseball values and conceits. With each year, the pastoral walls of the Hall had become more deaf to the howling winds of change on the outside. Almost as a test of baseball's backbone, the institution's guardians, abetted by the silence of the owners and Commissioner Frick over the latest race question, ignored the Hall's critics.

Ken Smith, the director of the Hall of Fame for decades, responded in 1964 to the move to enshrine Satchel Paige. "Sure, Satch has done a lot for the game," Smith said. "But he just doesn't qualify for it on his major league record. We all love the guy. But it wouldn't be right to bend the rules."

Added Ford Frick: "If you make one exception, you have to make many"—which, of course, had much the same ring as the old protestations against integration of the game.

Astonishingly, Jackie Robinson—whose animus toward the Negro leagues and their indentured servants, as he saw them, had not mellowed through the years—declared his opposition to the Paige nomination on eligibility grounds, unable or unwilling to see the parallels between his logic and that of those who had wanted to keep him from playing for the all-white Brooklyn Dodgers in 1947.

But the new permutations of the cause were now well beyond Jackie Robinson. A widening arc of baseball people had come to perceive the Hall of Fame issue as a different kind of test—that of baseball's sincerity in racial matters. More than ever, baseball had to make its sensibilities plain. In March 1965, Martin Luther King Jr. led three thousand people across the Edmund Pettus Bridge outside Montgomery, Alabama, and when this "Freedom March" reached Montgomery, the crowd had grown to over twenty-five thousand. Days later the Voting Rights Act was made into law; later that year, so was the Civil Rights Act. Baseball was either going to line up on the moral side of desegregation or have to stand with the dogs of de facto integration.

Providentially, the game caught a break that year. In December, Ford Frick retired as commissioner. His immediate replacement, a courtly former air force general named William "Spike" Eckert, seemingly was under orders from the owners not to do or say much of anything about any issue. Eckert could take this dishonorable treatment only until 1968, when he walked away from the job. And while the new commissioner, corporate lawyer Bowie Kuhn, was also reluctant to buck the owners' will, he would not allow baseball's racial weaseling to go on.

Knowing how sensitive breaking the final racial wall would be, Kuhn moved in the only way baseball change ever seems to come about—with deliberation and in secret. At the urging of the Baseball Writers' Association of America, Kuhn quietly empowered a ten-man committee to comb through hundreds of blackballers and nominate for Hall admission the first crop of four players—excluding Robinson and Roy Campanella, who had gone in the Hall, Robinson in 1962 and Campy in 1969, for their major league accomplishments.

The committee, it turned out, was a remarkably accurate cross section of Negro ball. Its members included favorite sons of the game like Campanella, Judy Johnson, and Monte Irvin, as well as its heralds, Wendell Smith and Sam Lacy. But there was also Eddie Gottlieb as proctor of its Caucasian caretakers and Alex Pompez of its racketeers.

When the panel reported in 1971, Satchel Paige was a unanimous choice as the first man to enter the Hall on the basis of his Negro league career. By happy coincidence, Paige became eligible in 1971, since his last appearance in organized ball had come with Greensboro in the Carolina League in 1966, allowing him to meet the five-year waiting period required of all Hall of Famers. By the time of his nomination, Paige had established a legacy of self-compiled "statistics" that alone formed an effective parable of blackball's epic history. Paige said he had pitched in around 2,500 games, winning around 2,000 of them, and hurled nearly 250 no-hit games. He had also become famous for the number one rule of his philosophy of life—"Don't look back; something might be gaining on you"—a sentiment shared by every Negro leaguer, whose sights were always on one game at a time.

Satch would go in alone, to be followed in 1972 by Josh Gibson and Buck Leonard, and in 1973 by Monte Irvin. (Irvin's nomination, which did not seem to be merited, was probably assured by the job of special assistant he held for many years in the commissioner's office.)

Kuhn made the surprise announcement of the "historic first" of Paige's induction on February 9, 1971, but he had worked behind the scenes for a good year arm-twisting in Cooperstown, coaxing the last den of racial hard-liners to accept the agreement he had made with the private trust that operated the Hall. Still, Kuhn felt he had to offer a concession to the old guard: The black entrants would be accorded all the pomp and circumstance of a regular induction ceremony, but their plaques would hang not in the main building on the National Baseball Museum but in a separate wing.

Attempting to explain the "special nature" of these honors, Kuhn admitted that "technically" Satchel Paige should not be in the Hall of Fame. Then, trying to tiptoe around what he had just said, he added, "But I've often said the Hall of Fame isn't a building but a state of mind."

If Kuhn believed that this slight was small enough to be buried under the huzzahs that he had torn down baseball's very last racial barrier, he must have been stunned when black and white sportswriters attacked him for condoning a new "separate but equal" Hall of Fame. In April, *Ebony* magazine gave Kuhn credit only for "the biggest shortchange of them all. When it comes to baseball, the so-called All-American game, Satchel Paige and other black stars who were kept out of organized baseball for so many years do not belong in any anteroom. They belong in the Hall of Fame proper....Black people will not in this day and age settle for just a half a loaf."

Admirably, Kuhn heard the call to reason and rewrote the occupancy guidelines at the Hall. When Satchel Paige arrived in Cooperstown for the August 9 ceremonies, he saw his plaque go up on the wall in the main building. Over the next five years, the committee would select other players deserving of entry into the Hall of Fame: James "Cool Papa" Bell in 1974, Judy Johnson in 1975, Oscar Charleston in 1976. In 1977, the committee disbanded, leaving future Negro league nominations to the Veterans' Committee. That year, John Henry Lloyd and Martin Dihigo were inducted, followed by Rube Foster in 1981, Ray Dandridge in 1987, and Leon Day in 1995. (Wendell Smith would go into the writers' wing of the Hall in 1994.)

But it was Satchel Paige's induction that carried baseball's racial armistice into history and into reality, at least on its fields of play, if not its front offices. Squinting through thick eyeglasses, the court jester now regal in his old age, Paige walked a straight line right down the middle of the once-rigid enemy camp that was white baseball. He began, "Since I've been here I've heard myself called some very nice names. And I can remember when some the men in [the Hall of Fame] called me some ba-a-a-a-d names, when I used to pitch against them."

He went on, "They'd make fun about my not running, about being slow to the mound. But I never rushed myself. I knew they couldn't start the game 'til I got out there."

Then, the poet laureate of blackball cut to the heart of what this day meant, not just for himself but for anyone who'd ever worn the bedraggled uniform of the Negro leagues.

"Today," he said, "baseball has turned Paige from a second-class citizen to a second-class immortal."

Way back when, Harlem's poet laureate Langston Hughes wrote of African Americans waiting without end to hear "one blaring note of sun." On August 9, 1971, in the dim afterlife of that joyous and cruel American anomaly known as the Negro baseball leagues, Leroy Paige had played that one blaring note at last. It sounded like a rapture. And the sun was bright and felt hot.

Index